D0262195

TAXATION SUMMARY

IRISH TAXATION INSTITUTE

The Irish Taxation Institute (ITI) is the leading representative body for taxation affairs in Ireland. Our membership comprises qualified tax advisers, accountants, barristers, lawyers, and other corporate and business professionals. Our mission is to support an efficient, fair and competitive tax system that promotes an understanding of and expertise in taxation, and encourages economic and social progress.

Our 5,500 members work with corporate leaders, Government, State agencies, representative groups, professional organisations and the general public. Through our membership of the Confédération Fiscale Européenne, we monitor and influence legislation and tax policy developments in the EU and internationally.

For over 40 years, ITI has been Ireland's foremost provider of qualified tax advisers through our three-year (AITI) and one-year (TMITI) tax qualification courses. Our professional development programme provides continued education, appropriate advice, specialist seminars and other support services for members. This ensures qualified tax advisers remain professionally competent throughout their working lives.

Through our nationwide branch network and comprehensive committee structure, our members are actively involved in developing and advancing research on taxation, economic and social policy. Drawing on this expert team, ITI produces a comprehensive suite of taxation publications covering the full range of tax topics.

ITI is governed by a 21-member Council made up of senior business executives and is managed by a dynamic executive team.

Titles in Print:

- A Practitioner's Guide to Revenue Audits
- Buying and Selling a Business
- Capital Acquisitions Tax
- Capital Allowances and Property Incentives
- Case Law for the Tax Practitioner
- Corporation Tax
- Direct Tax Acts
- Double Taxation Agreements – Vols. 1 & 2
- FINAK
- From Bóraimhe to Bit – The Art of Taxation
- Income Tax
- Irish Taxation – Law and Practice
- Law of Capital Acquisitions Tax
- Law of Value-Added Tax
- Money Laundering: Guidelines on the Money Laundering Legislation for Tax Advisers
- One Size Fits All? EU Taxation Policy
- Pensions: Revenue Law and Practice
- PRSI and Levy Contributions
- Residential Property Tax Legislation
- Stamp Acts
- Tax Implications of Marital Breakdown
- Taxation of Property Transactions
- Taxation Summary
- Taxes Consolidation Act 1997: The Busy Practitioner's Guide
- Taxing Financial Transactions
- Taxing GAAP and IFRS
- The Law and Practice of Irish Stamp Duty
- The Taxation of Capital Gains
- The 2002 Revenue Audit Code of Practice
- Trust and Succession Law
- Valuation of Shares in Unlisted Companies for Tax Purposes
- Value-Added Tax
- VAT on Property
- Who's Afraid of the ECJ? Implications of the European Court of Justice Decision on Ireland's Corporation Tax Regime
- World Tax Conference Papers 2001

Taxation Summary

32nd edition | Finance Act 2008

Joe Martyn
Paul Reck

Edited by

Terry Cooney

Irish Taxation Institute
South Block
Longboat Quay
Grand Canal Harbour
Dublin 2

Telephone: +353 1 6631700
Fax: +353 1 6688387
E-mail: info@taxireland.ie
Web: www.taxireland.ie

First edition 1977
Twenty-ninth edition 2005
Thirtieth edition 2006
Thirty-first edition 2007
Thirty-second edition 2008

A catalogue record for this book is available from the British Library

This book is a summary of the extensive volume of statute and case law in the Republic of Ireland and is not intended as a detailed exposition of that law and practice.

While every effort has been made to ensure the accuracy of the material in this book, neither the Institute nor the Editor accepts any responsibility for loss or damage occasioned by any person acting, or refraining from acting, as a result of this material. Any views or opinions expressed are not necessarily subscribed to by the Institute. Professional advice should always be sought before acting on any interpretation of the legislation in this book.

ISBN 978-1-84260-170-9
10 9 8 7 6 5 4 3 2 1

Printed and bound in Italy by Legoprint – Lavis (TN)

FOREWORD

I am delighted to present this latest edition of the Irish Taxation Institute's longest-running title, *Taxation Summary*. Longevity is the surest indicator of enduring quality, and this can certainly be said in the case of this book, which is now in its thirty-second edition.

With over fifty helpful charts and tables, and a useful wallchart that sets out the major rates and allowances, *Taxation Summary* is sure to prove an invaluable assistance to practitioners, students and interested readers again this year.

The book's undiminished popularity is a testament to the excellent work of its authors, Joe Martyn and Paul Reck, and the precision of its editor Terry Cooney. A sincere thank you is owed to each of them for their contributions to this update.

JIM RYAN
President
Irish Taxation Institute

Contents

LIST OF CHARTS

Chart No.		Contents	Page

Urban Renewal

Historic Rates

CHART 1

Income Tax Allowances

	90/91	91/92	92/93	93/94	94/95	95/96
	IR£	IR£	IR£	IR£	IR£	IR£
Single Person	2,050	2,100	2,100	2,175	2,350	2,500
Married Couple	4,100	4,200	4,200	4,350	4,700	5,000
Widowed person (in year of bereavement)	4,100	4,200	4,200	4,350	4,700	5,000
Widowed person (subsequent years)	2,550	2,600	2,600	2,675	2,850	3,000
Widowed person with dependent child (additional)	1,550	1,600	1,600	1,675	1,850	2,000
First year after bereavement	-	1,500	1,500	1,500	1,500	1,500
Second year after bereavement	-	1,000	1,000	1,000	1,000	1,000
Third year after bereavement	-	500	500	500	500	500
Single Parent – additional	2,050	2,100	2,100	2,175	2,350	2,500
Income Limit of Child	720	720	720	720	720	720
Incapacitated Child	600	600	600	600	600	600
Income Limit of Child	720	2,100	2,100	2,100	2,100	2,100
Dependent Relative allowance	110	110	110	110	110	110
Income Limit	3,566	3,777	3,877	4,133	4,149	4,270
Blind Person	600	600	600	600	600	600
Both Spouses Blind	1,400	1,400	1,400	1,400	1,400	1,400
Age allowance: Single/Widowed Person	200	200	200	200	200	200
Married	400	400	400	400	400	400
Employed person taking care of incapacitated person	5,000	5,000	5,000	5,000	5,000	5,000
Employee allowance	800	800	800	800	800	800
PRSI allowance	286	286	286	286	286	140

CHART 1 (*continued*)

	96/97	97/98	98/99	99/00		00/01
				@ Standard Rate 24%	@ Marginal Rate 46%	@ Standard Rate 22%
Single Person	2,650	2,900	3,150	4,200	-	4,700
Married Couple	5,300	5,800	6,300	8,400	-	9,400
Widowed person (in year of bereavement)	5,300	5,800	6,300	8,400	-	9,400
Widowed person (subsequent years – without dependent child)	3,150	3,400	3,650	4,200	500	5,700
Widowed person with dependent child (additional)	2,150	2,400	2,650	1,050	2,650	4,700
First year after bereavement	1,500	1,500	5,000	-	5,000	10,000
Second year after bereavement	1,000	1,000	4,000	-	4,000	8,000
Third year after bereavement	500	500	3,000	-	3,000	6,000
Fourth year after bereavement			2,000	-	2,000	4,000
Fifth year after bereavement			1,000	-	1,000	2,000
Single Parent – additional	2,650	2,900	3,150	1,050	3,150	4,700
Income Limit of Child	720	720	720	-	720	720
Incapacitated Child	700	700	800	-	800	1,600
Income Limit of Child	2,100	2,100	2,100	-	2,100	2,100
Dependent Relative allowance	110	110	110	-	110	220
Income Limit	4,440	4,601	4,848	-	5,152	5,536
Blind Person	700	700	1,000	-	1,500	3,000
Both Spouses Blind	1,600	1,600	2,000	-	3,000	6,000
Age allowance: Single/Widowed Person	200	400	400	-	400	800
Married	400	800	800	-	800	1,600
Incapacitated Person – employment of carer	7,500	7,500	8,500	-	8,500	8,500*
Home Carers allowance (Max)	-	-	-	-	-	3,000
Employee allowance	800	800	800	1,000	-	1,000
PRSI allowance	-	-	-	-	-	-

*Relief available at marginal rate.

CHART 2

Income Tax Credits

	Tax Year 2001	Tax Year 2002	Tax Year 2003	Tax Year 2004	Tax Year 2005	Tax Year 2006	Tax Year 2007	Tax Year 2008
	IR£	€	€	€	€	€	€	€
Single Person	814	1,520	1,520	1,520	1,580	1,630	1,760	1830
Married Couple	1,628	3,040	3,040	3,040	3,160	3,260	3,520	3660
Widowed Person								
– in year of bereavement	1,628	3,040	3,040	3,040	3,160	3,260	3,520	3660
– without dependent children	962	1,820	1,820	1,820	1,980	2,130	2,310	2430
– with dependent children	814	1,520	1,520	1,520	1,580	1,630	1,760	1830
Widowed Parent								
– first year after bereavement	2,000	2,600	2,600	2,600	2,800	3,100	3,750	4000
– second year after bereavement	1,600	2,100	2,100	2,100	2,300	2,600	3,250	3500
– third year after bereavement	1,200	1,600	1,600	1,600	1,800	2,100	2,750	3000
– fourth year after bereavement	800	1,100	1,100	1,100	1,300	1,600	2,250	2500
– fifth year after bereavement	400	600	600	600	800	1,100	1,750	2000
One-Parent Family								
– widowed person	814	1,520	1,520	1,520	1,580	1,630	1,760	1830
– other person	814	1,520	1,520	1,520	1,580	1,630	1,760	1830
Incapacitated Child Max	238	500	500	500	1,000	1,500	3,000	3660
Dependent Relative Max	33	60	60	60	60	80	80	80
Income Limit	4,989	9,352	9,852	10,373	10,997	11,912	12,745	13,473
Blind Person	444	800	800	800	1,000	1,500	1,760	1830
Both Spouses Blind	888	1,600	1,600	1,600	2,000	3,000	3,520	3660
Age Credit:								
– Single/Widowed Person	119	205	205	205	205	250	275	325
– Married	238	410	410	410	410	500	550	650
PAYE Max	296	660	800	1,040	1,270	1,490	1,760	1830
Home Carer Max	444	770	770	770	770	770	770	900
Trade Union Subscriptions		45	26	40	40	60	60	70
Employment of Carer for Incapacitated Person Max	7,400 @ Marginal Rate	30,000 @ Marginal Rate	30,000 @ Marginal Rate	30,000 @ Marginal Rate	30,000 @ Marginal Rate	50,000 @ Marginal Rate	50,000 @ Marginal Rate	50,000 @ Marginal Rate

CHART 3

Income Tax Rates

(see Chart 42 for earlier years)

Tax Year	Single/ Widowed	Married Couple	Rate
1990/91	6,500 3,100 Balance	13,000 6,200 Balance	30% 48% 53%
1991/92	6,700 3,100 Balance	13,400 6,200 Balance	29% 48% 52%
1992/93	7,475 Balance	14,950 Balance	27% 48%
1993/94	7,675 Balance	15,350 Balance	27% 48%
1994/95	8,200 Balance	16,400 Balance	27% 48%
1995/96	8,900 Balance	17,800 Balance	27% 48%
1996/97	9,400 Balance	18,800 Balance	27% 48%
1997/98	9,900 Balance	19,800 Balance	26% 48%
1998/99	10,000 Balance	20,000 Balance	24% 46%
1999/00	14,000 Balance	28,000 Balance	24% 46%

CHART 3 (continued)

(see Chart 42 for earlier years)

Tax Year	Single/ Widowed	Married Couples, One Income	Married Couples, Two Incomes	One-Parent Family	Rate
	£	£	£	£	
2000/01	1–17,000 Balance	1–28,000 Balance	1–34,000* Balance	1–20,150 Balance	22% 44%
** Note: Transferable between spouses up to a maximum of £28,000 for any one spouse.*					
	£	£	£	£	
2001	1–14,800 Balance	1–21,460 Balance	1–29,600* Balance	1–17,131 Balance	20% 42%
** Note: Transferable between spouses up to a maximum of £21,460 for any one spouse.*					
	€	€	€	€	
2002	1-28,000 Balance	1-37,000 Balance	1-56,000* Balance	1-32,000 Balance	20% 42%
** Note: Transferable between spouses up to a maximum of €37,000 for any one spouse.*					
	€	€	€	€	
2003	1-28,000 Balance	1-37,000 Balance	1-56,000* Balance	1-32,000 Balance	20% 42%
** Note: Transferable between spouses up to a maximum of €37,000 for any one spouse.*					
	€	€	€	€	
2004	1-28,000 Balance	1-37,000 Balance	1-56,000* Balance	1-32,000 Balance	20% 42%
** Note: Transferable between spouses up to a maximum of €37,000 for any one spouse.*					
	€	€	€	€	
2005	1-29,400 Balance	1-38,400 Balance	1-58,800* Balance	1-33,400 Balance	20% 42%
** Note: Transferable between spouses up to a maximum of €38,400 for any one spouse.*					
	€	€	€	€	
2006	32,000 Balance	41,000 Balance	64,000* Balance	36,000 Balance	20% 42%
** Note: Transferable between spouses up to a maximum of €41,000 for any one spouse.*					
	€	€	€	€	
2007	34,000 Balance	43,000 Balance	68,000* Balance	38,000 Balance	20% 41%
** Note: Transferable between spouses up to a maximum of €43,000 for any one spouse.*					
	€	€	€	€	
2008	35,400 Balance	44,400 Balance	*70,800 Balance	39,400 Balance	20% 41%
** Note: Transferable between spouses up to a maximum of €44,400 for any one spouse.*					

See 1.7.11 for special 20% rate applying to profits from dealing in or developing residential development land.

CHART 4

Exemption Limits

Single & Widowed	98/99 £	99/00 £	00/01 £	2001 £	2002 €	2003 €	2004 €	2005 €	2006 €	2007 €	2008 €
Under 65 Years	4,100	4,100	4,100	3,034	5,210	5,210	5,210	5,210	5,210	5,210	
over 65 and under 75	5,000	6,500									
75 and over	5,500	6,500									
65 and over			7,500	6,290	13,000	15,000	15,500	16,500	17,000	19,000	20,000

Married Couples	98/99 £	99/00 £	00/01 £	2001 £	2002 €	2003 €	2004 €	2005 €	2006 €	2007 €	2008 €
Under 65 Years	8,200	8,200	8,200	6,068	10,420	10,420	10,420	10,420	10,420	10,420	
over 65 and under 75	10,000	13,000									
75 and over	11,000	13,000									
65 and over			15,000	12,580	26,000	30,000	31,000	33,000	34,000	38,000	40,000

Note: The income limits are increased for each dependent child as follows:

	98/99 £	99/00 £	00/01 £	2001 £	2002 €	2003 €	2004 €	2005 €	2006 €	2007 €	2008 €
First and Second Child	450	450	450	333	575	575	575	575	575	575	575
Third and Subsequent Child	650	650	650	481	830	830	830	830	830	830	830

*Marginal Relief rates	40%	40%	40%	40%	40%	40%	40%	40%	40%	40%	40%

*Marginal relief restricts the amount of tax payable to the amount by which total income exceeds the exemption limit, at the above marginal relief rate.

CHART 5

PRSI Rates and Levies

EMPLOYEE – CLASS A1				
	PRSI			*HEALTH CONTRIBUTION*
	Employer Rate	*Employee*		*Employee Rate*
		Income €	*Rate*	
2007	10.75%	0 – 48,800	4%	2%
	10.75%	48,801 – 100,100	NIL	2%
	10.75%	100,101 onwards	NIL	2.5%
2008	10.75%	0 – 50,700	4%	2%
	10.75%	50,701 – 100,100	NIL	2%
	10.75%	100,101 onwards	NIL	2.5%

Notes:

Employers PRSI is 8.5% on earnings of €365 pw or less in 2007 and 2008.

For 2007 and 2008 an additional 0.5% Health Contribution has been introduced on earnings exceeding €1,925 per week (equivalent to €3,850 per fortnight and €8,342 per month).

Employees are exempt from PRSI on the first €127 per week or €26 per week for employees on a modified PRSI rate. Employees earning €352 or less per week in 2008 (€339 in 2007) are exempt from PRSI and Health Contribution. However, where earnings exceed €352 per week in 2008 (€339 in 2007), the employee's PRSI Free Allowance remains at €127 per week or €26 per week for employees on a modified PRSI rate. Employees earning €500 or less per week in 2008 (€480 in 2007) are exempt from Health Contribution of 2%.

Recipients of a Social Welfare Widow's or Widower's Pension, Deserted Wife's Benefit/ Allowance or One-Parent Family Payment are exempt from paying the 2% Health Contribution. All Medical Card holders (including people aged 70 or over) are also exempt from this contribution.

SELF-EMPLOYED			
	INCOME	*PRSI (Min)*	*HEALTH CONTRIBUTION*
2007	If income < €24,960	3% (€253)	NIL
	€24,960 – €100,100*	3%	2%
	Over €100,100	3%	2.5%
2008	If income < €26,000	3% (€253)	NIL
	€26,000 – €100,000*	3%	2%
	Over €100,000	3%	2.5%

*The exemption from Health Contribution only applies if the income is less than €24,960 in 2007 and €26,000 in 2008; otherwise, the 2% applies to all income up to €100,100.

In the case of Schedule E, income on which PRSI is calculated is net income after superannuation. In the case of Schedule D, income is after capital allowances but before pension contributions. There is no liability to PRSI where reckonable income is below €3,174. This test is applied separately to the income of husband and wife.

CHART 6
Mortgage Interest Relief

For the tax year 2008, the maximum allowable amounts are as shown hereunder.

	Maximum Allowable @ Standard Rate	
2008	**First Time Buyers* €**	**Other €**
Single Person	10,000	3,000
Married / Widowed	20,000	6,000

* *First time buyers who claimed mortgage interest relief for the first time in the tax year 2002 or later. The increased limit applies for a period of seven years beginning with the tax year in which mortgage interest was claimed for the first time.*

For the tax years 2002 *et seq.*, tax relief is granted at source (see 1.5.1).

CHART 7

Specified Amounts for the Restriction of Capital Allowances and Leasing Charges for Passenger Motor Vehicles

(see Chart 49 for earlier years)

Chargeable Periods Ending	SPECIFIED AMOUNT
	€
Between 1/1/2002 - 31/12/2005 inclusive	22,000
Between 1/1/2006 - 31/12/2006 inclusive	23,000
On or after 1/1/2007	24,000

CHART 8

Civil Service Motor Travel Rates

(For individuals who are obliged to use their cars in the normal course of their duties).

RATES PER KILOMETRE (1 mile = 1.609 kilometres)

MOTOR CARS			
Effective from 1 July 2006 to 30 June 2007			
Official Motor Travel in a Calendar Year	**Engine Capacity**		
	Up to 1,200cc	1,201cc to 1,500cc	1,501cc and over
Up to 6,437km	52.16 cent	61.66 cent	78.32 cent
6,438km and over	26.97 cent	30.96 cent	36.65 cent
Effective from 1 July 2007 to 30 June 2008			
Official Motor Travel in a Calendar Year	**Engine Capacity**		
	Up to 1,200cc	1,201cc to 1,500cc	1,501cc and over
Up to 6,437km	52.16 cent	61.66 cent	78.32 cent
6,438km and over	27.08 cent	30.96 cent	36.65 cent
Effective from 1 July 2008			
Official Motor Travel in a Calendar Year	**Engine Capacity**		
	Up to 1,200cc	1,201cc to 1,500cc	1,501cc and over
Up to 6,437km	52.16 cent	61.67 cent	78.76 cent
6,438km and over	28.29 cent	31.49 cent	37.94 cent

MOTORCYCLES		
Effective from 1 February 2006 to 30 June 2007		
Engine Capacity		
150cc or less	**151cc to 250cc**	**251cc and over**
15.35 cent	21.46 cent	28.33 cent

Effective from 1 July 2007				
	Engine Capacity			
	150cc or less	**151cc to 250cc**	**251cc and over**	**601 cc and over**
Up to 6,437km	18.92 cent	26.35 cent	31.13 cent	37.96 cent
6,438km and over	11.89 cent	16.94 cent	19.48 cent	22.59 cent

CHART 8 (continued)

Reduced Motor Travel Rates

(For individuals who are not obliged to travel in the normal course of their duties but who occasionally use their car for business purposes).

Effective from 1 January 2003 to 30 June 2008		
Engine Capacity up to 1200cc [cent]	**Engine Capacity 1201cc to 1500cc [cent]**	**Engine Capacity 1500cc and over [cent]**
19.52	21.88	23.87
Effective from 1 July 2008		
19.52	22.18	25.99

CHART 9

Civil Service Subsistence Rates

(a) Domestic Subsistence Rates

• Effective from 1 July 2006 to 30 June 2007

Class of Allowances	Night Allowances			Day Allowances	
	Normal Rate	Reduced Rate	Detention Rate	10 hours or more	5 hours but less than 10 hours
A Rate	€140.44	€129.48	€70.21	€41.55	€16.95
B Rate	€132.18	€113.05	€66.12	€41.55	€16.95

Salary levels corresponding to above classes:

A – Salary exceeds €63,109 per annum
B – Salary is below €63,109 per annum

• Effective from 1 July 2007 to 30 June 2008

Class of Allowances	Night Allowances			Day Allowances	
	Normal Rate	Reduced Rate	Detention Rate	10 hours or more	5 hours but less than 10 hours
A Rate	€144.45	€133.17	€72.21	€43.13	€17.60
B Rate	€141.60	€121.11	€70.83	€43.13	€17.60

• Effective from 1 July 2008

Class of Allowances	Night Allowances			Day Allowances	
	Normal Rate	Reduced Rate	Detention Rate	10 hours or more	5 hours but less than 10 hours
A Rate	€145.32	€133.97	€72.64	€44.81	€18.28
B Rate	€143.58	€122.81	€71.82	€44.81	€18.28

Salary levels corresponding to above classes:

A – Salary exceeds €66,302 per annum
B – Salary is below €66,302 per annum

Normal Rate - up to 14 nights
Reduced Rate - next 14 nights
Detention Rate - next 28 nights
Special Rules apply to absences over 56 nights

(b) Foreign Subsistence Rates

Details of quantum of Civil Service subsistence rates for certain foreign countries are available from any regional Revenue office.

CHART 10

(a) Interest on Overdue Tax

Rates of Interest		
0.5% per month or part of a month		To 31.7.71
0.75% per month or part of month	From 1.8.71	To 30.4.75
1.5% per month or part of a month	From 1.5.75	To 31.7.78
1.25% per month or part of a month	From 1.8.78	To 31.3.98
1.00% per month or part of a month	From 1.4.98	To 31.8.02
0.0322% per day or part of a day	From 1.9.02	To 31.3.05
0.0273% per day or part of a day	From 1.4.05	

Note:

In the cases of income tax, corporation tax, capital gains tax, gift tax and inheritance tax remaining unpaid on or after 1 April 2005, the basis for the calculation of interest will be by reference to a daily rate for all periods of delay, whether before or after 1 April 2005, instead of a monthly basis for periods up to 31 August 2002 and a daily basis thereafter. In the case of stamp duties, due to the variation in the rates which applied for various purposes in the past, the new rate will only apply for periods of delay arising on or after 1 April 2005.

The reduced rate from 1 April 2005 and the measures outlined above will not apply to indirect taxes, such as excise duties and VAT, and taxes such as PAYE, relevant contracts tax, professional fees withholding tax, DIRT and other withholding and exit taxes which are collected by employers and others on a fiduciary basis.

(b) Interest on Tax Overpaid

Rates of Interest		
1.50% per month or part of a month	From 6.4.76	To 5.7.78
1.25% per month or part of a month	From 6.7.78	To 26.5.86
1.00% per month or part of a month	From 27.5.86	To 31.7.90
0.60% per month or part of a month	From 1.8.90	To 31.3.98
0.50% per month or part of a month	From 1.4.98	To 31.8.02
0.0161% per day or part of a day	From 1.9.02	To 31.10.03*
0.011% per day or part of a day	From 1.11.03*	

* See 1.1.13 for details in relation to the period for which interest will be paid.

CHART 11

Average Rates of Exchange IR£/£Stg.

Year ended	Rate	Year ended	Rate
5.4.1980	.94995	5.4.1991	.9318
5.4.1981	.84582	5.4.1992	.9288
5.4.1982	.81138	5.4.1993	1.0095
5.4.1983	.83307	5.4.1994	.9737
5.4.1984	.80780	5.4.1995	.9981
5.4.1985	.84080	5.4.1996	1.033
5.4.1986	.8441	5.4.1997	1.023
5.4.1987	.9374	5.4.1998	.9016
5.4.1988	.9055	5.4.1999	.8695
5.4.1989	.8527	5.4.2000	.8128
5.4.1990	.9101	5.4.2001	.7801
		P/E 31.12.2001	.785

Divide £Stg by these factors to obtain IR£ equivalent

Average Rates of Exchange versus Irish Pound

	1999/00	2000/01	2001
US dollar	1.3093	1.1511	1.1252
Sterling	0.8128	0.7801	0.7850
Danish krone	9.4444	9.4706	9.4571
Japanese yen	145.73	127.638	137.75
Swiss franc	2.0342	1.9534	1.9087
Swedish krona	11.0248	10.9017	11.8583
Norwegian krone	10.3975	10.3306	10.1508
Canadian dollar	1.9262	1.7327	1.7481
Australian dollar	2.0323	2.0790	2.1916
Greek drachma	416.91		

Average Rates of Exchange versus Euro*

	2002	2003	2004	2005	2006	2007
US dollar	0.946	1.1312	1.2439	1.2441	1.2556	1.3705
Sterling	0.629	0.6919	0.6786	0.6838	0.6817	0.6843
Danish krone	7.43	7.4307	7.4399	7.4518	7.4591	7.4506
Japanese yen	118.10	130.97	134.44	136.85	146.02	161.25
Swiss franc	1.467	1.5212	1.5438	1.5483	1.5729	1.6427
Swedish krona	9.16	9.1242	9.1243	9.2822	9.2544	9.2501
Norwegian krone	7.51	8.0033	8.3697	8.0092	8.0472	8.0165
Canadian dollar	1.484	1.5817	1.6167	1.5087	1.4237	1.4678
Australian dollar	1.738	1.7379	1.6905	1.6320	1.6668	1.6348

* €1 = IR£0.787564 – Changeover date 1/1/2002

CHART 12

Specified Amounts (Preliminary Tax)

INCOME TAX		
Year of Assessment	*Paying Direct*	*Paying by Direct Debit*
2004 *et seq*	90% or 100% of p.y.	105% of p.p.y.
2003	90% or 100% of p.y.	142% of p.p.y.
2002	90% or 135% of p.y.	105% of p.p.y.
2001	90% or 74% of p.y.	78% of p.p.y.
1990/01 - 2000/01	90% or 100% of p.y.	105% of p.p.y.

CHART 13

Preferential Loans (Specified Interest Rates)

Tax Year	1997/98	1998/99	1999/00	2000/01	2001	2002	2003	2004	2005	2006	2007	2008
Residential Home Loan	7%	7%	6%	4%	6%	5%	4.5%	3.5%	3.5%	3.5%	4.5%	5.5%
Other Loan	11%	11%	10%	10%	12%	12%	11%	11%	11%	11%	12%	13%

CHART 14

Retention Tax on Payments for Professional Services

The persons who are required to deduct tax from payments for professional services are as follows and include, where any person is a body corporate, any subsidiary resident in the State are listed in Schedule 13 TCA 1997 as follows:

A Minister of the Government

A local authority within the meaning of section 2(2) of the Local Government Act, 1941

A body established under the Local Government Services (Corporate Bodies) Act, 1971

Primary Care Reimbursement Service

The Attorney General

The Comptroller and Auditor-General

The Director of Public Prosecutions

The Commissioner of Valuation

The Chief Boundary Surveyor

The Director of Ordnance Survey

The Revenue Commissioners

The Public Appointments Service

The Commissioners of Public Works in Ireland

The Clerk of Dáil Éireann

The Legal Aid Board

A vocational education committee or a technical college established under the Vocational Education Act, 1930

Teagasc

A harbour authority

An Foras Áiseanna Saothair

Údarás na Gaeltacha

The Industrial Development Agency (Ireland)

An Bord Tráchtála - The Irish Trade Board

Shannon Free Airport Development Company Limited

The National Tourisim Development Authority

An institution of higher education within the meaning of the Higher Education Authority Act, 1971

The Radiological Protection Institute of Ireland

A voluntary public or joint board hospital to which grants are paid by the Minister for Health in the year 1988/89 or any subsequent year of assessment

An authorised insurer within the meaning of section 145 of the Income Tax Act, 1967

(continued on following page)

CHART 14 (continued)

An Bord Glas
An Bord Pleanála
Dublin Airport Authority public limited company
Arramara Teoranta
Blood Transfusion Service Board
Bord na gCon
Bord Gáis Éireann
Bord Iascaigh Mhara
Bord na Móna plc
Coillte Teoranta
Córas Iompair Éireann
Custom House Docks Development Authority
Electricity Supply Board
Housing Finance Agency public limited company
Irish National Petroleum Corporation Limited
Irish National Stud Company Limited
National Building Agency Limited
National Concert Hall Company Limited
An Post National Lottery Company
Nítrigin Éireann Teoranta
An Post
Radio Telefís Éireann
Royal Hospital Kilmainham Company
The Environmental Protection Agency
Forbairt
Forfás
The Irish Aviation Authority
The National Economic and Social Council
The National Economic and Social Forum
The National Road Authority
Temple Bar Properties Limited
The Irish Film Board
An educational institution established by or under Section 3 of the Regional Technical Colleges Act 1992 as an Institute of Technology
The Dublin Institute of Technology
An Bord Bia
Area Development Management Limited
The Combat Poverty Agency

(continued on following page)

CHART 14 (continued)

The Commissioners of Irish Lights

Dublin Transportation Office

The Higher Education Authority

The Independent Radio and Television Commission

Horse Racing Ireland

The Labour Relations Commission

The Marine Institute

The Pensions Board

The Commission for Communications Regulation

The Law Reform Commission

National Standards Authority of Ireland

Enterprise Ireland

Dublin Docklands Development Authority

A Referendum Commission established by order made under section 2(1) of the Referendum Act 1998

Office of the Ombudsman

The Standards in Public Office Commission

The Office of the Information Commissioner

The Central Fisheries Board

A regional fisheries board established by virtue of an order made under Section 10, Fisheries Act, 1980

A County Enterprise Board

Western Development Commission

The Equality Authority

Commissioners of Charitable Donations and Bequests for Ireland

Commission for Electricity Regulation

Any Regional Authority established by an order made under Section 43 (1), Local Government Act, 1991

The Eastern Regional Health Authority, the Health Boards Executive or an area health board established under the Health (Eastern Regional Health Authority) Act, 1999

Irish Sports Council

An Bord Uchtála

National Disability Authority

Aquaculture Licences Appeals Board

Office of the President

Director of the Equality Tribunal

Data Protection Commissioner

(continued on following page)

CHART 14 (continued)

Competition Authority

Chief State Solicitor

Central Statistics Office

Commission to Inquire into Child Abuse

National Sports Campus Development Authority

Digital Media Development Limited

Citizens Information Board

Human Rights Commission

Pensions Ombudsman

The Dublin Institute for Advanced Studies

Pre-Hospital Emergency Care Council

Refugee Appeals Tribunal

Sustainable Energy Ireland – The Sustainable

Energy Authority of Ireland.

The Health Insurance Authority.

Commission for Aviation Regulation.

Railway Procurement Agency.

The National Council on Ageing and Older People.

National Qualifications Authority of Ireland (NQAI)

BreastCheck, The National Breast Screening Programme

The National Council for the Professional Development of Nursing and Midwifery

Mater and Children's Hospital Development Ltd

The National Consultative Commission on Racism and Interculturalism

Office of Tobacco Control

The Marine Casualty Investigation Board

National Treasury Management Agency as regards the performance of functions by it conferred on, or delegated to, it by or under Part 2 10 of the National Treasury Management Agency (Amendment) Act 2000 (State Claims Agency)

National Development Finance Agency

The National Council for Curriculum and Assessment

The State Examinations Commission

Children Acts Advisory Board

National Treatment Purchase Fund Board

The Mental Health Commission

Crisis Pregnancy Agency

Irish Medicines Board

(continued on following page)

CHART 14 (continued)

National Educational Welfare Board
Oifig Choimisinéir na dTeangacha Oifigiúla
The Health Service Executive
Commission for Public Service Appointments
Commission for Taxi Regulation
National Council for Special Education
National Library of Ireland
An Education Support Centre established under section 37 of the Education Act 1998
The Road Safety Authority
Grangegorman Development Agency
The Railway Safety Commission
The Teaching Council
EirGrid
The Further Education and Training Awards Council
The Irish Auditing and Accounting Supervisory Authority
Limerick Northside Regeneration Agency
Limerick Southside Regeneration Agency
The Health Information and Quality Authority
Telifís na Gaeilge
Food Safety Authority of Ireland
National Social Work Qualification Board
Sea-Fisheries Protection Authority
National Centre for Partnership Performance
National Economic and Social Development Office

CHART 15

Tax and Interest as Preferential Debt

(In winding up of insolvent companies and on appointment, under floating charge, of a receiver)

Type of tax	Preferential Debt	Legislation
Income Tax	Tax for any twelve months assessed up to 5 April/31 December next before "the relevant date" and all interest thereon	Sections 98 and 285 Companies Act 1963
Corporation Tax	Do	S974 TCA 1997
Capital Gains Tax	Do	S982 TCA 1997
VAT	Tax for the last twelve months ending before "the relevant date"	S62 FA 1976
Interest on VAT	All	Do
PAYE & PRSI	Tax for the last twelve months ending before the "relevant date"	S994 TCA 1997 S995 TCA 1997
Interest on PAYE & PRSI	Do	Do
Deductions on Construction Contracts	Do	S1000 TCA 1997

NOTES:

(a) "the relevant date" means

(i) where the company is ordered to be wound up compulsorily, the date of the appointment (or first appointment) of a provisional liquidator or, if no such appointment was made, the date of the winding-up order, unless in either case the company had commenced to be wound up voluntarily before that date; and

(ii) Where sub-paragraph (i) does not apply, the date of the passing of the resolution for the winding up of the company.

(b) No preferential debt exists as to (a) Capital Acquisitions Tax, (b) Wealth Tax and (c) interest on these taxes.

(c) Where a person holds a fixed charge on the book debts of a company and the company fails to pay PAYE and VAT, the holder of the fixed charge will on notification from the Revenue Commissioners, become liable to pay the PAYE and VAT.

The amount payable is subject to an overall limit of the amount collected under the fixed charge after the date of notification from the Revenue Commissioners.

(d) PAYE and PRSI includes:

(i) amounts deducted for the income tax month in which the "relevant date" occurs.

(ii) amounts which, apart from the provisions of Regulation 31A of the Income Tax (Employments) Regulations 1960 would otherwise have been due to be remitted at the "relevant date".

CHART 16

Income Tax Time Limits

(References are to Taxes Consolidation Act 1997 unless otherwise stated)

Section	Topic	Claim etc	Claim to be made within
S930	Error or Mistake	All	Four years of end of year of assessment
S787	Retirement Annuity premiums	Against income of previous year	31 October of following year
S298	Capital allowances on plant and machinery	Lessor	Two years of end of year of assessment
S305	Excess of capital allowances over income from leasing plant or industrial buildings	Set-off of excess against other income of the year of assessment	Two years of end of year of assessment
S381	Trading / Professional Losses	Set-off against other income of year of assessment	Two years of end of year of assessment
S865	Irish repayment claims	All	Four years of end of year of assessment
S195	Artists, Writers etc.	Exemption from income tax	Year of assessment
S1023	Husbands and wives	Separate assessment	1 April in year of assessment (continues until withdrawn)
S1016	Husbands and wives	Single assessment	Year of assessment (continues until withdrawn)
S503	Investment in corporate trades	Set off against income of year of assessment	Two years of end of year of assessment
S66	Trading etc profits	Second and Third Year Adjustment	On submission of Third Year Return

CHART 17

Rates of Corporation Tax – General

(See Chart 44 for Rates from 01/01/1977)

ACCOUNTING PERIOD	STANDARD RATE	HIGHER* RATE	LOWER** RATE
1/4/1991 to 31/3/1995	40%	n/a	n/a
1/4/1995 to 31/3/1997	38% (First £50,000 @ 30%)	n/a	n/a
1/4/1997 to 31/12/1997	36% (First £50,000 @ 28%)	n/a	n/a
Y/E 31/12/1998	32% (First £50,000 @ 25%)	n/a	n/a
Y/E 31/12/1999	28% (First £100,000 @ 25%)	n/a	n/a
Y/E 31/12/2000	24%	25%	12.5%
Y/E 31/12/2001	20%	25%	12.5%
Y/E 31/12/2002	16%	25%	12.5%
Y/E 31/12/2003 & onwards	12.5%	25%	n/a

Note:

** Higher rate applies to Case III, Case IV, Case V and Income from mining and petroleum activities and dealing in non-residential land.*

***Lower rate applies to trading profits less than £50,000. Marginal relief applies where trading profits are between £50,000 and £75,000 for the year 2000.*

Lower rate applies to trading profits less than £200,000/€254,000 from 1 January 2001. Marginal relief applies where trading profits are between £200,000/€254,000 and £250,000/€317,500.

A special rate of 20% applies to profits arising from dealing in or developing residential land (See Chart 18)

See 2.2 with regard to the 10% "manufacturing rate".

CHART 18

Rates of Corporation Tax – Property Dealing & Development

Year	Non-Residential Land	Residential Land	Developed Residential	Developed Non-Residential	Construction Services
2000	25%	20%	20%*	24%	24%*
2001	25%	20%	20%	20%	20%
2002	25%	20%	16%	16%	16%
2003 *et. seq*	25%	20%	12½%	12½%	12½%

* *For the year 2000, in the case of the sale of a completed residential unit, an apportionment will be required on a 'just and reasonable basis' to establish the percentage of profit attributable to the sale of serviced land (to include all works on the land prior to laying of foundations) which will be taxable at the 20% rate, and to establish the percentage attributable to construction work which is taxable at the 24% rate.*

CHART 19

Corporation Tax - Preliminary Tax

The payment date for the payment of preliminary corporation tax was brought for ward from sixmonths after the end of the accounting period to the 21st of the month before the end of the accounting period, over a transitional period of five years. During the transitional period the preliminary tax may be paid in two instalments, ensuring that the total of the two instalments is at least 90% of the final liability for the period in question.

A summary of the minimum first instalments payable is as follows:

	Standard Company	"Small" Company* Option
A/C Period Ending In	**Minimum % of Final Liability**	**Minimum % of Prior Period Liability**
2002	18%	20%
2003	36%	40%
2004	54%	60%
2005	72%	80%
2006 *et seq.*	90%	100%

** A company is regarded as a "small"company if its corresponding corporation tax liability for the preceding chargeable period does not exceed.*

(i) €50,000 in respect of preliminary tax payable on or before 6 December 2006.

(ii) €150,000 in respect of preliminary tax payable after 6 December 2006.

(iii) €200,000 in respect of preliminary tax payable on or after 6 December 2007.

New companies that do not expect their corporation tax liability for the first year to exceed the following limits are not obliged to pay preliminary tax in that first year:

(i) €150,000 in respect of accounting periods in respect of which preliminary tax is payble between 7 December 2006 to 5 December 2007.

(ii) €200,000 in respect of accounting periods in respect of which preliminary tax is payble on or after 6 December 2007.

CHART 20

Corporation Tax Payment Dates and Form CT1 Filing Dates

Accounting Periods Ended	1st Instalment	2nd Instalment	Balance of Tax (if any) and CT1 Filing Date
1 January 2002 - 31 July 2002	28th June 2002	On a date 6 months after the accounting period ends but not later than 28th day of the month in which that day falls.	On a date 1 month from the notice of assessment. (Form CT1 is due on a date 9 months after the end of the accounting period).
1 August 2002 - 31 December 2002	On a date 31 days before the end of the accounting period but not later than 28th day of the month in which that day falls.	On a date 6 months after the accounting period ends but not later than 28th day of the month in which that day falls.	On a date 1 month from the notice of assessment. (Form CT1 is due on a date 9 months after the end of the accounting period).
1 January 2003 - 1 July 2003	On a date 31 days before the end of the accounting period but not later than 28th day of the month in which that day falls	On a date 6 months after the accounting period ends but not later than 28th day of the month in which that day falls	Together with the Form CT1 on a date 9 months after an accounting period ends but no later than 21st day of that month
2 July 2003 - 31 December 2005	On a date 31 days before the end of the accounting period but not later than 21st day of the month in which that day falls	On a date 6 months after the accounting period ends but not later than 21st day of the month in which that day falls	As above
1 January 2006 onwards	as above	no second instalment	As above

Notes

Special rules apply for accounting periods of less than one month and one day. In this situation the payment of the first instalment is due on the last day of the accounting period but not later than 28th day of the month or 21st day of the month as appropriate

The rules above relate to the payment of corporation tax including corporation tax on chargeable gains. If capital gains tax is due as in the case of development land the payment dates for capital gains tax apply.

CHART 21

Manufacturing Relief and Investment in Corporate Trades (Section 443 TCA 1997)

Type of Company	10%	RICT
Manufacturing	Yes	Yes
Manufacturing Services	Yes	Yes
90% Related Sales Company	Yes	No
"New" Shannon Company	Yes	Yes
Fish, Engineering	Yes	Yes
Services, Ship Building	Yes	Yes
Data Processing and Computer Software Development Services	Yes	Yes
Services qualifying for IDA Employment Grants	No	Yes
Designated Funds	No	Yes
R & D Company	Yes	No
Financial Services in Custom House Dock Area	Yes	No
Shipping Activities	Yes	Yes
Tourist Activities	No	Yes
Export Sales of Trading Houses	Yes	Yes
Plant Cultivation by "Micro Propagation and Plant Cloning"	Yes	Yes
Factory Ships	Yes	No
Services Re Data Processing	Yes	Yes
Construction and Leasing of Advance Factories	No	Yes
Internationally Traded Service	No	Yes
Film Production for Cinema or TV	Yes	No
Meat Processing in EC approved Factory	Yes	Yes
Fish Processing	Yes	Yes
Remanufacture or Repair of computer equipment or subassemblies	Yes	Yes
Repair or maintenance of Aircraft, Aircraft Engines or Components	Yes	Yes
Service Activities to Ships and Off-Shore Platforms etc	Yes	No
Certain Agricultural or Fishery Society Activities	Yes	No
Newspaper Advertising	Yes	No
Recycling Activities	No	Yes

Note: With effect from 1 January 2003, the requirement that a company engaged in manufacturing must be entitled to claim manufacturing relief in order to qualify for the purposes of the BES no longer applies.

CHART 22

Corporation Tax Time Limits

(References are to Taxes Consolidation Act 1997 unless otherwise stated)

Section	Topic	Claim etc	Claim to be made within
S307	Plant and Machinery Industrial Buildings	Disclaimer of Initial Allowances	Two years of the end of the accounting period for which the claim arises
S308	Excess Case V Capital Allowances	Against other profits of same accounting period or preceding accounting period	Two years of the end of the accounting period in which the excess arises
S83	Excess management expenses of investment companies	Against franked investment income of same accounting period	Two years of the end of the accounting period in which the excess arises
S396	Trading losses	Against other profits of same accounting period or preceding accounting period	Two years of the end of the accounting period in which the loss is incurred
S399	Case V losses	Against other Case V income of preceding accounting period	Two years of the end of the accounting period in which the loss is incurred
S157	Trading losses	Against franked investment income of same accounting period or preceding accounting period	Two years of end of the accounting period in which the loss is incurred
S429	Group Relief and Consortium Relief	For surrender of trading losses and other amounts eligible for relief	Two years from the end of the accounting period of the surrendering company
S882	New Companies	Advise Inspector of commencement etc	Within thirty days of commencement
S883	Liability to Corporation Tax	Notification to Inspector	Twelve months from end of accounting period

CHART 23

Indexation Factors for Capital Gains Tax

Tax Year Expend -iture Incurred	Indexation Factor for Disposals in Tax Year																	
	1987/ 88	1988/ 89	1989/ 90	1990/ 91	1991/ 92	1992/ 93	1993/ 94	1994/ 95	1995/ 96	1996/ 97	1997/ 98	1998/ 99	1999/ 00	2000/ 01	2001	2002	2003	2004 *et seq.*
1974/75	4.756	4.848	5.009	5.221	5.355	5.552	5.656	5.754	5.899	6.017	6.112	6.215	6.313	6.582	6.930	7.180	7.528	7.528
1975/76	3.842	3.916	4.046	4.217	4.326	4.484	4.568	4.647	4.764	4.860	4.936	5.020	5.099	5.316	5.597	5.799	6.080	6.080
1976/77	3.309	3.373	3.485	3.633	3.726	3.863	3.935	4.003	4.104	4.187	4.253	4.325	4.393	4.580	4.822	4.996	5.238	5.238
1977/78	2.837	2.892	2.988	3.114	3.194	3.312	3.373	3.432	3.518	3.589	3.646	3.707	3.766	3.926	4.133	4.283	4.490	4.490
1978/79	2.621	2.672	2.760	2.877	2.951	3.059	3.117	3.171	3.250	3.316	3.368	3.425	3.479	3.627	3.819	3.956	4.148	4.148
1979/80	2.365	2.410	2.490	2.596	2.663	2.760	2.812	2.861	2.933	2.992	3.039	3.090	3.139	3.272	3.445	3.570	3.742	3.742
1980/81	2.047	2.087	2.156	2.247	2.305	2.390	2.434	2.477	2.539	2.590	2.631	2.675	2.718	2.833	2.983	3.091	3.240	3.240
1981/82	1.692	1.725	1.782	1.857	1.905	1.975	2.012	2.047	2.099	2.141	2.174	2.211	2.246	2.342	2.465	2.554	2.678	2.678
1982/83	1.424	1.451	1.499	1.563	1.603	1.662	1.693	1.722	1.765	1.801	1.829	1.860	1.890	1.970	2.074	2.149	2.253	2.253
1983/84	1.266	1.290	1.333	1.390	1.425	1.478	1.505	1.531	1.570	1.601	1.627	1.654	1.680	1.752	1.844	1.911	2.003	2.003
1984/85	1.149	1.171	1.210	1.261	1.294	1.341	1.366	1.390	1.425	1.454	1.477	1.502	1.525	1.590	1.674	1.735	1.819	1.819
1985/86	1.082	1.103	1.140	1.188	1.218	1.263	1.287	1.309	1.342	1.369	1.390	1.414	1.436	1.497	1.577	1.633	1.713	1.713
1986/87	1.035	1.055	1.090	1.136	1.165	1.208	1.230	1.252	1.283	1.309	1.330	1.352	1.373	1.432	1.507	1.562	1.637	1.637
1987/88	-	1.020	1.054	1.098	1.126	1.168	1.190	1.210	1.241	1.266	1.285	1.307	1.328	1.384	1.457	1.510	1.583	1.583
1988/89	-	-	1.034	1.077	1.105	1.146	1.167	1.187	1.217	1.242	1.261	1.282	1.303	1.358	1.430	1.481	1.553	1.553
1989/90	-	-	-	1.043	1.070	1.109	1.130	1.149	1.178	1.202	1.221	1.241	1.261	1.314	1.384	1.434	1.503	1.503
1990/91	-	-	-	-	1.026	1.064	1.084	1.102	1.130	1.153	1.171	1.191	1.210	1.261	1.328	1.376	1.442	1.442
1991/92	-	-	-	-	-	1.037	1.056	1.075	1.102	1.124	1.142	1.161	1.179	1.229	1.294	1.341	1.406	1.406
1992/93	-	-	-	-	-	-	1.019	1.037	1.063	1.084	1.101	1.120	1.138	1.186	1.249	1.294	1.356	1.356
1993/94	-	-	-	-	-	-	-	1.018	1.043	1.064	1.081	1.099	1.117	1.164	1.226	1.270	1.331	1.331
1994/95	-	-	-	-	-	-	-	-	1.026	1.046	1.063	1.081	1.098	1.144	1.205	1.248	1.309	1.309
1995/96	-	-	-	-	-	-	-	-	-	1.021	1.037	1.054	1.071	1.116	1.175	1.218	1.277	1.277
1996/97	-	-	-	-	-	-	-	-	-	-	1.016	1.033	1.050	1.094	1.152	1.194	1.251	1.251
1997/98	-	-	-	-	-	-	-	-	-	-	-	1.017	1.033	1.077	1.134	1.175	1.232	1.232
1998/99	-	-	-	-	-	-	-	-	-	-	-	-	1.016	1.059	1.115	1.156	1.212	1.212
1999/00	-	-	-	-	-	-	-	-	-	-	-	-	-	1.043	1.098	1.138	1.193	1.193
2000/01	-	-	-	-	-	-	-	-	-	-	-	-	-	-	1.053	1.091	1.144	1.144
2001	-	-	-	-	-	-	-	-	-	-	-	-	-	-	-	1.037	1.087	1.087
2002	-	-	-	-	-	-	-	-	-	-	-	-	-	-	-	-	1.049	1.049
2003 *et seq.*	-	-	-	-	-	-	-	-	-	-	-	-	-	-	-	-	-	1.00

NOTE: No indexation is available for expenditure made within 12 months prior to the date of disposal.

CHART 24

Capital Gains Tax Rates

(*See Chart 43 for earlier years*)

Date of Disposal	Development Land Sold for Residential Development	Development Land (other than for Residential Development)	Foreign Life Assurance Policies and Offshore Funds[1]	All Other Assets (Normal Rate)[2]
1/12/1999 onwards	20%	20%	40%	20%
23/4/1998 to 30/11/1999	20%	40%	40%	20%
12/2/1998 to 22/4/1998	40%	40%	40%	20%
3/12/1997 to 11/2/1998	40%	40%	20%	20%

Notes:

1. The rates quoted for offshore funds are for the chargeable gains on disposals of interests in offshore funds which are "distributing funds" (funds which are not non-qualifying funds), since gains on disposals of interests in non-qualifying offshore funds are taxed as income (and not capital gains tax). See page 126 in relation to tax other than capital gains tax.
2. The "All Other Assets" do not include the assets of certain special investment products (special portfolio investment accounts, special investment schemes and special investment policies) where gains on disposals are charged to capital gains tax at 20% from 6 April 1999 within the fund (and not on the beneficiary). The rate was 10% before 6 April 1999.

CHART 25

Capital Acquisitions Tax Rates

(*see Chart 52 for earlier years*)

Rates from 30 January 1991 to 10 April 1994

Slice	Cumulative Slice	Rate of Tax %	Tax Thereon	Cumulative Tax
Threshold Amount	Threshold Amount +	nil	nil	nil
10,000	10,000	20	2,000	2,000
40,000	50,000	30	12,000	14,000
50,000	100,000	35	17,500	31,500
Balance		40		

Rates from 11 April 1994 to 30 November 1999

Slice	Cumulative Slice	Rate of Tax %	Tax Thereon	Cumulative Tax
Threshold Amount	Threshold Amount +	nil	nil	nil
10,000	10,000	20	2,000	2,000
30,000	40,000	30	9,000	11,000
Balance		40		

Rates from 1 December 1999

Slice	Rate of Tax %
Threshold Amount	Nil
Balance	20%

CHART 26

Capital Acquisitions Tax Class Thresholds

(see Chart 53 for earlier years)

Relationship to donor/ testator	Gift or inheritance in								
	From 1/12/1999 to 31/12/2000	2001	2002	2003	2004	2005	2006	2007	2008
	£	£	€	€	€	€	€	€	€
Child or minor child of deceased child or parent where s116 FA 1991 applies	300,000	316,800	422,148	441,198	456,438	466,725	478,155	496,824	521,208
Lineal ancestor (other than a parent where s116 FA 1991 applies) lineal descendant (other than a child or minor child of a deceased child), brother, sister, child of brother or sister	30,000	31,680	42,215	44,120	45,644	46,673	47,815	49,682	52,121
Any other person	15,000	15,840	21,108	22,060	22,822	23,336	23,908	24,841	26,060

CHART 27

Rates of Stamp Duty

(1) Residential Property (effective from 5 November 2007)

(see Chart 57 for earlier years)

Consideration (or Aggregate Consideration) exceeds €127,000	Rate
First €125,000	NIL
Next €875,000	7%
Excess over €1,000,000	9%

Note: To fully preserve the exemption that applied prior to the introduction of the above rates, transactions where the consideration (or aggregate consideration) does not exceed €127,000 continue to be exempt from Stamp Duty.

Section 91 SDCA 1999 provides for an exemption from stamp duty for purchasers of certain smaller new residential properties where the purchaser is an owner-occupier but not a first-time buyer, and section 92 provides for a reduction in stamp duty for similar purchasers of certain larger new residential properties.

First Time Buyers – Instruments executed on or after 31 March 2007

Finance (No. 2) Bill 2007 provides for the abolition of stamp duty for all owner-occupying first-time buyers of houses and apartments, whether new or second-hand. The change applies to instruments executed on or after 31 March 2007. It also provides for a refund procedure for persons who, by virtue of this change, became entitled retrospectively to relief or additional relief. Such persons will be entitled to claim a repayment of duty paid from the Revenue Commissioners.

(2) Non-residential Property (effective from 4 December 2002)

Value	Rate
Up to €10,000	0%
€10,001 – €20,000	1%
€20,001 – €30,000	2%
€30,001 – €40,000	3%
€40,001 – €70,000	4%
€70,001 – €80,000	5%
€80,001 – €100,000	6%
€100,001 – €120,000	7%
€120,001 – €150,000	8%
Over €150,000	9%

CHART 28

VAT Fourth Schedule Services

If Supplier is	and Recipient is	The Place of Supply is	The Person liable for Irish VAT is
Foreign	Irish Business	Ireland	Irish Business Recipient
Foreign	Irish Private	Abroad	No Irish Liability
Irish	Irish Business or Private	Ireland	Irish Supplier
Irish	Business outside Ireland	Abroad	No Irish Liability
Irish	Private in EU	Ireland	Irish Supplier
Irish	Private outside EU	Abroad	No Irish Liability

The above rules are modified where the supplier has an establishment in the country of the recipient.

NOTE: VAT FOURTH SCHEDULE SERVICES include:
Services that are taxed where received viz:

(i) Transfers and assignments of copyrights, patents, licences, trade marks and similar rights;

(ia) Hiring out of movable goods other than means of transport;

(ii) Advertising services;

(iii) Services of consultants, engineers, consultancy bureaux, lawyers, accountants and other similar services, data processing and provision of information (but excluding services connected with immovable goods);

(iiia) Telecommunications services in certain circumstances. The definition of telecommunications services was modified in the Finance Act 2000;

(iiib) Radio and television broadcasting service;

(iiic) Electronically supplied services;

(iiid) The provision of access to, and of transport or transmission through, natural gas and electricity distribution systems and the provision of other directly linked services.

(iv) Acceptance of any obligation to refrain from pursuing or exercising in whole or in part, any business activity or any such rights as are referred to in paragraph (1);

(v) Banking, financial and insurance services (including re-insurance, and financial fund management functions but not including the provision of safe deposit facilities) in certain circumstances;

(vi) The provision of staff;

(vii) The services of intermediaries who act in the name and for the account of a principal when procuring for him any services specified in paragraphs (i) to (vi).

CHART 29

VAT Exempted Activities

The main exempted activities are:

Admission to sporting events.
Circus admissions.
Certain lettings of immovable goods.
Medical, dental and optical services.
Certain agency services.
Insurance services.
Certain banking and stock exchange activities.
Transport of passengers and their baggage.
Betting.
Funeral undertaking.
Certain theatrical and musical performances.
Certain welfare and non-profit making activities.
Management of collective investment undertakings, including the functions of collective portfolio management, as listed in Annex II to Directive 2001/107/EC, where those functions are supplied by the person with responsibility for the provision of those functions for the undertaking.
Chiropody.
Educational services including pre-school education facilities.
Certain child-care and homecare services

CHART 30

VAT Zero Rate

The main zero-rated goods and services are:

Most food and drink of a kind used for human consumption, most exports of goods and services relating to exports of goods, oral medicine, fertilizers, most articles of personal clothing and footwear suitable for children under 11 years of age, certain services relating to marine safety, certain books and booklets including atlases, certain medical equipment and appliances, certain navigation services and supplies to certain international bodies.

CHART 31

VAT 10% Rate

The goods and services liable at this rate are:

Domestic dwellings for which a contract with a private individual has been entered into before 25 February 1993, short term hire of cars under an agreement made before 25 February 1993 and at charges fixed at the time of the agreement, lettings of hotel and holiday accommodation under an agreement made before 25 February 1993 and at charges fixed at the time of the agreement.

CHART 32

VAT 13.5% Rate

The main goods and services liable at this rate are:

Immovable goods, services consisting of the development of immovable goods, concrete and concrete blocks, hotel and holiday accommodation, short term hiring of cars, boats, tents, caravans, mobile homes, tour guide services, fuel for power and heating, coal, peat, timber, electricity, gas, heating oil, hotel and restaurant meals, admissions to cinemas, cabaret, certain live theatrical and musical performances and to certain exhibitions, waste disposal, general agricultural and veterinary services, use of commercial sporting facilities, car driving instruction, care of the human body, general repair and maintenance services, certain imports and supplies of works of art, antiques and collectors' items, certain green fees, brochures, periodicals and newspapers, live poultry and live ostriches, animal insemination services, livestock semen, cooked food purchased at takeaway, supermarket, garage or other outlet, children's car safety seats, micanthus, rhizomes, seeds, bulbs, noots and similar goods used for the agricultural production of dio fuel and non oral contraceptive products.

CHART 33

VAT 21% Rate

The main goods and services liable at this rate are:

Adult clothing and footwear including materials for their manufacture, household durable and non-durable goods, drink and certain foods, goods for personal use, sport and recreational goods, educational goods, agricultural goods, non-oral medicines, most building materials, office equipment and stationery, most services such as telecommunication services, accountancy services (including farm accountancy services), legal services, advertising services, other goods and services not liable at another rate.

(*See Chart 47 for Historic VAT Rates.*)

CHART 34

VAT Thresholds

Persons supplying services	€25,500 - 1/7/1994 - 30/4/2006 €27,500 - 1/5/2006 - 28/2/2007 €35,000 - 1/3/2007 - 30/4/2008 €37,500 from 1/5/2008
Persons supplying goods	€51,000 - 1/7/1994 - 30/4/2006 €55,000 - 1/5/2006 - 28/2/2007 €70,000 - 1/3/2007 - 30/4/2008 €75,000 from 1/5/2008
Persons making intra-Community acquisitions	€41,000
Persons making mail order or distance sales into the State	€35,000

In the case of supplies in the State and intra-Community acquisitions, registration is obligatory where the appropriate turnover threshold is exceeded or is likely to be exceeded in any 12-month period.

The distance sales threshold is based on a calendar year.

There is no VAT registration threshold in respect of the cross border receipt of Fourth Schedule services by a person for business purposes.

See Chart 48 for earlier thresholds.

CHART 35

VAT Multiplier

VAT multiplier to be used when valuing an interest in immovable goods from 1990 to-date.

DATE ISSUE	*REDEMPTION YIELD*	*MULTIPLIER*
21 May 1991	9.30 per cent	10.75
24 January 1992	9.11 per cent	10.98
14 June 1993	7.37 per cent	13.57
15 October 1993	6.87 per cent	14.56
17 August 1994	8.56 per cent	11.68
15 May 1995	8.52 per cent	11.74
19 April 1996	6.93 per cent	14.43 (Note 1)
17 September 1997	6.26 per cent	15.97
11 May 1999	4.26 per cent	23.47 (Note 2)
29 January 2002	5.14 per cent	19.45
1 March 2003	3.377 per cent	29.61
1 February 2004	4.702 per cent	21.27

1. The operative date for the multiplier of 14.43 is 26 March 1997.
2. The operative date for the multiplier of 23.47 is 30 June 1999.

CHART 36

Capital Allowances

Initial Allowances

Expenditure Incurred	Plant and Machinery	Industrial Buildings	Hotels	Farm Buildings
1.4.71 - 5.4.74	100%	20%	10%	–
6.4.74 - 15.1.75	100%	20%	10%	20%
16.1.75 - 5.4.80	100%	50%	10%	20%
6.4.80 - 31.3.88	100%	50%	10%	Nil
1.4.88 - 31.3.89	*75%	*50%	10%	Nil
1.4.89 - 31.3.91	*50%	*50%	10%	Nil
1.4.91 - 31.3.92	*25%	*25%	10%	Nil
1.4.92 onwards	Nil	Nil	Nil	Nil

* A rate of up to 100% applies to qualifying services companies in the Customs House Docks Area or in the Shannon Customs Free Area, subject to varying time limits.

Writing Down and Wear and Tear Allowances

Expenditure Incurred	Plant and Machinery	Industrial Buildings	Hotels	Farm Buildings
1.4.71 - 5.4.74	Up to 100%	2%	10%	10%
6.4.74 - 15.1.75	Up to 100%	2%	10%	10%
16.1.75 - 1.2.78	Up to 100%	4%	10%	10%
2.2.78 - 5.4.80	Up to 100%	Up to 100%	Up to 100%	10%
6.4.80 - 31.3.88	Up to 100%	Up to 100%	Up to 100%	Up to 30%
1.4.88 - 31.3.89	*Up to 75%	*Up to 75%	Up to 75%	Up to 30%
1.4.89 - 31.3.91	*Up to 50%	*Up to 50%	Up to 50%	Up to 50%
1.4.91 - 31.3.92	*Up to 25%	*Up to 25%	Up to 25%	Up to 25%
1.4.92 - 26.1.94	15%	4%	10%	10%
27.1.94 - 31.12.00	15%	4%	15%	15%
1.1.01 - 3.12.02	20%	4%	15%	15%
4.12.02 onwards	12.5%	4%	4%**	15%

* A rate of up to 100% applies to qualifying services companies in the Customs House Docks Area or in the Shannon Customs Free Area, subject to varying time limits.

** See 1.20.14 re transitional provisions which extend the 15% in certain circumstances

CHART 37

Urban Renewal Area Allowances – 1986 Scheme*

	Dublin Areas	Custom House Docks	Temple Bar	Other Areas
Commercial Property				
Owner Occupier: Free Depreciation or Initial Allowance and Annual Allowance**	50% 25% 2%	100% 50% 4%	100% 50% 4%	100% 50% 4%
Lessor: Free Depreciation or Initial Allowance and Annual Allowance**	n/a 25% 2%	n/a 50% 4%	n/a 50% 4%	n/a 50% 4%
Qualifying Period	31.07.94	24.01.99	05.04.99	31.07.94
Residential Property				
Owner Occupier:**	5% p/a for 10 years	Old: 10% pa for 10 years	New: 5% pa for 10 years Old: 10% pa for 10 years	5% pa for 10 years
Lessor:	"Section 23" type relief applies with unrestricted set off against total rental income			
Qualifying Period	As above for each area			
Plant and Machinery				
Accelerated allowances expenditure incurred between 01.04.91 and 01.04.92	25%	25%*	25%	25%
Expenditure incurred after 01.04.92	n/a	n/a*	n/a	n/a

* See 2001 edition for full details of the various property tax incentive schemes.

See paragraph 1.27 in relation to "specified reliefs" under Chapter 2A TCA 1997, in the context of the limitation of the amount of certain reliefs used by certain high-income individuals.

CHART 38

Urban Renewal Area Allowances – Designated Area/Street From 1.8.1994

	DESIGNATED AREA	DESIGNATED STREET
INDUSTRIAL PROPERTY		
OWNER OCCUPIER		
Accelerated Allowance	50%	50%
Initial Allowance	25%	25%
Annual Allowance*	4%	4%
Maximum	100%	100%
LESSOR		
Initial Allowance	25%	25%
Annual Allowance*	4%	4%
Maximum	100%	100%
COMMERCIAL PROPERTY		
OWNER OCCUPIER		
Accelerated Allowance	50%	50%
Initial Allowance	25%	25%
Annual Allowance*	2%	2%
Maximum	50%	50%
LESSOR		
Initial Allowance	25%	25%
Annual Allowance*	2%	2%
Maximum	50%	50%
RESIDENTIAL PROPERTY		
OWNER OCCUPIER		
Construction*	5% p.a. (10 yrs)	Nil
Refurbishment*	10% p.a. (10 yrs)	10% p.a. (10 yrs)
LESSOR		
Construction	100%	Nil
Conversion	100%	100%
Refurbishment	100%	100%
DOUBLE RENT ALLOWANCE	YES	NO

See paragraph 1.27 in relation to "specified reliefs" under Chapter 2A TCA 1997, in the context of the limitation of the amount of certain reliefs used by certain high-income individuals.

CHART 39

1998 Urban and Rural Renewal Schemes

Industrial – Construction or Refurbishment	**Urban Scheme**	**Rural Scheme**
Owner Occupier		
Free Depreciation	50%	50%
or		
Initial Allowance	50%	50%
and		
Annual Allowance up to 100%*	4%	4%
Lessor		
Initial Allowance	50%	50%
and		
Annual Allowance up to 100%	4%	4%

Commercial – Construction or Refurbishment	**Urban Scheme**	**Rural Scheme**
Owner Occupier		
Free Depreciation	50%	50%
or		
Initial Allowance	50%	50%
and		
Annual Allowance up to 100%*	4%	4%
Lessor		
Initial Allowance	50%	50%
und		
Annual Allowance up to 100%	4%	4%

Residential	
Owner Occupier	
Construction:	5% deduction against total income for 10 years*
Refurbishment:	10% deduction against total income for 10 years*
Lessor	
Section 23-type relief available in respect of expenditure on the construction, conversion or refurbishment expenditure.	

See paragraph 1.27 in relation to "specified reliefs" under Chapter 2A TCA 1997, in the context of the limitation of the amount of certain reliefs used by certain high-income individuals.

CHART 40

2000 Town Renewal Scheme

Industrial – Construction or Refurbishment	**Allowances**
Owner Occupier	
Free Depreciation	50%
or	
Initial Allowance	50%
and	
Annual Allowance up to 100%*	4%
Lessor	
Initial Allowance	50%
and	
Annual Allowance up to 100%*	4%

Commercial – Construction or Refurbishment	**Allowances**
Owner Occupier	
Free Depreciation	50%
or	
Initial Allowance	50%
and	
Annual Allowance up to 100%*	4%
Lessor	
Initial Allowance	50%
and	
Annual Allowance up to 100%*	4%

Residential
Owner Occupier
Construction: 5% deduction against total income for 10 years*
Refurbishment: 10% deduction against total income for 10 years*
Lessor
Section 23-type relief available in respect of expenditure on the construction, conversion or refurbishment expenditure.

See paragraph 1.27 in relation to "specified reliefs" under Chapter 2A TCA 1997, in the context of the limitation of the amount of certain reliefs used by certain high-income individuals.

CHART 41

Summary of Terminating Property Investment Schemes and Incentives

Scheme	Extension to 31-12-2006 Existing conditions	Extension to 31 July 2008		Cap on expenditure 75% 2007 50% 2008	Section	
		Work = 15% costs by 31/12/06	Binding contract by 31/7/06		FA 2006	TCA 1997
Hotels ('accelerated' allowances)	Full and valid planning application by 31/12/04	Local authority to certify	Yes	Yes	26 27	270/316 268/272/274
Holiday Camps ('accelerated' allowances)	Full and valid planning application by 31/12/04	Local authority to certify	Yes	Yes	26 27	270/316 268/272/274
Registered Holiday Cottages	Full and valid planning application by 31/12/04	Local authority to certify	Yes	Yes	26 27	270/316 268/272/274
Multi-storey Car Parks	15% project costs by 30/9/03 - certified by 31/12/03	Architect/quantity surveyor to certify	No	Yes	26 29	270/316/344
Sports Injury Clinics	No existing conditions No previous termination date	Architect/quantity surveyor to certify	No	Yes	26 28	270/316/268
Nursing Home Residential Units (contracts pre 1 May 2007)	No existing conditions	Work = 15% costs not required	No	100% to 24/3/07 75% 25/3/07 - 31/12/07 50% 1/1/08 - 31/7/08	26 37	270/316/268
Nursing Home Residential Units (contracts on or after 1 May 2007)	No existing conditions	Extension to 30/4/10	N/A	Companies 75% 1/5/07 - 30/4/10 Individuals 50% 1/5/07 - 30/4/10	FA07 s28	268/270/272/274 /316
Third Level Educational Buildings	Application to Minister for Finance by 31/12/04	Architect/quantity surveyor to certify	No	Yes	26 34	270/316/843

CHART 41 *(continued)*

Urban Renewal	15% project costs by 30/6/03 - certified by 30/9/03	Local authority to certify commercial/industrial Architect/quantity surveyor to certify residential	For commercial/industrial only	Yes	25 26 30	372AL/372AS 270/316 372A/372B/372BA/372C/372D
Rural Renewal	Full and valid planning application by 31/12/04	Local authority to certify commercial/industrial Architect/quantity surveyor to certify residential	For commercial/industrial only	Yes	25 26 31	372AL/372AS 270/316 372L/372M/372N
Town Renewal	Full and valid planning application by 31/12/04	Local authority to certify commercial/industrial Architect/quantity surveyor to certify residential	For commercial/industrial only	Yes	25 26 33	372AL/372AS 270/316 372AA/372AB/372AC/372AD
Living over the Shop	Full and valid planning application by 31/12/04	Architect/quantity surveyor to certify	No	Yes	25 26 30	372AL/372AS 270/316 372A/372B/372BA/372C/372D
Park and Ride (including commercial/residential)	Full and valid planning application by 31/12/04	Architect/quantity surveyor to certify	No	Yes	25 26 32	372AL/372AS 270/316 372U/372V/372W
Student Accommodation	Full and valid planning application by 31/12/04	Architect/quantity surveyor to certify	No	Yes	25	372AL/372AS
General rented residential	No existing conditions No previous termination date	Work = 15% costs not required	No	Yes	11 25	372AM 372AL/372AS

CHART 42

Historic Income Tax Rates 1980/81 – 1989/90

1980/81

Single/Widow(er)	*Married Couple*
1,000 @ 25%	2,000 @ 25%
4,000 @ 35%	8,000 @ 35%
2,000 @ 45%	4,000 @ 45%
2,000 @ 55%	4,000 @ 55%
Bal @ 60%	Bal @ 60%

1981/82

Single/Widow(er)	*Married Couple*
1,000 @ 25%	2,000 @ 25%
4,500 @ 35%	9,000 @ 35%
2,000 @ 45%	4,000 @ 45%
2,000 @ 55%	4,000 @ 55%
Bal @ 60%	Bal @ 60%

1982/83

Single/Widow(er)	*Married Couple*
1,000 @ 25%	2,000 @ 25%
3,000 @ 35%	6,000 @ 35%
2,000 @ 45%	4,000 @ 45%
2,000 @ 55%	4,000 @ 55%
Bal @ 60%	Bal @ 60%

1983/84

Single/Widow(er)	*Married Couple*
1,000 @ 25%	2,000 @ 25%
3,000 @ 35%	6,000 @ 35%
2,000 @ 45%	4,000 @ 45%
2,000 @ 55%	4,000 @ 55%
2,000 @ 60%	4,000 @ 60%
Bal @ 65%	Bal @65%

1984/85

Single/Widow(er)	*Married Couple*
4,000 @ 35%	8,000 @ 35%
2,000 @ 45%	4,000 @ 45%
2,000 @ 55%	4,000 @ 55%
2,000 @ 60%	4,000 @ 60%
Bal @ 65%	Bal @ 65%

1985/86

Single/Widow(er)	*Married Couple*
4,500 @ 35%	9,000 @ 35%
2,800 @ 48%	5,600 @ 48%
Bal @ 60%	Bal @ 60%

1986/87 and 1987/88

Single/Widow(er)	*Married Couple*
4,700 @ 35%	9,400 @ 35%
2,800 @ 48%	5,600 @ 48%
Bal @ 58%	Bal @ 58%

1988/89

Single/Widow(er)	*Married Couple*
5,700 @ 35%	11400 @ 35%
2,900 @ 48%	5,800 @ 48%
Bal @ 58%	Bal @ 58%

1989/90

Single/Widow(er)	*Married Couple*
6,100 @ 32%	12,200 @ 32%
3,100 @ 48%	6,200 @ 48%
Bal @ 56%	Bal @ 56%

CHART 43

Historic CGT Rates From 1980/81

1980/81 and 1981/82	
Standard Rate	30%
Ownership period 3-6 years	25.5%
6-9 years	21%
9-12 years	16.5%
12-15 years	12%
15-18 years	7.5%
18-21 years	3%
More than 21 years	0%
These reduced rates applied to assets other than development land, mineral assets and shares deriving their value therefrom.	They were not available to companies or individuals remitting foreign gains
On or after 26 March 1982	
Ownership period 1 year	60%
1-3 years	50%
More than 3 years	40%
Development land	
Before 26 March 1982	45% (or 40% in the case of compulsory purchase)
26 March 1982 - 5 April 1990	
Ownership period 1 year	60%
1-3 years	50%
All other cases	50% (or 40% in the case of compulsory purchase)
1986/87- 1989/90	
Ownership period 1 year	60%
1-3 years	50%
3-6 years	35%
More than 6 years	30%
1990/91 and 1991/92	
Ownership period 1-3 years	50%
3-6 years	35%
More than 6 years	30%
Development land	50% (or 40% in the case of compulsory purchase)
1992/93 - 1997/98 (3 December 1997)	40% (all gains)
After 3 December 1997	20% (see legislation for conditions and exclusions)
Note that a reduced rate of 27% existed from 1994/95 to 1996/97 for certain shares.	This 27% rate became 26% for disposals between 6 April 1997 and 3 December 1997

CHART 44

Historic Corporation Tax Rates 1977-1995

Period	Standard Rate
1/1/1977 - 31/12/1981	45%
1/1/1982 - 31/03/1988	50%
1/4/1988 - 31/03/1989	47%
1/4/1989 - 31/03/1991	43%
1/4/1991 - 31/03/1995	40%

CHART 45

Historic PRSI Rates for the Self Employed

1987/88 – 2005

Year	Upper Limit	Minimum PRSI Payment	PRSI Free Allowance	Rate %
1987/88	N/A	N/A	N/A	N/A
1988/89	£16,200	£208	N/A	3
1989/90	£16,700	£208	N/A	4
1990/91	£17,300	£208	N/A	5
1991/92	£18,000	£234	N/A	5
1992/93	£19,000	£234	N/A	5
1993/94	£20,000	£250	N/A	5
1994/95	£20,900	£250	N/A	5
1995/96	£21,500	£230	£520	5
1996/97	£22,300	£215	£1,040	5
1997/98	£23,200	£215	£1,040	5
1998/99	£24,200	£215	£1,040	5
1999/00	£25,400	£215	£1,040	5
2000/01	£26,500	£215	£1,040	5
2001	N/A	£200	N/A	3
2002	N/A	€254	N/A	3
2003	N/A	€254	N/A	3
2004	N/A	€254	N/A	3
2005	N/A	€254	N/A	3

Notes:

(i) Each individual is treated separately for PRSI. For married couples, income for each spouse should be calculated separately.

(ii) Individuals over 66 years are exempt from charge to PRSI.

(iii) No liability to PRSI arises above the upper income limit figure.

CHART 46

Historic Levy Rates (PAYE Employees & Self Employed) 1987/88 – 2005

Year	Earnings Threshold	Employment & Training %	Income %	Health %	Total %
1987/88	N/A	1	N/A	1.25	2.25
1988/89	N/A	1	N/A	1.25	2.25
1989/90	N/A	1	N/A	1.25	2.25
1990/91	N/A	1	N/A	1.25	2.25
1991/92	N/A	1	N/A	1.25	2.25
1992/93	N/A	1	N/A	1.25	2.25
1993/94	N/A	1	1	1.25	3.25
1994/95	£8,996	1	N/A	1.25	2.25
1995/96	£9,256	1	N/A	1.25	2.25
1996/97	£9,776	1	N/A	1.25	2.25
1997/98	£10,244	1	N/A	1.25	2.25
1998/99	£10,764	1	N/A	1.25	2.25
1999/00	£11,284	N/A	N/A	2.00	2.00
2000/01	£14,560	N/A	N/A	2.00	2.00
2001	£10,640	N/A	N/A	2.00	2.00
2002	€18,512	N/A	N/A	2.00	2.00
2003	€18,512	N/A	N/A	2.00	2.00
2004	€18,512	N/A	N/A	2.00	2.00
2005	€20,800	N/A	N/A	2.00	2.00

Notes:

(i) Each individual is treated separately for levies. For married couples, income for each spouse should be calculated separately.

(ii) Individuals over 70 years are exempt from charge to levies.

(iii) The earnings threshold above is calculated weekly, e.g., for 2002 and 2003 the amount is €56 per week. If reckonable income is below the weekly amounts (annualised above) in the years 1994/95 to 2003 inclusive then no liability to levies arises.

(iv) An upper income limit applies to the health levy for the year's 1987/88 to 1990/91 inclusive. No liability to the Health levy arises above the upper income limit figure.

CHART 47

Historic Vat Rates

Date	General Rates %	Livestock Rates %
1 May 1987	Zero, 10, 25	1.7
1 March 1988	Zero, 10, 25	1.4
1 March 1989	Zero, 10, 25	2.0
1 March 1990	Zero, 10, 23	2.3
1 March 1991	Zero, 10, 12.5, 21	2.3
1 March 1992	Zero, 10, 12.5, 16, 21	2.7
1 March 1993	Zero, 10, 12.5, 21	2.5
1 March 1996	Zero, 10, 12.5, 21	2.8
1 March 1997	Zero, 10, 12.5, 21	3.3
1 March 1998	Zero, 10, 12.5, 21	3.6
1 March 1999	Zero, 10, 12.5, 21	4.0
1 March 2000	Zero, 10, 12.5, 21	4.2
1 January 2001	Zero, 10, 12.5, 20	4.3
1 March 2002	Zero, 10, 12.5, 21	4.3
1 January 2003	Zero, 10, 13.5, 21	4.3
1 January 2004	Zero, 10, 13.5, 21	4.4
1 January 2005	Zero, 10, 13.5, 21	4.8

CHART 48

Historic Vat Thresholds

Date	Thresholds					
	Services		Goods			
	£	€	£	€	£	€
1 November 1972	*1,800	2,285.53	*6,000	7,618.43	*12,000	15,236.86
1 November 1979	*3,000	3,809.21	*9,000	11,427.64	*18,000	22,855.29
20 November 1981	15,000	19,046.07	30,000	38,092.14		
1 July 1983	12,000	15,232.86	25,000	31,743.52		
24 May 1989	15,000	19,046.07	32,000	40,631.62		
1 July 1994	20,000	25,394.76**	40,000	50,789.52**		

* Equivalent to six consecutive two-monthly taxable periods.

** Rounded to €25,500 and €51,000.

CHART 49

Historic Specified Amounts for the Restriction of Capital Allowances and Expenses Passenger Motor Vehicles*

PROVIDED FOR USE	RELEVANT LIMIT ALL CARS £
Up to 15/5/1973	No Limit
16/5/1973 - 28/1/1976	2,500
29/1.1976 - 5/4/1986	3,500
6/4/1986 - 27/1/1988	4,000
28/1/1988 - 25/1/1989	6,000
26/1/1989 - 29/1/1992	7,000
30/1/1992 - 26/1/1994	10,000

	NEW CARS* £	SECOND HAND CARS* £
27/1/1994 - 8/2/1995	13,000	10,000
9/2/1995 - 22/1/1997	14,000	10,000
23/1/1997 - 2/12/1997	15,000	10,000
3/12/1997 - 2/12/1998	15,500	10,000
3/12/1998 – 30/11/1999	16,000	10,000
EXPENDITURE INCURRED		
1/12/1999 - (Note 1)	16,500	10,000

* In the case of running expenses the increased limits apply to all cars.

CHARGEABLE PERIODS ENDING (Note 2)	**All Cars**
Between 1/1/2001 - 31/12/2001 inclusive	IR£17,000 (€21,585)
Between 1/1/2002 - 31/12/2005 inclusive	€22,000
Between 1/1/2006 - 31/12/2006 inclusive	€23,000
On or after 1/1/2007	€24,000

Note 1 The limits of £16,500 / £10,000 apply for expenditure incurred between 01 December 1999 and the last day of the accounting period preceding:

(i) the accounting period ending on or after 01 January 2001, for companies, and

(ii) the income tax basis period ending on or after 1 January 2001, for individuals.

Note 2 The restriction in respect of motor running expenses does not apply for chargeable periods ending on or after 1 January 2002.

CHART 50

Historic Tax Credits on Dividends – Republic of Ireland

Period	Tax Credit Normal Dividend	Tax Credit Manufacturing Dividend
5/4/1976 to 5/4/1978	35/65	N/A*
6/4/1978 to 5/4/1983	30/70	1/18
6/4/1983 to 5/4/1988	35/65	1/18
6/4/1988 to 5/4/1989	32/68	1/18
6/4/1989 to 5/4/1991	28/72	1/18
6/4/1991 to 5/4/1995	25/75	1/18
6/4/1995 to 5/4/1997	23/77	1/18
6/4/1997 to 2/12/1997	21/79	1/18
3/12/1997 to 5/4/1999	11/89	1/18

Note: Tax credits were abolished with effect from 6 April 1999.

CHART 51

Historic Tax Credits on Dividends – UK

Period	Tax Credit	Tax Credit Repay to R.I.
1979/80 to 1985/86	30/70	15/30
1986/87	29/71	14/29
1987/88	27/73	12/27
1988/89 to 1992/93	25/75	10/25
1993/94 to 1998/99	20/80	5/20

Note:

(1) The tax credit is calculated by reference to the net dividend

(2) Repayment to R.I. shareholders is calculated by reference to the tax credit.

(3) Tax credits were abolished with effect from 6 April 1999.

CHART 52
Historic Capital Acquisitions Tax Rates
Position Up To 25 March 1984

There were four separate tables for different classes of relationship, and these were as follows:

TABLE 1
Applicable where the donee or successor is the spouse, child, or minor child of a deceased child, of the disponer

Slice £	Cumulative Slice £	Rate of Tax %	Tax Thereon £	Cumulative Tax £
150,000	150,000	Nil	Nil	Nil
50,000	200,000	25	12,500	12,500
50,000	250,000	30	15,000	27,500
50,000	300,000	35	17,500	45,000
50,000	350,000	40	20,000	65,000
50,000	400,000	45	22,500	87,500
Excess		50		

TABLE II
Applicable where the donee or successor is a lineal ancestor or a linear descendant (other than a child, or a minor child of a deceased child) of disponer.

Slice £	Cumulative Slice £	Rate of Tax %	Tax Thereon £	Cumulative Tax £

(a) the taxable gift of inheritance is taken on or before 31 March 1978.

Slice £	Cumulative Slice £	Rate of Tax %	Tax Thereon £	Cumulative Tax £
15,000	15,000	Nil	Nil	Nil
3,000	18,000	5	150	150
5,000	23,000	7	350	500
10,000	33,000	10	1,000	1,500
10,000	43,000	13	1,300	2,800
10,000	53,000	16	1,600	4,400
10,000	63,000	19	1,900	6,300
10,000	73,000	22	2,200	8,500
15,000	88,000	25	3,750	12,250
15,000	103,000	28	4,200	16,450
15,000	118,000	31	4,650	21,100
15,000	133,000	34	5,100	26,200
15,000	148,000	37	5,550	31,750
15,000	163,000	40	6,000	37,750
15,000	178,000	43	6,450	44,200
15,000	193,000	46	6,900	51,100
15,000	208,000	49	7,350	58,450
Excess		50		

CHART 52 (*Continued*)

(b) The taxable gift or inheritance is taken on or after 1 April 1978

Slice £	Cumulative Slice £	Rate of Tax %	Tax Thereon £	Cumulative Tax £
30,000	30,000	Nil	Nil	Nil
3,000	33,000	5	150	150
5,000	38,000	7	350	500
10,000	48,000	10	1,000	1,500
10,000	58,000	13	1,300	2,800
10,000	68,000	16	1,600	4,400
10,000	78,000	19	1,900	6,300
10,000	88,000	22	2,200	8,500
15,000	103,000	25	3,750	12,250
15,000	118,000	28	4,200	16,450
15,000	133,000	31	4,650	21,100
15,000	148,000	34	5,100	26,200
15,000	163,000	37	5,550	31,750
15,000	178,000	40	6,000	37,750
15,000	193,000	43	6,450	44,200
15,000	208,000	46	6,900	51,100
15,000	223,000	49	7,350	58,450
Excess		50		

TABLE III

Applicable where the donee or successor is a brother or a sister, or a child of a brother or of a sister, of the disponer

(a) the taxable gift or inheritance is taken on or before 31 March 1978.

Slice £	Cumulative Slice £	Rate of Tax %	Tax Thereon £	Cumulative Tax £
10,000	10,000	Nil	Nil	Nil
3,000	13,000	10	300	300
5,000	18,000	12	600	900
10,000	28,000	15	1,500	2,400
10,000	38,000	19	1,900	4,300
10,000	48,000	23	2,300	6,600
10,000	58,000	27	2,700	9,300
10,000	68,000	31	3,100	12,400
15,000	83,000	35	5,250	17,650
15,000	98,000	40	6,000	23,650
15,000	113,000	45	6,750	30,400
Excess		50		

CHART 52 (*Continued*)

(b) The taxable gift or inheritance is taken on or after 1 April 1978

20,000	20,000	Nil	Nil	Nil
3,000	23,000	10	300	300
5,000	28,000	12	600	900
10,000	38,000	15	1,500	2,400
10,000	48,000	19	1,900	4,300
10,000	58,000	23	2,300	6,600
10,000	68,000	27	2,700	9,300
10,000	78,000	31	3,100	12,400
15,000	93,000	35	5,250	17,650
15,000	108,000	40	6,000	23,650
15,000	123,000	45	6,750	30,400
Excess		50		

TABLE IV
Application where the donee or successor does not stand to the disponer in a relationship referred to in Table I, II and III.

Slice £	Cumulative Slice £	Rate of Tax %	Tax Thereon £	Cumulative Tax £

(a) the taxable gift or inheritance is taken on or before 31 March 1978.

Slice £	Cumulative Slice £	Rate of Tax %	Tax Thereon £	Cumulative Tax £
5,000	5,000	Nil	Nil	Nil
3,000	8,000	20	600	600
5,000	13,000	22	1,100	1,700
10,000	23,000	25	2,500	4,200
10,000	33,000	30	3,000	7,200
10,000	43,000	35	3,500	10,700
10,000	53,000	40	4,000	14,700
10,000	63,000	45	4,500	19,200
15,000	78,000	50	7,500	26,700
15,000	93,000	55	8,250	34,950
Excess		60		

(b) the taxable gift or inheritance is taken on or after 1 April 1978.

Slice £	Cumulative Slice £	Rate of Tax %	Tax Thereon £	Cumulative Tax £
10,000	10,000	Nil	Nil	Nil
3,000	13,000	20	600	600
5,000	18,000	22	1,100	1,700
10,000	28,000	25	2,500	4,200
10,000	38,000	30	3,000	7,200
10,000	48,000	35	3,500	10,700
10,000	58,000	40	4,000	14,700
10,000	68,000	45	4,500	19,200
15,000	83,000	50	7,500	26,700
15,000	98,000	55	8,250	34,950
Excess		60		

CHART 52 (*Continued*)

Table from 26 March 1984

Slice	Cumulative Slice	Rate of Tax %	Tax Thereon	Cumulative Tax
Threshold Amount	Threshold Amount +	nil	nil	nil
10,000	10,000	20	2,000	2,000
40,000	50,000	30	12,000	14,000
50,000	100,000	35	17,500	31,500
50,000	150,000	40	20,000	51,500
50,000	200,000	45	22,500	74,000
Balance		55		

CHART 53

Historic Capital Acquisitions Tax Class Thresholds

Relationship to donor/ testator	Gift or inheritance in										
	1989 or earlier	1990	1991	1992	1993	1994	1995	1996	1997	1998	1999
	£	£	£	£	£	£	£	£	£	£	£
Child or minor child of deceased child or parent where s116 FA 1991 applies	150,000	156,000	161,400	166,350	171,750	174,000	178,200	182,550	185,550	188,400	192,900
Lineal ancestor (other than a parent where s116 FA 1991 applies) lineal descendant (other than a child or minor child of a deceased child), brother, sister, child of brother or sister	20,000	20,800	21,520	22,180	22,900	23,200	23,760	24,340	24,740	25,120	25,720
Any other person	10,000	10,400	10,760	11,090	11,450	11,600	11,880	12,170	12,370	12,560	12,860

CHART 54
Probate Tax Exemption Thresholds

	Person dying in							
	1993	**1994**	**1995**	**1996**	**1997**	**1998**	**1999**	**From 1/12/99–6/12/00**
Exemption	10,000	10,150	10,390	10,650	10,820	10,980	11,250	40,000

CHART 55

(1) Residential Property Tax Limits

	INCOME YEAR ENDED 5 APRIL £	VALUATION AS AT 5 APRIL £
1983	20,000	65,000
1984	22,030	65,622
1985	23,395	66,491
1986	24,468	68,728
1987	25,307	69,971
1988	25,795	74,321
1989	26,654	82,772
1990	27,800	91,000
1991	28,500	96,000
1992	27,500	90,000
1993	28,100	91,000
1994	25,000	75,000
1995	29,500	94,000
1996	30,100	101,000

(2) Residential Property Tax Valuethreshold for Certificate of Clearanc e

VALUATION DATE*	THRESHOLD £
5 April 1997	115,000
5 April 1998	138,000
5 April 1999	200,000
5 April 2000	300,000
5 April 2001	342,000
	€
5 April 2002	438,000
5 April 2003	1,000,000
5 April 2004	1,140,000
5 April 2005	1,300,000
5 April 2006	1,389,000

* The relevant valuation date is the valuation date preceding the date of the contract, or where the date of the contract is 5 April in a year, that date.

A Certificate of Clearance is not required for contracts dated on or after 1 February 2007 or for contracts dated before 1 February 2007 where the sale is to be completed on or after 1 February 2007.

CHART 56

Residential Property Tax Rates for Year Ended 5 April 1994

For residential property valued between £75,000 and £100,000 a flat rate of tax was payable as follows:

Valuation not exceeding £	Tax due £
80,000	25
85,000	75
90,000	125
95,000	175
100,000	225

For residential property valued at over £100,000 tax was charged on the excess of the value over £75,000 as follows:

First £25,000	@ 1%	£250.00
Next £50,000	@ 1.5%	£750.00
Balance	@ 2%	–

CHART 57

Historic Rates of Stamp Duty on Residential Property

Value	Owner-Occupiers & Investors	First-Time Buyers who are Owner-Occupiers of Second-Hand Property		
		Instrument Executed		
	From 6/12/2001	*Pre 2/12/2004	Between 2/12/2004 and 30/3/2007	On or after 31/3/2007
Up to €127,000	Nil	Exempt	Exempt	Exempt
€127,001 -€190,500	3%	Exempt	Exempt	Exempt
€190,501 -€254,000	4%	3%	Exempt	Exempt
€254,001 -€317,500	5%	3.75%	Exempt	Exempt
€317,501 -€381,000	6%	4.5%	3%	Exempt
€381,001 -€635,000	7.5%	7.5%	6%	Exempt
Over €635,000	9%	9%	9%	Exempt

CHAPTER 1 INCOME TAX

1.1 Administration of Tax System

1.1.1 Legislation

The legislation on income tax in the Republic of Ireland is contained in the Taxes Consolidation Act 1997.

1.1.2 The Revenue Commissioners

The care and management of direct taxes such as income tax and corporation tax, and of indirect taxes such as customs and excise duty and value-added tax, is entrusted to the Revenue Commissioners. The Revenue Commissioners are appointed by the Taoiseach. Inspectors of Taxes are appointed by the Revenue Commissioners and are deployed throughout the country in various tax districts with a separate division for large cases. Responsibility for issuing annual tax returns and for the making of assessments rests with Inspectors of Taxes. Payment of income tax and corporation tax is made through the office of the Collector General.

1.1.3 Fundamental concepts

Year of Assessment – Income tax is charged for a year of assessment.

The year of assessment ran from 6 April in one calendar year to 5 April in the following year, for all tax years up to and including the year 2000/01.

With effect from 1 January 2002 the year of assessment was aligned with the calendar year and runs from 1 January to 31 December.

The first calendar tax year, 1 January 2002 to 31 December 2002 was preceded by a short transitional tax "year" running from 6 April 2001 to 31 December 2001.

Total Income – This is total income from all sources as computed in accordance with the provisions of the TCA 1997 (it is also called "net statutory income").

Taxable Income – This is total income less allowances, reliefs and deductions.

Schedules – Income from various sources is grouped for assessment purposes under various schedules. The TCA 1997 contain the rules for measuring the income assessable under the various schedules.

Basis of Assessment – All income is assessable to income tax on a current year basis.

1.1.4 Self-assessment

Self assessment was introduced for individuals with effect from 1988/89.

1.1.5 Chargeable Person

TCA97 s951 For income tax purposes, a person who is within the scope of the self assessment system is "chargeable person". This mainly refers to self-employed persons but includes those with a source of investment or rental income where the tax due cannot be recovered by restricting their tax credits under the PAYE system.

Section 14 FA 2005 amended the definition of a "chargeable person" for Self-Assessment purposes. The legislation now permits Revenue the discretion to look at an individual's gross non-PAYE income when deciding if the individual will be regarded as a "chargeable person."

For the years of assessment 2005 *et seq.*, an individual with PAYE income who also has substantial gross income from a non-PAYE source(s), even where this income has been reduced to NIL or to a negligible amount because of deductions, losses, allowances or other reliefs, is regarded as a "chargeable person" and is required to make a return under the Self-Assessment system.

In their publication *Tax Briefing* (Issue 62), Revenue indicated that an individual who is in receipt of income chargeable to tax under the PAYE system but who is also in receipt of gross non-PAYE income in excess of €50,000, which is covered or largely covered by losses, capital allowances and other reliefs, will now be regarded as a "chargeable person" within the Self-Assessment system. This €50,000 limit applies to gross income from all sources and not from each separate source.

Excluded from the definition of "non-PAYE income" for the purposes of this section are:

(i) Social Welfare Payments and Pensions;

(ii) Legally enforceable maintenance payments received.

Where the above sources of income can be accommodated by coding against the individual's tax credits, the individual will not be deemed to be a "chargeable person" for income tax Self-Assessment.

An individual, in receipt of both income chargeable tax under the PAYE system and income from other non-PAYE sources, will not be regarded as a "chargeable person" if the total gross income from all non-PAYE sources is less than €50,000 and the net assessable income is less than €3,174, provided the tax due on this income is collected via the PAYE system by coding against their tax credits for the year.

TCA97 s895 In addition to the foregoing, where a resident person, either directly or indirectly, opens a foreign bank account of which he is the beneficial owner, he is regarded as a chargeable person for the year of assessment during which the account is opened.

TCA976 s128 Where a person is chargeable to tax under Schedule E on a gain arising from the exercise, assignment or release of a right (e.g., exercise of a share option) that person is regarded as a chargeable person for the year. An exception to this is where the person is exempted in writing by the Inspector of Taxes from the obligation to file a tax return.

Where a person acquires a "foreign life policy" as defined in s730 H(1) TCA, they are deemed to be chargeable persons for that chargeable period. In addition, in order to avail of the more favourable tax regime for policyholders of such foreign life policies, any income payment or gain on disposal must be correctly included in the relevant tax return. Such a return must be submitted by the specified return date for the chargeable period in which the income arises, or in which the disposal is made, as appropriate.

Similarly, where a person acquires a material interest in an offshore fund, as defined in s743 TCA, they are deemed to be chargeable persons for that chargeable period. In addition, in order to avail of the more favourable tax regime, a timely return of income and gains must be made to Revenue.

TCA97 s896 Where a person acquires an offshore product, being a material interest in an offshore fund or a foreign life policy, to which s730 or s743 above do not apply, the person shall still be deemed to be a chargeable period.

See paragraph 1.1.6 below dealing with directors.

1.1.6 Directors

TCA97 s951 All directors are regarded as chargeable persons even where the director's only income is a salary subject to PAYE. However, Revenue Statement of Practice SP-IT/1/93, removes from the definition of chargeable persons non proprietary directors, provided the director is not otherwise a chargeable person and any non-PAYE income is taken into account in determining the amount of their tax credits and standard rate cut-off point. A proprietary director is a director of a company who is the beneficial owner of, or is able, either directly or indirectly to control more than 15% of the ordinary share capital of the company.

1.1.7 Returns

TCA97 s950 Individuals must file a return of income for each tax year not later than 31 October in the year following the tax year.

Special Arrangements for tax returns for the tax year 2007.

Taxpayers who both file and pay the total liability due through Revenue Online Service (ROS) will be offered a 17-day extension to the normal filing date of 31 October 2008 and accordingly the deadline for these taxpayers will be 17 November 2008.

For this purpose "total liability due" means any balance of income tax for the tax year 2007, capital gains tax for the "initial period of the tax year 2008", i.e., from 01 January 2008 to 30 September 2008 and preliminary income tax for the tax year 2008.

1.1.8 Surcharge

TCA97 s1084 If a return for a particular year of assessment is not submitted before the "specified date", the tax liability for that year is increased by a surcharge on the amount of tax assessed. This surcharge is calculated on the full tax payable for the year and does not take account of any payments on account.

The surcharge is calculated as follows:

(a) 5% of the amount of tax subject to a maximum of €12,695 where the return is submitted before the expiry of two months after the specified date, and

(b) 10% of the amount of tax subject to a maximum of €63,458 where the return is not submitted within two months after the specified date.

In the case of new businesses, the surcharge provisions apply from the second filing date only.

Finance Act 2004 provided for the application of a surcharge where a taxpayer who is claiming certain specified reliefs fails to give the additional information which will now be required to be included on the annual tax return forms with effect from the tax year 2004. The surcharge will only arise where, after the filing of the tax return, the taxpayer becomes aware, or it is brought to his/her attention, that the additional information has not been included on the return and the taxpayer fails to provide the required information without undue delay. Where a surcharge applies in these circumstances it will be the 5% surcharge which is subject to the normal maximum of €12,695.

Where a surcharge is applied, it must be included in the assessment so that the taxpayer can appeal against the surcharge to the Appeal Commissioners if the taxpayer is aggrieved with it.

1.1.9 Expression of doubt

TCA97 s955 Where a taxpayer is in doubt as regards a matter to be included in a return, his obligations with regard to the matter will be fulfilled if he draws the Inspector's attention to the matter in question. This provision does not apply where the Inspector or the Appeal Commissioners are of the opinion that the doubt was not genuine and the taxpayer was acting with an avoidance or evasion of tax motive.

1.1.10 Assessments

TCA97 s954-5 In general, assessments are not made until after a return has been submitted and will be based on the amounts included in the return. Where a person defaults in making a return or the Inspector is dissatisfied with the return, he may make an assessment. A time limit of four years applies to the making of assessments where a full return has been made.

The Inspector may elect not to make an assessment where he is satisfied that the correct tax has been paid. In such cases the taxpayer will be notified by the Inspector of his decision.

1.1.11 Payment of income tax

TCA97 s958 For the years of assessment 2002 *et seq.* the due date for payment of preliminary tax is 31 October in the year of assessment.

In order to avoid any possible interest charges in relation to preliminary tax or any balance of tax payable on an assessment, the taxpayer must pay by the due date for preliminary tax a minimum of:

(a) 90% of the final tax payable for that tax year – "the 90% rule", or

(b) 100% of the final tax payable for the previous tax year.

It should be noted that when calculating (b) above:

- any relief claimed under the business expansion scheme must be ignored and
- any relief for investments in films must be ignored.

Preliminary tax may be paid by means of direct debit. In this instance the taxpayer can base the amount of preliminary tax to be paid on 105% of the final tax payable for the pre-preceding for year.

During the first year of arranging the direct debit scheme, the taxpayer must meet his/her preliminary tax obligation by a minimum of three equal instalments and during the following year by way of eight equal instalments. The Collector General has discretion to vary the number of instalments for subsequent years. The taxpayer will not be treated as having paid the full amount of the preliminary tax unless all the instalments are met.

When the preliminary tax requirements have been met, the balance of tax assessed must be paid on or before 31 October in the year following the year of assessment (See 1.1.5 re: special arrangements for 2007).

Where the preliminary tax requirements have not been met, the due date for the balance of tax assessed is the date when the preliminary tax is due. However, where the taxpayer elects to pay preliminary tax at 100% of the previous years liability, and there is an underpayment in the previous year because of a computational error resulting in the preliminary tax payment being less than the required 100%, interest and penalties will not be imposed where the taxpayer tops up the preliminary tax to 100% before 31 December in that tax year.

In the case of a couple who are jointly assessed, preliminary tax is based on the couple's liability for the relevant year rather than the individual spouse's liability for that year.

1.1.12 Appeal procedures

(a) General

TCA97 s932-s944 A taxpayer aggrieved by an assessment to income tax or corporation tax or by a determination of the Revenue Commissioners in relation to these taxes has the right to appeal against such an assessment or determination. The appeal must be lodged in writing with the Inspector of Taxes within 30 days of the issue of the assessment or determination. If the matter is not subsequently settled by agreement between the Inspector and the taxpayer the appeal will eventually be heard by an Appeal Commissioner.

Appeal Commissioners are appointed by the Minister for Finance.

An application for adjournment of the hearing of an appeal by the Appeal Commissioners may not be refused if made:

(a) within 9 months from the end of the tax year to which the assessment relates, or

(b) within 9 months from the date on which the notice of assessment was given to the appellant, whichever of these dates is the earlier.

Where such an application has been refused by the Appeal Commissioners and:

(i) the appellant has not made a return of income, or

(ii) the appellant has made a return of income, but all the statements of profits and gains, schedules and other evidence relating to such return have not been furnished by the appellant,

the Commissioners shall make an order dismissing the appeal. They may, however, determine the appeal if they are satisfied that sufficient information has been furnished to enable them to do this. The distinction between dismissal and determination is of the utmost importance as the right of re-hearing of appeals by the Circuit Court is confined to those which have been determined by the Appeal Commissioners. An appellant whose appeal is dismissed by the Appeal Commissioners has the right to appeal to the High Court and to the Supreme Court if he considers that, having regard to the evidence available the dismissal of the appeal was unreasonable. The Revenue Commissioners and taxpayers have the right to take a case on a point of law to the High Court and to the Supreme Court.

Following a Supreme Court decision during 2006, Finance Act 2007 introduced a number of changes to the income tax appeal provisions.

The Act provides that where a determination of the Appeal Commissioners is to be reheard by a Circuit Court Judge, or a case is to be stated for the opinion of the High Court, the Inspector will not be obliged to amend the assessment under appeal until the appeal process has been fully completed. Accordingly, in those circumstances tax will be neither collected nor repaid by the Revenue Commissioners on the basis of the Appeal Commissioners determination. These amendments apply to appeals determined by the Appeal Commissioners, or by a judge of the Circuit Court, on or after 2 April 2007.

The Appeal Commissioners may publish details of their decisions in such cases as they consider appropriate, generally where the point of issue may be of interest to tax practitioners and taxpayers. The identity of the taxpayer involved may not be divulged in such publication.

(b) Self assessment

The normal appeal procedures apply, but an appeal will not be allowed against an assessment made by reference to the taxpayer's own figures or figures agreed by him.

Where an estimated assessment is made in the absence of a return, an appeal will be allowed only after the return has been submitted and the tax due on the basis of the return has been paid. The grounds for appeal must be stated in the notice of appeal.

A person will not be entitled to rely on any ground of appeal at a hearing unless it was included in the appeal notice or the Appeal Commissioners or Judge hold that the ground could not have been reasonably stated in the appeal notice.

(c) 1995 Amendments

The 1995 Finance Act introduced additional appeal provisions with effect from 8 June 1995. These are as follows:

(a) Where an Inspector of Taxes proposes not to accept a notice of appeal as being valid, he must notify the appellant in writing of his reasons.

(b) A taxpayer will be entitled to appeal directly to the Appeal Commissioners against an Inspector's refusal to accept a notice of appeal.

(c) Where an Inspector proposes to withdraw a listing of an appeal on the grounds that the appeal may be settled by agreement without recourse to an appeal hearing, he must obtain the agreement of the appellant.

(d) Where a taxpayer feels there is a delay by the Inspector in listing an appeal, he will be able to apply directly to the Appeal Commissioners for an early listing.

(e) The grounds on which the Appeal Commissioners may dismiss an appeal were extended to cover situations of non-cooperation by the appellant with requests for information by the Appeal Commissioners.

(d) Late Appeals

Where a taxpayer fails to lodge an appeal within 30 days of the date of issue of a notice of assessment, the assessment becomes final and conclusive. If, however, the taxpayer was prevented from giving timely notice of appeal due to absence, sickness or other reasonable cause he may apply to the Inspector of Taxes for admission of a late appeal. An application made later than 12 months after the date of the notice of assessment will not be admitted unless the appellant pays the tax charged in the assessment together with accrued interest and submits his return of income and such other information as is necessary to enable the appeal to be determined. Any overpayment of tax arising by reason of the determination of such an appeal will be refunded together with any interest paid thereon. An application for admission of a late appeal will not be entertained in the situations listed below until the relevant action has been completed:

(a) where court proceedings have been initiated for recovery of tax charged in an assessment; or

(b) where a certificate has been issued to a County Registrar or Sheriff in respect of tax charged in an assessment.

It should be noted that:

(i) Failure to attend or to be represented before the Appeal Commissioners results in the assessment becoming final and conclusive. There is, however, provision for the Appeal Commissioners to re-admit the appeal.

(ii) The tax charged in an assessment which has been determined by the Appeal Commissioners becomes payable at the time of determination. This is the position even though an application for re-hearing of the appeal by the Circuit Court has been made.

1.1.13 Interest on overdue tax

The rate of interest on overdue tax is 0.0273% per day or part of a day from 1 April 2005 (see Chart 10 for earlier rates).

1.1.14 Interest on overpayments/refunds/time limits

The Finance Act 2003 fundamentally changed the entitlement of taxpayers to apply for refunds of tax overpaid and their entitlement to interest in respect of their refunds. A summary of the changes is as follows:

TCA97 s865 (1) Refunds of tax

The timeframe within which a taxpayer may make a claim for a refund of tax has been shortened as follows:

(i) Chargeable periods ending on or before 31 December 2002

(a) If this claim was made before 31 December 2004, the claim will be on time if it is made within 10 years of the end of the chargeable period (or such other shorter time limit applying, e.g., 6 years for error or mistake – see below*).

(b) If the claim is made on or after 1 January 2005, the claim will be on time if it is made within 4 years of the end of the chargeable period.

(ii) Chargeable periods ending on or after 1 January 2003.

The claim must be made within 4 years of the end of the chargeable period.

* It is important to note that if the timeframe in other provisions of TCA 1997 under which a claim for a refund of tax is being made, is shorter than those set out above, then the shorter timeframe will apply. However, if these other provisions contain a longer timeframe for claiming a refund of tax than the measures set out above, then their timeframe(s) is restricted downwards to the above limits.

The Finance Act 2003 also introduced the concept of a "valid claim" for payment. A valid claim will only be deemed to be made where all necessary information has been submitted which the Revenue Commissioners reasonably require to certify the claim.

TCA97 s865A (2) Interest on repayments

The rate of interest is calculated on a daily basis at 0.011% in respect of repayments made on or after 1 November 2003 (see Chart 10 for earlier rates). This annualises at approximately 4.015% in contrast to the previous rate of 5.87%.

In the case of preliminary tax (in relation to income tax, and capital gains tax for individuals) the new provisions on interest on repayments will apply to tax paid on or after 1 November 2003. The old arrangements will apply to preliminary tax payments made before that date, provided the Return for the chargeable period in respect of which the preliminary tax was paid was lodged with the Collector General on or before 31 October 2004.

The period from which interest runs will depend on whether the overpayment is as a result of Revenue's mistake or the taxpayers. Where the overpayment arises because Revenue has mistakenly applied the law and a claim for repayment is made within the requisite time limit, interest shall commence to run from the day after the end of the chargeable period in which the overpayment arises, or, if later, the date of payment.

Where the overpayment cannot be ascribed to a mistaken application of the law by the Revenue Commissioners the overpayment will carry interest from the day which is 6 months after the day on which "a valid claim" (as defined) for the repayment had been filed with Revenue. Section 121 Finance Act 2007 provided for a reduction from 6 months or 183 days to 93 days to the period which must elapse after a receipt of "a valid claim" before Revenue is required to pay interest on repayments, in respect of repayments arising on or after 2 April 2007. The overpayment of tax will not be subject to withholding tax and is exempt from income tax. Interest will not be paid where the overall amount due is less than €10.

TCA97 s956(i)(c) (3) Audit look back period

The period in which Revenue can schedule an audit of a particular tax return has been reduced from 6 years after the end of the chargeable period within which the relevant return is filed to 4 years. However, the restriction is removed where Revenue has reason to believe that a return was filed negligently or fraudulently.

The reduction from 6 years to 4 years has effect in relation to enquiries and actions referred to in section 956(1)(b) TCA 1997 made on or after 1 January 2005 (per S.I. 508 of 2003).

TCA97 s955 (2) (4) Amending of assessments

The period within which Revenue is entitled to amend an assessment in respect of a full and true return has also been reduced from a period ending 6 years after the end of the chargeable period within which the relevant return is filed to 4 years.

The reduction from 6 years to 4 years has effect in relation to enquiries and actions referred to in section 956(1)(b) TCA 1997, made on or after 1 January 2005 (per S.I. 508 of 2003).

(5) Reduction of time frame from 10 years to 4 years

The following provisions have had their respective time frames reduced from 10 years to 4 years (effective in relation to the making of assessments on or after 1 January 2005 (per S.I. 508 of 2003):

- Section 401(6) TCA 1997 – assessment to disallow relief for trading losses where there has been a change of ownership in a company and a change in the nature of its trade.
- Section 504(3) – assessment to withdraw BES relief.
- Section 599(4)(b) – assessment to capital gains tax on "child" where assets disposed of so as to contravene retirement relief claimed by parent.
- Section 611(1)(c) – assessment to capital gains tax where relief claimed in respect of a disposal to the State, public bodies or charities.
- Section 919(5)(c) – assessment to corporation tax.
- Section 924(2)(b) – additional assessments to income tax.

1.1.15 Power of attachment

TCA97 s1002

The Revenue Commissioners have power to attach amounts due to a tax defaulter by a third party. The features of the Power of Attachment are as follows:

(a) The Power of Attachment relates to amounts due other than wages and salaries.

(b) The taxes which may be recovered in this manner are income tax, corporation tax, capital gains tax, value-added tax, self-employed PRSI, health contributions, levies employers' PRSI, customs and excise duties, capital acquisitions tax and stamp duty.

(c) The Notice of Attachment will be issued by the Revenue Commissioners to the third party and will show the taxpayer's name and address along with the aggregate of taxes, interest and penalties outstanding.

(d) The debtor who receives the notice must, within 10 days, make a return to the Revenue Commissioners of the amount of debt, if any, owing to the defaulter. Where however the debt exceeds the amount of outstanding taxes, etc. it is sufficient to advise a debt equal to that amount.

(e) The recipient of the notice must also pay over to the Revenue Commissioners within the period of 10 days, the amount specified in the Return.

(f) If the amount specified in the Notice is greater than the debt outstanding, the amount of the debt must be paid over. If, however, a further debt becomes due during the "relevant period of the Notice of Attachment" (as defined), a further return and payment must be made within 10 days. This process continues until all outstanding tax, etc. has been paid.

(g) A "debt" is the aggregate amount of money due by the debtor to the taxpayer at the time of receipt of the Notice of Attachment. It also includes balances (including accrued interest) owing by financial institutions to the taxpayer.

(h) Attachment orders can be placed on joint deposit accounts with financial institutions. Unless evidence to the contrary is produced within 10 days of the notice of attachment, a joint account will be deemed to be held equally for the benefit of each party to the account. Where contrary evidence is produced within the time limit, the amount of the deposit shown to be held by the defaulter will be regarded as a debt due to him and liable to be attached.

(i) Where a Notice of Attachment issues to a debtor, he may not make any disbursements except to the extent:

(i) that the disbursement will not reduce the debt below the amount of tax, etc. shown in the Notice, or

(ii) this disbursement is made pursuant to a Court Order.

(j) A Notice of Attachment cannot include amounts due to the Revenue Commissioners unless a period of 14 days has expired from the date on which the default commenced, and the Revenue Commissioners have given 7 days' prior notice of the intention to attach the outstanding amount.

(k) A Notice of Attachment may be revoked by the Revenue Commissioners by the issue of a Notice of Revocation where the taxpayer makes good his default.

(l) Copies of Notices of Attachment and Notices of Revocation will be given promptly by the Revenue Commissioners to the taxpayer. In addition, the taxpayer will receive details from the debtor of every payment made to the Revenue Commissioners out of debts due to him, and the Revenue Commissioners will issue receipts to both taxpayer and debtor.

(m) The debtor is indemnified against claims by the taxpayer, and is to be regarded as having made payment to the taxpayer.

(n) The Revenue Commissioners may issue two or more notices of attachment to two or more debtors of the defaulter at the same time. However, the aggregate of the amounts on the notices of attachment must not exceed the total amount of tax defaulted on by the taxpayer.

(o) Any interest on unpaid tax to be collected by attachment is to be specified in the notice of attachment.

1.1.16 Fixed charge on company book debts

TCA97 s1001 The Revenue Commissioners are entitled to require the person holding a fixed charge on the book debts of a company to pay any relevant amount for which the company is liable (but which it has failed to pay) in respect of certain taxes. The "relevant amount" is defined as any amount which the company is liable to remit to the Collector General in respect of PAYE/PRSI and value-added tax. The amount which the holder of the fixed charge (the lender) can be demanded to pay must not exceed the aggregate amount of all moneys, etc. which the lender has received, directly or indirectly, from the company in payment or part payment of any liabilities due by the company to the lender. Further, only such amounts received by the lender from the company after the date on which he or she is notified by the Revenue Commissioners to make the payment under the section can be demanded by the Commissioners. The effect of section 1001 is to reduce the value of the security the lender has obtained by the fixed charge.

It is also provided that the holder of the charge may, within 21 days of the creation of the fixed charge, furnish to the Revenue Commissioners certain details in relation to the charge as set out in subsection 3(c) of section 1001 TCA97. If the holder of the fixed charge does this, it cannot be liable for any relevant amount which the company was liable to pay before the date on which the holder is notified in writing by the Revenue Commissioners. In those circumstances, on receiving notification from the Revenue Commissioners, the holder of the fixed charge may become liable only for payment of any relevant amount which the company subsequently fails to pay.

1.1.17 Offset between taxes

TCA97 s1006A

The Revenue Commissioners may set a claim for repayment of any tax or duty or interest against any outstanding liabilities in respect of any tax or duty or interest on overdue tax. In addition, Revenue may also withhold repayment of tax pending the submission of outstanding tax returns.

1.2 The Unified System of Personal Taxation

TCA97 s1015-s1027

The unified system makes no distinction between earned and unearned income. The system provides that having ascertained the income for tax purposes, there are to be deducted the various allowances, reliefs and deductions to arrive at a figure which represents taxable income. The taxable income is then subjected to rates of tax which graduate from lower to higher levels depending on the taxable income. Relief is then granted for any tax credits. Rates of tax on taxable income for the years from 1990/91 to 2008 inclusive are shown in Chart 3. Earlier rates are shown in Chart 47.

1.2.1 Joint assessment

Joint assessment is automatic, unless either spouse gives notice of election for single assessment to the Revenue Commissioners before the end of the tax year. Such notice, when given, continues until withdrawn by the spouse who gave notice. Where a wife is living with her husband, the income of each spouse is taxed as if it were the income of the husband, but with the distinction that the bands of income chargeable at the lower rates are increased as compared with the single taxpayer. The amount of the increase in the lower rate bands depends on whether or not the married couple have one or two incomes. (See Chart 3.)

The assessment may be raised on the wife:

- if the husband and wife jointly elect before 1 April for the years of assessment 2002 *et seq.*;
- if they marry in 1993/94 or later and they have not elected nor been deemed to have made an election for the husband to be assessed and for the previous year the income of the wife exceeds that of the husband.

Repayments of tax will be allocated between spouses.

1.2.2 Single assessment

Where a wife is living with her husband, and an election for single assessment is made before the end of the tax year, each spouse is treated as a single person with no right of transferring allowances or reliefs between them. This has also become known as separate treatment.

1.2.3 Separate assessment

A claim may be made for separate assessment of the income tax liability where the joint assessment basis applies. The claim must be made before 1 April in the year of assessment or before 1 April in the following year in the case of marriage.

1.2.4 Separated spouses

Tax is not deducted at source from legally enforceable maintenance payments. Such payments are deductible for tax purposes in the hands of the payer and chargeable to income tax under Case IV of Schedule D in the hands of the recipient. Both spouses are assessed to income tax as single persons subject to a right of election by separated spouses of a marriage which has not been dissolved or annulled to elect for joint assessment under the provisions of section 1018. The election for joint assessment may be made only where both spouses are resident in the State.

If the election is made, the husband is assessed to income tax without regard to the maintenance payments and is granted the married man's allowance. If the spouses each have income in their own right, apart from maintenance payments, the income tax applicable to their respective incomes is calculated by the separate assessment procedure but treating the husband's income as undiminished by the maintenance payments. These provisions apply to payments made under maintenance arrangements made after 7 June 1983. In the case of maintenance arrangements made before that date, the new provisions do not apply unless:

(a) a new arrangement is entered into, or

(b) both parties jointly elect in writing and the new provisions apply from the date of (a) or (b).

Where a payment is made for the use or benefit of a child for whom the payer was entitled to child allowance, the payment is:

(a) to be made without deduction of income tax,

(b) to be treated as the income of the payer, and

(c) the payer's income tax liability is to be calculated without any deduction for the payment.

1.2.5 Divorced persons

In certain circumstances divorced couples may opt for joint assessment for income tax purposes in relation to maintenance payments. Both partners must be resident in the State and remain unmarried. The divorce must have been granted under section 5 of the Family Law (Divorce) Act, 1996 or if a foreign divorce, it must be recognised as valid in the State.

1.2.6 Individualisation

TCA97 s15 The concept of individualisation was first put forward by the Minister for Finance in his Budget 2000 speech when he stated – "One of the main difficulties with the present band structure is that a single person's tax band is doubled for all married couples. I am, therefore proposing the radical change of moving to individualisation of the standard rate band over this and the next two Budgets. This will ultimately involve each individual having his or her own standard rate band".

For the tax year 2008 the following tax bands apply:

Single Person	€35,400
Married Couple – One Income	€44,400
Married Couple – Two Income	€70,800

The €70,800 band for the two income couple is transferable from one earning spouse to the other, subject to a maximum individual band of €44,400 for either spouse. The €44,400 limit arises from the fact that this is the maximum band that applies in the case of married, one income couples and represents the target level ultimately for the individualisation of the lower rate tax band. Allowing transferability up to €44,400 ensures that nobody will have a lower effective band than under the pre-individualisation system.

1.3 Personal Tax Credits and Reliefs

A full tax credit system was introduced with effect from 6 April 2001. This system replaced the old tax free allowance based system and equalises the value of tax allowances to all taxpayers. Accordingly, every €1,000 of a personal tax allowance is now equivalent to a tax credit of €200 (i.e., €1,000 @ 20%) for each taxpayer.

The personal allowances available for the years 1990/91 to 2000/01 inclusive are set out in Chart 1, while the tax credits available for the tax years 2001 to 2008 are set out in Chart 2.

1.3.1 Personal tax credits

(a) Married tax credit

TCA97 s490

The married credit is due for the year of assessment, where:

(i) a husband and wife are assessed to tax jointly, or

(ii) where the couple are living apart but one is wholly or mainly maintained by the other during the year of assessment and is not entitled in computing the amount of his or her income for tax purposes for that year to make any deduction in respect of sums paid for the maintenance of the other.

Married couples are taxed as single persons in the year of assessment in which the marriage takes place. If the total of the tax paid as single persons exceeds what would have been paid if they were married for the whole year, they will be entitled, on making a joint claim, to repayment. The repayment is calculated by the formula:

$$\frac{A \times B}{12}$$

where –

A = the tax gained by the election

B = the number of income tax months from the date of marriage to the end of the income tax year (part of a month is treated as a month)

The repayment is allocated proportionately to the tax paid by each. A claim for repayment must be made in writing after the end of the year of marriage and made jointly.

(b) Widowed tax credit

TCA97 s462-s463

The widowed tax credit is available to a widowed person. A widowed person whose spouse has died in a given tax year is entitled to the widowed person's "bereaved in year" tax credit, for that year only. This tax credit is the same as the married person's tax credit but is not available to a surviving spouse who is the subject of a joint assessment for the same year.

A widowed person with dependent children is also entitled to:

(i) the single parent tax credit (see below) and

(ii) the following additional tax credits for the tax year 2008:

- €4,000 in the first year after bereavement
- €3,500 in the second year after bereavement
- €3,000 in the third year after bereavement
- €2,500 in the fourth year after bereavement
- €2,000 in the fifth year after bereavement

In determining whether a child is qualifying or not, the conditions applicable to the single parent tax credit (see below) will apply.

TCA97 s462 (c) Single tax credit

The single tax credit is available to other individuals (other than married or widowed).

TCA97 s462 (d) One-parent family tax credit

This tax credit may be granted to a person who is not entitled to the married tax credit. It is separate from the extra tax credit mentioned above which applies to widowed individuals with dependent children. The tax credit is granted to either

(i) a widowed person, or

(ii) any other person

who for any year of assessment proves that a qualifying child (as defined below) resided with him or her for the whole or part of that year of assessment.

The credit is not available to an unmarried couple who are living together.

The tax credit is granted in addition to the personal tax credit so that when the single parent and single tax credits are combined they will equal the married tax credit.

A qualifying child for this allowance is a child who:

(i) is born in the year of assessment, or

(ii) at the commencement of the year of assessment, is under the age of 18 years, or

(iii) if over 18 years of age:

- is receiving full-time instruction at any university, college, school or other educational establishment, or
- is permanently incapacitated by reason of mental or physical infirmity from maintaining himself, and if he has reached 21 years of age was so incapacitated before reaching that age, and

– is a child of the claimant or a child in the custody of the claimant who is maintained by the claimant at his own expense for the whole or part of the year of assessment.

"Child" includes a step child, a child whose parents have not married, a child who has been informally adopted, and an adopted child, in respect of whom an adoption order under the Adoption Acts 1952 to 1976 is in force.

The restriction of the credit where the qualifying child has income was abolished with effect from 6 April 2001.

1.3.2 Age tax credit

TCA97 s464 Claimable by a person where he or his spouse is at least 65 years of age during the year of assessment.

1.3.3 Incapacitated child tax credit

TCA97 s465 Child tax credit is available only in respect of incapacitated children.

The tax credit is granted if the claimant proves that he has living at any time during the year of assessment any child who:

(i) is under 18 years of age and is permanently incapacitated by reason of mental or physical infirmity, or

(ii) if over the age of 18 is permanently incapacitated from maintaining himself, and was so before he reached the age of 21 years, or was in full-time education at the time he became permanently incapacitated.

The credit is available for each qualifying child.

The restriction of the credit where the qualifying child has income was abolished with effect from 6 April 2001.

Where a credit is claimed in respect of a child who has not reached 18 years of age, it is only granted if there is the expectation that, if the child was over 18 years of age, he would be incapacitated from maintaining himself.

Where a credit is claimed in respect of a child who has reached 18 years of age, it is restricted to the actual amount spent on the maintenance of the child, if this is less than the maximum credit for the year of assessment.

Where two or more individuals are entitled to relief in respect of the same child, i.e., where the child is maintained jointly by both persons, each person may claim a proportion of the child credit relative to the amount expended by him or her on the maintenance of the child.

"Child" includes a stepchild, and a child in respect of whom an adoption order under the Adoption Acts 1952 to 1976 is in force.

It should be noted that a dependent relative credit cannot be claimed in respect of a child for whom a child credit has been claimed.

1.3.4 Dependent relative credit

TCA97 s466 Claimable if a person maintains at his own expense:

(a) a relative of his or his wife who is incapacitated by old age or infirmity from maintaining himself, or

(b) his or his wife's widowed mother, or

(c) his son or daughter who is resident with him and upon whom he is dependent by reason of old age or infirmity.

If the income of the dependent relative exceeds a specified limit no tax credit is due. For the tax year 2008 the specified limit is €13,473.

1.3.5 Home carer's credit

TCA97 s466A Claimable by married persons who are jointly assessed and where one spouse works at home to care for children, the aged or incapacitated persons. In general, the allowance will be granted where a number of conditions are met:

(a) the claimant is married and assessed to tax under joint assessment rules,

(b) one or more qualifying persons (child, elderly person or incapacitated person) normally resides with the claimant and the claimant's spouse (or, in the case of an aged or incapacitated relative, resides nearby) and is cared for by the claimant or the claimant's spouse (described as the "carer spouse"), and

(c) for the tax year 2008, the carer spouse's income is not in excess of €5,080. A reduced tax credit applies where the income is between €5,080 and €6,880. No account is taken of any carer's allowance from the Department of Social Community and Family Affairs in calculating the home carers income.

Only one credit is granted irrespective of the number of qualifying persons being cared for.

Where the credit has been granted and, in a particular year, the income of the carer spouse exceeds the permitted limit, the credit will be granted for that year if the claimant qualified for the allowance in the immediately preceding year.

The credit and the increased standard rate tax band for certain two earner couples are mutually exclusive but a person may opt for whichever is the more beneficial.

1.3.6 Employed person taking care of incapacitated individual

TCA97 s467 Claimable by an individual where he/she employs a person to take care of a family member who is totally incapacitated by old age or infirmity.

Where two or more persons employ the carer, the allowance will be apportioned between them. Carers may be employed on an individual basis or through an agency.

The maximum allowance for the tax year 2008 is €50,000 and relief is granted at the marginal rate. Relief may be granted in the first year in which the individual or the relative of the individual becomes totally incapacitated.

1.3.7 Blind person's tax credit

TCA97 s468 Claimable by a person where he or his spouse is blind during the year of assessment. Where both husband and wife are blind, the credit is doubled. An additional allowance of €825 at the marginal rate is available for a guide dog.

1.3.8 Medical expenses

TCA97 s469 ***Tax years up to and including 2006***

Income tax relief is available at the marginal rate in respect of certain medical expenses incurred by an individual on behalf of either:

(i) himself/herself

(ii) a relative, as defined

(iii) any other person over 65 years of age or permanently incapacitated (mental or physical).

Relatives include:

a) husband, wife, ancestor, lineal descendant, brother or sister,

b) mother or father of the individual's spouse,

c) brother or sister of the individual's spouse,

d) spouse of the individual's son or daughter; and

e) a child, not being the child of the individual, who for the year of assessment:

  i) is in the custody of the individual and is maintained by the individual, at the individual's own expense for the whole or part of the year of assessment, and

  ii) is under 18 years of age; or

  iii) if over 18 years of age, at the commencement of the year of assessment, is receiving full time instruction at any university, college, school or other educational establishment.

The amount of expenses qualifying for relief is the excess of the cost over €125 for an individual or over €250 for an individual and his/her relatives/other persons.

Tax years 2007 et seq.

With effect from the tax year 2007, the requirement that there be a defined relationship between the taxpayer and the person on behalf of which the tax relief is being claimed, has been abolished. Accordingly, there is no longer a requirement that persons are related to each other in order to claim relief for medical expenses.

In addition, the two tier *de minimis* limits of €125 and €250 for health expense claims have been abolished and accordingly the full amount of qualifying expenses defrayed will qualify for tax relief.

Health expenses

Only health expenses incurred in the provision of "health care" qualify for relief. Section 469 TCA 97 defines "health care" as meaning the prevention, diagnosis, alleviation or treatment of an ailment, an injury, an infirmity, a defect or a disability.

Medical expenses include expenses incurred on:

- services of a practitioner,
- diagnostic procedures carried out on the advice of a practitioner,
- maintenance or treatment in a hospital or approved nursing home,
- drugs or medicine supplied on the prescription of a practitioner,
- physiotherapy prescribed by a practitioner,
- orthoptic treatment prescribed by a practitioner,
- transport by ambulance,
- supply or repair of medical, surgical or dental appliances used on the advice of a practitioner, e.g., glucometer machine, hearing aid, orthopaedic bed/chair, wheelchair/wheelchair lift, exercise bicycle, computer, false eye, wig.
- non-routine dental treatment,
- maternity care (from 2001),
- cost of educational psychological assessments and speech and language therapy services for children (from 2001),
- certain travelling and home expenses in the case of kidney dialysis patients. (See *Tax Briefing* Issues 55 and 63),
- certain expenditure on telephone, overnight accommodation, travel, hygiene products and special clothing in the case of child oncology patients and children with permanent disabilities. (See *Tax Briefing* Issues 55 and 63),
- cost of gluten free food for coeliacs, and food products manufactured specifically for diabetics, on confirmation from a doctor that the taxpayer is a coeliac sufferer/diabetic.
- *In Vitro* fertilisation treatment,

Routine dental and ophthalmic treatment is specifically excluded from the relief.

Health Care Outside the State

With regard to treatment outside the State, the following expenses qualify for tax relief:

(i) The cost of qualifying treatment carried out by a practitioner (GP, consultant or dentist) provided such practitioner is entitled under the laws of the country in which the care is provided to practise medicine or dentistry there; and

(ii) the cost of maintenance or treatment in a hospital, nursing home or clinic is allowable provided that the institution is on the Revenue approved list.

Where the relevant qualifying health care is only available outside of the state, the cost of reasonable travelling and accommodation expenses are also allowable. In such cases, the expenses of one person accompanying the patient may also be allowed where the condition of the patient requires it. Where the patient is a child, the expenses of one parent may generally be allowed and, exceptionally, of both parents where it is clear that both have to be in attendance.

Tax Briefing Issue 68 contains detailed guidelines and procedures in relation to health expenses.

1.3.9 Medical insurance

TCA97 s470

Relief is available in respect of premiums paid to an authorised insurer under a contract which provides specifically for the payment of actual medical expenses resulting from sickness of the person, his wife, child or other dependants.

Relief is granted at the standard rate of tax and with effect from 6 April 2001 relief is granted at source and need not be claimed by the taxpayer. The premium paid to the insurer will be reduced by an amount equal to the standard rate of income tax, while the insurer will be repaid the equivalent of the standard rate reduction by the Revenue Commissioners.

1.3.10 Dental insurance

TCA97 s470

With effect from 1 January 2004, relief is available at the standard rate in respect of premiums paid on dental insurance policies for non-routine dental treatment provided by those who provide dental insurance only.

1.3.11 Long term care policies

TCA97 s470A

Relief is available at the standard rate in respect of premiums paid on qualifying insurance policies designed to cover – in whole or in part – for future care needs of individuals who are unable to perform at least two activities of daily living or are suffering from severe cognitive impairment.

Activities of daily living means one or more of the following – washing, dressing, feeding, toileting, mobility and transferring.

Relief is granted at source which will allow the subscriber to deduct the tax relief from the gross premium due. The amount deducted will be refunded by Revenue to the insurer.

Qualifying policies, which must be approved by Revenue, may be taken out by an individual in relation to himself or herself, his or her spouse and children and other relatives. Policies must generally be renewable, be standalone and must not provide for a termination lump sum payment or surrender for cash.

1.3.12 Permanent health benefit schemes

TCA97 s471 Premiums and other contributions under permanent health insurance schemes are allowed as deductions for income tax purposes. The amount on which relief is granted is not to exceed 10% of the total income for the year of assessment. Any benefits payable under such schemes are charged to tax under PAYE.

Relief is also available for premia paid to foreign health insurers if the individual first took out the insurance while resident in a Member State of the European Union.

1.3.13 Employee tax credit

TCA97 s472 An individual, who is in receipt of emoluments chargeable to income tax under Schedule E, may claim this credit. In the case of joint assessment and where each spouse is in employment the credit is available to each spouse.

The credit is not applicable to emoluments paid by his company to a proprietary director.

The credit may be claimed by children of proprietary directors and the self-employed who are full-time employees in the business of their parents and where certain conditions are fulfilled. The conditions are:

(a) PAYE must be operated in respect of the employment, and

(b) the individual's income from the employment must be at least €4,572.

1.3.14 Revenue job assist

TCA97 s472A On taking up a qualifying employment, a long-term unemployed individual (unemployed for at least a continuous period of 12 months) may claim, for a three-year period, both a tapering personal allowance and a tapering child allowance in respect of each qualifying child. The amounts which may be claimed at the marginal rate are:

Personal Allowance		Child Allowance
Year 1	€3,810	€1,270 for each qualifying child
Year 2	€2,540	€850 for each qualifying child
Year 3	€1,270	€425 for each qualifying child

The three-year period for the employee may commence with either the tax year in which the employment commences or the following tax year.

The allowances are granted by way of a deduction from the emoluments from the qualifying employment.

This allowance is also available for persons who have been in receipt of either disability allowance or blind persons pension for 12 months or more.

See 2.12.2 for double deduction available to employers.

1.3.15 Seafarers allowance

TCA97 s472B Seafarers who are absent from the state on a sea-going ship for at least 161 days per year are entitled to a tax free allowance of €6,350 per annum.

1.3.16 Trade union subscriptions

TCA97 s472C A tax credit may be claimed in respect of subscriptions paid for membership of a trade union.

For the tax years 2008 *et seq.* the credit is €70 per annum. The full credit of €70 may be claimed regardless of the actual amount of the subscriptions paid. Any person who is a member of a trade union at any time in a particular tax year will be entitled to the credit. Where a person is a member of more than one trade union, he/she will only be entitled to one credit.

Employers are permitted to share employees PPS numbers with trade unions in certain circumstances to enable the trade unions make returns to the Revenue Commissioners of their members who qualify for the credit.

1.3.17 Rents paid by certain tenants

TCA97 s473 Tax relief at the standard rate may be claimed by tenants for rent paid in respect of rented residential accommodation which is their sole or main residence.

For the tax year 2008, the maximum credits available are as follows:

Persons under 55 years	Max Tax Credit	Rent Limit
Single	€400	€2,000
Married/Widowed	€800	€4,000
Persons 55 years and over		
Single	€800	€4,000
Married/Widowed	€1,600	€8,000

1.3.18 Third-level tuition fees

TCA97 s473A Tax relief at the standard rate is available in respect of certain third level tuition fees paid to approved colleges.

An approved college is:

(a) a college or institute of higher education in the State which provides approved courses;

(b) a university or similar institution of higher education in another EU Member State which is maintained or assisted by recurrent grants from public funds of any EU Member State or, is a duly accredited university or institution of higher education of that Member State;

(c) a college or institution in another EU Member State which provides distance education in Ireland in approved courses or;

(d) a university or similar institution of higher education outside Ireland and the EU Member States which is maintained or assisted by public funds of that country or is a duly accredited university or institution of that country.

An approved course is:

(a) a full-time or part-time undergraduate course provided by an approved college which is of at least two academic years duration or;

(b) a postgraduate course of study provided by an approved college, leading to a postgraduate award based on a thesis or on the results of an examination or both,

- which is not less than one academic year but not more than four academic years duration and
- which requires the individual undertaking the course to have a degree or an equivalent qualification.

Qualifying fees, in relation to an approved course and an academic year, means the amount of fees chargeable in respect of tuition to be provided in relation to that course in that year.

Academic year, in relation to an approved course means a year of study commencing on a date not earlier than 1st day of August in a year of assessment.

For the tax years up to and including 2006, the relief is granted where an individual pays the qualifying fees on his or her own behalf or on behalf of a dependent. A dependent, in relation to an individual, means a spouse or child of the individual or a person in respect of whom the individual is or was the legal guardian. With effect from the tax year 2007, the requirement that there be a defined relationship between the taxpayer and the subject of the tax relief claim, has been abolished. Accordingly, there is no longer a requirement that the persons are related in order to claim the relief.

Fees which are met from any other sources, e.g., grant, scholarship or otherwise, do not qualify for the relief.

In the case of married couples, the allowance may be claimed by either spouse except in cases where separate assessment applies. Relief is allowable on qualifying fees, per course, per academic year, e.g., if a taxpayer has paid qualifying fees in respect of three dependents attending college in an academic year, he/she is entitled to relief up to the maximum limit in respect of each of these dependants.

The maximum limit for qualifying fees is €5,000 for the academic years 2005/06, 2006/07, 2007/08 and 2008/09.

1.3.19 Fees paid for training courses

TCA97 s476 Tax relief at the standard rate may be claimed in respect of tuition fees ranging from €315 to €1,270 in respect of approved training courses in the areas of information technology and foreign languages. To qualify for the relief an individual must receive a certificate of competency on completion of the course. For the tax years 2007 *et seq.*, the relief will be given to the person responsible for paying the fees. Prior to that, relief was available in respect of fees paid by an individual in respect of his/her dependent, to include his spouse or child.

1.3.20 Service charges

TCA97 s477 Tax relief at the standard rate may be claimed in respect of local authority service charges which are paid in full and on time by the person liable for them or by another person who resides on the premises to which the service charges relate.

The credit applies in respect of service charges paid in the preceding calendar year.

Finance Act 2006 revised the tax relief provisions in respect of service charges to take account of the introduction of the pay-by-use principle for local authority waste charges.

A general upper limit of €400 per annum applies with effect from 1 January 2006, irrespective of how the charge is determined. However, a transitional arrangement applies in respect of those taxpayers who have paid fixed charges in excess of €400 during 2005. In such cases relief may be claimed in 2006 on the actual amount paid.

In all cases the maximum ceiling of €400 will apply from 2007 onwards.

1.3.21 Heritage items

TCA97 s1003 A tax credit is granted in respect of qualifying donations of heritage items to the State. The credit can be obtained against taxes such as income tax, corporation tax, capital gains tax, gift tax or inheritance tax.

With effect from 26 March 2004, the minimum value of an item qualifying for tax credit must be €150,000 or, in the case of a collection, at least one item in the collection must be worth at least €50,000. However, Finance Act 2008 removed the minimum value limit of €50,000 in respect of any one item for collections consisting wholly of manuscript or archival material. In order to qualify, such collections are required to have been in existence for at least 30 years and each item must have been part of the collection for that period also.

The tax credit granted is by reference to the lesser of the independent valuation of the item obtained by the Revenue Commissioners and the valuation tendered by the prospective donor or the price paid for the item by the donor.

TCA97 s1003A Section 122 Finance Act 2006 provides a new scheme of tax relief for heritage property donated to the proposed Irish Heritage Trust. "Heritage property" will include buildings, gardens and contents of buildings insofar as they are historically associated with the buildings. The relief will apply to a person who makes a gift of heritage property to the Trust and will take the form of a payment on account of an amount equal to the value of the property against the person's tax liabilities.

The taxes to which the measure will apply are income tax, corporation tax, capital gains tax, gift tax and inheritance tax and may relate to past, current and future liabilities.

Section 122 Finance Act 2007 extended the relief to include the donation to the Trust of a particular collection of paintings and furniture which had been displayed previously in Fota House in County Cork and which is to be housed there again when Fota House is donated to the Trust. By having the collection in question treated as part of the contents of Fota House, the donor of the collection will be entitled to avail of section 1003A even though that donor is not the donor of Fota House.

To qualify for relief, the heritage property will have to be approved by the Minister for the Environment, Heritage and Local Government by reference to certain criteria. While there is a ceiling of €6m on the aggregate value of the heritage properties that can be approved in any one year, as the Trust was unable to avail of the relief in 2006, the annual limit was increased from €6m to €10m for the tax year 2007 only and from €6m to €8m for the tax year 2008 only.

The Revenue Commissioners will publish in their annual report each year descriptions and values of the heritage properties in respect of which relief is given under this section.

It should be noted that tax relief for donations of heritage items is a "specified relief" under Chapter 2A TCA 1997 in the context of the limitation on the amount of certain reliefs used by certain high income individuals – see paragraph 1.27.

1.3.22 Donations to charities and other approved bodies

TCA97 Sch26A, s848A A taxpayer aggrieved by an assessment to income tax or corporation for donations to charities and other approved bodies.

Relief may be claimed by both individuals and companies and the minimum aggregate donations to any charity or approved body in any year is €250.

With effect from 1 January 2006, relief also applies to donations of quoted securities. Where income tax or corporation tax relief is claimed in respect of donations of quoted securities, capital gains tax relief under section 611 TCA 1997 will not be available.

The legislation differentiates between donations made by PAYE taxpayers, self-employed tax payers and companies as follows:

(i) *PAYE taxpayers*

Relief is granted on a "grossed up" basis to the approved body rather than by way of a separate claim for tax relief by the donor. For example, if an individual who pays tax at the higher rate (41%), gives a donation of €590 to an approved body, the body will be deemed to have received €1,000 less tax of €410. The approved body will therefore be able to claim a refund of €410 from Revenue.

The donor must supply an "appropriate certificate" to enable the approved body to reclaim the tax.

(ii) *Self-employed taxpayers*

A claim for relief in respect of the donation is made when filing his/her tax return and there is no grossing up arrangement.

The donation will not reduce a persons relevant earnings for the purposes of calculating retirement annuity relief.

(iii) *Companies*

A claim for the donation can be made as a trading expenses or an expense of management for the accounting period in which it is made and there is no grossing up arrangement. The claim must be included in the companies tax return and where the donation is made in a short accounting period, it will be reduced proportionately.

With effect from 6 February 2003, an upper limit is placed on the level of tax relief which may be given in respect of donations in a single tax year by an individual to approved bodies with which the individual is associated. Where the aggregate of donations in a single tax year by an individual to approved bodies with which he/she is associated exceeds 10% of his/her total income, relief will not be given in respect of the excess.

An individual is regarded as being associated with an approved body if he/she is an employee or member of that approved body or of an associated approved body. Two approved bodies are regarded as being associated with each other if the same person or a similar group of persons has control over or can direct the activities of both approved bodies.

It should be noted that tax relief for donations is a "specified relief" under Chapter 2A TCA 1997 in the context of the limitation on the amount of certain reliefs used by certain high income individuals – see paragraph 1.27.

Approved bodies

Schedule 26A TCA 1997, sets out the list of bodies which are approved for the purposes of the relief. They are:

(1) A body approved for education in the arts, (see below)

(2) A body approved as an eligible charity; (see below)

(3) An institute of higher education within the meaning of section 1 of the Higher Education Authority Act 1971, or any body established for the sole purpose of raising funds for such an institution;

(4) An institution in receipt of public funding which provides courses under a scheme approved by the Minister under the Local Authorities (Higher Education Grants) Act, 1968 to 1992, and also applies to any body raising funds for such institutions;

(5) An institution of higher education which provides courses validated by the Higher Education Training Awards Council;

(6) An institution or body which provides primary education up to the end of sixth standard based on a programme prescribed by the Minister for Education and Science,

(7) An institution or body which provides post primary education up to the level of either or both the Junior Certificate or Leaving Certificate based on a programme prescribed by the Minister for Education and Science;

(8) A body for the promotion of the universal declaration of human rights;

(9) US – Ireland Alliance Limited;

(10) The Irish Heritage Trust, designated for that purpose by the Minister for Finance.

Approved body for education in the arts

An "approved body" means any body or institution which may be approved of by the Minister for Finance and which:

(a) provides any course one of the conditions of entry to which is related to the results of the Leaving Certificate Examination, a matriculation examination of a recognised university in the State or an equivalent examination held outside the State, or

(b) (i) is established on a permanent basis solely for the advancement of one or more approved subjects,

(ii) contributes to the advancement of that subject or those subjects on a national or regional basis, and

(iii) is prohibited by its constitution from distributing to its members any of its assets or profits.

Approval of a body as an eligible charity

An eligible charity means any body in the State which holds an authorisation which is in force.

The authorisation cannot be issued unless it is shown to the satisfaction of the Revenue Commissioners that:

(1) It is a body of persons or a trust established for charitable purposes only;

(2) That the income of the body or trust is applied for charitable purposes only;

(3) Before the date of making the application the body or trust has been granted exemption as a charity for a period of not less than two years;

(4) It provides such information to the Revenue Commissioners as they may reasonably require;

(5) It complies with such conditions (if any) as the Minister for Social, Community and Family Affairs may from time to time specify for this part of the Act.

An eligible charity must furnish information including audited accounts comprising an income and expenditure account or a profit and loss account and a balance sheet for its most recent accounting period.

The authorisation shall be for such period as the Revenue Commissioners may determine but for a period not exceeding five years.

1.3.23 Donations to certain sports bodies

TCA97 s847A The 2002 Finance Act introduced a scheme of tax relief for donations made on or after 1 May 2002, to certain sports bodies for the funding of capital projects.

To be eligible for the relief the following conditions apply:

(i) The project must be approved by the Minister for Tourism, Sport and Recreation.

(ii) The estimated aggregate cost of the project must not be greater than €40m.

(iii) The sports body must hold a certificate from the Revenue Commissioners that the body is, in the opinion of the Revenue Commissioners, a body of persons to which section 235 TCA 1997, applies, i.e., its income is exempt from tax because it is a body established for and existing for the sole purpose of promoting athletic or amateur games or sports and such income is applied solely for these purposes.

(iv) The sports body must also possess a valid tax clearance certificate.

Approved project

A project must fall within one of the following categories:

(i) The purchase, construction or refurbishment of a building or part of a building to be used for sporting activities by the approved sports body.

(ii) The purchase of land to be used for sporting activities by the approved sports body.

(iii) The purchase of permanently based equipment for use by the approved sports body for sporting activities.

(iv) The improvement of playing pitches, surfaces or facilities by the approved sports body.

(v) The repayment of, or the payment of interest on, funds borrowed by the approved sports body on or after 1 May 2002 for any of the above four activities.

Qualifying donations

The minimum donation in any year to any sports body is €250. The donation must satisfy the following conditions:

(i) It is made to an approved sports body for the sole purpose of funding an approved project and will be applied for that purpose.

(ii) Apart from the provisions of section 847A TCA 1997, the donation would not be tax deductible nor is it a relevant donation for the purposes of section 848A.

(iii) The donation is not made subject to a condition regarding repayment and the donor (or any person connected with the donor) is not entitled to any benefit either directly or indirectly as a consequence of making a donation.

(iv) The donation is not made conditional on the approved sports body acquiring property otherwise than by way of a gift by the donor.

(v) Only donations made by Irish resident individuals will qualify for the relief.

(vi) In the case of a donation made by an individual who is taxable solely through the PAYE system, the donation must be accompanied by an appropriate certificate, verifying that the individual has paid the quantum of tax certified in the certificate (see below).

Tax relief

The legislation differentiates between donations made by PAYE taxpayers, self-employed taxpayers and companies as follows:

(i) PAYE taxpayers

Relief is granted on a "grossed up" basis to the approved body rather than by way of a separate claim for tax relief by the donor. For example, if an individual who pays tax at the higher rate (41%), gives a donation of €590 to an approved body, the body will be deemed to have received €1,000 less tax of €410. The approved body will therefore be able to claim a refund of €410 from Revenue.

The donor must supply an "appropriate certificate" to enable the approved body to reclaim the tax.

(ii) Self-employed taxpayers

A claim for relief in respect of the donation is made when filing his/her tax return and there is no grossing up arrangements.

The donation will not reduce a person's "net relevant earnings" for the purposes of calculating retirement annuity relief.

(iii) Companies

A claim for the donation can be made as a trading expense or an expense of management for the accounting period in which it is made and there is no grossing up arrangement. The claim must be included in the company's tax return and where the donation is made in a short accounting period, it will be reduced proportionately.

It should be noted that tax relief for donations to certain sports bodies is a "specified relief" under Chapter 2A TCA 1997, in the context of the limitation on the amount of certain relief used by certain high-income individuals - see paragraph 1.27.

1.3.24 Relief on the retirement of certain sports persons

TCA97 s480A The 2002 Finance Act introduced a specific tax relief for the tax years 2002 *et seq.*, for certain retiring sports persons who are resident in the State.

The sports persons included are athletes, badminton players, boxers, cyclists, footballers, golfers, jockeys, motor racing drivers, rugby players, squash players, swimmers and tennis players.

The main features of the relief are as follows:

(i) The individuals must be resident in the State in the year of retirement.

(ii) The relief is applied by allowing a deduction of 40% against gross earnings (before deducting expenses) for up to any 10 tax years back to and including the tax year 1990/91, for which the sportsperson was resident in the State.

(iii) The earnings to which the relief applies are earnings deriving directly from actual participation in the sport concerned such as prize money, performance fees etc, but not other earnings such as sponsorship fees, advertisement income, income from interviews, newspaper or magazine articles or the right to use the sportspersons name to promote or endorse products or services.

(iv) The relief will be given by way of repayment of tax and is to be claimed in the year in which the sportsperson ceases permanently to be engaged in that sport.

(v) The relief will be clawed back if the sportsperson recommences to be engaged in that sport, though this does not prevent a subsequent claim for the relief if and when the sportsperson finally does retire at a later time.

(vi) The repayment will not carry interest.

(vii) The relief cannot create or augment a loss.

(viii) The relief will not affect the calculation of "net relevant earnings" for the purpose of ascertaining maximum pension contributions.

1.3.25 Pension contributions

(a) Retirement annuity contracts (RAC)

TCA97 Pt30 The maximum amounts on which tax relief may be claimed in respect of qualifying premiums, for the tax years 2006 *et seq.* are as follows:

Age	% of NET Relevant Earnings
Up to 30 years	15%
30 but less than 40	20%
40 but less than 50	25%
50 but less than 55	30%
55 but less than 60	35%
60 years or over	40%

Individuals who are engaged in specified occupations and professions – primarily sports professionals – qualify for a minimum 30% deduction irrespective of age.

There is an earnings cap on the amount of net relevant earnings as follows:

Tax Year	Maximum NRE
	€
2006	250,000
2007	262,382
2008	275,238

Earnings in excess of the above amounts will not be taken into account in calculating the allowable contribution. The cap is adjusted annually in line with an earnings index declared by the Government.

Contributions may be made until an individual reaches 75 years of age.

Accumulated funds can be transferred from one insurer to another.

Where, in any year part of the premium cannot be fully relieved because of the operation of the limits, that part is carried forward and added to the qualifying premium of the following year.

"Net relevant earnings" are earnings from trades, professions and non-pensionable employments, less certain payments and deductions. The earnings of a husband and wife are treated separately for purposes of determining relevant earnings and the relief is available in respect of each spouse with non-pensionable earnings.

For the tax years up to and including 2001, where a self-employed individual who was making contributions under an RAC, became an employee and joined an occupational pension scheme, it was necessary to terminate the RAC, unless the individual continued to have a source of self-employment income.

For the tax years 2001 *et seq.*, where a qualifying premium is paid after the end of a year of assessment but before 31 October in the year following the year of assessment (the specified return date), it may be treated as paid in the year of assessment. An election for such treatment must be made before 31 October in the year following the year of assessment.

For the tax years 2002 *et seq.*, the individual may continue to make contributions to an existing RAC or indeed, take out a further RAC, but without tax relief. The contributions to the RAC will be carried forward indefinitely, until such time, if any, that the employee acquires a source of self-employment income against which the contributions may be offset subject to the normal rules.

(b) Additional voluntary contributions (AVC)

Employees in occupational pension schemes are entitled to tax relief on the aggregate annual contributions to the scheme, including AVC contributions, based on the limits shown in the table for RACs in paragraph 1.3.22.

A similar earnings cap of €275,238 (see (a) above) for the tax year 2008 applies to income that qualifies for relief.

(c) Personal retirement savings accounts

A Personal Retirement Savings Account (PRSA) is a long-term savings account designed to assist people save for their retirement. The main features are as follows:

(i) Tax relief at the marginal rate is available on PRSA contributions subject to the maximum allowable contributions as a percentage of net relevant earnings as shown in the table in paragraph 1.3.20 for retirement annuity contracts. Where tax relief cannot be given in full in a tax year because of insufficient income on the operation of the limits, the unrelieved contributions can be carried forward to a later year for tax relief purposes.

(ii) Where an employer does not provide an occupational pension scheme, he/she must provide access to at least one PRSA with effect from 15 September 2003.

(iii) Employers may also contribute to an employees PRSA and obtain tax relief for their contribution.

(iv) PRSA's are available from PRSA providers whose products have been approved jointly by the Pensions Board and the Revenue Commissioners.

(v) Contributions made by an employer to a PRSA are aggregated with an employees contribution for the purpose of calculating the maximum tax-relieved contribution.

(vi) Employees who are not in pensionable employment may claim relief on contributions up to €1,525 per annum, regardless of the limits.

(vii) For the tax year 2008 a similar earnings cap of €275,238 (see (a) above) applies to income that qualifies for relief.

(viii) Where contributions are made between the end of the tax year and the following 31 October, the taxpayer can opt to have these contributions treated as having been made in the previous tax year.

(ix) No tax is charged on investment income or gains earned by a PRSA.

(x) Withdrawals cannot be made from a PRSA until the contributor reaches the age of 60, but they must commence before age 75. In certain circumstances withdrawals can be taken earlier. On retirement, the following options apply to contributors to a PRSA:

- They may take up to 25% tax free.
- They may opt to invest the funds in an annuity or retain the funds in a PRSA and withdraw these as they wish. Such withdrawals are subject to PAYE.
- Where the latter option is chosen, a minimum of €63,500 must be used to purchase an annuity payable immediately or left in the PRSA until age 75, unless he/she has a pension or annuity for life of at least €12,700 per annum (including any Social Welfare Pension to which they are entitled).
- Alternatively, the value of the assets in the PRSA may be transferred to an Approved Retirement Fund (ARF). If this option is chosen, a minimum of €63,500 must be used to purchase an annuity payable immediately or kept in an Approved Minimum Retirement Fund (AMRF) until age 75, unless the contributor is actually in receipt of "specified income" for life of at least €12,700 per annum (including any Social Welfare Pension to which he/she is entitled). The funds in an ARF may be withdrawn at any time or invested in an annuity. Where the funds are withdrawn, tax will be deducted by the manager of the ARF under PAYE.

(xi) Where death occurs before benefits are taken from a PRSA, the PRSA fund will pass in its entirety to the contributors estate, free of income tax. Inheritance tax will apply as normal.

(xii) Where death occurs after draw-down of benefits has commenced, the taxation rules for the PRSA fund will be similar to the taxation rules for an ARF, following death of the ARF holder (see page 42), i.e.:

- Generally the amount distributed is treated as the income of the deceased for the year of death.
- But where the distribution is made to another ARF in the name of the ARF holder's spouse or to a child of the ARF holder who is under 21 at the date of death of the ARF holder, no income tax liability will arise.
- Where the distribution is made from the ARF following the death of the surviving spouse or where the distribution is made to a child of the ARF holder who is over 21 at the date of death of the ARF holder, tax will be deducted under PAYE

at the standard rate of income tax for the year in which the distribution is made. No further tax liability will arise in respect of such a distribution.

(xiii) Contributions to both an RAC and a PRSA

Where an individual is not in pensionable employment, and already contributes to a Retirement Annuity Contract (RAC), his/her contributions to an RAC and a PRSA are added together when calculating the maximum tax relief.

(xiv) PRSA contributions by those in pensionable employment

When an individual is already in pensionable employment, he/she can only take out a PRSA and get tax relief on the contributions to it against the income from this employment, where the PRSA is linked to his/her main pension scheme. This is known as an Additional Voluntary PRSA (AVC PRSA).

In determining the maximum tax relief, the same limits which apply to PRSA's and RAC's also apply to the total of an individuals own pension contributions to the main pension scheme (either ordinary contributions or additional voluntary contributions) and to his/her AVC PRSA contributions.

However, as total pension and AVC PRSA contributions must be limited to the amount required to provide the maximum benefits permitted in line with Revenue limits, the actual limit in any contributor's own circumstances may be less than the percentages shown on page 35. In addition, the maximum tax-free lump sum arising from an AVC PRSA must be in line with the occupational pension scheme rules.

Where an individual has additional relevant earnings arising from non-pensionable employment, he/she may contribute in respect of these to a normal PRSA in the usual way and claim tax relief up to the appropriate limits.

(xv) Limit to relief for pensions contributions

The limits to tax relief for contributions set out on page 35 apply to all pension contributions made by an individual and contributions made by his/her employer to a PRSA. For this purpose, pension contributions mean contributions to a PRSA, to an RAC, to an employer sponsored pension scheme or to a statutory pension scheme. In addition, the maximum income on which the aggregate tax relief for contributions can be calculated is €275,238 for the tax year 2008 (see (a) above for earlier limits). To the extent that aggregate contributions exceed the allowable amount, the contributions are carried forward to the following year and treated as paid in that year.

TCA97 **(d) SSIA-related pension incentive**

Part 36B Finance Act 2006 introduced a new Pension Incentive Scheme to encourage those on lower incomes to roll over some or all of their

SSIA proceeds into an approved pension product and to continue the savings habit with regular savings into a pension. The new incentive will involve a tax credit of €1 for every €3 invested, up to a maximum of €2,500, along with a proportion of the tax deducted from the SSIA at maturity. The investment in the pension product must be made within three months of the SSIA maturing.

In order to qualify for the incentive, the following criteria will apply:

- An individual's income must not exceed €50,000 in the year prior to the year in which the SSIA matures.
- Tax relief cannot be claimed under normal tax rules for SSIA amounts up to and including €7,500 which are reinvested in an approved pension product.
- An individual cannot use this incentive to replace any amounts that he/she has already committed to contribute to a pension product.
- An SSIA Maturity Statement, which is obtained from the SSIA provider, must be forwarded to the pension provider.
- The individual must sign a declaration that the conditions set out above are and will be fully complied with.

The scheme operates from 1 June 2006.

Finance Act 2007 provides for a claw back of tax credits where a person availing of the credits invests funds in a pension product and withdraws any funds from the pension product within one year. Where the withdrawal takes place before 10 April 2007, the pension investor will be assessed to income tax directly. Where the withdrawal takes place on or after 10 April 2007, the pension administrator is required to deduct a claw back amount ("retained amount") from any payment made. This amount will be in the same proportion to the amount withdrawn as the total tax credits bear to aggregate of the total tax credits and the amount of SSIA funds invested in the pension product. For example, if a person seeks to withdraw an amount equivalent to the value of the SSIA funds invested and the associated tax credits from the pension product, the total amount of the tax credit previously granted will be clawed back.

(e) EU pension plans

TCA97 Part 30 Section 21 Finance Act 2005 amended Part 30, TCA 97 by providing for tax relief for contributions to EU pension plans in certain circumstances, with effect form 1 January 2005.

It also introduced a new Chapter 2B into the TCA 97 which provides for a statutory scheme of relief for contributions paid by a migrant worker who comes to the State and who wishes to continue to contribute to a pre-existing "overseas pension plan" concluded with a pension provider in another EU Member State. To qualify for the relief, certain conditions and information requirements must be met as set out in the section.

(f) Options on retirement

General

Prior to 6 April 1999, the accumulated pension premiums had to be used to purchase a life annuity.

From 6 April 1999, a number of new options were introduced for the self employed and proprietary directors (5% of voting shares) on retirement, as follows:

(i) They may take up to 25% of their pension fund tax free (subject to the limits provided for in Finance Act 2006 on lump sum payments that can be made tax-free on or after 7 December 2005) – See Finance Act 2006 changes on page 43.

(ii) Have the remainder of the fund, or €63,500 if less, transferred to an Approved Minimum Retirement Fund (AMRF). However, this will not be necessary if the individual is actually in receipt of "specified income" of €12,700 per annum. The amount invested in the AMRF cannot be drawn down until the individual reaches 75 years of age.

(iii) As an alternative to having an amount invested in an AMRF, the individual may opt to have the amount invested in a retirement annuity payable immediately.

(iv) The balance of the funds may be either taken by the individual and taxed under the PAYE system or invested in an Approved Retirement Fund (ARF).

Where a person has purchased a life annuity since 2 December 1998, he/she may opt for the new arrangements, with the agreement of the relevant assurance company.

Individuals whose pension date has passed but who have not yet invested in an annuity, can now, subject to meeting all other criteria, avail of the new options up to the date on which the rules of their pension scheme require that the fund must be used to purchase an annuity.

With effect from 6 April 2000, all employees who make additional voluntary contributions (AVCs) will be entitled to avail of the new options as regards that part of their pension fund which has been built up from such contributions.

TCA97 s780 With effect from 5 December 2001, refunds of employee pension contributions are taxed at the standard rate of income tax (Previously they were taxed at 25%)

Approved (Minimum) Retirement Funds

The main features of ARFs and AMRFs are as follows:

(a) Any income or gains arising within an ARF/AMRF are exempt from tax as long as they are held within an ARF/AMRF. However, any payments out of the fund, whether of capital, income or gains, will be chargeable to tax under the PAYE system.

(b) Finance Act 2003 extended the circumstances in which assets in an ARF are treated as having been distributed. With effect from 6 February 2003, assets will be treated as distributed in so far as they have been used for the following purposes:

- to make a loan or to secure a loan to the ARF holder or to a connected person;
- to acquire property from the ARF holder or a connected person;
- to acquire property to be used as holiday property or as a residence by the ARF holder or a connected person; where the property is acquired on or after 6 February 2003 for some other purpose (e.g., letting) and is subsequently used as holiday property or as a residence by the ARF holder or a connected person the distribution will arise at the time the property comes to be used for this purpose and will include any ARF assets used in the repair or improvement of the property;
- to acquire shares or other interests in a closely held company in which the ARF holder or a connected person is a participator;
- to acquire any tangible moveable property;
- Finance Act 2006 further extended the circumstances in which assets in an ARF are treated as having been distributed with effect from 2 February 2006, to include the acquisition of property for use in connection with any business of the ARF-holder or of a person connected to the ARF-holder.

In addition, the sale of assets in the ARF to the ARF-holder or a connected person will also be regarded as a distribution of the value of the assets in question.

Insofar as ARF assets are treated as distributed they are no longer regarded as ARF assets. Similarly, where the acquisition of assets is treated as giving rise to a distribution, the assets will not be regarded as assets in the ARF.

Similar rules on distributions for ARF's outlined above will also apply to AMRF's.

(c) Finance Act 2006 provided for a 3% annual imputed distribution which will apply to the value of assets held in an ARF at 31 December each year. The main features of this provision are as follows:

- The imputed distribution will apply to ARFs created on or after 6 April 2000 where the ARF-holder is 60 years of age or over for the whole of the tax year.

- The 3% rate will be phased in over the period 2007 to 2009, with 1% applying in 2007, 2% in 2008 and the full 3% in 2009 and each subsequent year.
- Actual distributions made during the year from the ARF (and from an AMRF of the ARF-holder) may be deducted from the imputed distribution to arrive at the net imputed amount, if any, to be regarded as a distribution.
- The net imputed amount, if any, is to be regarded as a notional distribution from the ARF, which is calculated as a percentage of the value of the assets in the ARF as at 31 December each year. It is regarded as a distribution made not later than February in the year following the year in which the ARF assets are valued. This means that any tax due must be remitted to Revenue not later than mid-March.
- Where an ARF-holder has more than one ARF, all of which are not managed by the same qualifying fund manager (QFM), the ARF-holder may nominate one of the QFMs for the purposes of operating the new provisions. In those circumstances, the nominee must act as if all of the ARFs and the actual distributions from them were, respectively, managed and distributed by the nominee. The nominee must then account for any tax due on the overall net imputed amount in the normal way.

It should be noted that the above provisions do not apply to AMRFs.

(d) An ARF or an AMRF must be held by a qualifying fund manager, as listed.

(e) Where the individual reaches 75 or dies, the AMRF becomes an ARF.

(f) The ARF becomes part of the estate of the individual.

A summary of the tax treatment of assets in an ARF, following death is as follows:

ARF inherited by	Income Tax due	CAT due
Surviving spouse	No tax due on the transfer to an ARF in the spouses name	No
Children (under 21)	No tax due	Yes*
Children 21 and over	Yes @ Standard Rate	No
Others	Yes @ Marginal Rate	Yes*

Death of surviving spouse		
Children (under 21)	No	Yes*
Children (over 21)	Yes @ Standard Rate	No
Others	Yes @ Standard Rate	Yes*

**Normal capital acquisitions tax thresholds apply.*

TCA97 Ch 2C

Finance Act 2006 Changes

Sch 23B

Chapter 2C TCA 1997 imposes a limit or ceiling on the total capital value of pension benefits that an individual can draw in their lifetime from tax-relieved pension products (including all Public Sector pension schemes), where those benefits come into payment for the first time on or after 7 December 2005. This is called the "standard fund threshold" in the legislation and is set at €5,000,000. This limit is adjusted annually from 2007 in line with an earnings index declared by Government and the maximum tax-free lump sum payable (i.e., 25% of "the standard fund threshold") is adjusted accordingly, as follows:

Period	Standard Fund Threshold	Maximum Tax Free Lump Sum (25%)
	€	€
07/12/05 – 31/12/06	5,000,000	1,250,000
Year Ending 31/12/2007	5,165,000	1,291,250
Year Ending 31/12/2008	5,418,085	1,354,521

In certain circumstances, a higher threshold (called the "personal fund threshold") may apply. This arises if, on 7 December 2005, the capital value of an individual's pension rights on that date, which the individual had not become entitled to on that date, exceeds the standard fund threshold and certain notification requirements have been met by 7 June 2006. The personal fund threshold is also adjusted annually from 2007.

The restriction applies to a single lump sum, or, where more than one lump sum is paid to an individual over time, to the aggregate value of those lump sums.

The restriction does not apply to lump sum death-in-service benefits.

On or after 7 December 2005, on each occasion an individual becomes entitled to receive a benefit under a pension arrangement for the first time (called in the legislation a "benefit crystallisation event" (BCE)), they use up part of their standard or personal fund threshold. At each BCE, a capital value must be attributed to the benefits that crystallise and the value is then tested by the pension scheme administrator against the individual's appropriate fund threshold. In respect of defined benefit type arrangements, for the purposes of placing a capital value on the uncrystallised pension rights of an individual and for establishing the capital value of benefits taken in respect of those rights, a valuation factor of 20 must be used, unless the pension scheme administrator can justify the use of a different factor to Revenue.

When the capital value of a BCE either on its own or, when aggregated with BCEs that have been taken earlier, exceeds the individual's fund threshold, a "chargeable excess" arises equal to the amount by which the fund threshold is exceeded. The whole of the amount of the chargeable excess is then subject to an up-front income tax charge of 41% (previously 42%) payable by the pension scheme administrator in the first instance (although both the administrator and the individual are made jointly and severally liable to the charge). This charge is without prejudice to any other income tax charge that might arise on the balance of the chargeable excess as and when benefits are taken under the scheme whether by way of pension, annuity, taxable cash lump sum or distribution from an ARF or AMRF.

When calculating the amount crystalised by a benefit crystallisation event in relation to an individual under a pension scheme which is subject to a pension adjustment order (PAO), the benefit payable under the PAO is to be included in the calculation as if the PAO had not been made. In other words, any benefit arising under the PAO is deemed to be a benefit arising to the individual for the purposes of determining whether the individual's standard fund threshold or personal fund threshold has been exceeded. This applies regardless of whether the benefit under the PAO is paid as a designated benefit from the member spouse's scheme or in some other form following payment of a transfer amount in accordance with the Family Law Acts.

As a transitional measure, responsibility for accounting for and remitting any tax due on a chargeable excess arising during the period between 7 December 2005 and 31 March 2006 rests with the individual entitled to the benefits giving rise to the tax charge. However, certain reporting requirements are imposed on pension scheme administrators where the capital value of BCEs made by them during that period are substantial.

TCA97 s779A

(g) Use of pension assets

With effect from 2 February 2006, where the assets of an occupational pension scheme are used for the purposes of certain transactions, the use of the assets will be treated as a pension paid under the scheme and subject to tax. The transactions concerned are the same as those which, if undertaken in the context of an ARF, would be regarded as distributions from the ARF (see (b) above). The transactions include the acquisition by the scheme of property to be used as a holiday property or as a residence by the scheme member or a connected person. Insofar as the use of assets of a scheme are treated as a pension paid under the scheme, they will no longer be regarded as assets of the scheme, and where scheme assets are used in the acquisition of certain property, the property assets concerned will not be regarded as assets of the scheme.

1.4 General and Age Exemptions

TCA97 s187 Exemptions from income tax are available to individuals with low incomes. The exemption limits are increased for individuals aged 65 years or over. Marginal relief applies where the income does not greatly exceed the relevant exemption limit.

1.4.1 General exemption

Total exemption from income tax for the tax year 2007 is available to an individual under 65 years of age whose "total income" does not exceed the following specified amounts for the year:

- €5,210 in the case of a single, widowed or a married person singly assessed
- €10,420 in the case of a married couple who are jointly assessed.

Arising from increases in personal tax credits in recent years, the general exemption limits outlined above are largely redundant. As a result, section 5, Finance Act 2008, provided for the cessation of the general exemption limits and the associated system of marginal relief with effect from 1 January 2008. (See Chart 3 for limits prior to 2007.)

1.4.2 Age exemption

TCA97 s188 Total exemption from income tax is available to individuals who are aged 65 years or over and whose income for the tax year 2008 does not exceed the following specified amounts for the year:

Single and widowed	€20,000
Married couples (either spouse aged 65 or over)	€40,000

The exemption limits are increased by €575 for each of the first two qualifying children that a claimant proves has lived with him/her at any time during the tax year and by €830 per child for each subsequent child.

The definition of a "qualifying child" is the same as for the "Single Parent Tax Credit" (see paragraph 1.3.1). See Chart 4 for earlier limits.

1.4.3 Marginal relief

Marginal relief is available where the total income exceeds the above limits, but is less than twice the specified amount. This marginal relief restricts the maximum amount of tax payable to 40% of the amount by which the individual's total income exceeds the exemption limit.

1.5 Interest Payable

1.5.1 Mortgage interest

TCA97 s244-s245 The maximum allowable mortgage interest for individuals for the tax year 2008 is set out in Chart 6. An individual who sells his only or main residence and acquires another is entitled to claim additional interest on the bridging loan up to the maximum of his marital status class threshold.

From 1 January 2002 relief is granted at source. The qualifying interest element of a mortgage repayment is reduced by an amount equal to the standard rate of income tax while the mortgage lender will be repaid an equivalent amount by Revenue.

The scheme only applies to residences situated in the State and only to loans secured on residences (mortgage loans). Other allowable interest will continue to be relieved by way of deduction against taxable income.

1.5.2 Interest on loans applied in acquiring shares/lending money to a company

TCA97 s244-s252 Relief is given to individuals for interest on loans applied in acquiring shares in or lending money to a "qualifying company". Interest is not given on loans granted on or after 29 January 1992 to acquire shares in quoted companies.

A qualifying company is a company:

(i) which exists wholly or mainly for the purpose of carrying on a trade or trades, or

(ii) whose business consists wholly or mainly of the holding of stocks, shares or securities of a company referred to in (i) above.

Relief in respect of loans applied in acquiring shares in or lending to companies:

(i) whose income consists wholly or mainly of profits or gains chargeable under CASE V of Schedule D, or

(ii) whose business consists wholly or mainly of the holding of stocks, shares or securities of a company referred to in (i) above was abolished in respect of loans taken out on or after 7 December 2005.

Relief is available to individuals who work for the greater part of their time in the management or conduct of the business of the company or of a connected company and who have a "material interest" (more than 5% of the equity) in the company.

Relief is also available to full-time or part-time directors and employees, even if the "material interest" test is not satisfied.

The tables below show the relief available in respect of loans taken out before and on or after 7 December 2005.

Loan taken out before 7 December 2005:

	Unquoted Trading or Rental Company	**Unquoted Holding Company of a Trading and Rental company**
Full-time director/employee	Unrestricted	Unrestricted
Part-time director/employee	Unrestricted	None

Loan taken out on or after 7 December 2005:

	Unquoted Trading Company	**Unquoted Holding Company of a Trading company**
Full-time director/ employee	Unrestricted	Unrestricted
Part-time director/ employee	Unrestricted	None

Where the investment in the company is by way of loan, relief is available only if the money lent is used wholly and exclusively for the trade or business of the company or a connected company.

No relief is available where during the period from the making of the loan to the date the interest is paid, the company or any person connected with it makes any loan to the individual or person connected with him, unless such loans are in the ordinary course of business which includes the lending of money.

Where an individual recovers any capital from the company or a connected company without using that amount in reduction of the loan, relief will cease to be given for that amount of the loan.

Capital is treated as being recovered from the company or a connected company where:

(a) the individual receives value for the sale of any part of the ordinary share capital of the company or of a connected company or consideration by way of repayment of any part of the ordinary share capital, or

(b) the company or a connected company repays the loan or advance, or

(c) the individual receives consideration for the assignment of any debt due to him from the company or from a connected company.

(See below re: restrictions applying to certain partnerships.)

Relief may not be claimed in respect of interest paid on a loan applied in acquiring shares for which BES/Film relief has been claimed.

Relief may not be claimed unless the loan is applied for bona fide commercial purposes and not as part of a scheme or arrangement the main purpose or one of the main purposes of which is the avoidance of tax.

It should be noted that tax relief for interest on loans to lend to or invest in qualifying companies is a "specified relief" under Chapter 2A TCA 1997 in the context of the limitation on the amount of certain reliefs used by certain high-income individuals – see paragraph 1.27.

1.5.3 Interest on loans applied in acquiring an interest in a partnership

TCA97 s253

Relief is given to individuals for interest on loans applied in purchasing a share in or lending money to a partnership provided the money is used wholly and exclusively for the purposes of the trade or profession carried on by the partnership.

Interest paid on the loan is available for relief if throughout the period from the application of the loan until the interest was paid, the individual personally acts in the conduct of the trade or profession and he has not recovered any capital from the partnership in the period.

Where the individual recovers any capital from the partnership without using the amount recovered in reduction of the loan, relief will cease to be given for that amount of the loan.

Capital is treated as having been recovered where:

(a) the individual receives consideration for the sale of any part of his interest in the partnership, or

(b) the partnership returns any amount of capital to him or repays any loan made by him, or

(c) the individual receives any consideration for assigning any debt due to him by the partnership.

TCA97 s1013

With effect from 29 February 2000, non-active partners are restricted as to the offset of interest paid after that date – see paragraph 4.1.7.

It should be noted that tax relief for interest on loans to acquire an interest in or lending to a partnership is a "specified relief" under Chapter 2A TCA 1997 in the context of the limitation on the amount of certain reliefs used by certain high-income individuals – see paragraph 1.27.

1.5.4 Interest – anti-avoidance

TCA97 s817A

Where interest is paid under any arrangement, the sole or main benefit of which is to obtain a reduction in tax, no relief shall be given.

TCA97 s817C

Where interest paid by a person to a connected person is a trading expense of the payer and not a trading receipt of the recipient, the interest will not be deductable as a trading expense until it has been accounted for as income of the connected person for tax purposes. The provision does not apply where the recipient of the interest is both non-resident and not under the ultimate control of Irish residents.

1.5.5 Payment of interest net

TCA97 s246 Where annual interest is paid by companies or where such interest is paid by individuals to persons whose usual place of abode is outside the State, tax at the standard rate must be deducted and paid over to Revenue.

The following are exceptions to this rule:

(a) Interest paid in the State on an advance from a bank or building society carrying on a bona fide banking business in the State.

Finance Act 2002 provided that interest paid to other financial services companies who make loans in the ordinary course of business may be paid without the withholding of tax provided certain conditions are met as follows:

(i) The interest is paid in the State on a loan from a company in whose hands the interest is chargeable as trading income

(ii) The interest arises from a loan made by a company in the ordinary course of a trade which includes the lending of money, and

(iii) The company receiving the interest has fulfilled the notification requirements to both the Revenue Commissioners and the paying company.

(b) Interest paid by such a bank or building society to non residents in the ordinary course of its business.

(c) Interest on any securities in respect of which the Minister for Finance has authorised that payment be made gross, i.e., Government loan interest.

(d) Interest paid by companies where the Revenue Commissioners have authorised the payment to be made gross, i.e., co-op interest.

(e) Interest paid which is a distribution under section 130.

(f) Interest paid by a qualifying company based in the IFSC to a non resident person.

(g) Interest paid by a company or an investment undertaking in the course of a trade or business to companies which are resident in another EU Member State or in a country with which Ireland has a double taxation agreement.

(h) Interest paid by companies to investment undertakings within the gross roll-up regime. The investment undertakings concerned are not themselves taxable and already have an exemption from dividend withholding tax and DIRT.

1.5.6 Interest to a 75% Group Company

TCA97 s452

Finance Act 2007 provides that in certain circumstances interest paid by a company to a non-resident 75 per cent parent or associated company will not be treated as a distribution of its profits and will therefore be a deductible trading expense. In certain cases double taxation can arise where the interest is disallowed as a trading expense under the distribution rule and is also taxed in the hands of the recipient as interest. Subject to the conditions of the section being met, a company paying yearly interest to a non-resident 75 per cent parent or associated company may treat such interest as a deductible trading expense.

The section as drafted does not avoid withholding tax for non-treaty territories and does not deal with short interest. (See also 2.2.1)

1.6 Schedule C

TCA97 s32-s51 Assessments under Schedule C may be made on persons entrusted with the payment of certain interest, annuities, dividends, etc., payable out of Public Revenue, and on bankers or dealers who engage in cashing or selling coupons.

1.6.1 Exemptions

There is no assessment where interest is paid on securities in respect of which the Minister for Finance has authorised that payment be made gross, or where interest is paid by companies which have been authorised by the Revenue Commissioners to make such payments gross.

No tax is chargeable in respect of the dividends on any securities of any territory outside the State which are payable in the State to non-residents of the State.

1.7 Schedule D - Cases I and II

Tax is charged on the annual profit or gains arising from any trade (Case I) or from any profession (Case II). The tax treatment of these items is almost identical and therefore they can be considered together. The expression "annual profits or gains" is not defined in the Tax Acts.

TCA97 s3 Trade includes "every trade, manufacture, adventure or concern in the nature of trade". This definition has been held by the courts to embrace profits arising not alone from trading in the normal sense of the word but also from isolated transactions, and activities such as the conducting of professional examinations. Profits from dealing in or developing land are assessable under Case I as are profits from farming.

TCA97 s81 Only deductions authorised by the Tax Acts are allowed in computing the profits of a trade or profession. No deduction is allowed for:

(a) any expense, not being money wholly and exclusively laid out or expended for the purposes of the trade or profession;

(b) any disbursements or expenses of maintenance of the parties or their families or any sums expended for any other domestic or private purposes;

(c) rent of any dwelling-house except where such part thereof is used for the purposes of the trade or profession;

(d) any sum expended over and above repairs to premises, implements, utensils or articles employed for the purposes of the trade or profession;

(e) any loss not connected with or arising out of the trade or profession;

(f) any capital withdrawn from, or any sum employed or intended to be employed as capital in the trade or profession;

(g) any capital employed in improvements to premises occupied for the purposes of the trade or profession;

(h) any interest which might have been made if any such sums as aforesaid had been laid out at interest;

(i) any debts, except bad debts proved to be such to the satisfaction of the Inspector and doubtful debts to the extent that they are respectively estimated to be bad;

(j) any sum recoverable under an insurance or contract of indemnity;

(k) any annuity or other annual payment payable out of the profits or gains;

(l) any royalty or other sum paid in respect of the user of a patent.

(m) expenditure involving crime.

1.7.1 Pre-trading expenses

TCA97 s82

An allowance may be claimed in respect of pre-trading expenses in the case of a trade or profession which is set up and commenced on or after 22 January 1997, provided that the expenses:

(i) were incurred for the purpose of the trade or profession, and

(ii) were incurred within three years of commencement, and

(iii) are not otherwise allowable in computing profits.

Where an allowance is granted for pre-trading expenses, it is treated as if the expenditure was incurred on the date on which the trade/ profession commenced.

The pre-trading expenditure which is allowed cannot be used for the purpose of set off against income of the individual other than that arising from the trade or profession in respect of which the expenditure was incurred.

1.7.2 Entertainment expenses

TCA97 s840

No deduction is granted in respect of any expenses incurred on or after 26 March 1982 in providing business entertainment. "Business entertainment" means entertainment of any kind including the provision of accommodation, food and drink or any other form of hospitality in any circumstances whatsoever.

1.7.3 Motor expenses

TCA97 s376

Running expenses

The restriction on the tax deduction in respect of running expenses on cars where the cost of the car exceeded a specified amount was abolished for expenditure incurred in accounting periods ending on or after 1 January 2002 for companies and in income tax basis periods ending on or after 1 January 2002 for individuals (see Chart 49 for the relevant specified amounts).

Leasing charges

(i) Cars Leased before 1 July 2008

TCA97 s377

Leasing charges are restricted where the cost of the car exceeds a specified amount. Leasing charges incurred in accounting periods ending on or after 1 January 2007 for companies and income tax basis periods ending on or after 1 January 2007 for individuals, in respect of cars costing in excess of €24,000 (the specified amount) are restricted by an amount which bears to the leasing charge, the same proportion as the cost of the vehicle less the specified amount (€24,000) bears to the cost of the vehicle (see Chart 7 for relevant specified amounts). This may be expressed by the formula:

$$A \times \frac{B - €24{,}000}{B}$$

where:

A = Qualifying Leasing Charges

B = Cost of the vehicle

(ii) Cars leased on or after 1 July 2008.

TCA97 s380M Finance Act 2008 introduced a new scheme of relief for leasing charges for business cars which seeks to limit the availability of allowances for leasing charges by reference to the carbon emission levels of cars. Cars are categorised by reference to carbon dioxide (CO_2) emissions as follows:

Category A Vehicles	Category B/C vehicles	Category D/E Vehicles	Category F/G Vehicles
0 – 120 g/km	121 – 155g/km	156 – 190g/km	191g/km +

In the case of cars in Categories A/B/C, the leasing charges will be increased or reduced, as the case may be, in the proportion which the specified amount (i.e., €24,000) bears to the cost of the car. Accordingly, such cars will benefit from a proportionately higher deduction than the actual leasing charges where the cost of the car is less than €24,000.

In the case of cars in Categories D/E, where the cost of the car is less than or equal to the specified amount (i.e., €24,000), the leasing charges will be reduced by 50%. Where the cost of the car is greater than €24,000, the leasing charges will be reduced in the proportion which 50% of the specified amount (€24,000) bears to the cost.

Cars in Categories F/G do not qualify for a deduction for leasing charges.

1.7.4 Basis of assessment

TCA97 s65 Current year basis was introduced with effect from the year of assessment 1990/91. This replaced the preceding year basis which obtained for the years to 1989/90 inclusive, and which is dealt with in early editions of this book. Where business profits are computed by reference to annual accounts the charge to tax for a year of assessment is based on the profits of an accounting period ending in the year of assessment.

The year of assessment ran from 6 April in one calendar year to 5 April in the following year, for all tax years up to and including the year 2000/01.

With effect from 1 January 2002 the year of assessment is aligned with the calendar year and runs from 1 January to 31 December.

The first calendar tax year, 1 January 2002 to 31 December 2002 was preceded by a short transitional tax "year" running from 6 April 2001 to 31 December 2001.

1.7.5 Commencement years

TCA97 s66

First year: For the tax years 2002 *et seq*. the profits assessable are those from the date of commencement to the following 31 December.

Second year: For 1998/99 and subsequent years of assessment, the profits to be assessed in the second year are as follows:

(a) If there is only one set of accounts made up to a date within that year and these accounts are for a full 12 months, the full amount of the profits of the one year ending on that date;

(b) If the accounts are for less than one year or there are more than one set of accounts made up to a date or dates within that tax year, the full amount of the profits of the one year ending on the later or latest of those dates;

(c) In any other case, the actual profits for the tax year.

If the actual profits of the second year (calculated on a 31 December basis) are lower than those of the first 12 months' trading, the difference can be set against the profits of the third year of assessment. When the profits of the third year of assessment are insufficient to absorb the full amount of the difference, any balance can be carried forward as a loss available for set off against profits of subsequent years of assessment.

Third and subsequent years: The assessment for these years is on a current year basis.

1.7.6 Cessation years

TCA97 s67

Final year: For the tax years 2002 *et seq*., the profits assessable are those from the preceding 1 January to the date of cessation.

Penultimate year: Where the actual profits of the penultimate year of assessment (calculated on a 31 December basis) exceed the assessed profits calculated on a current year basis, the assessment for the penultimate year is revised to the actual profits.

TCA97 s958(A)

Where an assessment has to be revised and an additional tax liability arises, the obligation is on the taxpayer to include it in the self assessment tax return for the year in which the cessation occurred.

1.7.7 Short-lived businesses

TCA97 s68 Where a business commences and ceases within three tax years, the aggregate taxable profits for the three years of assessment may not exceed the profits actually earned in the period. An election for this treatment must be made before the specified return date for the year of cessation.

1.7.8 Period of computation of profits

(a) If only one account is made up to a date within the year of assessment and that account is for a period of one year, these accounts will form, as indicated above, the basis of assessment for that year.

(b) If the accounting date is changed, the profits for a year ending on the new date will be adopted.

(c) If more than one set of accounts are made up to different dates in the tax year, the profits for a year ending on the later of those dates will be adopted.

(d) In any other case the assessment will be based on the profits for the year ended 31 December, i.e., the actual year of assessment.

(e) Where there has been a change of accounting date or where two or more sets of accounts are prepared and the rule outlined at (b) or (c) above is adopted, Revenue can review the assessment for the previous tax year as follows:

  (i) The review will be a comparison between the assessment for the previous year of assessment and profits of a one year period ending on the corresponding accounting date in the previous year.

  (ii) Where the profits for that year exceed the profits assessed, Revenue will increase the assessment of the previous year of assessment.

  (iii) This previous tax year review will apply even where that year is the second year in which a trade or profession is carried on.

1.7.9 Basis of assessment – changeover to calendar year basis of assessment

TCA97 s65-67 A number of provisions were introduced by the Finance Act 2001 to facilitate the changeover to a calendar year of assessment – for example:

(a) For the year of assessment 2001, the profits assessable were based on 74% of the profits of a period of account ending in that year or a period of account deemed to be ending in that year.

(b) Where accounts are made up for a period of one year ending on a date falling in the period from 1 January 2002 to 5 April 2002, those accounts formed the basis of assessment for both the tax year 2001 and the tax year 2002. The assessment for the tax year 2001 was based on 74% of the profits of those accounts.

(c) Special provisions also apply to take account of the mismatch between the length of the year of assessment for the tax year 2001 (9 months) and the length of previous and subsequent years of assessment (12 months), in the following circumstances:

(i) where two or more sets of accounts are made up to different dates in the year of assessment,

(ii) when accounts are made for a period not ending in the year of assessment,

(iii) where there is a change in the accounting date,

(iv) in commencement situations, and

(v) in cessation situations.

1.7.10 Losses

TCA97 s381-s390

Losses under Cases I and II may be utilised as follows:

Set off against Other Income – the loss incurred in a year of assessment may be deducted from any other income chargeable to tax in that year.

Carry Forward – Any loss not relieved under section 381 can be carried forward and set-off against the profits of the same trade or profession in subsequent years.

Terminal Loss – Terminal loss relief can be claimed in respect of a loss incurred in the last 12 months of a trade or profession. This loss can be carried back against profits from the same trade or profession "for the three years of assessment last preceding that in which discontinuance occurs". Capital allowances can be used to create or augment the loss.

TCA97 s392

Capital allowances of a year of assessment may be utilised to create or augment a loss. This is subject to the proviso that such capital allowances must first be set-off against any balancing charge assessable in the year of assessment to which they relate. There are provisions also to ensure that capital allowances can be used to create or augment a loss only to the extent that they have not otherwise been effectively relieved.

1.7.11 Residential development land

TCA97 s644a

Profits or gains arising after 1 December 1999, from dealing in or developing residential development land in the course of a business are taxable at 20%.

Where such profits or gains form part of other profits or gains there is provision for a suitable apportionment.

The income from dealing in or developing residential land is ring-fenced and there is no offset for personal allowances or credits e.g., BES relief, film relief, etc., against the income taxable at the 20% rate.

However, the taxpayer has the option to have these profits taxed at the normal rate and not to claim the benefit of the 20% rate.

Construction operations are excluded from the 20% rate.

See paragraph 2.1.3 re: Corporation Tax Rates applying to development land.

1.7.12 Withholding tax on payments for professional services

TCA97
s520-s529

Income tax at the standard rate is deducted from payments made for professional services by government departments, state bodies, local authorities, etc.

Services which are regarded as professional services are:

(a) medical, dental, pharmaceutical, optical, aural or veterinary

(b) architectural, engineering, quantity surveying and related services

(c) accountancy, auditing, finance and consultancy services

(d) legal services provided by solicitors and barristers and other legal services

(e) geological

(f) training services provided on behalf of FAS.

The bodies who are required to deduct tax are shown at Chart 16.

Section 15 Finance Act 2005 provides for a statutory exemption in relation to the operation of Professional Services Withholding Tax on relevant payments by accountable persons to accountable persons who are exempt from tax or who are exempt charities.

Credit for tax withheld is to be granted as follows:

Corporation Tax:

Against liability of accounting period for which tax is withheld.

Income Tax:

Against liability of the year for which period of withholding tax is credit period. Provision is made for interim refunds which will only be permitted if the Inspector of Taxes considers that hardship would otherwise arise. There are three categories to be considered under this provision:

(a) Ongoing Business

It is a condition that the profits for tax purposes of the immediately preceding accounting period must have been agreed and the tax paid. The interim refund will be restricted by the amount of the liability for the previous year and any other outstanding amounts for VAT, PAYE and PRSI.

(b) Commencing Business

A commencing business would be unable to satisfy the condition at (2) above and in order to cater for this, a formula is provided under which the Inspector may make a refund. The refund will be the lesser of the amounts at (i) and (ii) below:

(i) tax at standard rate on an amount determined by the formula:

$$E \times \frac{A}{B} \times \frac{C}{P}$$

Where:

E = Estimated expenses for the basis period
A = Estimated payments from which tax withheld for the basis period
B = Estimated total income for the basis period
C = Number of months covered by claim
P = Number of months in basis period

(ii) The tax withheld.

(c) Cases of Particular Hardship

In a case where any of the condition already outlined cannot be fulfilled, the Revenue Commissioners may waive one or more of the conditions. In such circumstances the amount of the refund is at the discretion of the Revenue Commissioners.

The Revenue Commissioners may raise assessments on accountable persons if such persons either refuse or neglect to pay over withholding tax.

1.7.13 Accounting for work in progress (UITF 40)

UITF 40, which was issued on 10 March 2005 by the Urgent Issues Task Force of the Accounting Standards Board, can have the effect of increasing the value of work in progress for most professional firms. The change to the basis results in a once-off increase in profit in the year of change. Finance Act 2006 provides for this increase to be taxed over five years. If there is a cessation to the trade, any amount not taxed is taxed in the year of cessation.

The relief is available where the change is made in a chargeable period ending in the two-year period beginning on 22 June 2005. UITF 40 confirmed the accounting position which some business had adopted before this date. The legislation provides no relief for those businesses.

1.8 Schedule D – Case III

TCA97 s18 Tax is charged under this Case on the following items:

(a) Interest, annuities and other annual payments, excluding bank and certain other deposit interest receivable under deduction of tax.

(b) All discounts.

(c) Profits on securities bearing interest payable out of the public revenue other than such as are charged under Schedule C.

(d) Interest on any securities issued or deemed within the meaning of section 36 to be issued under the authority of the Minister for Finance, in cases where such interest is paid without deduction of tax.

(e) Dividends paid on Credit Union regular share accounts only. Dividends/interest paid on Credit Union special share accounts are liable to DIRT.

(f) Income arising from foreign securities and possessions to the extent that it has not suffered Irish tax at source. Examples are rents from property situated abroad, dividends and interest from UK companies, income from foreign employment's or businesses and interest from foreign securities. In certain circumstances, only remittances into Ireland out of foreign income chargeable to income tax under Case III are liable to Irish income tax.

TCA97 s267M Section 20 Finance Act 2005 provides that deposit interest received by individuals from lending institutions (banks, building societies, etc.) in other EU countries will be subject to tax at the same rate as deposit interest received by individuals from lending institutions in Ireland, provided that the tax on such interest is discharged by the return filing date for the year concerned.

This means that, where the liability on such interest is discharged by the return date, individuals who are taxable in Ireland and who receive interest income from other EU countries will, for the tax years 2005 *et seq.*, be taxed at the standard rate of income tax on the income instead of at the marginal rate. Such interest will be regarded as income chargeable to tax under Schedule D – CASE IV.

1.8.1 Basis of assessment

TCA97 s70 The basis of assessment is the actual basis.

1.9 Schedule D – Case IV

TCA97 s18

Tax is charged under this Case in respect of any annual profits or gains not falling under any other Case of Schedule D or under any other Schedule.

Examples of items charged under this Case are as follows:

(a) Profits from the sale of a certificate of deposit or of an assignable deposit.

(b) Shares received in lieu of cash dividends.

(c) Income deemed to be that of an individual as a result of a transfer of assets abroad.

(d) Gains from certain disposals of land.

(e) Copyright royalties not chargeable under Case I and II.

(f) Post-cessation receipts of a trade or profession.

(g) Certain income from which tax has or is deemed to have been deducted e.g., annuities, building society interest receivable and bank and certain other deposit interest receivable.

(h) Companies are liable to income tax under Case IV Schedule D in accordance with certain provisions of the Tax Acts. These include:

   (i) distributions made by companies out of capital profits;

   (ii) distributions made by newly resident companies out of profits earned before residence begins;

   (iii) recovery of tax credits previously repaid through loss relief and now being foregone through claiming the loss against profits of subsequent accounting periods.

(i) Profits or gains from an unknown or unlawful source or activity.

(j) Withdrawal of relief on investment in corporate trades.

(k) Liability to corporation tax on dividends on certain preference shares.

(1) Certain disposals of land where there is a right to reconvey.

(m) Interest element included in sale proceeds from certain Government stocks.

(n) Income from UCITS and Unit Trusts.

(o) Guaranteed dividends.

TCA97 s267M (p) Interest received from lending institutions (banks, building societies, etc.) in other EU countries in certain circumstances.

1.9.1 Basis of assessment

TCA97 s74

The basis of assessment is the actual basis.

1.10 Deposit Interest Retention Tax

1.10.1 Companies and pension funds

TCA97 s256

Companies and pension funds are permitted to open deposit accounts on which interest is paid without deduction of DIRT.

The company or pension scheme must be the beneficial owner of the interest and must provide the relevant deposit taker with a tax reference number, or in the case of a pension scheme the number assigned by the Revenue Commissioners to the employer to whom the pension scheme relates.

1.10.2 Individuals

TCA97 s256

(1) DIRT Accounts

There are two rates of DIRT as follows:

(i) Standard rate DIRT accounts

(a) Ordinary deposit accounts

DIRT is deducted at the standard rate (20%) from interest paid or credited to ordinary deposit accounts on an annual or more frequent basis. This DIRT is regarded as satisfying the individuals full liability to tax in respect of that interest. However, the interest is included in computing total income for the purposes of the Tax Acts and accordingly falls within the definition of reckonable income for the purposes of PRSI and Health Contribution.

(b) Special term accounts

The 2001 Finance Act provided for the introduction of Special Term Accounts which attract favourable tax treatment.

The tax treatment of these accounts differs according to the term of the investment – the Medium Term account runs for three years and the Long Term account runs for five years.

These accounts are deposit based and the legislation specifically prohibits returns that are linked in any way to stocks, shares, debentures, listed or unlisted securities. The list of relevant deposit takers as set out in section 256 TCA 1997 has been extended to include Credit Unions. However, the Credit Union version of these accounts are known as Special Term Share Accounts.

The following exemptions from tax will apply in respect of these accounts:

(a) The first €480 pa of interest earned on the Medium Term accounts, and

(b) the first €635 pa of interest earned on the Long Term accounts.

DIRT at the standard rate will be levied on the excess and this DIRT is regarded as satisfying the individuals full liability to tax in respect of that interest. However, the interest is included in computing total income for the purposes of the Tax Acts.

(ii) Increased rate DIRT accounts

DIRT is deducted at the standard rate (20%) increased by 3% (i.e., a total of 23%) from interest paid or credited on any deposit account opened on or after 23 March 2000 and where the amount of interest cannot be determined until it is paid.

This DIRT is regarded as satisfying the individuals full liability to tax in respect of that interest. However, the interest is included in computing total income for the purposes of the Tax Acts and accordingly falls within the definition of reckonable income for the purposes of PRSI and Health Contribution.

(2) DIRT Exempt Accounts

With effect from 2 April 2007, deposit interest can be paid by the deposit taker without deduction of DIRT where:

(i) At any time in a year of assessment, the individual beneficially entitled to the interest or his or her spouse is 65 years of age or over and their total income does not exceed the relevant income tax exemption limit. The individual concerned is required to make a declaration to that effect to the relevant deposit taker,

(ii) The deposit taker obtains a notification to that effect from the Revenue Commissioners. This applies where the individual beneficially entitled to the interest or his or her spouse is permanently incapacitated or where the persons entitled to the interest are trustees of a special trust for permanently incapacitated individuals who are exempt from tax under section 189A(2) TCA 97.

1.10.3 Deposit taker

DIRT is deducted by a "relevant deposit" taker who is:

TCA97 s256

(a) A person who holds a licence under section 9, Central Bank Act, 1971, or a person who holds a licence or similar authorisation under the law of any other Member State of the EC which corresponds to a licence granted under section 9, or

(b) A building society within the meaning of the Buildings Societies Act 1989, or a society established in accordance with the law of any other Member State of EC.

(c) A Trustee Savings Bank within the meaning of the Trustee Savings Bank Acts, 1863 to 1979

(d) A Credit Union

(e) The Post Office Savings Bank.

The following are not regarded as relevant deposit takers:

(a) Friendly societies

(b) Industrial and provident societies

(c) Investment trust companies

(d) Unit trusts.

1.10.4 Returns and payments

TCA97 s258 Deposit takers are, subject to certain exceptions, obliged to account for DIRT on an annual basis in respect of all relevant interest accrued but not actually paid or credited by them in a year of assessment.

1.10.5 Charities

TCA97 s256 Charities are exempt from the retention tax. To receive gross interest the charity must provide to the relevant deposit taker the reference number assigned to it by the Revenue Commissioners known as the charity (CHY) number. Where, however, an exempted charity suffers retention tax, it may claim a repayment.

1.10.6 Repayment to elderly and incapacitated individuals

TCA97 s267 Repayment of retention tax may be made to an individual who is not liable or fully liable to income tax and who satisfies the Revenue Commissioners that:

(a) at some time during the tax year he or his spouse was aged 65 years or more, or

(b) throughout the tax year or from some date during the tax year he or his spouse was or became permanently incapacitated by reason of mental or physical infirmity from maintaining himself or herself.

See 1.10.2 above for DIRT-exempt accounts.

1.10.7 Non-resident depositors

TCA97 s263 Deposit accounts held by non-residents are exempt from the retention tax. A declaration must be made to the appropriate bank before interest can be paid without retention tax.

1.10.8 Credit unions

TCA97 Pt8 Ch3 There are four types of account which members may hold in credit unions and the tax treatment of each account is as follows:

(i) Regular Share Accounts

Members must declare dividends to Revenue and pay tax thereon at the marginal rate.

(ii)Deposit Accounts

Deposit interest is liable to DIRT at the standard rate.

(iii) Special Share Accounts

Dividends are liable to DIRT at the standard rate.

(iv) Special Term Share Account

A member may hold shares in a special term share account for a term of either 3 or 5 years. An exemption from DIRT and income tax will apply for the first €480 of dividends received where the funds are invested for a minimum of 3 years and for the first €635 of dividends received where the funds are invested for 5 years. Any dividends received in excess of those amounts will be liable to DIRT at the standard rate.

A person may not hold a special term share account and a special term deposit account at the same time.

Annual returns with details of the special term account holders must be provided by Credit Unions to Revenue.

1.10.9 Reporting requirements

See paragraph 4.3.9

1.11 Special Investment Products

1.11.1 Special Investment Policies (SIP)

Special Investment Policies or SIPs cannot be commenced after 31 December 2000.

Please see the 31st or earlier editions of this book for more details in relation to SIPs.

1.11.2 Special Investment Schemes (SIS)

Investments can no longer be made in Special Investment Schemes. As they have been wound up, Finance Act 2003 provided for unused capital losses in the final year to be set back against capital gains arising in the 3 previous years of assessment prior to the year of cessation. This amendment was introduced in recognition of the fact that capital losses forward may be unutilised due to the winding up. As is the case with terminal loss relief, the capital losses must first of all be used in the penultimate year of assessment, then the pre-penultimate year of assessment and anything left over can then be offset against the earliest of the 3 years of assessment.

Please see the 31st or earlier editions of this book for more details in relation to SISs.

1.11.3 Special Portfolio Investment Accounts (SPIA)

TCA97 s838, s839

These accounts contain a portfolio of shares and securities and when introduced in the Finance Act 1993, had a favourable tax treatment and the gains and losses were ring-fenced within the account (see earlier editions for full details).

No SPIAs can be opened after 5 April 2001 and they are being phased out and to assist this, any unrelieved losses of the SPIA at the time of its closing can be appropriated by the holder of the SPIA as if they were his or her own losses and offset against gains in the same year of assessment or a later year.

1.11.4 Special Saving Incentives Accounts (SSIA)

TCA97 Pt36A s848B-U

Accounts under the special savings incentive scheme must be opened between 1 May 2001 and 30 April 2002.

The main features of the scheme are as follows:

(a) Every resident person who is aged 18 or over can have an account, but only one account – it will be a criminal offence to open more than one account.

(b) In the first year of the account the person must save an amount agreed with the managing institution, which amount cannot be less than €12.50, and not more than €254 in any one month.

(c) After the first year there is no obligation to save a fixed regular amount but, in any one month, the amount saved cannot exceed €254.

(d) The incentive to save, which the scheme provides, is that for every €1 saved in an account, the Exchequer will contribute 25 cent to the account or €1 for every €4 saved.

(e) The accounts must be operated by qualifying savings managers which include banks, building societies, credit unions, life assurance companies, etc.

(f) A saver may switch from one manager to another.

(g) The term of the account is 5 years.

The closing date will be regarded as the fifth anniversary of the end of the month in which a subscription was first made, (e.g., first subscription made on 15 March 2002, closing date is 31 March 2007) or the day of death of the qualifying individual, whichever event occurs first.

(h) Where an account has run its full term of 5 years, the original investment and the Exchequer's contribution may be withdrawn tax free and the income earned during the period will be taxed at 23%.

(i) If withdrawals are made during the 5 year period, tax at 23% will apply to the total amount of the withdrawals.

(j) Tax at 23% will also apply to the total amount in the account, if the account "ceased". This will arise on any of the following events:

  (i) account withdrawn within 5 years;

  (ii) a missed subscription during year one;

  (iii) if any of the matters declared at the opening of the account ceased to be materially correct;

  (iv) if at the end of the SSIA term a declaration is not made to Revenue Commissioner in the correct format (see (o) page 68) and within the specified time limit.

(k) Funds held in such accounts are exempt from income tax, capital gains tax, DIRT and withholding tax during the life of the account. Accordingly they have the benefit of a "gross roll up" form of investment.

(l) A declaration is required to be made in writing by the person opening the account to include name and address, PPS number, date of birth, confirmation of residency in the State, etc.

(m) A person cannot use borrowings to invest in a SSIA or to defer repayments of sums already borrowed to provide for the investment.

(n) A person must indicate on their return of income that they have opened an SSIA.

(o) On maturity, the account holder must make and sign a declaration in writing, to include name, address, PPS number and date of birth. The declaration must also declare that at all times in the period from which the SSIA was opened until the date the declaration is made, the account holder was the beneficial owner of the funds held in the SSIA, had only one SSIA, was resident or ordinarily resident in the State, subscribed to the SSIA without recourse to borrowings and did not assign or otherwise pledge the funds held in the SSIA as security for a loan.

The period in which the declaration can be completed commences 60 days before, and ends 30 days after, the fifth anniversary of the day on which the SSIA was commenced.

(p) Each institution managing an SSIA, must, if requested, issue to an SSIA holder a statement which sets out the details of his or her SSIA when it matures. This statement is being made a requirement in order to facilitate those who wish to invest some or all of their SSIA funds in a pension product under the new "pensions incentive tax credits" scheme contained in Finance Act 2006 (see paragraph 1.3.25).

1.11.5 Investment in life assurance and investment undertakings

TCA97
s730B-730GB
s739B-739G

A new regime for taxing investors on the return from investments in life policies and investment undertakings was introduced by the Finance Act 2000. The new regime applies to new life policies issued from 1 January 2001, or from the date the company commenced business if not commenced on 1 April 2000. The new regime applies from 1 April 2000 to the acquisition of units in investment undertakings operating from the IFSC, and from the date of the first issue of units for other undertakings which had not issued any units before 1 April 2000.

The categories of funds which are covered by the legislation include unit trusts established under the 1990 Acts, UCITS established under the regulations of the EC Directive, Part XIII Companies and Investment Limited Partnerships established under the Act of 1994.

The general thrust of the legislation is to provide that no tax is paid on the income and gains accruing to an investor within a life company or undertaking, but that tax is generally withheld at the rate of 23% on payments out of the company or fund, to individuals resident or ordinarily resident in Ireland, or in respect of profits on disposals by such individuals.

Finance Act 2006 introduced new provisions for automatic exit tax for Irish investors after holding units in Irish or offshore funds for eight years. Similar rules apply in relation to the gross roll-up regime for life assurance companies – see below.

A 20% rate of withholding tax applies to distributions by undertakings for a year or lesser period.

No further income tax is payable by the individual.

Payments may be made by a fund or a life assurance company without deduction of exit tax where the payments are being made to:

- A Credit Union, subject to a declaration.
- The Court Service who administer the investment of the funds lodged in court. A change in the court appointed manager does not give rise to an exit charge.
- The National Pensions Reserve Fund, subject to a declaration.
- Securitisation companies, subject to a declaration.

Payments made by a money market fund to an Irish-resident company, including a securitisation company, can avoid the exit tax withholding by quoting their tax reference number in the same way as they would to a bank in relation to DIRT.

Finance Act 2006 confirms that non-Irish investors (i.e., individuals who are neither resident nor ordinarily resident, or non-resident companies) in Irish funds do not have a CGT exposure in relation to any payments made out of Irish funds. This clarification removes a theoretical exposure for non-residents in this area with effect from 3 March 2006.

1.11.6 Offshore life and collective investment products

TCA97 s594 s730H-730K s740-747A s740B-747F

Depending on the location of the Life company or collective fund, the return from investment in such offshore investment products may be taxed at 23%, 40% (CGT) or income tax marginal rates.

Broadly, the distinction is whether the issuing entity is located in;

(i) an EU State other than Ireland, a signatory to the European Economic Area Agreement and an OECD State having a tax treaty with Ireland, or

(ii) elsewhere.

The tax rate of 23% only applies to investment returns from entities located in a State as specified and then only if included in a tax return which is made on time. The 23% rate applies to individuals and companies where the conditions are satisfied.

The higher rates of tax apply in the case of products issued by entities located eleswhere and in cases where there is an incorrect or late return.

Where an offshore fund is reconstructed/amalgamated, the cancellation of the original units or shares will not be taxable and the cost of the new units or shares will be taken to be the cost of the old units or shares.

Where an offshore fund is reconstructed/amalgamated, the cancellation of the original units or shares will not be taxable and the cost of the new units or shares will be taken to be the cost of the old units or shares.

Losses which arise on the disposal of an interest in an offshore fund cannot be offset for tax purposes against any gains of the investor with effect from 3 February 2005.

Finance Act 2006 introduced new provisions for automatic exit tax for Irish investors after holding units in Irish or offshore funds for eight years. Similar rules apply in relation to the gross roll-up regime for life assurance companies — see below.

1.11.7 Automatic exit tax for Irish investors having held units in Irish or offshore funds for eight years

Finance Act 2006 provided that Irish and offshore funds automatically apply an exit tax to units held by Irish investors in such funds for eight years. Investors are deemed to have disposed of such units at the expiration of the eight-year period. This would mean that, assuming an investor holds their units indefinitely, an exit tax will be applied every eight years to the increased values in their units since the last exit tax applied.

In respect of domestic funds, the exit tax applies to any chargeable event occurring after 31 March 2006. This means that any units acquired by Irish investors in Irish funds since the introduction of the gross roll-up regime on 1 April 2000 will be subject to this exit tax. Therefore, the first exit tax will have arisen on 1 April 2008.

For offshore funds, the provisions will apply to units acquired on or after 1 January 2001, which means that the first such exit tax will apply from 1 January 2009.

Finance Act 2008 amended the 2006 legislation to assist the funds industry in administrating the legislation from 2009 onwards. The practical changes to the operation of the eight-year disposal rule included the following:

(a) If the Irish fund has less than 10% of its value held by Irish investors, then the fund does not have to calculate and apply the deemed disposal tax on the eight anniversary. Instead the Irish investor will be required to disclose such a gain in their tax return under self assessment. The fund will be required to make an election to benefit from this *de minimis* rule and to report certain detail in respect of unit holders.

(b) Rather than having to perform the eight-year deemed disposal calculation using daily net asset values, the new rules provide that an irrevocable election can be made to use net asset values on 30 June or 31 December prior to the chargeable event.

(c) Irish investors can claim refunds directly from the Irish Revenue rather than the fund in respect of tax that has been withheld in respect of their units and paid over as part of the eight year deemed disposal calculation. The overpayment can be claimed back from the Irish Revenue provided that the Irish investors in the fund hold less than 15% of the value of the fund.

Similar new rules apply in relation to the gross roll-up regime for life assurance companies with a deemed disposal event after eight years. This provision applies to life policies taken out after 1 January 2001. As a result, the first deemed disposal event will occur on 1 January 2009.

Section 730D(2A) TCA 1997 provides that a gain shall not arise on the happening of a chargeable event under the gross roll up regime in relation to a life policy where the assurance company has established a branch in an EU or EEA Member State and has received written approval from the Revenue Commissioners that exit tax will not apply.

Finance Act 2008 extends this exemption to situations where the life assurance company carries on business on a freedom of service basis (as provided for in Regulation 50 of the EC [Life Assurance]) Framework Regulations 1994 (S.I. No. 360 of 1994), or under an equivalent arrangement in an EEA State and the risk resides in an EU or EEA Member State. Written approval from the Revenue Commissioners is also required.

The legislation allows tax paid under the new chargeable event of eight years to be offset against tax due in respect of the subsequent maturity surrender or assignment of the policy.

1.11.8 Personal Portfolio Investment Undertakings (PPIU)

TCA97 Pt27 s747A-B

Finance Act 2007 introduced some significant changes to the offshore funds regime. For funds established on or after 20 February 2007, the gross roll up regime will only apply to four categories of offshore fund, i.e., UCITS, Unit Trust Schemes, Investment Companies and Investment Limited Partnerships and only in circumstances where the funds in question are comparable with regulated funds operating in Ireland. In all other cases, income and gains will be taxed under general taxation principles. Where Irish investors held an interest in an off-shore fund (under the pre-Finance Act 2007 rules) on 20 February 2007 grandfathering provisions have been introduced.

The Act also introduced new anti-avoidance legislation in relation to individuals who invest in off-shore funds under the new rules. This anti-avoidance provision introduced a new definition of a personal portfolio investment undertaking (PPIU). The new measure seeks to impose a higher rate of tax on income and gains arising from Irish or off-shore funds to Irish individual investors who come within this definition of a PPIU. In broad terms a PPIU is defined as a fund held by individual investors where the selection of some or all of the assets held by the fund is influenced by the investor or a person connected with the investor.

The table below shows the tax position for investments in offshore funds which are effected on or after 20 February 2007. If the investment is in a regulated fund, then consideration must be given to whether or not the investment is a PPIU. If it is regarded as a PPIU then the tax rate applicable to all distributions is 43%. If it is not a PPIU then the gross roll up regime continues to apply. If the investment is made in a non regulated vehicle, then the investment is taxable under first principles, i.e., marginal income tax on distributions and capital gains tax on gains.

Offshore Investments Post 20 February 2007		
Regulated/Acceptable Entity e.g., Irish QIF, Luxembourg SIF	PPIU	43% on all distributions (61% for offshore investment where not correctly included in tax return)
	Non PPIU	Income taxable at 20% Exit tax at 23%
Unregulated Foreign Entity e.g., French SARL	PPIU Non PPIU	Marginal rates apply to income distributions and CGT at 20% applies to gains.

Finance Act 2008 amends sections 615 and 617 TCA 1997 to restrict the availability of capital gains tax relief on reconstructions and amalgamations and of group relief on transactions that involve the transfer of assets from existing Irish companies (which are subject to corporation tax) to Irish "gross-roll-up" funds structured as variable capital companies under Part XXIII of the Companies Act 1990.

The restrictions apply as respects a transfer or disposal on or after 18 February 2008.

1.12 Schedule D – Case V

TCA97 s18 Tax is charged under Case V in respect of rents from any premises in the State.

1.12.1 Deductions

TCA97 s97 In arriving at the chargeable income the following expenses may be deducted from the gross rents receivable:

(i) Rent payable on the property.

(ii) Rates payable on the property.

(iii) Goods provided and services rendered in connection with the letting of the property.

(iv) Repairs, insurance, maintenance and management of the property.

(v) Interest accruing on or after 1 January 2002 (or before 23 April 1998), on money borrowed to purchase, improve or repair the property. For these purposes, interest is deemed to accrue on a day to day basis. (See 2001 edition in relation to interest paid during the period 23 April 1998 to 31 December 2001 inclusive, which was not allowed as a deduction in certain circumstances.)

However, in the case of an individual, for the tax years 2006 *et seq.*, a deduction for such interest will not be allowed unless it can be shown that the registration requirements of Part 7 of the Residential Tenancies Act 2004 have been complied with in respect of all tenancies that existed in relation to that premises in that chargeable period. In this regard, a written communication from the Private Residential Tenancies Board confirming the registration of a tenancy will be accepted as evidence that the registration requirements have been met.

In the case of a company, the above registration requirements apply for accounting periods beginning on or after 1 January 2006.

Finance Act 2003 disallowed interest relief against rental income with effect from 6 February 2003, in contrived arrangements involving one spouse buying out the other spouse's interest in the family home using a loan, the letting of that property and the purchase by the couple of a second residence, again using a loan. It does not apply in the case of legal arrangements between separated or divorced spouses.

TCA97 s284 (vi) Capital allowances (see below).

TCA97 s328 (vii) Expenditure on rented accommodation (see below).

(viii) Accountancy fees incurred in preparing the rental accounts.

(ix) Certain mortgage protection premiums for the tax years 2002 *et seq.*

1.12.2 Capital allowances

TCA97 s284 Capital allowances (wear and tear) may be claimed for the years 1997/98 *et seq.* in respect of capital expenditure incurred on the provision of machinery or plant (fixtures and fittings) where:

(i) the expenditure is incurred wholly and exclusively in respect of a house which is used solely as a dwelling which is or is to be let as a furnished house, and

(ii) the furnished house is provided for renting or letting on bona fide commercial terms on the open market.

The rates of wear and tear applying are as follows:

Expenditure Incurred	Rate	Basis
Pre-01/01/01	15%	Straight Line
01/01/01 - 03/12/02	20%	Straight Line
04/12/02 onwards	12.5%	Straight Line

Finance Act 2000 provided a legal basis for setting excess allowances arising in charging rental income, against non-rental income. An individual on joint assessment can set excess capital allowances against the income of a spouse, where the individual's own income is insufficient. The excess to be set off is calculated after deducting any unused allowances for previous years from the relevant income, while respecting the €31,750 limit on the offset of excess capital allowances in the case of passive investors.

1.12.3 Refurbishment of certain rented accommodation

TCA97 s380G-J Allowances may be claimed for expenditure incurred on the refurbishment of certain residential properties.

The premises must, both before and after the refurbishment, contain one or more residential units to qualify for this relief.

Refurbishment is described as "any work of construction, reconstruction, repair or renewal including the provision of improvement of water, sewerage or heating facilities, carried out in the course of the repair or restoration or maintenance in the nature, repair or restoration of the house for the purposes of complying with regulations governing Standards for Rental of Houses".

The refurbishment expenditure may be set off against all rental income whether arising from the property on which the work was carried out or other rental income, over a seven year period - 15% per annum for the first six years and 10% in year seven.

The relief is available in respect of all qualifying premises, irrespective of where they are located.

1.12.4 Expenditure on rented accommodation – "section 23"

TCA97 s325-s329

Certain expenditure incurred on the construction, refurbishment or conversion of a house or flat for letting is allowable as a deduction against the rental income from the property or other Irish properties.

The relief applies to new, refurbished or converted property, measuring between 35 and 125 square metres in the case of a house and 30 to 90 square metres in the case of a flat which, without having been used for owner occupation, is let by its owner to a tenant on an arms length basis.

A certificate of reasonable cost provided by the Department of Environment is required in the case of expenditure on conversion of the cost of the house or flat built by the person who lets them.

A claw-back of relief will arise where the property ceases to be a qualifying premises or the lessor's interest passes to another party (including on death) within ten years of the first letting of the premises under a qualifying lease. Where a clawback occurs the original relief may be claimed by the new owner but cannot exceed the price paid by the new owner.

If the property is sold after the qualifying ten-year period, and provided that all the qualifying conditions have been met during that period, the original owner will continue to be entitled to any unutilised allowances, i.e., the allowances do not travel with the property.

The property must be let under a qualifying lease which means the following conditions must be satisfied:

(i) The lease must be a genuine rental agreement with regular payments by way of rent only.

(ii) The tenant cannot be granted an option to buy at less than market value.

Where a qualifying unit is erected by a speculative builder and sold to an investor who lets the property, the site cost together with a proportion of the builders profit will not be allowable as qualifying expenditure. Qualifying expenditure is arrived at by applying the formula:

$$\text{Purchase Price} \times \frac{\text{Builder's Development Cost}}{\text{Builder's Site Cost} + \text{Builder's Development Cost}}$$

The following is an example of how to compute qualifying expenditure:

	€
Cost of Site	5,000
Site Development Costs	2,000
Building Costs	20,000
Builders Profit	3,000
Purchase Price	30,000

Qualifying expenditure is, therefore, as follows:

$$€30{,}000 \times \frac{(€2{,}000 + €20{,}000)}{(€5{,}000 + €2{,}000 + €20{,}000)} = €24{,}444$$

It should be noted that "section 23" type relief is a "specified relief" under Chapter 2A TCA 1997 in the context of the limitation on the amount of certain reliefs used by certain high income individuals – see paragraph 1.27.

1.12.5 Rent-a-room relief

TCA97 s216A Where an individual rents a room (or rooms) in a "qualifying residence" and the gross income received, including sums arising for food, laundry or similar goods and services, does not exceed €10,000, in the tax year 2008 (previously €7,620) this income will be exempt from income tax. Where the income exceeds €10,000, the entire amount is taxable. Where more than one individual is entitled to the rent, the limit is divided between the individuals concerned.

The relief is available to individuals only. It does not apply to companies or partnerships. However, it can apply where individuals have the income jointly (for instance husband and wife where there is no partnership), where the limit can be divided between the individuals concerned. Individuals who rent as well as individuals who own their own home may avail of the relief.

A "qualifying residence" is a residential premises in the State, which is occupied by an individual as his/her principal private residence during the year of assessment.

Room rentals coming within the scope of this scheme will not affect the person's entitlement to mortgage interest relief or the capital gains tax exemption on the disposal of a principal private residence.

There is no deduction for expenses made in ascertaining the rental income received and if the income does not exceed the limit in the year then those profits/losses are treated as "nil" for the year of assessment.

This income is not liable to either PRSI or the 2% Health Levy but it must be included on an individuals annual income tax return.

An individual may, if they wish, elect to have any income/losses from this source assessed under the normal rules for rental income, e.g., if there is a rental loss on the room(s).

With effect from 1 January 2007, the exemption no longer applies where a child pays rent to a parent. While a child may still claim relief in respect of bona fide rent paid in the family home, the rent will not be exempt in the hands of the parent under the rent-a-room scheme.

1.12.6 Exemption of income from leasing of farm land

TCA97 s664

Exemption from income tax is granted in respect of certain leasing income obtained by a lessor of agricultural land. The conditions attaching to the relief are:

(a) The income must arise from the leasing of farmland;

(b) The lease must be in writing and for a definite term of five years or more;

(c) The land must be leased to an individual who is not connected with the lessor and who uses the farm land leased for the purpose of a trade of farming carried on solely by him or in partnership;

(d) (i) The land must be leased by an individual who is aged 40 years or more for the tax years 2004 *et seq.* (previously 55 years), or who is permanently incapacitated by reason of mental or physical infirmity from carrying on a trade of farming, and

(ii) has not, after 30 January 1985 leased the farm land from a connected person on terms which are not at arms length.

The limits are as follows:

Age of Lessor	Lease entered into	Term of Lease	Exemption Limit
55 or over	Between 23/01/96 and 31/12/03	7 years or more Between 5 and 7 years	€7,618.43 €5,078.95
40 or over	01/01/04 - 31/12/05	7 years or more Between 5 and 7 years	€10,000 €7,500
	01/01/06 - 31/12/06	7 years or more Between 5 and 7 years	€15,000 €12,000
	01/01/07 or after	10 years or more Between 7 and 10 years Between 5 and 7 years	€20,000* €15,000* €12,000

** The threshold relief of €20,000 per annum for leases exceeding 10 years will come into effect on the making of an Order to that effect by the Minister for Finance. Until the Order is made, all leases exceeding 7 years will qualify for the threshold relief of €15,000.*

The relief also applies with effect from 1 January 2005 in respect of rental income received in situations where land is leased along with entitlement to EU Single Farm Payments.

The leasing income of a husband and wife is treated separately for the purposes of the relief, whether they are jointly assessed or not.

1.12.7 Premiums on leases

TCA97 s98

Where a premium is received on the granting of a lease of less than 50 years duration a portion of the premium is treated as rent and assessed in the first year. The assessable portion of the premium is calculated as follows:

$$\text{Assessable Portion} = P - \left| \frac{P \times (N-1)}{50} \right|$$

where:
P = Amount of the premium and
N = The amount of each complete period of 12 months in the term of the lease.

Provided the lessee uses the premises for the purpose of a trade or profession or where he lets the premises he will receive an annual deduction, in computing his profits, for the portion of the premium assessable on the lessor divided by the number of years of the lease.

1.12.8 Reverse premiums

TCA97 s98A

A reverse premium is a payment or other benefit received by a person as an inducement to enter into a lease.

Reverse premiums received on or after 7 June 2001 are treated as revenue receipts. The premium is assessable as rent unless it is to be assessed as a receipt of a trade or profession.

The above treatment does not apply to the following:

(a) reverse premiums received by an individual in relation to a lease of the individual's only or main residence;

(b) where the reverse premium is made in consideration for a sale and leaseback transaction which is entered into on bona fide commercial terms and;

(c) where the reverse premium is already taxable as a receipt of a trade or profession under Case I or II of Schedule D.

1.12.9 Rents paid to non-residents

TCA97 s1041

Rents payable directly to persons whose usual place of abode is outside the State must be paid under deduction of tax at standard rate, and the tax paid over to the Revenue Commissioners.

The tenant should give the landlord a form R185 to show that the tax has been accounted for to Revenue. The landlord is chargeable on the gross rents less any allowable expenses in arriving at rental profit. Credit for the actual tax deducted from the rent by the tenant will be given.

Rents paid to agents in Ireland are not paid under deduction of tax. The agent will be assessed in the name of the non-resident landlord in the same manner as the non-resident landlord would have been assessed if he were resident in Ireland.

1.12.10 Losses

TCA97 s384 Case V losses incurred in a year of assessment can be carried forward and set off against Case V profits for any subsequent year of assessment.

TCA97 s105 Anti-avoidance measures exist to prevent the carry forward of losses against future rental income where those losses arise out of interest payments becoming due for a period during which the property is not occupied for the purpose of a trade or as a residence.

1.12.11 Transfer of a right to receive rent for a capital sum

TCA97 s106A A tax avoidance scheme used by individuals to reduce their exposure to income tax on rental income is counteracted by legislation in the Finance Act 2003. Under the scheme, a capital sum is paid to an individual in return for the transfer of a right to receive rent. Where the right to receive rent is transferred to a company the income from the right would be taxed at the corporation tax rate. The legislation provides that with effect from 6 February 2003:

(i) The capital sum will be taxed as income of the person who receives it in the year of assessment in which the person becomes entitled to it (or, if earlier, the year of assessment in which it is received), and

(ii) Any income arising to the person who pays the capital sum will be chargeable under Case V of Schedule D in respect of that income. Where that person is a company, the income will be subject to the 25% corporation tax rate.

1.12.12 Basis of assessment

TCA97 s75 The basis of assessment is the actual basis.

1.13 Property Tax Incentive Schemes – Overview

Tax-based property incentive schemes have been a feature of Irish tax legislation for almost 20 years. The first major tax-based incentive scheme was introduced in 1986. This scheme was targeted at the five major urban areas in the country. This scheme was ultimately replaced by the 1994 Urban Renewal Scheme, which in turn was replaced by the 1998 Urban Renewal Scheme. In addition, 1998 saw the introduction of the first Rural Renewal Scheme. In more recent times, Urban Renewal has been extended to smaller towns. This legislation was introduced in Finance Act 2000 and is commonly referred to as the Town Renewal Scheme. This latter scheme is aimed at towns with a population between 500 and 6,000.

Following on from a review by the Government of the cost to the Exchequer of property-based tax reliefs, Finance Act 2006 introduced provisions for the phasing out of many reliefs by 31 July 2008. A number of reliefs, most notably in the healthcare and childcare sectors, are to remain, but certain amendments are introduced for buildings that are first used on or after 1 February 2007.

The following is a list of the reliefs to be phased out:

- Urban renewal relief
- Multi-storey car parks
- Town renewal relief
- Holiday camps
- Rural renewal relief
- Hotels
- Living over the shop scheme
- Sports injury clinics
- Park-and-ride
- Registered holiday cottages
- Student accommodation
- General rental refurbishment schemes
- Specified residential units for nursing homes
- Third-level educational buildings.

Finance Act 2006 extended the reliefs to 31 December 2006, provided the relevant existing conditions with regard to extension certificates, planning permission, etc. have been satisfied.

In addition, where 15% of the qualifying construction/refurbishment costs (excluding site cost) have been incurred by 31 December 2006, and previous conditions have been met, the qualifying period is extended to 31 July 2008 (other than specified residential units for nursing homes, see 1.20.19), with allowances being available on a reduced basis. In the case of the reliefs set out above (other than specified residential units for nursing homes - see 1.20.19), relief is available as follows:

- 100% for expenditure incurred in the 12 months ended 31 December 2006
- 75% for expenditure incurred in the 12 months ended 31 December 2007
- 50% for expenditure incurred in the eight months ended 31 July 2008.

In the case of hotels and the commercial and industrial elements of the Urban, Rural and Town Renewal Schemes, there is an additional requirement to make an application for certification to the relevant local authority by 31 January 2007. It must include details of actual expenditure incurred by 31 December 2006 and a projection of the balance of capital expenditure to 31 July 2008. The amount of expenditure taken into account in calculating allowances available is capped at the projected expenditure included in the application. In addition, a binding contract must be entered into in writing by 31 July 2006.

It should be noted that the relief for property-based tax incentives schemes is a "specified relief" under Chapter 2A TCA 1997, in the context of the limitation on the amount of certain relief used by certain high-income individuals - see paragraph 1.27.

In addition to the foregoing schemes, certain other targeted reliefs have been introduced over the years. A scheme of capital allowances existed for many years in respect of the Temple Bar Area. Additionally, a scheme, referred to as the Enterprise Area Scheme, was introduced to help foster the development of business parks throughout the country. This scheme also targeted the development of such facilities in areas adjacent to major airports.

Finally, schemes have also existed to develop certain seaside resort areas and also certain islands. The qualifying periods in respect of most of the schemes referred to above have now come to an end. The following sections focus on the schemes which are still available.

The schemes which have now expired are not dealt with in detail in this edition. A list of these schemes is set out hereunder. Readers requiring further information in relation to these schemes should review the Finance Act, 2001 edition of this book (references noted below):

Scheme	Section Reference
1986 Urban Renewal Scheme	1.13
Temple Bar Scheme	1.14
1994 Urban Renewal Scheme	1.15
Enterprise Area Schemes	1.16
Resort Area Scheme	1.17
Designated Islands	1.18
Dublin Docklands	1.19
Double Rent Relief	1.13.4

It should be noted that while the qualifying periods in respect of these schemes may have expired, persons who invested during the qualifying periods may well have an ongoing entitlement to claim an annual allowance. Additionally, it should be noted that in the context of most designated properties a claw-back provision applies which is triggered if a property is sold within a period of 13 years from first use.

1.14 Urban Renewal – 1998 Scheme

TCA97 s372B The 1998 Finance Act together with the Urban Renewal Act 1998, provided for a scheme of incentives for certain urban areas.

A total of 43 towns and cities have been designated on the basis of Integrated Area Plans (IAPs) submitted by local authorities.

The qualifying periods for these incentives are as follows:

Residential premises	1 March 1999 to 31 July 2008*
Industrial/Commercial premises	1 July 1999 to 31 July 2008**

* The duration of the qualifying period has been amended in recent Finance Acts. Finance Act 2006 extended the deadline date to 31 December 2006. In order to qualify for this extension the relevant local authority must have given a certificate in writing on or before 30 September 2003 stating that it is satisfied that not less than 15% of the total project costs had been incurred on or before 30 June 2003. The application for such a certificate must have been received by the local authority on or before 31 July 2003.

Finance Act 2006 further extended the availability of allowances to 31 July 2008 where the existing conditions set out above are satisfied and at least 15% of the construction expenditure (excluding site cost) has been incurred by 31 December 2006.

** As for the residential relief, the qualifying period in respect of commercial development was also extended to 31 December 2006. In order to qualify for this extension it was necessary for the relevant local authority to give a written certificate on or before 30 September 2003 stating that it was satisfied that not less than 15% of the project costs had been incurred on or before 30 June 2003. The application for such a certificate must have been received by the local authority on or before 31 July 2003.

The Finance Act 2006 extension to 31 July 2008 is dependent on the existing conditions set out above being satisfied and a certificate being obtained from the relevant local authority that at least 15% of the construction expenditure (excluding site cost) was incurred by 31 December 2006. There is also a requirement to have a written binding contract in place in respect of the construction/refurbishment work by 31 July 2006.

The level of allowances available in respect of expenditure attributable to work done in 2007 and 2008 are restricted to 75% and 50% respectively as set out in section 1.13 above.

1.14.1 Restrictions on relief

In order to meet the European Commission rules regarding State Aid, the capital allowances provided under this Scheme do not apply to:

(a) Construction or refurbishment expenditure incurred on or after 6 April 2001 of which any part is met by grant assistance or any other assistance which is granted by or to through the State, any board established by statute, any public or local authority or any other agency of the State.

(b) Expenditure incurred in relation to the construction or refurbishment of a building or structure and where one of the following trades or activities is carried on wholly or mainly from that premises:

  (i) In the sector of agriculture, including the production, processing and marketing of agricultural products,

  (ii) In the coal industry, fishing industry or motor vehicle industry, or

  (iii) In the transport, steel, shipbuilding, synthetic fibres or financial services sectors.

(c) In respect of expenditure incurred on the construction of a building where a property developer is entitled to the relevant interest in relation to that expenditure and either that person or a connected person incurred the expenditure on the construction of the building concerned.

(d) Finance Act 2003 introduced further approval procedures (for expenditure incurred on/after 1 January 2003) in the context of projects subject to the notification requirements under either the "Multisectoral framework on regional aid for large investment projects" dated 7 April 1998 or 19 March 2002. Under the new provisions any such projects will require specific European Commission clearance before allowances will be available. In practice this is likely to have limited application.

1.14.2 Location specific

Whilst the legislation sets out the framework as to the capital allowances available, it should be noted that there is a specific statutory instrument in place for each area. Before advising as to a specific project, care should be taken to review the relevant statutory instrument for any specific conditions that might apply to a given area.

1.14.3 Industrial buildings

TCA97 s372C Expenditure incurred on the construction or refurbishment of a qualifying industrial building will qualify for the following allowances:

Owner occupiers	Up to 50% Free Depreciation or 50% Initial Allowance 4% Annual Allowance Maximum 100%
Lessors	50% Initial Allowance 4% Annual Allowance Maximum 100%

Refurbishment expenditure only qualifies if it is equal to or more than 10% of the market value of the building before refurbishment.

1.14.4 Commercial premises

TCA97 s372D Allowances at the same rates as for industrial buildings (see above) may be claimed in respect of expenditure incurred for the construction or refurbishment of qualifying commercial buildings.

1.14.5 Balancing allowances/charges

A clawback of allowances will not occur on an event arising more than 13 years after the building was first used or more than 13 years after the expenditure on refurbishment was incurred.

1.14.6 Double rent allowance

TCA97 s372E Double rent allowance is not available under the 1998 Urban Renewal Scheme.

1.14.7 Rented residential accommodation

TCA97 Pt10 Ch11 "Section 23" type relief (see 1.12.4) is granted against all Irish source rental income for expenditure incurred on the cost of construction (excluding site cost) of rented residential accommodation.

TCA97 Pt10 Ch11 Relief is granted against all Irish source rental income for expenditure on the conversion into rented residential accommodation of a building which had not previously been in use as a dwelling or the conversion into two or more houses of a building which, prior to the conversion, had not been in use as a single dwelling.

1.14.8 Owner-occupied residential accommodation

TCA97 Pt10 Ch11 Relief is granted by way of deduction from total income of the owner occupier of an amount equal to 5% of construction expenditure and 10% of refurbishment expenditure incurred on owner-occupied residential accommodation. The individual incurring the expenditure must be the first owner and occupier of the property after the expenditure has been incurred.

The relief may be claimed in each of the first 10 years of the life of the dwelling following construction or refurbishment provided that the dwelling is the sole or main residence of the individual.

Many areas designated under the 1998 Urban Renewal Scheme for residential reliefs were only designated in respect of the owner/occupier relief described above but not designated for the "section 23" type relief (see 1.12.4) available to lessors. Finance Act, 2002 introduced an amendment extending "section 23" type relief to areas previously only designated for owner/occupier relief. In order to avail of this "section 23" relief it is necessary that a contract for the purchase of the residential unit in question had not been evidenced in writing prior to 5 December 2001 but that a contract for the purchase of the unit would be evidenced in writing on or before 1 September 2002.

1.15 Rural Renewal – 1998 Scheme

TCA97 s372L

The 1998 Finance Act provided for a new scheme of incentives targeted at the Upper Shannon Region – covering all of the counties of Leitrim and Longford and certain parts of Cavan, Roscommon and Sligo.

The qualifying periods for these incentives are as follows:

Residential Premises	
Lessors	1 June 1998 to 31 July 2008*
Owner Occupiers	6 April 1999 to 31 July 2008*
Industrial/Commercial premises	1 July 1999 to 31 July 2008*

*The deadline date in respect of the commercial and industrial incentives was extended by FA2006 to 31 December 2006. However, in order to qualify for this extension (the deadline was previously 31 December 2004) certain conditions need to be satisfied. Broadly, valid application for full planning permission must be made on or before 31 December 2004 and an acknowledgement of same must be issued by the planning authority. In the context of a development not requiring planning permission it will be necessary to show a detailed plan in relation to the development, a binding contract in writing under which the expenditure is incurred and finally that 5% of the development cost has been incurred, not later than 31 December 2004.

Finance Act 2006 extended the qualifying period to 31 July 2008 in the case of industrial buildings in certain circumstances, subject to a number of additional requirements. Where a certificate has been obtained from the relevant local authority that at least 15% of the construction expenditure (excluding site cost) was incurred by 31 December 2006, and a binding contract was in place by 31 July 2006, the deadline date is extended to 31 July 2008.

Similarly, in the context of residential reliefs for both lessors and owner occupiers the deadlines were also extended to 31 December 2006. The same criteria as set out above in the context of the commercial/industrial extension also apply to the residential extension.

The deadline is extended to 31 July 2008 where at least 15% of the construction expenditure (excluding site cost) was incurred by 31 December 2006. There is no requirement to have a binding contract in place by 31 July for residential aspects of a development.

The allowances available in respect of qualifying expenditure in 2007 and 2008 are restricted to 75% and 50% respectively.

1.15.1 Industrial buildings

TCA97 s372M Expenditure incurred on the construction or refurbishment of qualifying industrial buildings, including piers and jetties will qualify for the following allowances:

Owner Occupiers	Up to 50% Free Depreciation or
	50% Initial Allowance
	4% Annual Allowance
	Maximum 100%
Lessors	50% Initial Allowance
	4% Annual Allowance
	Maximum 100%

Refurbishment expenditure only qualifies if it is equal to or more than 10% of the market value of the building before refurbishment.

1.15.2 Commercial premises

TCA97 s372N Allowances at the same rates as for industrial buildings (see above) may be claimed in respect of expenditure incurred on the construction or refurbishment of qualifying commercial premises, including certain infrastructural projects such as the provision of sewerage facilities, water supplies or roads for public purposes where these have been approved by a local authority.

1.15.3 Restrictions on relief

TCA97 s372T In order to meet the European Commission rules regarding State Aid, the capital allowances provided under this Scheme do not apply to:

(a) Construction or refurbishment expenditure incurred on or after 6 April 2001 of which any part is met by grant assistance or any other assistance which is granted by or through the State, any board established by State, any public or local authority or any other agency of the State.

(b) Expenditure incurred in relation to the construction or refurbishment of a building or structure and where one of the following trades or activities is carried on wholly or mainly from that premises:

- (i) In the sector of agriculture, including the production, processing and marketing of agricultural products,
- (ii) In the coal industry, fishing industry or motor vehicle industry, or
- (iii) In the transport, steel, shipbuilding, synthetic fibres or financial services sectors.

(c) In respect of expenditure incurred on the construction of a building where a property developer is entitled to the relevant interest in relation to that expenditure and either that person or a connected person incurred the expenditure on the construction of the building concerned.

(d) Finance Act 2003 introduced further approval procedures (for expenditure incurred on/after 1 January 2003) in the context of projects subject to the notification requirements under the "Multisectoral framework on regional aid for large investment projects" dated 7 April 1998 or 19 March 2002. Under the new provisions any such projects will require specific European Commission clearance before allowances will be available. In practice this is likely to have limited application.

1.15.4 Balancing allowances/charges

A claw-back of allowances will not occur on an event arising more than 13 years after the building is first used or more than 13 years after the expenditure on refurbishment was incurred.

1.15.5 Double rent allowance

Double rent allowance is not available under the Rural Renewal Scheme.

1.15.6 Rented residential accommodation

TCA97 Pt10 Ch11

"Section 23" type relief (see 1.12.4) is granted against all Irish source rental income for the cost of construction (excluding site costs) of rented residential accommodation. Relief is granted against all Irish source rental income for the cost of conversion into rented residential accommodation of a building which had not previously been in use as a dwelling or the conversion into two or more houses of a building which, prior to the conversion had not been in use as a dwelling, or had been in use as a single dwelling.

Relief is granted against all Irish source rental income for expenditure incurred on refurbishment of a building which before and after refurbishment contains one or more residential units.

Leases must be for a minimum of three months and the accommodation must be the sole or main residence of the lessee throughout the period of the lease.

1.15.7 Owner-occupied residential accommodation

Owner occupiers of residential accommodation may claim a deduction of 5% per annum for 10 years in the case of construction expenditure and 10% per annum for 10 years in the case of refurbishment expenditure.

The individual incurring the expenditure must be the first owner and occupier of the dwelling after the expenditure has been incurred and the dwelling must be the sole or main residence of the individual.

1.16 Town Renewal – 2000 Scheme

TCA97 s372 The 2000 Finance Act introduced a renewal scheme for smaller towns. The scheme provides incentives in respect of industrial, commercial, rented residential and owner-occupied residential accommodation. It is envisaged that the scheme will apply to towns with a population of between 500 and 6,000. There will be a process of applying incentives to qualifying areas based on Town Renewal Plans prepared by county councils.

The qualifying periods for these incentives are as follows:

Residential Premises:	1 April 2000 to 31 July 2008*
Industrial/Commercial Premises:	6 April 2001 to 31 July 2008*

* The deadline date in respect of the commercial and industrial incentives was extended by FA2006 to 31 December 2006. However, in order to qualify for this extension (the deadline was previously 31 December 2004) certain conditions need to be satisfied. Broadly, valid application for full planning permission must be made on or before 31 December 2004 and an acknowledgement of same must be issued by the planning authority. In the context of a development not requiring planning permission it will be necessary to show a detailed plan in relation to the development, a binding contract in writing under which the expenditure is incurred and finally that 5% of the development cost has been incurred, not later than 31 December 2004.

Finance Act 2006 extended the qualifying period to 31 July 2008 in the case of industrial buildings in certain circumstances, subject to a number of additional requirements. Where a certificate has been obtained from the relevant local authority that at least 15% of the construction expenditure (excluding site cost) was incurred by 31 December 2006, and a binding contract was in place by 31 July 2006, the deadline date is extended to 31 July 2008.

Similarly, in the context of residential reliefs for both lessors and owner occupiers the deadlines were also extended to 31 December 2006. The same criteria as set out above in the context of the commercial/industrial extension also apply to the residential extension.

The deadline is extended to 31 July 2008 where at least 15% of the construction expenditure (excluding site cost) was incurred by 31 December 2006. There is no requirement to have a binding contract in place by 31 July 2006 for residential aspects of a development.

The allowances available in respect of qualifying expenditure in 2007 and 2008 are restricted to 75% and 50% respectively.

1.16.1 Industrial/commercial buildings

The expenditure incurred on the construction/refurbishment of a qualifying industrial/commercial building will now qualify for the following allowances:

Owner/Occupier:	Up to 50% Free Depreciation or
	50% Initial Allowance
	4% Annual Allowance
	Maximum 100%
Lessors:	50% Initial Allowance
	4% Annual Allowance
	Maximum 100%

Refurbishment expenditure only qualifies if it is equal to or more than 10% of the market value of the building before refurbishment.

1.16.2 Balancing allowances/charges

A clawback of allowances will not occur on an event arising more than 13 years after the building was first used, or more than 13 years after the expenditure on refurbishment was incurred.

1.16.3 Double rent allowance

No double rent allowances will be available under the Town Renewal Schemes.

1.16.4 Restrictions on relief

Capital allowances shall not be available under this scheme in any of the following cases:

(a) Where, in respect of expenditure incurred on the construction of a premises, a property developer is entitled to the relevant interest in relation to that expenditure and either that person or a person connected with him incurred the expenditure on the construction of the building concerned.

(b) In relation to expenditure incurred on or after 6 April 2001 on the construction or refurbishment of a building or structure where any part of that expenditure has been or is to be met, directly or indirectly, by grant assistance or any other assistance which is granted by or through the State, any board established by statute, any public or local authority or any other agency of the State.

(c) In relation to expenditure incurred on or after 6 April 2001 on the construction or refurbishment of a building unless the relevant interest in such expenditure is held by a small or medium size enterprise within the meaning of Annex 1 to Commission Regulations (EC) No. 70/2001 of 12 January 2001.

These regulations are reproduced in the Official Journal of the European Union, No. L10 of 13 January 2001.

With effect from 1 January 2005, the relevant interest referred to above could also be held by a micro, small or medium-sized enterprise within the meaning of the Annex to Commission Recommendation of 6 May 2003 concerning the definition of micro, small and medium-sized enterprises.

(d) Where the building or structure is used for the purposes of carrying on any of the following trades or activities:

  (i) In the sector of agricultrue, including the production, processing and marketing of agricultural products,

  (ii) In the coal industry, fishing industry or motor vehicle industry or

  (iii) In the transport, steel, shipbuilding, synthetic fibres or financial services sectors.

(e) Finance Act 2003 introduced further approval procedures (for expenditure incurred on/after 1 January 2003) in the context of projects subject to the reporting requirements under the "Multisectoral framework on regional aid for large investment projects" dated either 7 April 1998 or 19 March 2002. Under the new provisions any such projects will require specific European Commission clearance before allowances will be available. In practice this is likely to have limited application.

1.16.5 Rented residential accommodation

"Section 23" type relief (see 1.12.4) is granted against all Irish source rental income for expenditure incurred on the cost of construction (excluding site cost) of rented residential accommodation.

Relief is granted against all Irish source rental income for expenditure on the conversion into rented residential accommodation of a building which had not previously been in use as a dwelling, or the conversion into two or more houses of a building which, prior to the conversion, had not been in use as a single dwelling.

1.16.6 Owner occupied residential accommodation

Relief is granted by way of deduction from total income of the owner occupier of an amount equal to 5% of construction expenditure and 10% of refurbishment expenditure incurred on owner occupied residential accommodation. The individual incurring the expenditure must be the first owner and occupier of the property after the expenditure has been incurred.

The relief may be claimed in each of the first 10 years of the life of the dwelling following construction or refurbishment, provided that the dwelling is the sole or main residence of the individual.

1.17 Living Over the Shop Scheme

TCA97 s372BA The 2001 Finance Act introduced this scheme which is aimed at providing residential accommodation in the vacant space over commercial premises in the five cities of Cork, Dublin, Galway, Limerick and Waterford. It provides tax incentives similar to those available under the 1998 Urban Renewal Scheme – see 1.14.

The incentives will be applied by way or order of the Minister for Finance to specific lengths of streetscape in the five cities covered. Details of the streets designated are available from the relevant local authority.

The qualifying period for the scheme starts on 6 April 2001 and ends on 31 December 2006. In order to avail of the extension of the qualifying period from 31 December 2004 to 31 December 2006 the same planning criteria as set out at 1.16 need to be satisfied on or before 31 December 2004.

Finance Act 2006 extended the qualifying period to 31 July 2008 in certain circumstances. In the case of residential buildings where the 31 December 2004 planning application requirement is satisfied and at least 15% of the construction expenditure (excluding site cost) is incurred by 31 December 2006, the deadline is extended to 31 July 2008.

In the case of commercial buildings, in addition to the planning requirement, there are a number of additional requirements. Where a certificate has been obtained from the relevant local authority that at least 15% of the construction expenditure (excluding site cost) was incurred by 31 December 2006 and a binding contract was in place by 31 July 2006, the deadline date is extended to 31 July 2008. This is subject to the other conditions relating to State aid rules, etc. being satisfied.

The allowances available in respect of qualifying expenditure in 2007 and 2008 are restricted to 75% and 50% respectively.

The incentives are available in respect of buildings which front on to qualifying streets. They apply in respect of buildings which existed on 13 September 2000 and for replacement buildings where the original building has to be demolished following a demolition order or, in certain cases, due to structural reasons.

1.17.1 Residential accommodation

Expenditure incurred on the refurbishment, conversion or "necessary" construction of qualifying residential accommodation will qualify for allowances of up to 100% as set out below.

1.17.2 Rented residential accommodation

"Section 23" type relief (see 1.12.4) is granted against all Irish rental income for expenditure incurred on the cost of "necessary" construction (excluding site cost) of rented residential accommodation.

Relief is granted against all Irish rental income for expenditure on the conversion into rented residential accommodation of a building which had not previously been in use as a dwelling, or the conversion into two or more houses of a building which, prior to the conversion, had not been in use as a single dwelling.

1.17.3 Owner occupied residential accommodation

Relief is granted by way of deduction from total income of the owner occupier of an amount equal to 5% of construction expenditure and 10% of refurbishment expenditure incurred on owner occupied residential accommodation. The individual incurring the expenditure must be the first owner and occupier of the property after the expenditure has been incurred.

The relief may be claimed in each of the first 10 years of the life of the dwelling following construction or refurbishment, provided that the dwelling is the sole or main residence of the individual.

1.17.4 Necessary construction

"Necessary construction" means:

(i) construction of an extension to a building which does not exceed 30 per cent of the floor area of the building before the expenditure was incurred;

(ii) the extension must be necessary for the purpose of facilitating access to or providing essential facilities in one or more qualifying premises;

(iii) construction of an additional storey or storeys to the building which was or were, as the case may be, necessary for the restoration of enhancement of the streetscape;

(iv) construction of a replacement building (see below).

1.17.5 Replacement building

A "replacement building" is a building which fronts onto a qualifying street and which is constructed to replace an existing building where:

(i) a demolition notice was made on or after 13 September 2000 and before 31 March 2001; and

(ii) the replacement building is consistent with the character and size of the existing building;

(iii) the demolition of the existing building (being a single storey building) was required for structural reasons in order to facilitate the construction of an additional storey or storeys which were necessary for the restoration or enhancement of the streetscape.

1.17.6 Commercial premises

Expenditure incurred on the refurbishment or "necessary" construction of associated commercial property will also qualify for allowances provided that:

(i) the qualifying premises are comprised in the ground floor of an existing building or a replacement building

(ii) expenditure must be incurred on the residential element, being the upper floor or floors of the existing building or replacement building

(iii) the expenditure on the commercial element cannot exceed the expenditure on the residential element.

The allowances available are as follows:

Owner occupiers	Up to 50% Free Depreciation or
	50% Initial Allowance
	4% Annual Allowance
	Maximum 100%
Lessors	50% Initial Allowance
	4% Annual Allowance
	Maximum 100%

Commercial premises are confined to those used essentially for the retailing or supply of local goods and services.

1.17.7 Balancing allowances/charges

A claw-back of allowances will not occur on an event arising more than 13 years after the building was first used or more than 13 years after the expenditure on necessary construction/refurbishment was incurred.

1.17.8 Double rent allowance

Double rent allowance is not available.

1.17.9 Restrictions on relief

In order to meet the European Commission rules regarding State Aid, the capital allowances provided under this Scheme do not apply to:

(a) Construction or refurbishment expenditure incurred on or after 6 April 2001 of which any part is met by grant assistance or any other assistance which is granted by or to through the State, any board established by State, any public or local authority or any other agency of the State.

(b) Expenditure incurred in relation to the construction or refurbishment of a building or structure and where one of the following trades or activities is carried on wholly or mainly from that premises:

   (i) In the sector of agriculture, including the production, processing and marketing of agricultural products,

   (ii) In the coal industry, fishing industry or motor vehicle industry, or

   (iii) In the transport, steel, shipbuilding, synthetic fibres or financial services sectors.

(c) In respect of expenditure incurred on the construction of a building where a property developer is entitled to the relevant interest in relation to that expenditure and either that person or a connected person incurred the expenditure on the construction of the building concerned.

(d) Finance Act 2003 introduced further approval procedures (for expenditure incurred on/after 1 January 2003) in the context of projects subject to the notification requirements under the "Multisectoral framework on regional aid for large investment project" dated 7 April 1998 or 19 March 2002. Under the new provisions any such projects will require specific European Commission clearance before allowances will be available. In practice this is likely to have limited application.

1.18 Schedule E

The income chargeable under Schedule E consists, in general, of the emoluments of all offices and employments, together with pensions and annuities. Expenses allowances and benefits in kind, as well as ex-gratia payments and other compensation payments are assessable under Schedule E. Emoluments paid in respect of an office or employment either before its commencement or after its cessation are liable to income tax under Schedule E.

1.18.1 Social welfare benefits

TCA97 s126

Social Welfare benefits are not chargeable to income tax unless there is a specific charging provision or, in certain cases, where they are paid for more than 12 months. In the latter case they are regarded as a pension payable out of public Revenue, within the meaning of section 19 TCA 1997, and accordingly are assessable under Schedule E.

(a) Non-taxable Benefits

The following payments are not liable to income tax:

(i) Unemployment Assistance

(ii) Maternity Benefit

(iii) Children's Allowance (see section 194 TCA 1997)

(iii) Death Grant

(v) Disability Allowance (formerly known as Disabled Persons Maintenance Allowance)

(vi) Family Income Supplement

(b) Taxable Benefits

The following social welfare payments are taxable under Schedule E either by virtue of the specific charging provisions contained in section 126 TCA 1997 or under the general Schedule E provisions:

(i) Contributory Old Age Pension

(ii) Retirement Pension

(iii) Contributory Survivors Pension

(iv) Contributory Orphan's Allowance

(v) Invalidity Pension

(vi) One Parent Family Payment

(vii) Non-Contributory Widow's Pension

(viii) Non-Contributory Orphan's Pension

(ix) Social Assistance Allowance for Deserted Wives

(x) Social Assistance Allowance for Prisoners Wives

(xi) Carers Allowance

(xii) Non-Contributory Old Age Pension

(xiii) Blind Person's Pension

(xix) Disability Benefit*

(xv) Occupational Injuries Benefit

(xvi) Unemployment Benefit*

*Note: (a) The first €13 per week of unemployment benefit is not taxable.

(b) Child dependent allowances paid with unemployment benefit and disability benefit are not taxable.

(c) Persons in receipt of unemployment benefit due to short time working (e.g., where the individuals working week is cut to say, three days) are exempt from income tax in respect of any unemployment benefit received for days of unemployment.

(d) For the year 1997/98 disability benefit paid for the first 18 days (3 weeks) of illness is disregarded. This was increased to 36 days (6 weeks) for 1998/99 and subsequent years.

In practice, PAYE is not operated by the Department of Social, Community and Family Affairs on the grounds of impracticability. The first four pensions listed above are nonetheless deemed to be emoluments which qualify the individual for the PAYE allowance.

1.18.2 Basis of assessment

TCA97 s112 All income assessable under Schedule E is assessed on the actual income of the year of assessment, regardless of whether taxed under PAYE or not.

TCA97 s997 The Revenue may raise a Schedule E assessment on an individual tax payer where:

(a) The taxpayer requests it, or

(b) The emoluments paid are not the same as the emoluments which were previously deemed to have been paid, or,

(c) The emoluments may have been taxed incorrectly at the standard rate of tax.

In relation to (a) above, for years of assessment 2003 *et seq.*, the taxpayer must ask for the assessment to be raised within 4 years of the relevant year of assessment (as opposed to the old 5 years timeframe). In relation to (b) and (c) above the timeframe is reduced to 4 years from the existing five years with effect from 1 January 2005.

1.18.3 Deductions

TCA97 s114 The deductions available in computing income for Schedule E purposes are confined to expenses incurred wholly, exclusively and necessarily in the performance of the duties of the office or employment. There is no deduction for expenses incurred in placing an individual in a position to perform the duties of the office or employment, e.g., travel from home to place of employment. No deduction is allowed in respect of entertainment expenses.

TCA97 s284 In addition to the deduction for expenses, there is an allowance for wear and tear on any wasting asset used by an individual in the course of performing the duties of his office or employment, e.g., private motor car.

1.18.4 Round sum expense allowances

TCA97 s117 Where a round sum payment is made, the employer is obliged to deduct income tax under PAYE. The employee must then make a claim to the Inspector of Taxes justifying the expenses as having been incurred wholly, exclusively and necessarily in the performance of the duties of the office or employment. In certain circumstances the Inspector of Taxes may agree to dispense with the necessity to deduct income tax and thus avoid the procedure of an annual claim to expenses.

1.18.5 Benefits-in-kind

(a) Background

TCA97 s118 Subject to certain exceptions benefits-in-kind (e.g., private use of company car, free or subsidised accommodation and preferential loans) received from an employer, by an employee whose total remuneration (including benefits-in-kind) is €1,905 or more in a tax year, are taxable. Where the employee receiving such benefits is a director of the company concerned, the benefits are taxable regardless of the level of remuneration. The liability to tax also applies in respect of benefits provided by an employer for a member or members of an employee's family or household.

In addition, employees and directors are chargeable to tax in respect of "perquisites" from their employment, that is, remuneration in non-money form which is convertible into money or money's worth, e.g., vouchers in various forms, the payment of club subscriptions and medical insurance premiums on an employee's behalf.

For the tax years up to and including the tax year 2003, the income tax due on benefits was effectively collected by way of "coding-in" under the PAYE system, i.e., the employee's reliefs for use against "money" wages and salaries were restricted so as to increase the tax payable to the extent required to collect the tax on the benefits. This procedure no longer applies to most benefits after 31 December 2003.

(b) Summary of Procedures which Apply from 1 January 2004

The procedures which apply from 1 January 2004 to collect tax on benefits are as follows (by virtue of section 6 Finance Act, 2003 and sections 16 to 21 Social Welfare (Miscellaneous Provisions) Act, 2003):

(i) Income tax due on benefits must be collected by the employer through the operation of PAYE on the taxable value of the benefit.

(ii) PRSI is due on benefits and must be collected by the employer through the operation of PAYE on the taxable value of the benefit.

(iii) The notional pay liable to PAYE and PRSI in respect of benefits must be the best estimate that can reasonably be made by the employer, at the time the benefit is being provided, of the amount chargeable to tax in respect of the benefit.

(iv) Where the amount of the money, wages or salary payable to an employee is insufficient to collect the full amounts of PAYE and PRSI due on the notional pay, the employer is required to remit any shortfall, by reference to the full PAYE and PRSI due, in addition to the amounts collected from the money wages or salary.

(v) Any shortfall, in PAYE (but not PRSI) collected from money wages or salary, which is paid by the employer for a tax year (the "first" tax year) but not made good by the employee to the employer by the end of the tax year (concessionally extended to 31 March of the following year) will be regarded as a taxable benefit of the employee in the following tax year (i.e., the tax year following the first tax year) and subject to PAYE and PRSI.

(vi) Where as respects benefits provided to employees:

   (a) the amount which an employer is liable to remit to the Collector-General is in excess of the amount of tax which he or she has deducted or accounted for (in the case of insufficiency of money wages or salary), and

   (b) it is established that the amount deducted or accounted for was in accordance with the best estimate that could reasonably have been made by the employer when the benefits were being provided,

   the Revenue Commissioners may direct that the amount of the excess should be recovered from the employees. Where they so direct, the employer will not be liable for the balance due.

(vii) Where an employer provides an employee with a small benefit (that is, a benefit with a value not exceeding €250) PAYE and PRSI need not be applied to that benefit. No more than one such benefit given to an employee in a tax year will qualify for such treatment. Where a benefit exceeds €250 in value the full value of the benefit is to be subjected to PAYE and PRSI.

(viii) The employer's best estimate of the taxable value of a benefit is to be treated as notional pay in the pay period in which the benefit is provided and must be added to the money wages or salary for that pay period. It is the aggregate of the money wages or salary payment and the notional pay which must be used for the purposes of calculating PAYE and PRSI for that pay period. For example, if in a particular pay period an employee receives money wages or salary of €300 plus a voucher representing notional pay of €150, the pay for that period for PAYE and PRSI purposes is €450.

The employee's PAYE and PRSI liability, in respect of the €450, must be deducted from the money wages or salary for that pay period. In addition, employer's PRSI is also due on the €450.

(c) Valuation of Benefits

(i) General Rule

Except where there are specific statutory valuation rules, the amount of the taxable benefit (i.e., the notional pay) which is liable to PAYE and PRSI is the higher of:

- the expenses incurred by the employer in connection with the provision of the benefit to the employee, or
- the value realisable by the employee for the benefit in money or money's worth

less any amount made good to the employer by the employee.

(ii) Specific Statutory Valuation Rules

Specific statutory valuation rules must be used to determine the taxable value in relation to:

- Company cars
- Company vans
- Accommodation
- Employer owned assets, and
- Preferential loans.

TCA97 s121 **(d) Company Cars**

(a) General

Where a company car is available for the private use of an employee the employee is chargeable to PAYE and PRSI in respect of that use. The notional pay to which PAYE and PRSI must be applied is determined by reference to the "cash equivalent" of the private use of a company car. To arrive at the cash equivalent the employer must first apply a business mileage related percentage to the Original Market Value (OMV) of the vehicle supplied.

The percentages applicable are as follows:

Annual Business Mileage Thresholds	Cash Equivalent (% of OMV)
15,000 or less	30%
15,001 to 20,000	24%
20,001 to 25,000	18%
25,001 to 30,000	12%
30,001 and over	6%

The following steps are a guide to assist in the calculation of the amount of the taxable benefit on "notional pay" in respect of a company car.

(i) *Ascertaining the Original Market Value of the car*

The Original Market Value (OMV) of a car is the price (including any duty of customs, duty of excise or value-added tax chargeable on the car) which the car might reasonably have been expected to fetch, if sold in the State singly in a retail sale in the open market, immediately before the date of its first registration in the State or elsewhere. OMV includes vehicle registration tax (VRT).

Generally, the OMV is taken to be the list price of the vehicle, including VAT and VRT at the time of first registration. However, where a discount was received on the acquisition of the vehicle and such discount was normally obtainable in respect of a single retail sale in the open market, the list price may be reduced accordingly.

In cases where:

- An exceptionally large discount was obtained (e.g., a quantity or fleet discount), or
- The discount cannot be determined (e.g., a car has been traded in against a new car), or
- The car involved was purchased second-hand,

claims in respect of discounts are limited to the discounts normally obtainable in respect of a single retail sale on the open market. Reductions for discounts do not usually exceed 10% and higher percentages will not be accepted in the absence of documentary evidence in respect of single retail sales in the open market. Where an employer receives a discount in relation to the cost of the car (or a fleet of cars) the OMV is taken to be the VAT inclusive/VRT inclusive discounted price.

(ii) *Ascertain the business mileage for the year and calculate the cash equivalent using the appropriate percentage.*

The cash equivalent is calculated by applying the appropriate annual business mileage related percentage in the table above to the OMV.

For the purpose of determining the correct percentage, the total mileage for the year should be reduced by a minimum of 5,000 private miles to arrive at business mileage. The employer may accept lower levels of private mileage but only where documentary evidence can be provided in this regard by the employee to the employer.

(iii) *Deduct amounts made good by the employee to the employer*

Having ascertained the cash equivalent amount, any amount made good by the employee directly to the employer towards the cost of providing or running the car must be deducted in order to arrive at the amount of notional pay.

(b) Alternative basis for certain employees with low business mileage

In the case of certain employees whose annual business mileage does not exceed 15,000 miles, the cash equivalent of 30% of OMV may be reduced by 20% giving an effective cash equivalent of 24% of OMV.

This alternative basis is available where the following conditions are complied with. The employee:

- Works an average of not less than 20 hours per week.
- Travels at least 5,000 business miles per annum on the employer's business.
- Spends at least 70% of his or her working time away from the employer's premises.
- Retains a log book detailing business mileage, business transacted, business time travelled and date of journey, and the log book is certified by the employer as being correct.

(c) Company car not available for full year

Adjustments will be necessary where a car is not available for the full year, e.g., where:

- An employee receives a car after the start of the tax year, or
- An employee gives up a car before the end of the tax year.

Equally an adjustment will be required where a car is for some other reason not available for private use for part of the tax year, for example, where an employee is working abroad for an extended period. In this case, a car provided to an employee will not be regarded as available for private use for that part of the year in which the employee is outside the State for the purpose of performing the duties of the office or employment, provided the following conditions are met:

- The employee travels abroad without the car.
- The car is not available for use by the employee's family or household during the employee's period of absence outside of the State.

Where a car is not available for part of a year, the business mileage thresholds and the percentage cash equivalents used should be calculated by reference to the following fraction of the normal thresholds and percentages (as listed in the table on page 102). The fraction is:

$$\frac{\text{Number of days in the tax year car is available for private use}}{365}$$

This fraction may also be expressed as a percentage as follows:

$$\frac{\text{Number of days in the tax year car is available for private use}}{365} \times 100$$

(d) Change of car during the year

Where there is a change of company car during the year, the annual business mileage thresholds and the cash equivalent percentages must be calculated for each car separately.

(e) Cars in "car pools"

There will not be a charge to tax in respect of a car which is in a "car pool". A car can be treated as being in a car pool if:

- The car is made available to, and is actually used by, more than one employee and is not ordinarily used by one employee to the exclusion of the others, and
- Any private use of the car by the employees is merely incidental to business use, and
- It is not normally kept overnight at the home of any of the employees.

TCA97 s121A

(e) Company Vans

(a) General

Subject to certain conditions being met (see below), where a company van is available for the private use of an employee, the employee is chargeable to PAYE and PRSI in respect of that private use.

The private use of a company van will be exempt from benefit-in-kind if:

- The van is necessary in the performance of the duties of the employees employment.
- The employee is required to keep the van at his or her private residence when not in use.
- Private use of the van is prohibited and the employee spends at least 80% of his or her time away from his or her work premises.

A van means a mechanically propelled vehicle which:

- Is designed or constructed solely or mainly for the carriage of goods or other burden, and
- Has a roofed area or areas to the rear of the driver's seat, and
- Has no side windows or seating fitted in that roofed area or areas.

Where a crew cab or other similar type of vehicle meets all of these criteria it would be regarded as a van rather than a car.

(b) Cash equivalent of private use of van

The notional pay to which PAYE and PRSI must be applied is determined by reference to the "cash equivalent" of the private use of the van. The cash equivalent is 5% of the Original Market Value (OMV) of the vehicle supplied. The OMV must be calculated in the same manner as for cars as outlined above.

Where the van has been modified, e.g., where a refrigeration unit has been installed, the OMV of the van excluding such modifications should be used.

The cash equivalent may be reduced by any amount required to be made good, and actually made good, by the employee directly to the employer, in respect of any part of the cost of providing or running the van.

(c) Vans in "van-pools"

There will not be a charge to tax in respect of a van which is in a "van pool". A van can be treated as being in a van pool if:

- The van is made available to, and is actually used by more than one employee and is not ordinarily used by one employee to the exclusion of the others, and
- Any private use of the van by the employees is merely incidental to business use, and
- It is not normally kept overnight at the home of any of the employees.

TCA97 s118 **(f) Accommodation**

Where accommodation is owned and provided by the employer for use by an employee, the value of the taxable benefit to the employee is the aggregate of:

- Any expense (other than the cost of acquisition) incurred by the employer in connection with the provision of the accommodation, and
- The annual value of its use.

The annual value of the use of employer-owned accommodation is the annual rent which the employer might reasonably expect to obtain for the property if the property were rented on an arm's length basis and on the basis that the landlord be responsible for all repairs, insurance etc. and the tenant undertook to pay all the usual tenant's expenses.

As a general rule of thumb for calculating the market rent (the annual rent which the employer might reasonably expect to obtain) the employer may take a figure equal to 8% of the current market value of the property.

However, where a vouched lower figure is available, e.g., an auctioneer's estimate of the rent likely to be obtained, this figure may be used for the purposes of calculating the PAYE and PRSI due on the taxable benefit.

A taxable benefit will not arise where an employee (but not a director) is required by the terms of his or her employment to live in accommodation provided by the employer in part of the employer's business premises so that the employee can properly perform his or her duties ("better performance test") and either:

- The accommodation is provided in accordance with a practice which since before 30 July 1948 has commonly prevailed in trades of the class in question as respects employees of the class in question, or,
- It is necessary, in the particular class of trade, for employees of the class in question to live on the premises.

It is accepted that the "better performance test" is met in practice where:

- The employee is required to be on call outside normal hours, and
- The employee is in fact frequently called out, and
- The accommodation is provided so that the employee may have quick access to the place of employment.

Examples of such employees include:

(a) Managers or night care staff in residential or respite centres (where such centres are not nursing facilities).

(b) Governors and chaplains in prisons.

(c) Caretakers living on the premises (where they are in a genuine full-time caretaking job).

Where accommodation is rented, at a market rent, by an employer for an employee, the taxable benefit for PAYE and PRSI purposes is the actual amount of rent paid less any amount which the employee is required to make good and actually makes good to the employer in respect of the accommodation.

(g) Employer Owned Assets (Other than Company Cars, Vans and Accommodation

Where an asset (other than accommodation, company cars or vans), and including land which continues to belong to the employer, is provided by an employer for use by an employee, the annual value of the use of the asset is 5% of the market value of the asset when it was first provided as a benefit by the employer to that employee or any other employee. This is the amount that must be taken into account when calculating the taxable benefit which is to be included as notional pay for the purposes of PAYE and PRSI.

If any annual amount paid by the employer for the rent or hire of the assets is greater than the annual value as calculated above, the notional pay will be that annual amount paid by the employer.

The taxable benefit in respect of the asset will apply for each tax year for which an employee has the free use of an employer-owned asset. Where there is free use of an asset for part of the year only, the amount of the taxable benefit should be time-apportioned.

TCA97 s236 There is no charge to tax in respect of the loan of art objects kept in buildings of significance where the Revenue Commissioners have determined that the public have reasonable access to view both the object and the significant building.

TCA97 s122

(h) Preferential Loans

PAYE and PRSI apply to the benefit derived by an employee from certain loans at preferential rates of interest.

A "preferential loan" means a loan, made by an employer to an employee or the spouse of an employee, in respect of which no interest is payable, or interest is payable at a rate lower than the "specified rate". It does not however include such a loan where the rate of interest is not less than the rate of interest at which the employer in the course of the employer's trade makes equivalent loans for similar purposes at arm's length to persons other than employees or their spouses.

The specified rates for the tax year 2008 are:

Qualifying Home Loans	5.5%
All other loans	13%

See Chart 13 for previous rates.

PAYE and PRSI are to be applied to the difference between the amount of interest paid or payable on the preferential loan in the tax year and the amount of interest which would have been payable in the tax year if the loan had been subject to the specified rate. The charge to tax applies for each year in which there is a balance outstanding on the loan.

Section 10 Finance Act 2004 provided that in addition to existing employees, former employees are also within the scope of section 122 TCA 1997 as respects loans made on or after 4 February 2004.

TCA97 s118 Other Benefits

TCA97 s985A

(i) Company Shares

Where certain shares in a company are given by the company to an employee free of charge or at a discounted price or under a share scheme, the employee is chargeable to tax on the benefit accruing to him or her. However, PAYE and PRSI do not apply. Instead, the benefit must be returned on the employee's return of income form.

(j) Pension Contributions

PAYE and PRSI should not be applied to pension contributions paid by an employer in respect of an employee to Revenue-approved superannuation schemes and Personal Retirement Savings Accounts (PRSAs).

However, while PAYE and PRSI do not apply to an employer's contribution to an employee's PRSA, the contribution is nevertheless a taxable benefit in the employee's hands, subject to relief up to certain limits, and must be returned by the employer on form P11D.

(k) Medical Insurance

TCA97 s118 In the case of medical insurance premiums, the cost to the employer is based on the gross premium before tax relief at source (TRS) – the employer has to refund the TRS to Revenue.

Accordingly, the notional pay is the gross premium and the employee will be entitled to a standard rate tax credit in respect of the gross premium in his or her Certificate of Tax Credits.

(l) Meals and Meal Vouchers

Canteen Meals

A taxable benefit does not arise in respect of free or subsidised meals in staff canteens where meals are provided for the staff generally. The facility must be available to all employees. Otherwise, the exemption does not apply. In the event that a taxable benefit does arise, the running costs must be apportioned, in a reasonable manner between those employees entitled to use the canteen, and taken into account as notional pay for PAYE and PRSI purposes.

Meal Vouchers

Where an employer provides luncheon or meal vouchers to employees there is a taxable benefit and the face value of the vouchers (disregarding 19 cent per voucher) must be taken into account as notional pay for PAYE and PRSI purposes.

TCA97 s120A **(m) Crèche/Childcare Facilities**

Employer-provided facility

Where an employer provides free or subsidised childcare facilitates for employees, a taxable benefit does not arise where the childcare facility is provided on premises which:

(i) Meet certain requirements of the Child Care (Pre-School Services) Regulations 1996, and

(ii) Are made available:

- Solely by the employer.
- By the employer jointly with one or more other participants in a joint scheme and the employer is wholly or partly responsible for either:
  - financing and managing the facility, or
  - providing capital for the construction or refurbishment of the premises, or
- By any other person or persons and the employer is wholly or partly responsible for either:
  - financing and managing the facility, or
  - providing capital for the construction or refurbishment of the premises.

Independent Facility

Where the above conditions are not complied with, e.g., where an employer merely pays for or subsidises the cost to an independent crèche or child care facility, the cost borne by the employer is a taxable benefit and PAYE and PRSI must be applied accordingly. In such circumstances, where an employer makes a block payment to a crèche or childcare facility, the amount paid should be apportioned and treated as notional pay of the respective employees. The apportionment of the block payment should be based on the facts, including the number of children concerned for each employee, and should lead to a result which is fair and reasonable.

TCA97 s118 **(n) Sports and Recreational Facilities**

Facilities provided on the employer's premises

Where sports and recreational facilities are made available on the employer's premises for the use of employees generally, a taxable benefit is not treated as arising. The facility must be available to all employees. Where the facilities are not available to all employees there is taxable benefit. The taxable benefit should be computed by apportioning the running costs in a reasonable manner between those employees entitled to avail of the facilities.

Corporate Membership paid by the employer

Where a corporate subscription to sports or recreational facilities is paid by an employer on behalf of an individual employee or specified employees, the amount paid must be treated as notional pay for PAYE and PRSI purposes.

Where a "group" membership is paid by the employer on behalf of employees generally, the cost incurred by the employer should be divided equally among all the employees who are entitled to and indicate an intention to participate in the scheme. No cost should be attributed to an employee who specifically informs the employer that he does not wish to, and will not, participate in the group scheme.

(o) "En-Bloc" Payments

Where a block payment (or an en bloc payment) is made by the employer in providing a benefit on behalf of employees generally, the payment should be divided equally amongst the employees entitled to benefit from the payment. Employees who specifically indicate that they do not wish to, and will not, benefit should be left out of account.

(p) In-House Medical Plans/Corporate General Practitioner Services

Some employers operate in-house medical plans under which employees contribute to and claim from the plan. Employers will in some cases contribute to the plan to the extent that the aggregate claims by employees exceed the aggregate contributions made by employees in the relevant year. In other cases, employers may employ or pay a retainer to a general practitioner. In such circumstances PAYE and PRSI should not be applied to any benefit arising from the employer's contribution to the plan or payment of the general practitioner.

(q) Staff Discounts

Price above cost to the employer

A discount, given by an employer (e.g., an employer in the retail sector) on the purchase of goods by an employee, is not regarded as a taxable benefit if the sum paid by the employee is equal to or greater than the cost to the employer of acquiring or manufacturing the goods.

Price below cost to the employer

However, where goods are sold below the employer's cost, the difference between that cost and the price paid is a taxable benefit and PAYE and PRSI must be operated on this amount.

(r) Christmas Parties and Other Inclusive Events

Where an employer provides staff Christmas parties, special occasion meals or other inclusive events, such as sports days for staff, a taxable benefit will not be treated as arising where the expenses are reasonable.

(s) Travel Passes

PAYE and PRSI should not be applied to the value of certain monthly or annual bus, train, Luas and commuter ferry passes given to employees for use on a licensed passenger transport service.

(t) Car Parking

Car parking facilities provided by an employer to employees are not treated as giving rise to a taxable benefit.

(u) Work-related Supplies

Office accommodation, furniture, supplies or services provided for the director or employee on the business premises and used by him or her solely in performing the duties or his or her office or employment do not give rise to a taxable benefit. In other words, facilities used solely for business purposes are tax-free and PAYE and PRSI are not to be applied to their value.

(v) Laptops/Mobile Phones/Home High-Speed Internet Connections

Where an employer provides an employee with any of the above for business purposes and the employer bears the costs of its installation and use, a taxable benefit will not be treated as arising where private use is merely incidental to the business use of the item.

(w) Computers and Other Equipment provided in Employee's Home

A taxable benefit will arise on an employee in respect of a computer or other equipment provided in an employee's home for the employee's private use. The notional pay is calculated at 5% of the market value of the asset when first provided as a benefit.

However, a taxable benefit will not arise where the computer or other equipment is provided in the employee's home for business purposes and private use is incidental.

(x) Home Telephone provided by an Employer

Second Home Telephone Account

Where an employer provides a home telephone for business use to an employee and the employer bears the costs of the use of the phone, no taxable benefit will be treated as arising where private use is incidental.

Single Home Telephone Account

Where a home telephone is used for business and private use and the employer pays any associated costs such as the line rental and/or the monthly/bi-monthly telephone bill, a taxable benefit will arise. The amount to be taken into account as the notional pay is 50% of the cost to the employer, less any amount made good by the employee to the employer. However, where the private costs are lower, the notional pay may be restricted to those costs. Records in support of the notional pay, however computed, must be kept for inspection by Revenue, if required.

(y) Corporate Charge Cards

Business Use Only

Where the charge card is provided by the employer to the employee exclusively for business use, any annual membership or stamp duty paid by the employer in connection with the card will not be regarded as a taxable benefit.

Business and Private Use

Where the card can be used by the employee for private purchases, or other private payments, any amounts paid in respect of the employee's private purchases, or for other non-business purposes, and not made good by the employee to the employer will be taxable benefits and PAYE and PRSI will apply.

(z) Medical Check-ups

The provision of medical check-ups which employees are required to undergo by their employer will not be regarded as taxable benefits.

(aa) Course or Exam Fees

Refunds of course or exam fees to an employee which have been paid by the employee, or direct payments of course or exam fees by the employer, will not be treated as giving rise to a taxable benefit where the course undertaken is relevant to the business of the employer.

A course is regarded as relevant to the business of the employer where it leads to the acquisition of knowledge or skills, which are:

- necessary for the duties of the employment, or
- directly related to increasing the effectiveness of the performance of the employee's or director's present or prospective duties in the office or employment.

(bb) Professional Subscriptions

Where the employer pays a subscription to a professional body on behalf of an employee, or reimburses the employee who has paid such a subscription, a taxable benefit or emoluments will not be treated as arising if membership of that professional body is relevant to the business of the employer.

Membership of a professional body can be regarded as relevant to the business of the employer where it facilitates the acquisition of knowledge which is necessary for the duties of the employment, or directly related to the performance of the employee's or director's present or prospective duties in the office or employment.

Where membership of a professional body cannot be so regarded as relevant to the business of the employer, the subscription paid by the employer directly or by reimbursement will be regarded as a taxable benefit, to be included as notional pay or emoluments for PAYE and PRSI purposes.

(cc) Provision of Newspapers, Periodicals, etc.

Where an employer provides employees with free periodicals, newspapers, etc. which are generally related to the employer's business, a taxable benefit will not be treated as arising.

(dd) Examination Awards

Reimbursement of Expenses

Examination awards made to an employee, in the context of passing an examination, or acquiring a qualification which bears some relationship to the employees duties, will not be treated as giving rise to a taxable benefit. This treatment is subject to the condition that the award is an amount that can reasonably be regarded as a reimbursement of expenses likely to have been incurred in studying for the qualification or sitting the examination.

Special Increments

Special increments of salary awarded on passing an examination or other such "recognition" payments are chargeable as part of an employee's remuneration in the normal way.

(ee) Exceptional Performance Awards

Where an employer has a scheme in place to reward exceptional performance, any awards received under such schemes are taxable benefits. The treatment is as follows:

- Where the award is made in cash, it must pass through the payroll system and PAYE/PRSI must be applied to the amount of the award.
- Where the award is made by way of gift or voucher, the value of the gift or voucher is a taxable benefit to which PAYE and PRSI must be applied.

If an employer wishes to discharge the tax on the exceptional performance award made, whether in the form of cash or in the form of gifts or vouchers, so that the awards are made to the employees concerned "tax-free", the value of each award made must be grossed up for the purposes of computing the PAYE and the PRSI to be remitted to the employer.

(ff) Staff Suggestion Schemes

The previous practice regarding such schemes was withdrawn with effect from 1 January 2004. Awards made on or after that date under staff suggestion schemes are to be treated as giving rise to a taxable benefit and PAYE and PRSI must be applied to the value of the award.

(gg) Long Service Awards

A taxable benefit does not arise in respect of Long Service Awards where the following conditions are satisfied:

- The award is made as a testimonial to mark long service of not less than 20 years.
- The award takes the form of a tangible article(s) of reasonable cost,
- The cost does not exceed €50 for each year of service, and

- No similar award has been made to the recipient within the previous 5 years.

This treatment does not apply to awards made in cash or in the form of vouchers, bonds, etc. Where any of the conditions above are not met PAYE and PRSI must be applied to the value of the award.

(hh) Security Assets and Services

TCA97 s118A Subject to certain conditions, an exemption from a benefit-in-kind tax charge will arise in circumstances where an employer incurs expenses in providing a security asset or service for use by a director or employee. In order to qualify for the exemption there must be a credible and serious threat to the physical personal safety of the director or employee which arises wholly or mainly from his or her employment.

1.18.6 Salary sacrifice agreements

TCA97 s118B Section 118B TCA 1997 defines a salary sacrifice agreement as meaning any arrangement under which an employee foregoes the right to receive any part of his or her remuneration under their terms of employment and in return his/her employer agrees to provide him or her with a benefit. Any amount of remuneration foregone by an individual under any salary sacrifice arrangement and not within certain permitted exceptions shall be deemed to be an emolument of the individual and income tax shall be chargeable accordingly.

The section sets out certain exemptions from the charge to tax for salary sacrifice as follows:

(i) Any salary sacrifice in relation to travel passes issued by an approved transport provider under section 118 TCA 1997, and

(ii) Any salary sacrifice in relation to shares appropriated to employees or directors under an approved profit sharing scheme, which shares are exempt from a charge to tax by virtue of section 510(4) TCA 1997.

Where the salary sacrifice relates to the exempt matters outlined above, and there is an arrangement or scheme in place under which the employee is compensated by the provision of the exempt benefit and a payment of compensation, then the entire salary sacrifice will be treated as an emolument.

Any salary sacrifice entered into in respect of a bonus or commission or other emolument arising to an individual after the end of the year of assessment shall not be exempt even if applied in the year of assessment to the approved profit sharing scheme or in relation to a travel pass.

There is also a provision to catch employee benefits provided to spouses or dependents.

The above provisions apply with effect from 31 January 2008.

1.18.7 Employee share schemes

There are a number of schemes operated by employers whereby shares in the employer company are allocated to employees, or whereby employees are given options to acquire shares, as follows:

(i) Unapproved Share Option Schemes

TCA97 s128, s128A

When a share option is exercised, an individual is charged to income tax under Schedule E for the year of exercise on the difference between the price paid (i.e., the option price) and the market value at that date, and not the market value on the date on which the option was granted.

If the option is capable of being exercised more than seven years after its granting, Revenue reserves the right to tax the individual when the option is granted on any difference between the option price and the market value of the share on the date of grant.

Subsequently tax is also charged when the option is exercised but credit is available for any tax paid at the time the option was granted.

In addition any amount assessable to Irish income tax is deemed to be part of the cost for capital gains tax purposes.

Income tax arising from the exercise of share options is, in general, payable under self assessment in respect of the gain arising from share options.

The income tax payable on the exercise of share options between 6 April 2000 and 28 March 2003, may, on election, be deferred until 31 October following the year of disposal of the shares acquired by the exercise, or 31 October in the tax year following the tax year beginning seven years after the year of exercise, whichever is the earlier.

An election must be submitted by 31 October in the tax year following the year of exercise.

For options exercised in the period from 29 March 2003 to 29 June 2003 deferral of payment of income tax arising on the exercise of the option is not possible.

For share options exercised on or after 30 June 2003, the tax due (relevant tax) is payable within 30 days after the exercise of the share option. The option gain will be taxable at the higher rate of income tax for the year of exercise. Where on application in writing, the Revenue Commissioners are satisfied that the individual is likely to be chargeable to income tax at the standard rate only for the year of assessment, payment may be calculated at the standard rate. Each payment of relevant tax must be accompanied by a return. Interest will be charged on late payments on a daily basis. Relevant tax payable in respect of the exercise of an option will be taken into account in computing liability for the tax year in question, but is not regarded as a payment of preliminary tax. The option gains must be reported in the annual income tax return.

In the case of share options exercised before 6 February 2003, payment of the income tax liability arising on the exercise of the share options whether currently due or deferred may be deferred where the market value of the shares acquired by the exercise of the share option has fallen below the amount of the income tax arising on exercise of the option when the income tax is due for payment.

On election, a payment on account equal to the market value of the shares at specified dates may be made by a specified date with the balance of the income tax being deferred until the taxpayer, or his or her spouse, disposes of the option shares or any shares in a company.

There is no refund where income tax paid before 6 February 2003 exceeds the payment on account due under these rules. In addition, any other income tax liability arising from the exercise of share options (which does not qualify for the deferred payment on account arrangements) must have been paid or have been included in an instalment arrangement acceptable to the Collector General. Where the requirements of the relief are not fully complied with, the amount of unpaid tax is reinstated. Tax unpaid at death shall be discharged by the Revenue Commissioners.

An election must be made on or before 1 June 2003 in the form prescribed by Revenue to avail of these provisions.

The deadline for companies' returns of information regarding share options is 31 March after the end of the tax year.

Returns of information will also be required from the Irish employer where the share options are granted to a non-resident person.

Restricted Shares

Shares acquired by employees on the exercise of option rights and under other employee share offer schemes may be subject to a restriction or "clog" where disposal is prohibited for a number of years. Revenue (see *Tax Briefing* 31 – April 1998 and *Tax Briefing 35* - March 1999) recognises that a restriction on the sale of shares could be said to reduce the benefit acquired by the individual particularly, for example, where the individual would like to dispose of the shares immediately but is prohibited. Revenue are prepared, in cases where there is a genuine restriction, to allow the following % abatements on the gain chargeable to income tax:

No of years of restriction on sale	Abatement
1 Year	10%
2 Years	20%
3 Years	30%
4 Years	40%
5 Years	50%
Over 5 Years	55%

The prohibition on the disposal of shares must be for genuine commercial reasons and not simply used for the purpose of tax avoidance.

The award/grant of shares to employees/directors in companies other than the "employer" company or its parent company is not covered by the practice.

Residence

Revenue guidelines (see *Tax Briefing* 31 – April 1998) provide that the liability to tax is determined by the residence position of the employee at the time the option is granted although the legislation contains no such provision.

If the employee is resident in Ireland at the date of grant, Revenue maintains that he is liable to income tax under s128 at the date of grant, if applicable, and at the date of exercise regardless of whether or not he is resident in Ireland at the date of exercise.

However, Revenue accepts that the reverse applies if the employee is granted an option prior to arriving in Ireland but exercises the option while resident in Ireland. In this instance, no Irish income tax liability arises upon exercise as long as there is no connection between the Irish employment and the granting of the option and there is no tax planning or avoidance involved.

Finance Act 2005 provided for the introduction of major changes to the taxation treatment in Ireland of unapproved share options acquired by cross-border employees prior to moving to Ireland. These provisions became effective following the signing of a Commencement Order on 5 April 2007.

Revenue has published a Statement of Practice detailing how the new rules will be implemented, and the key changes are as follows:

(i) Options acquired on or after 5 April 2007 by overseas employees prior to moving to Ireland may be subject to tax on exercise.

(ii) Double taxation relief applies to share options exercised on or after 1 January 2004.

(iii) Changes have been made in relation to the capital gains tax base cost of certain shares acquired by mobile employees under an unapproved share option scheme.

(ii) Approved Share Option Schemes (ASOS)

TCA97 s519D The main features of ASOS are as follows:

(a) A company must apply in writing to the Revenue Commissioners for approval.

(b) Under an ASOS, employees will not be chargeable (as is the case with an unapproved scheme) to income tax on the exercise of the option, but will instead be chargeable to capital gains tax on the full gain (i.e., the difference between the amount paid for the shares and the amount received) on a disposal of the shares.

(c) The director or employee must not dispose of the shares within three years of the grant date.

(d) Where options are exercised on or after 15 February 2001, but before the scheme is approved by the Revenue Commissioners, those options will also be eligible provided the scheme is approved before 31 December 2001 and, at the time of both the grant and exercise, the scheme would have been approved had the legislation been in force on 15 February 2001.

(e) The scheme must be open to all employees and must provide that employees be eligible to participate in the scheme on "similar terms". Under the "similar terms" rule the options may be granted by reference to remuneration, length of service or other similar factors.

(f) The scheme must not contain features which would discourage qualifying employees from participating or have the effect of conferring benefits wholly or mainly on directors or higher paid employees of the company.

(g) In order to assist companies to retain key employees, the scheme may contain a "key employee" element where options can be granted which do not meet the "similar terms" conditions, provided at least 70% of the total number of shares over which rights are granted under the scheme in any one year are made available to all employees on "similar terms". Employees cannot participate in both elements of the scheme in the same year.

(h) Share used in the scheme must form part of the ordinary share capital of the company and, in general, must not be subject to restrictions that do not apply to other shares of the same class.

(i) The shares must be:

  (a) shares of a class quoted on a recognised stock exchange,

  (b) shares in a company which is not under the control of another company, or

  (c) shares in a company which is under the control of a company (other than a company which is, or if resident in the State would be, a close company within the meaning of section 430) whose shares are quoted on a recognised stock exchange.

(j) An employee shall not be permitted to transfer his/her rights but where a person dies before exercising these rights, they must be exercised within one year of that persons death.

(k) The three year holding period does not apply in the case of death.

(l) The price at which the shares may be acquired is to be stated at the time the option is granted and is not to be less than the market value of the shares at that time or if Revenue agrees the price at such earlier times as it approves.

(m) Any money expended by the company in setting up the scheme will be allowed as a deduction against profits or gains of the trade or as a management expense of the company.

(n) The Revenue may also approve a scheme for a group of companies.

(iii) Rights to Acquire Other Assets

TCA97 s128 The exercise of rights granted to employees and directors, to acquire other assets (other than shares dealt with above) may also give rise to a charge to tax.

(iv) Convertible Securities

TCA97 s128c Finance Act 2008 provides specific rules for the tax treatment of convertible securities acquired by directors and employees by reason of their office or employment, on or after 31 January 2008.

Prior to Finance Act 2008, the income tax charge on the acquisition of a convertible security was based on the market value of the security at the date of acquisition. This did not reflect the reality of the director or employee acquiring a security plus a right to convert that security subsequently into a more valuable security. Finance Act 2008 rectifies this by imposing an additional income tax charge on the occurrence of a number of events associated with such securities (including but not limited to conversion and disposal).

(v) Share Subscription Schemes

TCA97 s479 Where an eligible employee of a qualifying company subscribes for eligible shares in the company, he/she is entitled, in calculating the amount of his/her total income for the year of assessment in which the shares are issued, to a deduction of an amount equal to the amount of the subscription. The maximum lifetime deduction allowed for an employee is €6,350. Where the employee has previously been granted relief under s479 that was below this limit, the balance may be taken up in later years. The conditions for this relief are as follows:

(a) The individual subscribes for the shares at not less than market value.

(b) The deduction is granted for the tax year in which the shares are issued.

(c) The individual takes up new ordinary shares in the company.

(d) The shares are issued in a company which is resident in Ireland and not resident elsewhere and incorporated in the State and is a trading company or a holding company.

(e) With effect from 12 February 1998, where the individual sells the shares within 3 years of the date of acquisition, any income tax relief granted is withdrawn by reference to the tax year in which it was originally given.

(f) The relief will not be withdrawn where the employee ceases employment with the particular company, where he ceases to be a resident or where he ceases to be a full-time employee.

(g) An amount equivalent to the tax deduction granted is excluded from the base cost of the asset in calculating capital gains tax liability on the sale of the shares.

(vi) Approved Profit-Sharing Schemes (APSS)

TCA97 s509-s518 In general, the purposes of APSS's are as follows:

(a) To give companies a tax deduction, subject to certain restrictions, for the costs of providing shares for employees for the purposes of profit sharing schemes and for the costs of running the schemes.

(b) To give the recipient employee exemption from income tax on the grant to him of shares up to certain limits.

(c) To grant the employee favourable income tax treatment on any growth in the value of the shares.

The main features of such schemes are:

(a) The scheme must be established under a trust deed and the scheme and trust deed must be approved by Revenue Authorities.

(b) The costs to a company in setting up a scheme, in providing shares for employees under a scheme and the running costs thereof are, subject to certain limitations, tax deductible.

(c) Although trustees must hold the shares, they are appropriated to employees. An employee is exempt from income tax on shares received to the value of €12,700 in a tax year.

Subject to certain conditions, this may be increased, on a once off basis, to €38,100 in respect of shares which previously had been held in an ESOT as security for borrowings by the ESOT. In particular the shares in question must have been so held in the ESOT for a minimum period of 10 years. However, with effect from 31 January 2008, Revenue has the discretion to reduce the 10 year holding period where circumstances are appropriate.

Trustees are not liable to capital gains tax on the appropriation of shares, or on the sale of shares on the open market and to the extent that such proceeds are used to repay monies borrowed by those trustees including the payment of interest on such borrowings.

An individual, who has already had an appropriation of shares under the terms of an Approved Profit Sharing Scheme from his/her employer company in a particular year, can avail of another appropriation under the terms of a second company's scheme in the same year, where the first company has been taken-over by the second company. This will only be allowed in the year of the take-over and will be subject to the existing annual limits of €12,700/€38,100 applying to the aggregate value of the shares appropriated under both schemes.

(d) The employee must hold the shares for more than three years in order to avoid an income tax penalty. If the shares are sold within three years, income tax is charged at 100% of the value of the shares at the date of assignment.

If within the three year period the employee ceases to be an employee of the company, or has reached pensionable age as defined in section 2, Social Welfare (Consolidation) Act 1993, income tax is charged at 50% of the value of the shares.

However, with effect from 27 March 1998 this holding period will not apply where shares pass or are transferred from an employee share ownership trust (ESOT) to an approved profit sharing scheme (APSS) provided the following conditions are met:

(i) immediately prior to the transfer, the ESOT had held the shares for at least three years; and

(ii) the participating employee must have been a beneficiary of the ESOT for the three-year period ending on the date on which the shares are transferred.

Where the conditions are met, the participants will be able to dispose of his or her shares without any income tax implications immediately he or she receives them through the APSS.

Where the shares are held for a period of less than three years in an ESOT, the holding period in the APSS for the exemption to apply will be reduced proportionately.

(e) Scheme shares may, subject to certain conditions, be subject to a restriction imposed by a company's Articles of Association requiring employees to dispose of shares on leaving the company.

(f) A disposal of shares is treated as a disposal by the employee for purposes of capital gains tax. Any amount assessed to income tax is not deducted in computing capital gains.

(g) While the trustees hold the shares the employee is absolutely entitled to the shares as against the trustees and he is also entitled to any dividends which arise thereon.

(h) Participation in the scheme is determined on the following basis:

(i) Participation in the scheme is open to every full-time director or full time and part time employee chargeable to tax under Schedule E who has been such for a qualifying period (which must not exceed 3 years).

(ii) Shares may be appropriated only to an individual who, at the time is (or was within the preceding 18 months or 15 years, where certain conditions are met) a director or employee.

(iii) Shares may not be allotted to any individual who has a material interest (more than 15 per cent of the ordinary shares) in the company where it is a close company.

(iv) All participating directors or employees must be eligible to participate on similar terms.

(i) The shares must be ordinary shares of the company and must be quoted on a recognised Stock Exchange, or, if not so quoted, be shares in a company which is either controlled by a company whose shares are so quoted or be shares in a company not under the control of another company.

(j) An APSS may not be approved by the Revenue Commissioners unless they are satisfied that it is not intended solely to confer benefits on the directors and higher paid employees of a group of companies. In addition, the Commissioners may not approve an APSS if they consider that there are features in the scheme which would act as a disincentive to employees of the company to participate in the scheme.

Finance Act 2002 included a number of provisions to ensure that the transfer and appropriation of securities other than ordinary shares to the participants of an APSS, in the case of certain take-overs, takes place in a way which preserves the tax benefits of the participants.

(vii) Employee Share Ownership Trusts (ESOT)

An ESOT is effectively a mechanism where a company can store shares for long periods up to a maximum of 20 years. They are designed to work in conjunction with profit sharing schemes in that shares can be released from the ESOT each year into the company's profit sharing scheme.

TCA97 s519 The main features of ESOTs are as follows:

(a) The ESOT must be established by a company (the founding company) which must not be controlled by another company, and it must extend to all companies which the founding company controls. However, with regard to ESOTs approved on or after 27 March 1998, the founding company has the option of selecting the companies it wants to include in the ESOT.

(b) Three alternative forms of trustees are provided for, i.e., majority employee representation, a paritarian trust with equal company/employee representation or a single corporate trustee with equal company/employee representation on the board of directors.

(c) All employees and certain full-time directors (who work at least 20 hours per week) of the founding company or a group company who have been such for a qualifying period of not more than three years, and are chargeable to tax under Schedule E, must be eligible to be beneficiaries under the ESOT. However, a company at its discretion may include other employees, e.g., foreign based employees.

(d) Former employees and directors (within 18 months of their departure or 15 years where certain conditions are met) may also be included.

(e) Employees and directors cannot be beneficiaries if they have, or had within the previous 12 months, a material interest (i.e., 5% of the ordinary share capital) in the company.

(f) The functions of the trustees must be to acquire shares in the founding company (either out of contributions from the company or borrowings) for distribution to beneficiaries.

(g) Shares must be transferred to beneficiaries by the trustees within 20 years of their acquisition by the trustees.

(h) Sums of money received by the trustees (e.g., from the founding company, dividends, etc.) must be spent, normally within 9 months, on one or more qualifying purposes. With effect from 27 March 1998 the trustees are exempt from income tax arising on such income, if and to the extent that the income is spent by the trustees within the qualifying period, for one or more qualifying purposes. The trustees will, however, not be entitled to any tax credit in relation to exempt dividends.

(i) Shares or sums (or both) must be offered to all beneficiaries of the ESOT and the transfers be made at the same time on similar terms.

(j) An ESOT may not be approved by the Revenue Commissioners unless they are satisfied that it is not intended solely to confer benefits on the directors and higher paid employees of a group of companies.

(k) Section 18 Finance Act 2005 provides that certain payments made by an ESOT to beneficiaries will be treated as distributions, subject to the deduction of dividend withholding tax at source, where there is an associated approved profit sharing scheme.

The reliefs available are as follows:

(i) A company may claim a deduction for corporation tax purposes for:

(a) the costs (legal, etc.) of setting up an approved ESOT, and

(b) contributions to the trustees of an approved ESOT where the company, or a company it controls, has employees who are beneficiaries under the ESOT and the contributions are expended by the trustees during the "expenditure period" on one or more "qualifying purposes".

(ii) Dividends received by trustees of an approved ESOT in respect of securities held by them will not be liable to the surcharge under section 805 in respect of undistributed income.

(iii) The transfer of securities by the trustees of an approved ESOT to trustees of an approved profit sharing scheme will be exempt from capital gains tax in respect of any chargeable gain arising on such transfer.

(iv) Trustees will be exempt from capital gains tax on any gains from the sale of securities on the open market, if and to the extent that such proceeds are used to repay monies borrowed by the trustees, including the payment of interest on such borrowings.

(v) With effect from 6 April 2001, the payment of money or the transfer of securities by the trustees to the personal representatives of a deceased beneficiary of the trust, are exempt from tax. The exemption is in respect of capital gains tax on the trustees and income tax on the personal representatives and is conditional on the deceased beneficiary having been a participant in an approved profit sharing scheme (APSS) through which the securities would have passed to him/her had he/she lived.

Finance Act 2002 included a number of provisions to ensure that the transfer and appropriation of securities other than ordinary shares to the participants of an ESOT, in the case of certain take-overs, takes place in a way which preserves the tax benefits of the participants.

(viii) Save As You Earn (SAYE) Share Schemes

TCA97 s519A Sch12A There are two aspects to this scheme – an approved savings-related share option scheme and a certified contractual savings scheme. The latter scheme is used to fund the purchase of shares allocated to employees under the former scheme.

In brief the SAYE scheme allows employees to save a part of their after tax salaries – between €12 and €500 per month over a three year period and at the end of this period the savings can be used by the employees to purchase shares in their employers company. The upper limit of €500 was increased from €320 in respect of contributions made under a scheme entered into on or after 1 February 2008.

The shares can be purchased at a discount of 25% of their market value at the beginning of the three year savings period. No charge to income tax arises on the purchase at this discounted price.

TCA97 s519A Where an individual obtains a right to acquire shares in his/her employing company or a group company, no tax will be chargeable in respect of the receipt or exercise of that right except in certain circumstances where the option is exercised within 3 years of being obtained.

TCA97 s519B The cost of establishing a savings related share option scheme is allowed as a deduction for corporation tax purpose.

Any terminal bonus or interest earned on an individual's savings is exempt from tax, including DIRT.

TCA97 s519C Contractual savings schemes must be with "qualifying savings institutions" as listed.

TCA97 Sch 12A Certain conditions must be complied with in order for a savings-related share option scheme to be approved by the Revenue Commissioners. These conditions govern the type of company eligibility, type of shares, exercise of rights, acquisition of shares and the share price.

1.18.8 Treatment of unpaid remuneration

TCA97 s996 Remuneration which is allowed as a deduction in computing the Schedule D profits of an employer, but which has not been paid within 6 months of the end of his accounting period, is deemed to have been paid on the last day of the accounting period. This remuneration is, therefore, subject to the PAYE regulations regarding the collection of tax and the charging of interest on unpaid PAYE.

1.18.9 Credit for directors PAYE

TCA97 s997A Section 13 Finance Act 2005 provides that in the case of controlling directors of a company, (that is those who on their own or with others control more than 15% of the ordinary share capital of a company) a credit for tax deducted from emoluments paid to them by the company will not be given unless there is documentary evidence that the tax has been remitted to the Collector General. Any tax remitted by a company will in the first instance be treated as deducted from other employees and any tax remitted in respect of the directors referred to here will be treated as deducted from each director in the same proportion as the emoluments paid to each director bears to the aggregate amount paid to all such directors.

1.18.10 Payments in connection with the commencement of employment

Whether payments in connection with the commencement of an employment (commonly referred to as "inducement payments") are taxable under Schedule E as an emolument of the new office or employment depends on the facts of each particular case. As a general rule, it may be said that the payment will be an emolument of the new employment where the payment is made under the terms of a contract of service or is in effect made in consideration of future services to be rendered to the new employer. The payment may not be taxable, however, where it can be shown that the payment is in fact compensation for the loss of some right as a result of taking up the new employment.

1.18.11 Payments on retirement or removal from an employment

TCA97 s201 Where a payment not otherwise chargeable to income tax is made in connection with the termination of an office or employment, tax is to be charged only on the excess of the payment over the higher of (i) the basic exemption and (ii) an amount entitled the Standard Capital Superannuation Benefit calculated by the formula:

$$\frac{A \times N}{15} - L$$

where:

A = One year's average of the remuneration for the last 3 years of service.

N = Number of complete years of service.

L = Any tax-free lump sum received or receivable under an approved superannuation scheme.

With regard to payments made on or after 1 December 1998, the basic exemption is £8,000/€10,160 together with £600/€765 for each complete year of service in the employment in respect of which the payment is made.

In addition, the basic exemption may be increased by an additional €10,000 with effect from 1 January 2002 in a case where an individual is not a member of an occupational pension scheme or irrevocably gives up his right to receive a lump sum from such a scheme. If an individual receives or is entitled to receive a pension lump sum, then the additional exemption is reduced by the amount of the pension lump sum. The additional exemption may be claimed by an individual every ten years and approval must be obtained from the Inspector of Taxes before it can be paid without the deduction of PAYE.

Tax payable on the termination payment is the lower of the following:

(i) Income tax calculated on the basis of treating the lump sum (after deducting the exempt amount as mentioned above) as extra income earned in the year of assessment in which retirement, etc occurs, or

(ii) Income tax calculated on the basis of taxing the lump sum payment (after deducting the exempt amount) at a rate obtained by dividing the total tax payable for the three years of assessment (for the tax years 2005 *et seq.*, previously five years) immediately prior to the year of retirement etc by the taxable income of those three years. The extra tax payable on this basis is expressed by the formula:

$$P \times \frac{T}{I}$$

where:

P = The lump sum payment after deduction of the exempt amount.

T = Tax liability on income of the previous three years of assessment.

I= Taxable income of the previous three years of assessment.

TCA97 s201A Section 19 Finance Act 2005 introduced new reporting requirements, with effect from 25 March 2005, in relation to payments made on death or on account of injury or disability. Where an exemption from taxes is claimed the person by whom the payment was made must deliver to the Inspector of Taxes, not later than 46 days after the end of the year of assessment in which a payment was made the following particulars:

(a) The name and address of the person to whom the payment was made.

(b) The PPS number of the person who received the payment.

(c) The amount of the payment.

(d) The basis on which the payment is not chargeable to tax indicating, in the case of a payment made on account of injury or disability the extent of the injury or disability as the case may be.

1.18.12 Retraining and Redundancy

TCA97 s201 Finance Act 2008 provides an additional exemption of up to €5,000 for each eligible employee, who has more than two years full time continuous service, where an employer bears the cost of retraining workers as part of a redundancy package.

The retraining must be designed to improve skills or knowledge used in obtaining employment or setting up a business and the course must be completed within six months of the employee being made redundant.

The exemption applies in respect of retraining made available on or after 13 March 2008. It will not apply to spouses or dependants of the employer, and the employees must avail of the retraining rather than receive cash.

1.18.13 Exemptions

The exemptions from the charge to tax under Schedule E are:

(a) Payments made in connection with the termination of an office or employment by the death of the holder or made on account of injury to or disability of the holder.

(b) Payments made in connection with restrictive covenants before 24 April 1992.

(c) Payments from pension schemes where the contribution by the employer was assessed as emoluments.

(d) Payments to approved pension schemes.

(e) Certain allowances to members of the Defence Forces.

(f) Allowances to widows of members of the British Armed Forces in respect of children.

(g) Allowances under certain Army Pension Acts.

(h) Childrens allowances under Social Welfare Acts.

(i) Payments to Commonwealth representatives.

(j) Payments to Consular representatives.

(k) Scholarship income. (A benefit in kind may arise in certain circumstances.)

(1) Statutory redundancy payments.

(m) Certain payments in respect of thalidomide children.

(n) Lump sum payments made to employees under certain company restructuring schemes involving agreed pay restructuring.

(o) Payments to certain officers of the State as compensation for the extra cost of having to live outside the State in order to perform his or her duties.

1.18.14 Interest on PAYE repayments

Under changes introduced in the Finance Act 2003 and brought into effect on 1 November 2003 interest is now payable on some categories of PAYE repayments as follows:

- Where the repayment arises because of a mistaken assumption of the law by Revenue interest will be due for the period commencing on the day after the end of the tax year to which the repayment relates and ending on the date on which the tax is repaid.

- Where the taxpayer has made a valid claim to a repayment of tax overpaid for whatever reason, interest will be due for the period commencing on the day which is six months after the date on which the valid claim is made and ending on the date on which the tax is repaid.

Taxpayers must have made claims for repayments to Revenue for any year from 1994/95 to 1999/00 incl. on or before 31 December 2004. A repayment claim for 2000/01 must have been made on or before 5 April 2005.

Claims made after 31 December 2004 must be made to the tax office within 4 years of the end of the tax year to which they refer.

1.18.15 PAYE – electronic and telephone communications

TCA97 Ch 6 Pt 38

Finance Act 2005 contained enabling legislation to facilitate the extension to PAYE taxpayers of Revenue On-Line Service (ROS) which will enable them to file returns electronically and to avail of a range of electronic self-service options in relation to their tax affairs. In addition, in the context of an enhanced telephony service, a limited number of the self-service options is also being made available to PAYE taxpayers through an automated telephone system.

PAYE taxpayers using the extended ROS system will have the following self-service options made available to them:

- Amending personal details, e.g., change of address;
- Amending tax credit details;
- Claiming additional tax credits;
- Re-allocating tax credits between employments;
- Re-allocating tax credits between spouses;
- Claiming repayments and making payments;
- Requesting balancing statements;
- Requesting forms and leaflets.

An automated telephonic self-service facility will enable PAYE taxpayers to order forms and leaflets and claim low risk tax credits.

Both the new electronic and telephone self-service will be available to PAYE taxpayers on a secure basis, 24 hours a day, 7 days a week.

The legislation also provides that the Revenue Commissioners may make automatic repayments of tax to PAYE taxpayers where they are satisfied on the basis of the information available to them that tax has been overpaid.

The normal requirement that claims for personal reliefs should be accompanied by a return of income, will, in general, not apply where the claim is in relation to a relief to be used in the operation of PAYE or is in relation to a repayment of tax deducted under PAYE.

The requirement that a claim to repayment of tax must be the subject of a valid claim is being eased in relation to tax deducted under PAYE. In future, the Revenue Commissioners will be able to make automatic repayments of tax deducted under PAYE where they are satisfied on the basis of the information in their possession that tax has been overpaid.

TCA97 s886A A statutory obligation similar to that which applies to taxpayers in relation to business records will apply to taxpayers wishing to make claims to tax reliefs to keep and preserve, for a minimum of 6 years, any supporting documentation. The obligation to keep and preserve documents can be satisfied by retention of the information in them. The Revenue Commissioners will be able to subject any claim to detailed examination within a 4 year period and may call for any necessary documentation (either the originals or photocopies), of which copies or extracts may be made.

Where a tax inspector, under Regulation 37 of the PAYE Regulations, decides to issue a statement of liability to an employee rather than raising an assessment, the statement is, where the inspector so directs and notifies the employee at the time, to be treated as if it were an assessment. The provisions of the Income Tax Acts relating to appeals against assessments and collection of the tax charged in an assessment will also apply to the statement.

1.19 Deeds of Covenant

TCA s792

A deed of covenant is a legal instrument by which a person binds himself to make periodic payments of income to another person. The advantage to be derived from such a deed is that it enables the covenanter to divest himself of part of his statutory income by transferring it to the covenantee.

Any amount can be paid under a deed of covenant, however only covenants in favour of certain individuals qualify for tax relief, provided the covenant is capable of lasting more than 6 years.

The covenanter's total income is reduced by the gross amount which he covenants to pay. The payments are made under deduction of tax at the standard rate, currently 20%. The covenantee is able to obtain the benefit of his personal reliefs and tax credits (to the extent that these are not covered by other income) against the income received under the covenant, and, depending upon the amount of the gross payment, receive a repayment of the tax deducted or obtain a tax credit available for offset against his liability.

It should be noted that any express power contained in the covenant which enables the covenanter to revoke the covenant of his own accord will deprive it of its effectiveness as a method of saving tax.

1.19.1 Covenants - in favour of individuals

The tax status of covenants following the restrictions imposed by Finance Act 1995 is set out below.

TCA s794

Minor Children

Covenants in favour of the covenanter's own minor children are ineffective for tax purposes.

Unrestricted tax relief can be claimed on covenants in favour of permanently incapacitated minors, other than from parents to their own minor incapacitated children. (A minor for this purpose is an unmarried individual under 18 years).

TCA97 s792

Covenants to adults (persons aged 18 or over)

- Unrestricted tax relief can be claimed on covenants in favour of permanently incapacitated adults.
- Tax relief can be claimed on covenants in favour of adults aged over 65, but the relief is restricted to 5% of the covenanter's total income, i.e., gross income less certain deductions such as expenses, capital allowances, etc.

1.19.2 Covenants – other than those in favour of individuals

Relief for covenants for the conduct of research, teaching of natural sciences, promotion of human rights and payments to universities and other approved bodies for research in, or teaching of, approved subjects was repealed by section 45 Finance Act 2001. Relief now applies under "Donations to Approved Bodies". (Please see paragraph 1.3.22)

1.20 Capital Allowances

Capital allowances are granted for "chargeable periods" – accounting periods in the case of companies liable to corporation tax and years of assessment in the case of other persons liable to income tax. All capital allowances are granted by reference to events occurring in an accounting period (companies) or in a basis period for a year of assessment (other persons).

1.20.1 Wear and tear allowance

(i) Plant and machinery

TCA97 s285 This is an allowance for the wear and tear of plant and machinery in use for the purpose of a trade, profession, vocation, or employment at the end of a basis or accounting period. The allowance is calculated by reference to the cost of the item less grants.

The rates of wear and tear allowance applying to plant and machinery are as follows:

Expenditure Incurred	Rate	Basis
Pre 01/01/01*		
Pre 01/01/01* **See earlier editions for more details*	15%	Straight Line
01/01/01 - 03/12/02	20%	Straight Line
04/12/02 onwards	12.5%**	Straight Line

***However, the 20% rate will apply in the case of plant and machinery acquired under the terms of a binding contract evidenced in writing before 4 December 2002 and in respect of which capital expenditure was incurred on or before 31 January 2003*

For chargeable periods ending on or after 1 January 2002, a taxpayer has the option to elect, that the tax written down value of capital expenditure incurred on plant and machinery and motor vehicles beforé 1 January 2001, be "pooled together" and be written off at 20% per annum on a straight line basis over the following five years.

The election is irrevocable and must be included in the tax return for the first chargeable period in which a claim is made on the "pooled" basis.

TCA97 s291 Plant and machinery includes computer software or the right to use such software for the purposes of a trade – see below.

(ii) Motor vehicles

TCA97 s373-s376 The rate of wear and tear allowances which is applied to motor vehicles other than cars in use in a taxi or car hire business, is as follows:

Expenditure Incurred	Rate	Basis
Pre 01/01/01	20%	Reducing Balance
01/01/01 - 03/12/02	20%	Straight Line
04/12/02 onwards	12.5%*	Straight Line

**However, the 20% rate will apply in the case of motor vehicles acquired under the terms of a binding contract evidenced in writing before 4 December 2002 and in respect of which capital expenditure was incurred before 31 January 2003.*

See above for "pooling" arrangement for tax written down value of expenditure incurred before 1 January 2001.

(a) Cars purchased before 1 July 2008

The wear and tear allowance on new and second hand cars purchased during accounting periods ending on or after 1 January 2007 for companies and income tax basis periods ending on or after 1 January 2007 for individuals, are computed as though the cars had cost €24,000, i.e., the "specified amount" (See Chart 7 for previous specified amounts).

(b) Cars purchased on or after 1 July 2008

TCA97 s380L Finance Act 2008 introduced a new scheme of capital allowances for business cars which seeks to limit the availability of allowances by reference to the carbon emission levels of cars. Cars are categorised by reference to carbon dioxide (CO_2) emissions as follows:

Category A Vehicles	Category B/C Vehicles	Category D/E Vehicles	Category F/G Vehicles
0 – 120 g/km	121 – 155g/km	156 – 190g/km	191g/km +

For cars in Categories A/B/C, the cost of the car for capital allowances purposes will be an amount equal to the specified amount, i.e., €24,000, regardless of the cost of the car.

For cars in Categories D/E the cost of the car for capital allowances purposes will be:

- 50% of the retail price of the car where that retail price is less than or equal to the specified amount (i.e., €24,000), or
- 50% of the specified amount (i.e., €24,000) where the retail price is greater than the specified amount.

No capital allowances are available for cars in categories F/G.

In the event of a disposal of a car on which capital allowances have been claimed under the new regime outlined above, appropriate adjustments will be required in the calculation of any balancing allowance/charge.

(iii) Taxis and cars on short term hire

The rate of wear and tear applying to taxis and cars on short term hire is 40% on a reducing balance basis. The restriction by reference to the cost of €24,000, i.e., the "specified amount" etc. does not apply to these cars.

1.20.2 Transmission capacity rights

TCA97 s769A - s769F Finance Act 2000 introduced a scheme of allowances for expenditure incurred on the purchase of long-term rights to use advanced communications infrastructure. Capital allowances are already available in respect of investments in the physical infrastructure such as cabling and equipment. The allowances will apply to long-term rights to use wired, radio or optical transmission paths for the transfer of data and information. These rights, known as indefeasible rights of use, typically span periods of 10 to 25 years. The legislation provides that expenditure incurred by a company on such rights can be written off over the life of the agreement relating to the use of the rights subject to a minimum write off period of 7 years. The normal balancing allowance/balancing charge provisions apply where there is a sale of part or all of the rights or where the rights otherwise come to an end. The allowances will apply to expenditure incurred on or after 1 April 2000.

However, any capital expenditure incurred on or after 6 February 2003 in respect of licences issued on or after that date by the Commission for Communications Regulation under:

(a) the Wireless Telegraphy Acts 1926 to 1988, or

(b) the Postal and Telecommunications Services Act 1983

will not be eligible for the allowance.

Finance Act 2003 also contains anti-avoidance provisions to prevent entitlement to the allowance being artificially created as respects sales of capacity rights within groups of companies where the allowance was not properly due.

1.20.3 Capital allowances for computer software

TCA97 s288 Finance Act 2000 introduced a number of changes to clarify the position relating to balancing allowances and charges in cases where a licence or right to use computer software is granted to another person but the computer software itself is retained by the person granting the licence or right to use. The legislation, in effect, treats the grant of a licence or right to use computer software and the computer software itself as two separate assets for capital allowances purposes.

The legislation provides that only a portion of the tax written down value of the original cost of developing or acquiring the computer software concerned is attributed to the software which remains undisposed of. Similar apportionment of the original capital expenditure incurred and of the allowances already made, before the grant of the licence or right to use, is provided for in the section.

1.20.4 Accelerated Capital Allowances for Energy-Efficient Equipment

TCA97 s285A Finance Act 2008 introduced a new scheme to provide accelerated capital allowances in respect of expenditure by companies on certain energy-efficient equipment bought for the purposes of the trade. The scheme is limited to companies and will come into operation by way of an Order to be made by the Minister for Finance following clearance under State aid rules. (Please see paragraph 2.14 for more details).

1.20.5 Balancing allowances and charges – plant and machinery

(i) General

TCA97 s288 Balancing allowances and/or charges may arise when one or more of the following events occur in a period:

(a) an item of plant and machinery on which initial or writing-down allowance was granted is sold (see earlier editions for meaning of initial allowance); or

(b) such an item ceases permanently to be used for the purposes of the trade or profession; or

(c) the trade or profession ceases.

TCA97 s289 Where the sale proceeds realised on an item are less than its written-down value a balancing allowance arises on the difference.

Where the sale proceeds exceed the written-down value a balancing charge arises on the difference. With effect from 1 January 2002, a balancing charge will not arise in respect of plant and machinery where the disposal proceeds is less than €2,000. This does not apply where the disposal is to a connected person.

The balancing charge cannot exceed the aggregate of initial and wear and tear allowances previously obtained on the item. For purposes of computing balancing allowances and charges, the treatment of grants obtained on the purchase of an item will depend on whether the grants were taken into account in calculating wear and tear and/or initial allowances in the first instance. Where the grants were ignored in the first instance, they are treated on disposal of the item as capital allowances obtained, and are deducted from the written-down value. The calculation of the balancing allowance or charge is made by reference to the resultant figure. In a case where this resultant figure is negative, it is administrative practice to confine the balancing charge to the amount of the sale proceeds arising on the disposal. In situations where the grants have been deducted in computing wear and tear and/or initial allowances, the written-down value will reflect the deduction and the balancing charge arising on the disposal will be confined to the amount of the sale proceeds. The overriding limit on the balancing charge continues to be the aggregate of initial and wear and tear allowances previously obtained on the item.

(ii) Transfers at written-down values

Subject to certain conditions items qualifying for capital allowances may be transferred for tax purposes at their tax written-down values. In this way no balancing allowance or charge arises on the transfer. In computing a balancing allowance or charge on a subsequent disposal by the transferee, the allowances claimed by the transferor are taken into account.

TCA97 s289(6)(A) With effect from 6 February 2003, the provision whereby a balancing charge can be postponed where plant and machinery is gifted or sold at an undervalue will not apply where the donor/transferor is not a company and the recipient/transferee is a company. However, where both parties are connected for the purposes of the Taxes Acts, the provision will continue to apply.

(iii) Withheld balancing charge

TCA97 s290 A taxpayer may, for tax purposes elect to reduce the cost of the replacement of an item by any balancing charge arising on the disposal of the item. When the replacement is disposed of, any balancing allowance or charge arising will take account of the balancing charge previously withheld.

1.20.6 Writing-down allowance – industrial buildings

TCA97 s272 This is an allowance granted to a person who at the end of a basis or accounting period holds the "relevant interest" in an industrial building (as defined) in use for the purpose of a trade carried on by him.

The allowance is granted with effect from 1 April 1992 at 4% per annum, of the capital expenditure incurred on the construction of industrial buildings exclusive of grants. (See Chart 40 for allowances claimable in earlier years and special rates applying to farm buildings and hotels.)

Where free depreciation had been claimed prior to 1 April 1992, the 4% allowance will be applied to the balance of expenditure not claimed by means of free depreciation.

A purchaser of a qualifying building may claim the allowance (where applicable) provided that the previous owner(s) does not claim allowances and it is acquired within one year of first use. However, the amount in respect of which allowances may be claimed depends on whether or not the seller is a person who carries on a trade of the construction of buildings.

Where the expenditure on the construction was incurred by a non-builder, the person who acquires the building is deemed to have incurred construction expenditure on the date the purchase price is payable equal to the lower of:

(a) the actual construction expenditure, or

(b) the net price (as defined) paid by him.

If the seller is a builder, allowances may be claimed on the net price which in effect includes part of the builder's profit.

The net price paid is:

$$B \times \frac{C}{C + D}$$

where:

B = the purchase price

C = the construction expenditure

D = the site cost

TCA97 s268 Expenditure incurred on or after 23 April 1996 on industrial buildings situated outside the State does not qualify for any allowances. Certain transitional provisions applied in the case of foreign hotel projects due for completion by 30 September 1998.

TCA97 s268 The allowance is extended to expenditure incurred on or after 25 January 1984 on laboratories used wholly or mainly for mineral analysis in connection with the exploration for, or the extraction of, minerals (including oil and natural gas).

1.20.7 Balancing allowances and charges – industrial buildings

TCA97 s274 In general these follow on the same lines as for plant and machinery. No balancing allowance or charge can arise as a result of any event occurring more than 50 years after the building was first used, where the expenditure on the building was incurred prior to 16 January 1975. Where the expenditure was incurred on or after 16 January 1975, the period is 25 years. In the case of hotels the period is 50 years for expenditure incurred in the period 30 September 1956 to 31 December 1959, 10 years in the period 1 January 1960 to 25 January 1994 and 7 years in the period 26 January 1994 to 4 December 2002 (subject to transitional arrangements which may extend the qualifying period to 31 July 2008). The period is 25 years for all subsequent periods.

No balancing allowances arise on the sale of an industrial building where the seller and buyer are connected with each other or it appears that the sole or main object of the transaction was to obtain the balancing allowance.

1.20.8 Lessors

TCA97 s403 In general lessors deriving income from the leasing of plant and machinery or industrial buildings are entitled to the same capital allowances as those who purchase and use such items in their own businesses.

Section 403 TCA 1997 provides for a leasing ring-fence, under which losses incurred in the leasing of plant or machinery may not be used to shelter non-leasing income. Under the section, leasing is regarded as a separate trade, and any losses arising from an excess of capital allowances over gross leasing receipts in that trade, may not be set off against non-leasing income. In addition to the general ring-fence in section 403, section 404 TCA 1997 applies a second ring-fence in respect of leases that do not have a broadly even spread of payments over the term of the lease, often referred to as "balloon" leases. Losses from such leases cannot be taken outside of the single lease. These rules were modified by Finance Act 2006 so as not to have an unduly adverse impact on companies that carry on a trade that consists primarily of leasing.

Finance Act 2006 provides that losses and capital allowances may be offset against a wider range of income. This will apply to a company if the activities of the company or group of which it is a member consist wholly or mainly of the leasing of plant or machinery, and not less than 90% of the activities of the company consist of a combination of leasing plant and machinery and providing loans to fund the purchase of, or providing leasing expertise in relation to, plant or machinery of the type of asset that it leases. Such a company will be allowed to set losses and capital allowances from leasing against income from such activities.

Finance Act 2006 ensures that the leasing of a master film negative is subject to the section 403 ring-fence.

Balloon leasing ring-fence

TCA97 s404 Finance Act 2006 made a number of changes to section 404.

Firstly, it provides that a lease denominated in a foreign currency that fails the requirement to have an even spread of lease payments by reason only of exchange rate fluctuations will not be subject to the ring-fence.

Secondly, the ring-fence is modified in the case of long-term leases so that losses and capital allowances on such assets may be setoff against income from other long-term leases and, in the case of a company whose trade consists primarily of leasing, against its income from leasing and activities related to leasing or against such income of a connected company.

Thirdly, it provides that the alteration of certain leases that are not currently subject to the ring-fence under section 404 will not result in the lease becoming subject to the ring-fence, so long as the alteration does not involve a delay of more than 20 years in any payment under the lease. In addition, the alteration will not affect the tax treatment of a defeasance payment under the lease unless it involves a reduction in a payment which is not a payment calculated by reference to interest rates.

Finally, it provides that a lease will not be subject to the section 404 ring-fence if:

- The lease is a lease of an asset with a useful life not exceeding eight years and the lease period does not exceed five years;
- Apart from the first accounting period, the cumulative amount of lease payments up to the end of any accounting period equates to annual payments of approximately one-eighth of the original value of the asset; and
- Capital allowances on the leased asset are calculated by reference to the amount of use of the asset in the accounting period concerned.

TCA97 s80A An alternative tax mechanism for lessors of short life assets under finance leases was introduced in Finance Act 2004.

Under normal rules, income of a lessor under a finance lease is calculated by treating gross lease payments (capital and interest) as income and allowing deduction for capital allowances on the asset. Where the lease period is less than eight years, a timing mismatch occurs.

The 2004 changes allow lessors of such assets to account for them for tax purposes in accordance with accounting rules. This will result in the "interest element" only of lease payments being taxed but no capital allowances being available. It will not change the amount of tax paid but will involve a more even spread of the tax over the lease period.

To avail of the new treatment, an election must be made when filing the CT1.

1.20.9 Anti-avoidance

TCA97 s289 There are anti-avoidance provisions designed to prevent the obtaining of a tax advantage through transactions in plant and machinery or industrial buildings carried out other than at arms length.

1.20.10 Expenditure on dredging

TCA97 s303 There are reliefs on expenditure incurred on or after 30 September 1956 on "the removal of anything forming part of or projecting from the bed of the sea or of any inland water". The expenditure must be for the purposes of a qualifying trade. The reliefs are.

Initial Allowance 10%

Annual Allowance 2%

1.20.11 Scientific research – capital/non-capital expenditure

TCA97 s764-s765 The full amount of the expenditure is deductible as a trade expense for the period in which the expenditure is incurred.

1.20.12 Expenditure on patent rights

TCA97 s755 Subject to certain restrictions an allowance of one-seventeenth of the cost is granted for the period in which the expenditure is incurred and for the 16 subsequent chargeable periods.

1.20.13 Know-how

TCA97 s768 Section 768 TCA 1997 provides a tax deduction for expenditure incurred on "know-how" acquired for use in a trade carried on by a person. The section defines "know-how" as "industrial information and techniques likely to assist in the manufacture or processing of goods or materials, or in the carrying out of any agricultural, forestry, fishing, mining or other extractive operations".

The relief does not apply where a person acquires know-how as part of the acquisition of a trade or where the buyers and sellers fail a common control test.

Finance Act 2008 introduced the following anti-avoidance provisions to ensure that section 768 TCA 1997 operates as intended:

(i) Relief under section 768 is not available where the know-how is bought as part of a trade that is being acquired. In order to ensure that this provision operates in the manner intended, the requirement is extended so as to deny relief where two connected persons work together to acquire a trade, with one person buying the know-how used in the trade and the other person buying the remainder of the trade.

(ii) The tax relief will be limited to the expenditure incurred wholly and exclusively on the acquisition of know-how for bona fide commercial reasons and not as part of a tax avoidance scheme.

(iii) Provision is made to facilitate the consultation by the Revenue Commissioners of "experts" to assist them in the evaluation of claims for expenditure on "know-how". Before disclosing any information to any person the identity of the expert and the information to be disclosed must be made known to the claimant. If the claimant demonstrates to Revenue (or on appeal to the Appeal Commissioners) that the expert could prejudice the person's trade, then no disclosure will be made.

The above provisions apply with effect for any chargeable period ending on or after 31 January 2008, or any accounting period of a company ending on or after 31 January 2008.

1.20.14 Multi-storey car parks

TCA97 s344 Certain capital allowances are available on expenditure incurred on the construction or refurbishment of certain multi-storey car parks, where the relevant local authority certifies that the car park has been developed in accordance with criteria laid down by the Minister for the Environment.

The initial qualifying period commenced on 1 July 1995 and ended on 30 June 1998. However, the expiry date was extended to 30 September 1999 where the local authority gave a certificate, in writing, before 30 September 1998, that not less than 15% of the total cost of the multi-storey car park (including site cost) had been incurred by 30 June 1998.

Further extensions were granted in respect of multi-storey car parks outside the county boroughs of Cork and Dublin as follows:

(a) An extension to 31 December 2002 where at least 15% of the total cost of the project was incurred on or before 30 September 2001 and a certificate to this effect has been issued by the relevant local authority on or before 31 December 2001, and

(b) An extension to 31 December 2004 where at least 15% of the total cost of the project was incurred on or before 30 September 2003 and a certificate to this effect has been issued by the relevant local authority on or before 31 December 2003.

This 31 December 2004 deadline was extended to 31 July 2006 by Finance Act 2004 and further extended to 31 December 2006 by Finance Act 2006.

The deadline is extended to 31 July 2008 where at least 15% of the construction expenditure (excluding site cost) is incurred by 31 December 2006.

The allowances available in respect of qualifying expenditure in 2007 and 2008 are restricted to 75% and 50% respectively.

The allowances available are:

Owner Occupier	Up to 50% Year 1
	Maximum 50%*
Lessors	Up to 25% Year 1
	2% Annual Allowance
	Maximum 50%*

**These allowances were increased from 50% to 100% with effect from 1 August 1998, in cases where double rent relief is not available (see below).*

For the purposes of double rent relief, the latest date for entering into qualifying leases in respect of multi-storey car parks was 31 July 1998. However, this deadline was extended to 30 September 1999 where 15% of the total cost of the project was incurred on or before 30 June 1998.

As double rent allowance is no longer available (apart from the cases referred to in the preceding paragraph) the capital allowances available in respect of multi-storey car parks has been increased from 50% to 100% with effect from 1 August 1998.

Where the double rent allowance is available on leases entered into after 31 July 1998, the maximum allowance remains at 50%.

In the case of refurbishment, capital allowances will be available only if the amount expended on the refurbishment equals at least 20% of the site-exclusive market value of the car park immediately before the refurbishment.

It should be noted that the relief for expenditure on multi-storey car parks is a "specified relief" under Chapter 2A TCA 1997, in the context of the limitation on the amount of certain relief used by certain high-income individuals - see paragraph 1.27.

1.20.15 Airports

TCA97 s268

Capital expenditure incurred on or after 27 March 1998, on buildings used for the management or operation of an airport, such as terminal buildings, etc., will qualify for an industrial buildings allowance of 4% per annum. The tax life of such buildings is 25 years.

Allowances are also available in respect of existing airport buildings or structures with effect from 27 March 1998, on a net figure based on the original cost less the amount of capital allowances that would have been granted had those buildings qualified before 27 March 1998.

1.20.16 Hotels

TCA97 s268, s272

Capital expenditure incurred between 27 January 1994 and 3 December 2002 on any building or structure in use as a hotel qualifies for an annual industrial buildings allowance of 15% for the first 6 years and 10% in year 7.

With regard to capital expenditure incurred on or after 4 December 2002, subject to transitional provisions (see paragraph below), the allowance is reduced to 4% per annum.

Finance Act 2006 extended the transitional provisions. As a consequence, where a valid application for full planning permission is lodged with the relevant planning authority on or before 31 December 2004, and the expenditure is incurred on the hotel on or before 31 December 2006, capital allowances under the old regime (15%, etc.) will be available. It is important to note that written confirmation must be obtained from the planning authority that the planning application was lodged by the due date.

Finance Act 2006 introduced additional transitional provisions extending the availability of allowances under the "old" seven-year regime to 31 July 2008 in certain circumstances. Where a planning application was lodged by 31 December 2004, a certificate has been obtained from the relevant local authority that at least 15% of the construction expenditure (excluding site cost) was incurred by 31 December 2006, and a binding contract was in place by 31 July 2006, the deadline date is extended to 31 July 2008. This is subject to the other conditions relating to State aid rules, etc. being satisfied.

It should be noted that the amount of qualifying expenditure used to determine allowances available is capped at the level of actual expenditure incurred to 31 December 2006 and projected expenditure to 31 July 2008, as set out in the application for certification to the local authority.

Furthermore, the allowances available in respect of qualifying expenditure in 2007 and 2008 are restricted to 75% and 50% respectively.

Finance Act 2005 introduced the requirement that in order to qualify for allowances as an industrial building a hotel must be registered on the register of hotels under the Tourist Traffic Act. This condition applies in respect of expenditure incurred on or after 3 February 2005. It is, however, subject to the transitional provisions as set out above which preserves the old regime up to 31 July 2008.

Where capital expenditure is incurred on a hotel on or after 20 March 2001, the hotel will not be treated as an industrial building for capital allowances purposes, where any part of the expenditure is met directly or indirectly by way of a grant from the State or any other assistance which is granted by or through the State, any board established by statute, any public or local authority or any other agency of the State.

Where capital expenditure is incurred on the construction or refurbishment of a hotel and the construction or refurbishment commences on or after 6 April 2001, the hotel will not be treated as an industrial building for capital allowances unless Bord Fáilte has received a declaration from the hotel owner as follows:

(i) whether or not that person is a small or medium-sized enterprise within the meaning of Annex I to Commission Regulation (EC) No. 70/2001 on the application of Articles 87 and 88 of the EC Treaty to State aid to SMEs, or whether or not that person is a micro, small or medium-sized enterprise within the meaning of the Annex to Commission recommendation of 6 May 2003.

(ii) the person has undertaken to furnish to the Minister for finance (or to another Government Minister, agency or body nominated for that purpose by the Minister for Finance) upon written request, such further information as may be necessary to enable compliance with the reporting requirements of that Regulation or any other regulation or Directive under the EC Treaty governing the granting of State aid.

(iii) Finally, in the context of expenditure incurred on or after 1 January 2003, if the project is subject to the reporting requirements of the multisectoral framework on regional aid for large investment projects dated either 7 April 1998 or 19 March

2002 then the Minister for Finance is obliged to obtain approval for the potential allowances involved from the EU Commission. These provisions will only apply in the context of projects of at least €50,000,000.

Prior to Finance Act 2005 there was a requirement that sufficient information be provided to Bord Fáilte to determine the classification under EU State Aid Rules. Finance Act 2005 requires hotel owners to operate a self assessment procedure in this regard.

It should be noted that the relief for expenditure on hotels is a "specified relief" under Chapter 2A TCA 1997, in the context of the limitation on the amount of certain relief used by certain high-income individuals - see paragraph 1.27.

1.20.17 Holiday camps, holiday cottages, guest houses and holiday hostels

TCA97 s272 Capital expenditure incurred between 27 January 1994 and 3 December 2002 on any building or structure in use as a holiday camp registered with Bord Fáilte qualifies for an annual industrial buildings allowance of 15% for the first 6 years and 10% in year 7.

With regard to capital expenditure incurred on or after 4 December 2002, subject to transitional provisions, the allowance is reduced to 4% per annum.

Finance Act 2005 introduced a requirement that in order for a holiday camp to qualify for allowances it must be registered in the register of holiday camps under the Tourist Traffic Acts.

Capital expenditure incurred on or before 3 December 2002 on a holiday cottage registered with Bord Fáilte qualifies for an allowance of 10% per annum. However, Finance Act 2003 provided that a registered holiday cottage is no longer to be regarded as a building in use for the trade of hotel-keeping. Accordingly, subject to transitional provisions, capital expenditure incurred on or after 4 December 2002 on registered holiday cottages will not qualify for any allowances.

Finance Act 2006 further amended the transitional provisions such that the old allowance regime (15%, etc.) continued to be available until 31 December 2006. The extension to 31 December 2006 was subject to the same planning criterion (i.e., application on or before 31 December 2004) referred to at 1.20.14 above in the context of hotels.

Finance Act 2006 introduced additional transitional provisions extending the availability of allowances for holiday cottages and holiday camps to 31 July 2008. The conditions to be satisfied and restrictions on the quantum of allowances available are the same as those applicable to hotels, as set out at 1.20.14 above.

Finance Act 2005 introduced entitlement to industrial buildings allowance for guest houses and holiday hostels. Allowances are available at the rate of 4%per annum in respect of expenditure incurred on or after 3 February 2005 and in order to qualify for allowances the guest house/holiday hostel must be registered under the Tourist Traffic Acts.

It should be noted that the relief for expenditure on holiday camps, holiday cottages, guest houses and holiday hostels is a "specified relief" under Chapter 2A TCA 1997, in the context of the limitation on the amount of certain relief used by certain high-income individuals – see paragraph 1.27.

1.20.18 Caravan and Camping Sites

TCA 1997 s268 s272, s274

Finance Act 2008 introduced capital allowances for caravan and camping sites. Allowances are available at the rate of 4% per annum in respect of expenditure incurred on or after 1 January 2008. In order to qualify there is a requirement for the caravan/camping site to be appropriately registered with Fáilte Ireland.

It should be noted that the relief for expenditure on caravan/ camping sites is a "specified relief" under Chapter 2A TCA 1997, in the context of the limitation on the amount of reliefs used by certain high income individuals – see paragraph 1.27.

1.20.19 Hotel room ownership scheme

TCA97 s409

Anti-avoidance legislation exists to counteract any room ownership schemes entered into in connection with a hotel investment by a hotel partnership, whereby the partners claim capital allowances on their investment in the hotel and at the end of the tax life of the hotel, each partner receives a room or suite in the hotel.

Capital allowances are denied in respect of an investment in a hotel, by a partnership, where a room ownership scheme is in existence. It applies to hotel investments, the capital expenditure in respect of which is incurred on or after 26 March 1997. Transitional provisions apply in cases where contracts were entered into or planning permission was received prior to 26 March 1997.

1.20.20 Shannon Corridor Capital Allowances Scheme

TCA97 s372AW–AZ

Finance Act 2007 introduced a new tax relief for investment along the Mid-Shannon region, between Lough Ree and Lough Derg, covering parts of Clare, Galway, Offaly, Roscommon, Tipperary and Westmeath.

The relief is aimed at promoting the tourism facilities of the area and applies to investment in registered holiday camps and tourism infrastructure facilities.

The tax relief applies to the cost of construction or refurbishment of a qualifying building or structure that is situated wholly within the qualifying area and which is incurred within a three-year period from the date of the Ministerial Order giving effect to the relief. For refurbishment projects to qualify for relief the refurbishment expenditure must amount to at least 20% of the market value of the building/structure (excluding the site value) immediately before the expenditure was incurred.

Relief will not be given in relation to any expenditure which is met by grant aid or BES funding or where relief is available under any other provision in the Taxes Acts.

The relief is available by way of capital allowances over a seven-year period (15% in years 1-6 and 10% in year 7). The relief available in the Clare and Tipperary regions is reduced to 80% of the expenditure otherwise allowable. The allowances are available for offset primarily against rental income with a maximum of €31,750 available per annum against other income. The claw-back period is 15 years.

The Minister for Arts, Sport and Tourism (in consultation with the Minister for Finance) will issue guidelines on the types of project that will qualify for the relief and a new Mid-Shannon Tourism Infrastructure Board ("the Board") will be set up by the Minister for Arts, Sport and Tourism to grant approvals to qualifying projects having regard to the criteria set out in the guidelines.

One of the main restrictions of the relief is that tax relief on accommodation buildings is capped at the lesser of the expenditure on non-accommodation buildings or 50% (or less if so provided in the guidelines) of the total project expenditure. Therefore, standalone accommodation buildings will not qualify for relief.

In addition, neither licensed premises (apart from licensed restaurants) nor buildings in which gambling or gaming is carried on for consideration will qualify for the relief. The usual denial of relief to property developers who hold the relevant interest applies where the property developer or a connected party builds the building. Finance Act 2008 extended this restriction to include persons connected with a property developer. This extended restriction applies for expenditure incurred on or after 1 January 2008.

In order to qualify for the relief it is necessary to apply for pre-approval in principle for the project, from the Board, within one year of the provisions taking effect. In addition, it is also necessary to obtain certification from the Board after the building is brought into use that it meets the criteria set out in the guidelines. Detailed information as regards the investment must also be provided to the Board in order to qualify for relief.

The scheme will be notified to the EU Commission under the new regional aid block exemption guidelines and will take effect by way of Ministerial Order. The Act provides that different effective dates may apply to different parts of the new provisions.

Finance Act 2008 introduced certain amendments to reflect changes in EU Guidelines on national aid. In addition, the Act provides for a restriction of allowances where the claimant is subject to " recovery proceedings" by the EU relating to a previous matter.

It should be noted that the relief for expenditure under the Shannon Corridor Scheme is a "specified relief" under Chapter 2A TCA 1997, in the context of the limitation on the amount of certain relief used by certain high-income individuals – see paragraph 1.27.

1.20.21 Nursing homes

TCA97 s268; s272; s274

Capital expenditure incurred on or after 3 December 1997, on the construction, extension or refurbishment of buildings used as private, registered nursing homes and on the conversion of an existing building into such a nursing home qualifies for capital allowances at the rate of 15% per annum for the first 6 years and 10% in year 7.

The nursing home must be registered with a health board under the Health (Nursing Homes) Act 1990.

For buildings first used prior to 1 February 2007, the tax life is 10 years, and allowances will be clawed back if the building ceases to be used as a qualifying nursing home. For buildings first used on or after 1 February 2007, the relevant holding period is 15 years.

The capital allowances are subject to the €31,750 limit per year which an individual passive investor can set-off against non-rental income (see 1.20.35).

It should be noted that the relief for expenditure on nursing homes is a "specified relief" under Chapter 2A TCA 1997, in the context of the limitation on the amount of certain relief used by certain high-income individuals – see paragraph 1.27.

1.20.22 Housing units for the aged or infirm

TCA97 s268; s272; s274

Capital expenditure incurred up to 30 April 2010 on the construction or refurbishment of housing units associated with a registered nursing home, qualifies for capital allowances.

Allowances are available at the rate of 15% per annum for the first six years and 10% in year 7. Allowances are available in respect of 100% of the qualifying expenditure incurred up to 24 March 2007. The allowances available in respect of qualifying expenditure incurred for the remainder of 2007 and to 31 August 2008 are restricted to 75% and 50% respectively.

Finance Act 2007 introduced new expenditure restrictions and extended the qualifying period to 30 April 2010 for contracts entered into on or after 1 May 2007.

The level of qualifying capital expenditure incurred between 1 May 2007 and 30 April 2010 is capped at 50 per cent for individuals and 75 per cent for companies.

The objective of the scheme is the provision of residential units for older people who wish to maintain their independent living status within a sheltered caring environment.

The main conditions applying to this scheme are as follows:

(i) The residential units must be operated or managed by a registered nursing home and the nursing home will provide back-up medical facilities (including nursing) to the occupants of the units when required, and an onsite caretaker will also be available.

(ii) There must be a minimum of 10 (20 prior to 4 February 2004) housing units within the site of the nursing home. The units must be single storey houses or comprised in a two-storey building. Finance Act 2004 allows the units to be comprised in a building of one or more storeys. The units and any building in which they are comprised must be designed and constructed to meet the needs of persons with disabilities, including in particular the needs of persons confined to wheelchairs. Each unit must contain one or two bedrooms, a kitchen, a living room, bath or shower facilities, toilet facilities and a nurse call system linked to the nursing home.

(iii) The units must be leased to those who are certified by a medical doctor to require such accommodation by virtue of old age or infirmity. Alternatively, where units are leased to nursing homes and let to individuals certified by a doctor, these units will qualify for relief.

(iv) There must be a day care centre on site, which complies with Health Board requirements (although any development cost of providing this centre will not qualify for capital allowances).

(v) Not less than 20 per cent of the residential units must be made available to the relevant Health Board, and the general rates charged must be discounted by at least 10% in the case of the Health Board tenants.

The capital allowances will not be granted where any part of the expenditure is met directly or indirectly by grant assistance from the State, any body established by statute, any public or local authority or any other agency of the State.

Finance Act 2007 introduced certain additional conditions for contracts entered into on or after 1 May 2007 as follows:

(a) Residents of the units must not be connected with the lessor.

(b) Residents may include a spouse of an aged or infirm person.

(c) Certification must be obtained from the HSE on first letting that the residential unit meets the various conditions.

(d) Investors are required to submit a report to the HSE on an annual basis throughout the 20 year tax life indicating occupancy levels and confirming that certain conditions continue to be satisfied.

For buildings first used prior to 1 February 2007, the tax life is 10 years and allowances will be clawed back if the building ceases to be used as a qualifying building. For buildings first used on or after 1 February 2007, the relevant holding period is 15 years. For units relating to build/refurbishment contracts entered into on or after 1 May 2007 the tax life is extended to 20 years.

The capital allowances are subject to the €31,750 limit per year which an individual passive investor can set-off against non-rental income (see 1.20.35).

It should be noted that the relief for expenditure on housing units for the aged or infirm is a "specified relief" under Chapter 2A TCA 1997, in the context of the limitation on the amount of certain relief used by certain high-income individuals – see paragraph 1.27.

1.20.23 Private convalescent facilities

TCA97 s268; s272; s274

Capital expenditure incurred on or after 2 December 1998 on the construction, extension and refurbishment of a private convalescent facility qualifies for capital allowances at the rate of 15% per annum for the first 6 years and 10% in year 7.

The allowances also apply to expenditure incurred on the conversion of an existing building into a private convalescent facility.

The facilities are to be used as an alternative to hospital care for patients recovering from acute hospital treatment and must be approved by the relevant health board. Such approval will be subject to meeting certain requirements of the Health (Nursing Homes) Act 1990.

For buildings first used prior to 1 February 2007, the tax life is 10 years and allowances will be clawed back if the building ceases to be used as a qualifying convalescent facility. For buildings first used on or after 1 February 2007, the relevant holding period is 15 years.

The capital allowances are subject to the €31,750 limit per year which an individual passive investor can set-off against non-rental income (see 1.20.35).

It should be noted that the relief for expenditure on private convalescent facilities is a "specified relief" under Chapter 2A TCA 1997, in the context of the limitation on the amount of certain relief used by certain high-income individuals – see paragraph 1.27.

1.20.24 Childcare facilities

TCA97 s843A

Capital expenditure incurred on or after 2 December 1998, on the construction, extension and refurbishment of a building or part of a building used as a childcare facility qualifies for capital allowances at the rate of 15% per annum for the first 6 years and 10% in year 7.

Accelerated capital allowances, by way of initial allowance and accelerated writing down allowances (free depreciation), are available in respect of expenditure incurred on or after 1 December 1999. Property developers are (in certain circumstances) excluded from claiming the accelerated allowances. Finance Act 2008 extended this restriction to include persons connected with a property developer. This extended restriction applies for expenditure incurred on and after 1 January 2008.

The allowances also apply to expenditure incurred on the conversion of an existing building or part of a building for use as a childcare facility.

The premises must meet the required standards for such premises as provided in the Childcare Act 1991 and must be in use for the purpose of providing:

(i) A pre-school service, or

(ii) A pre-school service and a day care or other service to cater for children other than pre-school children.

The premises must not include any part of a building or structure in use as, or as part of a dwelling-house.

For buildings first used prior to 1 February 2007, the tax life is 10 years and allowances will be clawed back if the building ceases to be used as a qualifying childcare facility. For buildings first used on or after 1 February 2007, the relevant holding period is 15 years.

The capital allowances are subject to the €31,750 limit per year which an individual passive investor can set-off against non-rental income (see 1.20.35).

It should be noted that the relief for expenditure on childcare facilities is a "specified relief" under Chapter 2A TCA 1997, in the context of the limitation on the amount of certain relief used by certain high-income individuals - see paragraph 1.27.

1.20.25 Student accommodation

TCA97 s372AM Capital expenditure incurred in the period between 1 April 1999 and 31 December 2004 on the construction, conversion or refurbishment of rented residential accommodation for third level students, qualifies for "section 23" type relief.

Finance Act 2006 provided for an extension of the deadline date to 31 December 2006. In order to qualify for this extension a valid application for full planning permission must be made to the relevant planning authority on or before 31 December 2004.

Finance Act 2006 extended the qualifying period from the 31 December 2006 date above to 31 July 2008 in certain circumstances. Where the 31 December 2004 planning application requirement is satisfied and at least 15% of the construction expenditure (excluding site costs) is incurred by 31 December 2006, the deadline is extended to 31 July 2008.

The allowances available in respect of qualifying expenditure in 2007 and 2008 are restricted to 75% and 50% respectively.

The relief provides for a deduction of 100% of the construction, conversion or refurbishment expenditure, which may be off-set against all Irish rental income – whether derived from the premises in question or from other lettings.

The buildings must conform with guidelines issued by the Minister for Education and Science. These guidelines deal with various features of the scheme, including the institutions which qualify, conditions relating to the standards and location of accommodation and the categories of students whose accommodation will be covered.

The accommodation must be provided within an 8km radius of the main campus and must be approved by the relevant college.

Subject to transitional provisions, the Finance Act 2003 provided that the following three conditions must also be satisfied as respects expenditure incurred on or after 18 July 2002, in order for a building to be treated as qualifying student accommodation for the purpose of this relief:

(i) All the rent payable in respect of the letting of the house during the 10-year holding period for the relief must be paid to the investor. No other person must receive or be entitled to receive that rent or any part of that rent. Where the expenditure on the provision of the house is incurred by two or more investors, the share of the rent received by each investor must bear the same proportion to the total rent as the expenditure incurred by that investor on the provision of the house bears to the total expenditure incurred on such provision by all the investors.

(ii) Where borrowed money is used by an investor to fund the provision of the house, that money must be borrowed from a financial institution (and no other person). The investor must be personally responsible for the repayment of the loan, the payment of interest on the loan and the provision of any security required in relation to the loan. In addition, there must be no arrangement or agreement, whether or not known to the lender, whereby some other person agrees to be responsible for the obligations of the investor in relation to the loan.

(iii) Where the investor is claiming a tax deduction for management or letting fees payable in relation to the letting of the house, those fees must be bona fide fees which reflect the level and extent of the services provided and must not exceed an amount equal to 15% of the rent from the letting of the house.

There will be a clawback of allowances where the premises are sold within 10 years and a subsequent purchaser can claim the original allowances on a premises where a claw-back arises.

It should be noted that the relief for expenditure on student accommodation is a "specified relief" under Chapter 2A TCA 1997, in the context of the limitation on the amount of certain relief used by certain high-income individuals - see paragraph 1.27.

1.20.26 Third-level institutions

TCA97 s843 Capital expenditure incurred on construction of certain buildings ("qualifying premises" as defined) used for the purposes of third level education and the provision of machinery and plant qualifies for capital allowances, subject to certain conditions.

The premises must be in use for the purposes of third level education provided by an "approved institution" (as defined) and must be let to that institution. In addition, the approved institution must have raised at least 50% of the cost of the total expenditure before construction begins, and that expenditure must be approved by the Minister for Education with the consent of the Minister for Finance.

Allowances also apply to projects funded by the Research and Development Fund announced by the Minister for Education and Science in November 1998.

Allowances are granted at the rate of 15% per annum for the first 6 years and 10% in year 7 and may be claimed in respect of expenditure incurred between 1 July 1997 and 31 December 2006.

Finance Act 2006 extended the availability of allowances for expenditure incurred up to 31 July 2008 in certain circumstances. Provided the application for a certificate was made to the Minister for Finance by 31 December 2004 and at least 15% of the qualifying construction expenditure (excluding site cost) is incurred by 31 December 2006, the deadline date is extended to 31 July 2008.

The allowances available in respect of qualifying expenditure in 2007 and 2008 are restricted to 75% and 50% respectively.

No balancing charge will arise after seven years from the period when the premises were first used.

The capital allowances are subject to the €31,750 limit per year which an individual passive investor can set-off against non-rental income (see 1.20.35).

Prior to Finance Act 2005 the Minister for Finance was precluded from issuing after 31 December 2004 a certificate that a project conformed to the conditions of the section. Finance Act 2005 ensures that the Minister can issue such a certificate where an application had been received on or before 31 December, 2004.

It should be noted that the relief for expenditure on third-level institutions is a "specified relief" under Chapter 2A TCA 1997, in the context of the limitation on the amount of certain relief used by certain high-income individuals - see paragraph 1.27.

1.20.27 Private hospitals

TCA97 s268, s272, s274

Capital allowances may be claimed on expenditure incurred on or after 15 May 2002 on the construction or refurbishment of buildings used as private hospitals.

In order to qualify for the allowances, the hospital must meet certain conditions, the principal ones being:

(i) it must have the capacity to afford medical or surgical services all year round

(ii) it must provide a minimum of 70 in-patients beds, out-patients services, operating theatres and on site diagnostic and therapeutic services and have facilities to provide at least five specialist services ranging from accident and emergency to oncology and cardiology, etc. Finance Act 2006 extended the range of services to include mental health services.

(iii) 20% of the bed capacity must be available for public patients and it must provide a discount of at least 10% to the State in respect of fees charged to public patients.

(iv) Rooms used exclusively for the assessment or treatment of patients (but not consultant's room or offices) will qualify for the capital allowances

Capital allowances are available at 15% per annum for the first 6 years and 10% in year 7.

The allowances will be subject to a clawback if the building is sold or ceases to be a qualifying private hospital within 10 years.

Finance Act 2006 introduced a number of changes for hospitals first brought into use on or after 1 February 2007, including an extension of the holding period from 10 to 15 years. In addition, there is a requirement to provide certain details regarding the project e.g., amount of the capital expenditure, investor details, etc. to the Health Service Executive to facilitate an evaluation of the project.

Prior to Finance Act 2006, there was a requirement that the Health Service Executive provide annual certification for the seven-year period during which allowances are claimed. This has been extended to 10 years for existing hospitals and 15 years for those that are first used on or after 1 February 2007.

Finance Act 2003, extended the scheme of allowances available for private hospitals to hospitals providing acute services on a day-case basis, with effect from 28 March 2003.

To qualify, a day hospital must provide a minimum of 40 day-case beds as well as meeting all the other requirements applicable to private hospitals.

A hospital will not qualify for capital allowances where the "relevant interest" in the capital expenditure incurred on the construction is held by:

(i) A company,

(ii) The trustees of a trust,

(iii) An individual who is involved in the management of the hospital as either an employee or director or in any other capacity, or

(iv) A property developer where either the property developer or a connected person incurred capital expenditure on the building. Finance Act 2008 extended the construction to include persons connected with the property developer. This extended restriction applies for expenditure incurred on or after 1 January 2008.

The above will apply whether the relevant interest is held solely by any of the above persons or jointly or in partnership with another person or persons.

Up until 30 April 2004 a property was excluded from qualifying for capital allowances if any member of a group of investors fell within an excluded category of person.

Finance Act 2004 provided that with effect from 1 May 2004 it is only the excluded person within the investor group who will not be entitled to capital allowances while all other members of such a group will continue to qualify for capital allowances.

The capital allowances are subject to the €31,750 limit per year which an individual private investor can set off against non-rental income (see 1.20.35).

It should be noted that the relief for expenditure on private hospitals is a "specified relief" under Chapter 2A TCA 1997, in the context of the limitation on the amount of certain relief used by certain high-income individuals – see paragraph 1.27.

1.20.28 Mental health centres

TCA97 s268, s272, s274

Finance Act 2006 introduced a scheme of capital allowances for mental health centres on broadly the same terms as for private hospitals. To qualify, the centre must have a minimum of 20 in-patient beds and make available 20% of its capacity annually for the treatment of public patients.

Allowances are available at 15% per annum for the first six years and 10% in year 7. Allowances will be clawedback if the building is sold or ceases to be used as a qualifying mental health centre within 15 years.

It should be noted that the relief for expenditure on mental health centres is a "specified relief" under Chapter 2A TCA 1997, in the context of the limitation on the amount of certain relief used by certain high-income individuals – see paragraph 1.27.

1.20.29 Palliative Care Units

TCA97 s268 s272, s274

Finance Act 2008 introduced a scheme of capital allowances for palliative care units, broadly on the same terms as for private hospitals and mental health centres (see paragraph's 1.20.27 and 1.20.28 above). To qualify, the unit must be regarded as a hospital or hospice within the meaning of the Public Health (Tobacco) Act 2002 or other similar facility mainly involved in palliative care. The unit must have a minimum of twenty in-patient beds and make available 20% of its capacity annually for the treatment of public patient.

Allowances are available at 15% p.a. for the first six years and 10% in year seven. Allowances will be clawed back if the building is sold or ceases to be used as a qualifying specialist palliative care unit within 15 years.

It should be noted that the relief for expenditure on specialist palliative care units is a "specified relief" under Chapter 2A TCA 1997, in the context of the limitation on the amount of reliefs used by certain high income individuals.

1.20.30 Sports injury clinics

TCA97, s268, s272, s274

Capital expenditure incurred on the construction or refurbishment of buildings used as qualifying private sports injury clinics qualifies for capital allowances at the rate of 15% per annum for the first 6 years and 10% in year seven.

The qualifying period expires on 31 December 2006, subject to some transitional provisions introduced in Finance Act 2006. Where at least 15% of the construction expenditure (excluding site cost) is incurred by 31 December 2006, the deadline is extended to 31 July 2008.

The allowances available in respect of qualifying expenditure in 2007 and 2008 are restricted to 75% and 50% respectively.

In order to qualify for the allowances the following conditions must be met by the clinic:

(i) It does not provide healthcare services to a person pursuant to his or her entitlements under the Health Act 1970.

(ii) It is one in which the sole or main business carried on is the provision, by or under the control of medical or surgical specialists, of healthcare consisting of the diagnosis, alleviation and treatment of physical injuries sustained by persons in participating, or in training for participation, in athletic games or sports.

(iii) It has the capacity to provide day-patient, in-patient and out-patient medical and surgical services and in-patient accommodation of not less than 20 beds.

(iv) It contains an operating theatre or theatres and related on-site diagnostic and therapeutic facilities.

(v) It undertakes to the Health Board (in whose functional area it is situated)

(a) to make available 20% of its capacity annually for the treatment of public patients, and

(b) that the fees to be charged in respect of the treatment afforded to any such person should not be more than 90% of the fees to be charged in respect of similar treatment afforded to a person who has private medical insurance.

(vi) The Health Board must issue a certificate in writing each year for seven years stating that it is satisfied that the medical clinic complies with the conditions set out above. Finance Act 2006 extended the requirements to obtain HSE Certification from 7 to 10 years.

Rooms used exclusively in the clinic for the purpose of the assessment and treatment (but not consultant's rooms) qualify for the allowance.

A clinic will not qualify for the allowances where the "relevant interest" in the capital expenditure incurred in its construction or refurbishment is held by:

(i) a company;

(ii) the trustees of a trust;

(iii) an individual who is involved in the operation or management of the clinic concerned either as an employee or director or in any other capacity; or

(iv) a property developer where either such property developer or a person connected with him or her incurs the capital expenditure on the clinic.

The above will apply whether the relevant interest is held solely by any of the above persons or jointly or in partnership with another person or persons.

Up until 30 April 2004 a property was excluded from qualifying for capital allowances if any member of a group of investors fell within an excluded catagory of person.

Finance Act 2004 provided that with effect from 1 May 2004 it is only the excluded person within the investor group who will not be entitled to capital allowances while all other members of such a group will continue to qualify for capital allowances.

The tax life of qualifying clinics is 10 years and allowances will be clawed back if the building is sold or ceases to be a qualifying clinic within 10 years.

The capital allowances are subject to the €31,750 limit per year which an individual passive investor can set off against non-rental income (see 1.20.35).

It should be noted that the relief for expenditure on sports injury clinics is a "specified relief" under Chapter 2A TCA 1997, in the context of the limitation on the amount of certain relief used by certain high-income individuals – see paragraph 1.27.

1.20.31 Park-and-ride facilities

TCA97 s372

Various capital allowances are available in respect of qualifying expenditure incurred on park-and-ride facilities in the larger urban areas.

Park-and-ride facilities are defined as a building or structure served by a bus or train service with the purpose of providing, for members of the public intending to continue a journey by bus or rail without preference for any particular class of person and on payment of an appropriate charge, parking space for mechanically propelled vehicles. It also includes any area under, over or immediately adjoining any qualifying park-and-ride facility.

The scheme is subject to guidelines issued by the Minister for the Environment and Local Government. The local authorities empowered to certify areas for park-and-ride facilities are, Cork, Dublin, Galway, Limerick and Waterford Corporations, Dun Laoghaire/Rathdown, Fingal, Kildare, South Dublin and Wicklow County Councils and the Urban District Councils in Kildare, Meath and Wicklow.

The qualifying period is from 1 July 1999 to 31 December 2006. In order to qualify for the cut-off date of 31 December 2006 referred to above it is necessary that a valid application for full planning permission is lodged on or before 31 December 2004. Otherwise, the cut-off date for incurring qualifying expenditure is 31 December 2004.

Finance Act 2006 extended the qualifying period to 31 July 2008 in certain circumstances. Where the 31 December 2004 planning application requirement is satisfied and at least 15% of the construction expenditure (excluding site costs) is incurred by 31 December 2006, the deadline is extended to 31 July 2008.

The allowances available in respect of qualifying expenditure in 2007 and 2008 are restricted to 75% and 50% respectively.

The allowances available are as follows:

(a) Park-and-ride facilities

Expenditure incurred on the construction or refurbishment of qualifying park-and-ride facilities, qualifies for the following allowances:

Owner Occupier	100% Free Depreciation or 50% Initial Allowance 4% Annual Allowance Maximum 100%
Lessor	50% Initial Allowance 4% Annual Allowance Maximum 100%

In the case of refurbishment expenditure, the allowances are available only if the expenditure is not less than 10% of the value of the premises before refurbishment.

Where the local authority is unable to give the required certification for a qualifying park-and-ride facility due to a delay in the provision of the public transport element, then the availability of the capital allowances may be suspended until the public transport element is in place and the development is certified.

With regard to expenditure incurred on or after 7 February 2002, a property developer may not avail of capital allowances in relation to a park-and-ride facility or a commercial premises within the site of a park-and-ride facility.

The tax life of such facilities is 13 years.

(b) Commercial Premises

Expenditure incurred on the construction or refurbishment of certain commercial premises located on the site of a park-and-ride facility qualifies for the same allowances as shown above for park-and-ride facilities.

The definition of commercial premises is restricted to premises in use for the purposes of retailing of goods or the provision of services only within the State. Specifically excluded are buildings or structures in use as offices or for the provision of mail order or financial services.

However, the total amount of capital expenditure which qualifies for allowances is restricted, so that, only expenditure which, when combined with expenditure on any residential accommodation at a park-and-ride facility, does not exceed 50% of the total allowable expenditure at the facility, will qualify for relief.

(c) Rented residential accommodation

Expenditure incurred on the construction of certain rented residential accommodation located on the site of a park-and-ride facility qualifies for "section 23" (see 1.12.4) type relief. The relief is a deduction of 10% of the construction expenditures against all rental income whether it arises from the premises in question or from other lettings.

There is an overall limit on the amount of expenditure which will qualify for this relief, so that, only expenditure which, when combined with any expenditure on owner-occupier accommodation at a park-and-ride facility, does not exceed 25% of total allowable expenditure at the facility, will qualify for relief.

(d) **Owner-occupied residential premises**

Relief is available for expenditure incurred on the construction of owner-occupied residential accommodation located on the site of a park-and-ride facility.

A deduction of 5% of the expenditure incurred may be claimed by the owner occupier as a deduction from total income, for 10 years provided the dwelling is the sole or main residence of the individual.

There is an overall limit on the amount of expenditure which will qualify for this relief, so that, only expenditure which, when combined with any expenditure on "section 23" accommodation at a park-and-ride facility, does not exceed 25% of the total allowable expenditure at the facility, will qualify for relief.

It should be noted that the relief for expenditure on park-and-ride facilities is a "specified relief" under Chapter 2A TCA 1997, in the context of the limitation on the amount of certain relief used by certain high-income individuals – see paragraph 1.27.

1.20.32 Significant buildings and gardens

TCA97 s482

Relief from income tax is available to the owner or occupier of an "approved building" for certain expenditure incurred on or after 6 April 1982 on the repair, maintenance or restoration of that building or garden. The relief is allowed by treating the expenditure as if it were a loss in a separate trade carried on by the owner or occupier, and relief may be claimed under the normal sections applying to an individual who has incurred a Case I or Case II of Schedule D loss. For the tax years 1995/96 *et seq*. any unutilised portion of the "loss" may be carried forward for a period of up to two years.

Finance Act 2002 inserted a new section, section 409C into the TCA 1997 for the purpose of restricting the use, by passive investors, of relief under section 482 TCA 1997 (see below).

An Approved Building is defined as a building within the State which is determined:

(i) by the Commissioners of Public Works in Ireland, to be a building which is intrinsically of significant scientific, historical, architectural or aesthetic interest, and

(ii) by the Revenue Commissioners to be a building to which reasonable access is afforded to the public.

The question of reasonable access is decided in each individual case, however the following are the minimum requirements:

(i) access to the whole or a substantial part of the building is allowed at the same time;

(ii) access is allowed annually for 60 days (of which 40 days must be in the period from 1 May to 30 September and 10 of these 40 must be at weekends) in a reasonable manner and at reasonable times for periods at least averaging 4 hours a day;

(iii) the charge levied (if any) is reasonable;

(iv) the dates and opening hours applicable are advertised to the satisfaction of the Revenue Commissioners;

(v) authorised officers of the Revenue Commissioners have the power to make unannounced visits to ensure that the requirement of reasonable access to the property for the public is being met.

Relief will not be granted in respect of expenditure incurred in a chargeable period beginning on or after 23 May 1994 unless the claimant can prove that he/she has provided Bord Fáilte with the details of the dates and times which the building is open to the public by 1 November in:

(a) the chargeable period for which the claim is made, and

(b) in each of the five chargeable periods immediately preceding the chargeable period in which the claim is made or if shorter, each of the chargeable periods since 23 May 1994.

This information must be given to Bord Fáilte on the understanding that it may be published for the promotion of tourism.

Relief will not be granted for any chargeable period prior to the one in which the application for approval of the building is made to the Revenue Commissioners.

Relief is only allowed for expenditure not already relieved under any other provisions of the taxes acts, or reimbursed to the individual by a grant or other means. Either the Office of Public Works or the Revenue Commissioners may withdraw their determinations at any time if they feel the building ceases to qualify, which may give rise to a claw-back of relief granted in the five-year period prior to revocation.

The relief also applies to:

(i) expenditure incurred on or after 6 April 1993, on the cost of maintenance or restoration of an "approved garden". An approved garden is a garden, not attached to an approved building, which has been determined to be of significant horticultural, scientific, historical, architectural or aesthetic interest.

Where expenditure was incurred before the tax year 1997/98 in relation to an approved garden, in order to qualify for the relief, it must have been incurred by the person who owned or occupied the garden.

(ii) buildings which are in use as tourist accommodation facilities for at least six months in any calendar year, of which four months must be in the period 1 May to 30 September. To qualify the building must be approved by Bord Fáilte as a guest house and the Board must be notified of the opening times of the guest house.

(iii) expenditure of up to an aggregate of €6,350 p.a. on:

   (a) the repair, maintenance or restoration of an "approved object", in an approved building or garden subject to the objects being on display in the approved building or garden for a period of at least two years from the year in which the relief for the contents is claimed.

   (b) the installation, maintenance or replacement of a security alarm system, and

   (c) the provision of public liability insurance for an approved building or garden.

An approved object is an object (including a picture, sculpture, book, manuscript, piece of jewellery, furniture or other similar object) or a scientific collection which is owned by the owner or occupier of the approved building.

Relief for a chargeable period in respect of expenditure incurred on or after 12 February 1998 will be limited to the amount of that expenditure attributable to the actual work carried out during that chargeable period.

TCA97 s409C Subject to certain transitional arrangements an individual, who as a result of participating in a passive investment scheme, claims relief under section 482 as owner of such a building, will be limited to €31,750 in the amount by which he or she can reduce his or her taxable income. Broadly, a passive investment scheme is defined as an arrangement under which:

(i) A person (who will make a claim under section 482 as owner) takes an interest in a building from its original owner;

(ii) at that time, or in the next five years, the building is determined to be an approved building for the purposes of section 482; and

(iii) the arrangements are such that the original owner has influence over how expenditure on the building is to be incurred; or, the original owner is entitled to participate in the tax benefits; or the original owner may reacquire the interest.

It should be noted that the relief for expenditure on significant buildings and gardens is a "specified relief" under Chapter 2A TCA

1997, in the context of the limitation on the amount of certain relief used by certain high-income individuals – see paragraph 1.27.

1.20.33 Contributions to capital expenditure of local authorities

TCA97 s310 Capital allowances may be claimed by a person carrying on a trade in respect of capital sums contributed to a local authority, towards the cost of certain expenditure under an approved trade effluence scheme.

In addition, capital allowances may also be claimed in respect of contributions made to a local authority on or after 15 February 2001 for the purpose of funding new water supply infrastructures.

The allowances available may be either wear and tear or industrial buildings allowances and are granted as if the trader had incurred the capital expenditure himself/herself in the course of his/her trade.

This provision was subject to EU approval and a Ministerial Commencement Order and it came into effect on 22 October 2001.

1.20.34 Public service vehicles – taxis

TCA97 s286A Capital allowances may be claimed on expenditure incurred on the cost of taxi licences acquired on or before 21 November 2000.

The allowances are effectively backdated with the cost being deemed to have been incurred on 21 November 1997 where the licence was purchased prior to that date. Where the licence was purchased after that date, it is deemed to have been incurred on the date on which the trade commenced.

The allowance is a wear and tear allowance of 20% per annum over five years and is allowed against the trading income of the licence owner who drives the associated taxi.

The allowance cannot be claimed where the licence-owner rents out the licence and associated vehicle to another person, except in the case where a licence owner who operates a taxi trade involving the driving of the taxi also receives income from renting the licence and the associated vehicle on a part-time basis. In this case the cost will be allowed against both the trading and the rental income from the vehicle in question. Where more than one licenced vehicle is operated in such a manner, the capital allowances will only be available in respect of the cost of a licence relating to one vehicle. The capital allowances may not be utilised to reduce any other income of the licence holder in the event that the trading and rental income from operating the licences is insufficient to absorb the available capital allowances.

Where a licence is inherited from a deceased spouse who carried on a taxi trade, the licence holder may offset the capital expenditure incurred on the original acquisition of the licence against the rental income arising from the licence, even if there is no trading income from the licence.

Where inheritance tax or probate tax was paid in respect of a taxi licence, the value used for such tax purposes may be used instead of the actual capital expenditure cost, if that value is higher.

1.20.35 Restriction of capital allowances/losses

(a) General

TCA97 s409A; s409B

In the case of passive investors, the amount of capital allowances on qualifying buildings which can be set off against non-rental income, is restricted to €31,750 in a full tax year. There is no restriction on the amount which can set off against rental income. The restriction does not apply to companies, owner operators and active partners.

In the case of a partnership, where an individual is not an active partner and capital allowances have been used under section 392, to create or augment a loss in the partnership, the amount of the loss which may be set against other income is based on the formula:

A + €31,750

where

A = the amount of profits or gains of the individual trade in the year of loss before the capital allowances are taken into account.

Where an individual is a partner in two or more partnership trades, then those partnership trades in which he is not an active partner are deemed to be a single partnership trade.

The restriction applies to all types of commercial premises, including multi-storey car parks, which attract capital allowances under the various existing tax incentive schemes and the proposed new Urban and Rural Renewal Scheme.

Capital allowances on hotels are ring fenced and may be set off only against rental income in the case of individual investors. This restriction does not apply to owner operators or companies, or to certain hotels located in counties Cavan, Donegal, Leitrim, Mayo, Monaghan, Roscommon or Sligo.

Transitional arrangements have been provided for where certain commitments were made prior to 3 December 1997. Accordingly the restrictions outlined above will not apply where before 3 December 1997:

(i) In the case of construction, the foundation of the building was laid in its entirety;

(ii) In the case of refurbishment, work up to the value of 5 per cent of the total cost of the refurbishment was carried out;

(iii) The building was provided for the purposes of a project approved for grant assistance by an industrial development agency within a period of two years ending on 3 December 1997;

(iv) An application for planning permission on the building had been received by a planning authority before 3 December 1997;

(v) The individual can prove to the Revenue Commissioners that a detailed plan had been prepared and that discussions had taken place with the planning authority before 3 December 1997 and that this can be supported by an affidavit or statutory declaration by the planning authority and the expenditure is incurred by the person entitled to the capital allowances under an obligation entered into before 3 December 1997 or before 1 May 1998 pursuant to negotiations which were in progress before 3 December 1997;

(vi) Obligations will be treated as having been entered into before 3 December 1997 only if there was an existing and binding contract, in writing, under which the obligation arose;

(vii) Negotiations pursuant to which the obligation was entered into shall not be regarded as having been in progress unless preliminary commitments or agreements in writing, were entered into before that date.

See paragraph 4.1.7 in relation to restrictions applying in the case of both limited and general partnerships.

TCA97 s407

(b) Shipping Trades

Section 407 restricts the set-off of losses and capital allowances arising in respect of a shipping trade against non-shipping income, and as respects leasing, ensures that where a ship is leased for use in a shipping trade the capital allowances in respect of that ship can only be set against the income arising under that lease but not against other leasing income. The ring-fence on the use of losses and capital allowances in qualifying shipping trades applies until 31 December 2010.

1.21 Farming Taxation

TCA97 s654-s664

All farming carried on by individuals, with the exception of certain market gardening and other activities, is liable to income tax under Case I of Schedule D.

1.21.1 Averaging of farm profits

TCA97 s657

(a) General

An individual may elect that his/her farming profits chargeable to income tax are to be computed by reference to an average of the profits arising in each of the preceding three years, provided that he/she has been charged to tax under Schedule D Case I on the current year basis in each of the two preceding years. Where an election for averaging is made, the election remains in force for all future years, except where the individual decides to opt out of the averaging system. Finance Act 2001 contains special provisions to account for the fact that the tax year 2001 was only 9 months when calculating assessable profits on the income averaging basis.

(b) Losses

Where losses are taken into an averaging calculation and the result of that calculation is a loss, one-third of the loss is available for relief against other income under section 381 or for carry forward under section 382.

(c) Capital Allowances

Capital Allowances are not subject to averaging.

(d) Stock Relief

As Stock Relief is treated as if it were a trading expense, profits for averaging purposes are the profits after deduction of Stock Relief.

(e) Opting Out of Averaging

The individual may opt out of the averaging system only if he was charged to tax on the average basis for each of the three years of assessment immediately preceding the year for which he wishes to revert to the normal year basis.

If he wishes to revert to the normal year basis, no amendment is made in the average basis assessment for the last average year but the two years prior to the last average year are reviewed and if the existing assessment for either or both year(s) is less than the amount of the assessment for the last average year, an additional assessment for the difference is made for the year(s) affected.

(f) Cessation

Where all farming carried on by an individual ceases, the normal cessation provisions are applied irrespective of an election for the average basis.

(g) Time Limits

The time limit within which an election for the average basis may be made is within 30 days of the date of the notice of assessment to income tax on farming profits. Notification of opting out of the averaging system must be given on or before 31 October in the year following the year of assessment.

(h) Ineligible Farmers

The following individuals cannot elect for averaging:

TCA97 s657 (i) A farmer who, (or whose spouse) at any time in the year of assessment, is carrying on (either solely or in partnership) another trade or profession.

There is an exclusion where the trade carried on by the spouse consists solely of the provision of accommodation in the buildings on the farm land occupied by the farmer and the provision of such accommodation is ancillary to the farming of that land, i.e., the provision of farmhouse holidays.

(ii) A farmer who (or whose spouse) at any time in the year of assessment, is:

– a director (or employee) of a company carrying on a trade or profession, and

– is able to control (either directly or indirectly) more than 25% of the ordinary share capital of the company.

A farmer whose spouse is not living with him may elect for averaging notwithstanding that his wife may fall within the above categories.

(i) Milk Quota Partnership

With effect from 13 March 2008 where a farmer moves into a milk quota partnership, the partnership trade shall be treated for the purpose of averaging, as a continuation of the farmer's sole trade.

1.21.2 EU Single Payment Scheme

TCA97 s657A Section 29 Finance Act 2005 provided for new measures which apply to individuals who are engaged in the trade of farming in the year of assessment 2005 and who are in receipt of payments under the new EU Single Payment Scheme for farmers and certain terminated FEOGA Scheme payments in 2005. The new provisions do not apply to farmers who are already availing of farm income averaging.

The measures provide that where certain conditions are met and where the individual so opts, any payments received in 2005 under the terminated FEOGA schemes will be disregarded for tax purposes in 2005 and instead be deemed to arise in three equal instalments in 2005 and the two succeeding years of assessment and taxed accordingly. Should an individual permanently cease farming during that three-year period, any of these instalment payments which have yet to be taxed will be brought into charge under CASE IV of Schedule D for the year of cessation. Other than in a case of cessation, once an individual opts for this instalment arrangement, it cannot be altered during the three-year period.

Section 22 Finance Act 2007 extended the income averaging scheme outlined above to certain farmers who were in receipt of both old and new payments in the calendar year 2005, which may be taxable in the 2005 and 2006 years of assessment depending on the accounting year end.

1.21.3 EU restructuring aid for sugar beet growers

TCA97 s657B Finance Act 2007 introduced a new scheme for the taxation of EU Restructuring Aid for sugar beet growers.

Under the scheme, farmers in receipt of the restructuring payments will be allowed to average them over a period of six years for the purposes of calculating taxable income. An individual, who has carried on the trade of farming in 2007 or in any subsequent year, and is within the charge to tax under Case I of Schedule D, may elect to have any payments, which would be liable to income tax, to be chargeable in equal instalments for the year of assessment in which it is received and the five succeeding years of assessment (i.e., over six years).

Where a trade of farming is discontinued, then income tax shall be chargeable under Case IV of Schedule D for the year of assessment and spreading forward of the income can also apply subject to the individual having been taxed under Case I in 2007 or a subsequent year.

Any election to spread the payments must be made on or before 31 October in the year of assessment following the year in which the payments are made to the individual. Any election is irrevocable for the six year period.

1.21.4 Stock relief

TCA97 s665-9 **(a) General**

Individuals or companies carrying on the trade of farming may deduct 25% of any increase in stock values in a chargeable period or period of account as a trading expense incurred in that period.

The relief cannot increase or create a loss. Excess capital allowances or unused losses may not be carried forward from or before a period in which stock relief is claimed. The relief must be claimed in writing on or before the return filing date for the period to which it relates.

In the case of individuals, the relief will not apply for any year of assessment later than the year 2008 and in the case of companies it will not apply for any accounting period which ends after 31 December 2008.

Special provisions apply to commencements and certain other situations where opening stock may not be at a realistic value. In such circumstances the Inspector of Taxes is entitled to treat the farmer as having trading stock of such value as appears to him to be reasonable and just.

(b) Young Trained Farmers

In the case of "young trained farmers", as defined, in section 667A TCA 1997, the tax relief available is 100% of any increase in stock values for the year in which the individual begins farming and for three successive years.

This relief was due to expire on 31 December 2006 but was extended to 31 December 2008 subject to a Ministerial Order.

(c) Compulsory Disposal of Livestock.

Special relief applies to profits resulting from the disposal of livestock due to statutory disease eradication measures. This special relief is broadly as follows:

(i) In the case of disposals on or after 21 February 2001, the farmer may elect to have the profits treated as arising in four equal instalments in each of the four succeeding accounting periods, or on further election, in the accounting period of disposal and the three immediately succeeding accounting periods.

This option does not apply where a permanent discontinuance of the farming trade occurs. For disposals between 6 April 1993 and 20 February 2001, the deferral period was two years.

(ii) Where the receipts from the disposal are reinvested in livestock, the farmer may elect to claim stock relief at 100% (instead of the normal 25%) during the four year deferral period. However, if the receipts are not fully reinvested by the end of the four-year period, the aggregate stock relief for the four years is to be reduced to an amount that bears the same proportion to the aggregate stock relief as the expenditure actually incurred in the four-year period bears to the compensation received. This reduction is to take place, as far as possible, in the later years.

This special treatment is available in the case of total cattle herd depopulation arising from statutory disease eradication schemes. Where the disposal is due to brucellosis, a farmer is treated as having disposed of an entire herd where under the brucellosis eradication rules he disposes of all eligible animals (as distinct from the total herd), together with any other animals that must be disposed of in accordance with those rules.

Finance Act 2008 extended the relief where part of a livestock herd is disposed of under any underlying disease eradication scheme, with effect from 13 March 2008.

Finance Act 2001 extended the relief to all animals and poultry specified in Parts I and II of the First Schedule of the Diseases of Animals Act, 1996, where all animals or poultry of that particular kind of farming are disposed of. It also provides that the relief will apply to disposals on or after 6 December 2000 in such circumstances that compensation is paid by the Minister for Agriculture, Food and Rural Development in respect of that disposal.

1.21.5 Losses

TCA97 s662 Relief for farm losses against other income is claimable only where the farming is carried on, on a commercial basis with a view to the realisation of profits. The relief will only be available for three consecutive years and in special cases, four consecutive years.

If there is no other income, or if relief is denied because of the three/four year rule losses may be carried forward for set off against future farming profits.

1.21.6 Discontinued farm trades

TCA97 s656 A farmer ceasing to trade and a successor to that trade may jointly elect to transfer trading stock at book value.

1.21.7 Pollution control

TCA97 s659 Farm pollution control allowances are available to a farmer who has a farm nutrient management plan in place in respect of his farm and who incurs necessary capital expenditure for the control of pollution on certain buildings and structures.

The relief applies to expenditure incurred between 6 April 1997 and 31 December 2008. There is an accelerated allowance in year one of the lesser of €50,000 or 50% of qualifying expenditure with effect from 1 January 2006. (The previous limit was the lesser of €31,750 or 50% of qualifying expenditure). The balance of expenditure is written off over seven years in the case of expenditure incurred prior to 1 January 2005 and over three years in the case of expenditure incurred on or after 1 January 2005.

The year one allowance is regarded as a "floating allowance" to be taken in whole or in part at any time over the writing down period.

1.21.8 Milk quotas

TCA97
Pt23 Ch3
s669A–F

Capital allowances are available to farmers in respect of expenditure incurred on or after 6 April 2000, on the purchase of any qualifying milk quota.

The amount of expenditure which qualifies for relief is limited to the lesser of:

(i) the amount of the capital expenditure incurred on the purchase of a qualifying quota, or

(ii) the amount of capital expenditure which would have been incurred on the purchase of that milk quota if the price paid were set otherwise than by the Minister for Agriculture and Food for the purposes of a Milk Quota Restructuring Scheme in the area in which the land, with which that milk quota is associated, is situated.

The allowances are granted on a straight line basis over a seven year period.

Where a quota is subsequently sold or disposed of, the normal balancing allowance or charge provisions will apply.

1.21.9 Stallion stud fees

TCA97
Pt 23 Ch 4
s381, s669G-K

Section 26 Finance Act 2007 provided for the taxation of profits and gains arising from stallion stud fees with effect from 1 August 2008. It also introduced a new credit for income tax that is paid by an individual on exempt stallion fees and dividends as a result of the restriction of certain specified tax reliefs that were introduced by Finance Act 2006 (see paragraph 1.27).

The main provisions which will come into effect by way of Ministerial Order following clearance from the European Commission, can be summarised as follows:

(i) With effect from 1 August 2008, stallions are to be treated as stock in trade and income and gains arising from stallion stud fees or from the sale of stallions will be subject to income tax.

(ii) The normal expenses for the upkeep of stallions will be allowed as a tax deduction.

(iii) A tax deduction in respect of the purchase cost of the stallion will be provided over four years at 25 per cent per annum.

(iv) Stallions purchased on the open market on or after 1 August 2008 are to be valued for the purposes of the four year deduction at their purchase price.

In cases where stallions are standing at stud prior to 1 August 2008, or where stallions transfer to stud from racing or training or are bred on farms or held as stock in trade, the cost of the stallion for the purposes of the four-year deduction will be the prevailing market value as at 1 August 2008, or the date the stallion first stands at stud, as appropriate.

(v) Where a stallion is sold or dies there is provision for adjustment to the amount of the write down that has already been claimed. This adjustment will be calculated in much the same way as a balancing allowance/charge is calculated for capital allowances purposes.

(vi) A distinction will be made between stallion owners that hold interests in stallions in the course of a farming trade and those that hold such interests for passive investment purposes.

Stallion fees and profits arising to owners engaged in farming activities will be taxed under Schedule D Case I as ordinary income of the farming trade.

Where a loss arises to such owners, that loss will be available for offset against other income under the existing rules that apply to farming losses.

Stallion fees and profits arising to owners who are passive investors will be taxed under Schedule D Case IV. Where a loss arises to a passive investor, that loss may not be offset against any other income and must be carried forward for offset against future Case IV income arising from stallion activities.

(vii) Any additional tax paid in respect of exempt stallion stud fee income under the provisions introduced by Finance Act 2006 (restriction of specified reliefs, see paragraph 1.27) may be carried forward as a credit against income tax in future years.

1.21.10 Greyhound stud fees

TCA97 s233 The exemption from tax on profits or gains arising from greyhound stud fees was abolished with effect from 1 August 2008 (see paragraph 1.23.5).

1.22 Relevant Contracts Tax (RCT)

TCA97 s531 There are special rules relating to payments made by principal contractors to sub-contractors in respect of relevant contracts in the construction, forestry and meat-processing industries. These rules are commonly known as the Relevant Contracts Tax (RCT) system. Where relevant operations under a relevant contract are carried out in the State, then the RCT system applies regardless of whether or not:

(i) parties to the contract are non-resident in the State or are not liable to tax in the State in respect of those operations,

(ii) the contract is executed outside the State, and

(iii) payments under the contract are made outside the State.

The principal contractor must deduct tax (RCT) at 35% from such payments and remit this to the Collector-General unless:

(i) the sub-contractor produces a certificate authorising the receipt of the amount without deduction of tax (Form C2), and

(ii) the principal contractor obtains a Relevant Payments Card in relation to the sub-contractor.

The sub-contractor's Inspector of Taxes will issue such a certificate of authorisation if he is satisfied that:

(a) The applicant is or is about to become a sub-contractor engaged in the business of carrying out relevant contracts.

(b) The business is or will be carried on from a fixed place of business and has or will have such equipment, stock and other facilities as in the opinion of the Revenue Commissioners are required for the purposes of the business.

(c) Proper books and records will be kept in relation to the business.

(d) The applicant has paid all his due taxes, including interest and penalties, and delivered all necessary returns and supplied all information requested by his Inspector of Taxes for the "qualifying period", which includes the period from the beginning of the tax year to the date the application for Form C2 is made to the Inspector.

Where the contractor has been resident outside the State during the qualifying period and applies for a Form C2, he/she must satisfy Revenue that he/she has complied with the tax obligation of the country in which he/she were resident during the qualifying period.

(e) There is good reason to expect that the applicant will keep proper books and records in the future, and will also be tax-compliant in the future.

(f) The Inspector is satisfied, following "look through" procedures, in relation to the tax history of persons connected with the applicant. These "look through" procedures are similar to those applying in the case of applications for tax clearance certificates.

If the Inspector of Taxes refuses, for any reason, to issue Form C2, the sub-contractor can apply to the Revenue Commissioners who have powers to issue the certificate even though they may not be satisfied on one or more of the conditions. A sub-contractor has a right of appeal against a refusal by Revenue authorities to issue the certificate.

1.22.1 Principal contractor

A principal contractor is defined as one of the following:

(a) A person who, in respect of the whole or any part of the construction operations to which the contract relates is himself the contractor under another construction contract.

(b) A person carrying on a business which includes the erection of buildings or the manufacture, treatment or extraction of materials for use whether used or not in construction operations. Finance Act 2007 extended the list of principal contractors with effect from 1 May 2007 to include a person carrying on a business involving the development of land and a board or body established under Royal Charter that is funded wholly or mainly out of moneys provided by the Oireachtas.

(c) A person who is connected with a company carrying on such a business as is mentioned in paragraph (b) (a person being regarded for the purposes of this paragraph as being so connected if he would be regarded for the purposes of section 639 as being so connected).

Finance Act 2008 amended the connected persons rule contained in section 531(1)(c) TCA97. The amendment has the effect of eliminating from the definition of principal contractor, companies which are obliged to operate RCT because they are connected with a company engaged in the business of land development or construction. It is proposed that those companies will now not have to operate RCT where they engage a subcontractor solely to carry out work on their own business premises provided they are not themselves engaged in the land development or construction business. The effect of this amendment is that in the case of connected or group companies, where one of those companies is carrying on the business of land development or construction, other connected or group companies are not automatically regarded as principal contractors unless they themselves are carrying on the business of land development or construction.

The amendment also ensures that a person (which includes an individual) who is not engaged in a business of land development or construction, who is connected with a company carrying on forestry or meat processing operations, does not have to operate RCT, where that person engages a subcontractor solely to carry out construction operations in relation to a private dwelling or their own business premises. The effect of this amendment is to recognise a practice which has existed for some time.

(d) A local authority, a public utility society within the meaning of section 2, Housing Act 1966 or a body referred to in paragraphs 1 or 2 of section 12 (2)(a) or section 19 or 45 of that Act.

(e) A Minister of State.

(f) Any board established by or under statute, or with effect from 1 May 2007, any board or body established by or under Royal Charter and funded wholly or mainly out of moneys provided by the Oireachtas.

(g) A person who carries on any gas, water, electricity, hydraulic power, dock, canal or railway undertaking.

(h) A person carrying on a business of meat processing operations in an establishment approved and inspected in accordance with the European Communities (Fresh Meat) Regulations 1997 (S.I. No 434 of 1997) or as the case may be, the European Communities (Fresh Poultry Meat) Regulations 1996 (S.I. No 3 of 1996) or any person connected with a company carrying on such a business.

(i) a person carrying on a business which includes the loading, hauling, cleaning and grading operations in the meat and poultry industries.

(j) A person carrying on a business which includes the processing (including cutting and preserving) of wood from thinned or felled trees in sawmills or other like premises on the supply of thinned or felled trees for such processing.

1.22.2 Certified sub-contractor

A certified sub-contractor in relation to a principal means a sub-contractor:

(a) In respect of whom the principal holds at the time of making a payment under a relevant contract to the sub-contractor, a relevant payments card for the year in which the payment is made; and

(b) In respect of whom the principal has not received a cancellation notice from the Revenue Commissioners.

Uncertified subcontractor means a sub-contractor who is not a certified subcontractor.

1.22.3 Relevant contract

A relevant contract means a contract between a sub-contractor and a principal contractor where the sub-contractor is liable as follows:

(a) to carry out relevant operations; or

(b) be answerable for the carrying out of such operations by others; or

(c) to furnish his own labour or the labour of others in the course of such operations, i.e., employment agencies.

Where a person is an employee of the principal contractor a "Relevant Contract" does not exist between them. PAYE is operated on payments to the employee in the normal way.

Relevant operations are any of the following:

(i) The construction, alteration, repair, extension, demolition or dismantling of buildings or structures.

(ii) The construction, alteration, repair, extension, or demolition of any works forming or to form part of land including walls, roadways, power lines, aircraft runways, docks and harbours, railways, inland waterways, pipelines, reservoirs, watermains, wells, sewers, industrial plant and installations for purposes of land drainage.

(iii) The installation in any building or structure of systems of heating, lighting, air conditioning, sound proofing, ventilation, power supply, drainage, sanitation, water supply, burglar, fire-protection or telecommunications.

(iv) The external cleaning of buildings (other than cleaning of any part of a building in the course of normal maintenance) the internal cleaning of buildings and structures so far as carried out in the course of their construction, alteration, extension, repair or restoration.

(v) Operations which form an integral part of or are preparatory to or are for rendering complete such operations such as are described above including site clearance, earth moving, excavation, tunnelling and boring, laying of foundations, erection of scaffolding, site restoration, landscaping, and the provision of roadways and other access works.

(vi) Operations which form an integral part of or are preparatory to or are for rendering complete the drilling or extraction of minerals, or natural gas or the exploration or exploitation of natural resources.

(vii) The construction, alteration, repair, extension or demolition of telecommunications apparatus (with effect from 1 April 2002).

(viii) The haulage for hire of materials, machinery or plant for use whether or not in any of the aforesaid construction operations.

(ix) Forestry operations which include:

(a) the planting, thinning, lopping or felling of trees in woods, forests or other plantations, e.g., the maintenance of woods, forests and plantations and the preparation of land, including woods or forests which have been harvested for planting;

(b) the haulage or removal of thinned, lopped or felled trees;

(c) the processing (including cutting or preserving) of wood from thinned, lopped or felled trees in sawmills or other like premises;

(d) the haulage for hire of materials, machinery or plant for use, whether used or not, in any of the aforesaid operations.

(x) "Meat processing operations" which include:

(a) the slaughter of cattle, sheep or pigs;

(b) the division (including cutting or boning), sorting, packaging (including vacuum packaging) or branding of, or the application of any other similar process to the carcasses, or any part of the carcasses, of slaughtered cattle, sheep or pigs;

(c) the application of methods of preservation (including cold storage) to the carcasses, or any part of the carcasses, of slaughtered cattle, sheep or pigs;

(d) the loading or unloading of the carcasses, or any part of the carcasses of slaughtered cattle, sheep or pigs at any establishment where any of the operations referred to in paragraphs (a), (b) and (c) are carried on;

(e) the rendering of the carcasses of slaughtered cattle, sheep, pigs, domestic fowl, turkeys, guinea fowl, ducks or geese (with effect from 1 April 2002).

1.22.4 Gang system

A relevant contract is deemed to exist between the principal contractor and each member of a gang. The principal contractor making a payment to a group or gang must consider the tax status of each individual member of that group or gang and make payment in full or deduct tax accordingly from each element of the payment. Individual gang members must give the principal contractor details of the amount due to them.

1.22.5 Credit for tax deducted

The gross amount receivable under the contract is included in the computation of the profit of the sub-contractor and he is entitled to credit for, or repayment of, the tax suffered. During the course of a year of assessment the sub-contractor may apply for repayment of the tax deducted in that year on a monthly basis. The repayment will be confined to the amount of the tax suffered which appears to the Revenue Commissioners to exceed the proportionate part of the amount of tax for which the sub-contractor is estimated to be liable for that year of assessment. Any amount outstanding in respect of VAT, PAYE, PRSI and capital gains tax will however be deducted from the amount of the repayment.

Claims for repayment of excess RCT deducted are subject to the four-year time limit that applies to tax repayments generally. However, where the subcontractor submits the Form RCTDC outside the 4-year time limit for repayments, he/she is entitled to have the tax contained in the RCTDC taken into account and credited only against any outstanding tax liability on trading profits (from the trade which gave rise to the deduction) for the particular chargeable period. The sub-contractor will not be entitled to an offset against any other tax liability or to secure a repayment in respect of any balance remaining in the RCTDC.

1.22.6 Returns

Revenue can require principal contractors to make returns of all deductions made within nine days of the end of the income tax month and the tax deducted must be paid over to Revenue.

1.22.7 Payments to subcontractors

Where a person to whom a C2 has been issued wishes to receive payments without deduction of tax, the C2 must be produced in person to the principal contractor who then applies to Revenue for a payments card. On receipt of the payments card, the principal contractor may make payments without deduction of tax. The requirement for the sub-contractor to produce the C2 in person may be relaxed in two circumstances

(i) Where the sub-contractor has nominated a bank account to Revenue into which all payments are to be made by principal contractors, the principal will be entitled to apply for a payments card without having seen the sub-contractor's C2. The sub-contractor will have to notify the principal of details of his or her C2 and of the nominated bank account and the principal will have to undertake to make all payments directly into that bank account.

(ii) Where the principal contractor already holds a payments card in relation to a sub-contractor and the contract in relation to which the payments card was issued is ongoing at the end of the tax year, the principal will be allowed to apply for a payments card for the following year without having seen the sub-contractor's C2 for that year.

Finance Act 2006 placed Revenue practice of applying a payment limit in certain cases on a statutory basis. Where a payment limit is imposed and payments to the sub-contractor exceed the limit, the principal must deduct RCT from such excess payments to the sub-contractor as if the sub-contractor were an uncertified sub-contractor. Where a limit is applied, the sub-contractor concerned may apply to Revenue for an increased (or a reduced) limit or the removal of the limit. If a sub-contractor is not satisfied with any limit imposed in relation to him or her, he or she has the right of appeal to the Appeal Commissioners and the Courts.

1.22.8 Late payments by principal contractors

To combat the deliberate late payment of RCT, the Finance Act 2003 provides that where a principal contractor makes an RCT remittance for a tax year or a period included in a tax year and that remittance is not included in a monthly return, the remittance will be treated as a remittance for the first income tax month of the tax year. However, if within one month of interest (on late payment) being demanded by virtue of the operation of that rule, the principal contractor makes a return for the income tax month or months to which the remittance relates, then that rule will be disapplied and the remittance will be treated as a remittance or remittances for the income tax month or months in question. This will then enable interest to be charged on the basis of the due date for the RCT remittance for the month or months in question.

It also provides that where an amount of RCT is payable on foot of a yearly estimate notice issued by an Inspector of Taxes, interest on the overdue tax will be calculated on the basis that the tax was due for the first income tax month of the tax year to which the notice relates. There is provision for the Inspector of Taxes or, on appeal against the notice, for the Appeal Commissioners to determine the amount of RCT which was unpaid for each income tax month in the tax year to which the notice relates. Where the Inspector of Taxes or Appeal Commissioners so determine, the interest on overdue tax will be calculated on the basis of the due date for the RCT remittance for the month or months in question.

1.23 Exemptions

1.23.1 Artists

TCA97 s195

Certain earnings of individuals who are determined by the Revenue Commissioners to have produced a work or works generally recognised as having cultural or artistic merit are exempted from Irish income tax.

"A Work" is defined as an original and creative work, whether written, composed or executed as the case may be, which falls into one of the following categories:

(a) A book or other writing.

(b) A play.

(c) A musical composition.

(d) A painting or other like picture.

(e) A sculpture.

The exemption applies to an individual only. The relief will be granted to a person who has written, composed or executed the work or works jointly with another individual. The individual must be resident in Ireland and not resident elsewhere, or ordinarily resident and domiciled in Ireland and not resident elsewhere. If the Revenue Commissioners accept that the claim to exemption is valid, any profits or gains arising to the claimant from the publication, production or sale, as the case may be, of the work or works or a work of his in the same category as that work and which would, apart from the exemption, be included in an assessment under Case II of Schedule D, are to be disregarded for all purposes of the Tax Acts. There are detailed rights of appeal.

A formal claim for exemption must be made on a special claim form Artists 1 or 2 depending on the category of the claim, and the exemption will only apply from the tax year in which the claim is made. It should be noted that, notwithstanding the exemption granted or claimed for any year, a return of total income from all sources must be made for each year.

The Arts Council and the Minister for Arts, Culture and the Gaeltacht have drawn up guidelines for the correct operation of this provision.

Tax relief in respect of artistic income is restricted with effect from 2007 in accordance with Chapter 2A TCA 1997 in the context of the limitation on the amount of certain reliefs used by certain high-income individuals – see paragraph 1.27.

1.23.2 Patent royalties

TCA97 s234

The exemption from income tax afforded to individuals in respect of income arising from a qualifying patent (with the exception of those mentioned below) has been phased out completely with regard to patent income arising on or after 6 April 1994.

Income from a qualifying patent, paid on or after 11 April 1994, is exempt where the royalty or other sum is paid in respect of:

(i) a manufacturing activity of a company or of an incorporated enterprise, whether that activity is carried on in the State or elsewhere, or

(ii) a "non manufacturing" activity, to the extent that the income arises from bona fide "third party" payments, i.e., where the payer and payee of the royalty are not connected. Connected persons include spouses, in-laws, relatives, trustees, partners and companies controlled by another person or persons.

The exemption available under paragraph (i) above is restricted in the case of connected persons, to an amount which would have been payable if the payer and the beneficial recipient were independent persons acting at arms length. This restriction applies in respect of royalties paid on or after 23 April 1996.

The exemption from income tax also applies to dividends paid out of "manufacturing royalties" and bona fide "third party" exempt royalties in respect of "eligible shares" in a patent company.

Eligible shares are shares which are:

- fully paid up;
- carry no preferential right to dividends or assets on a winding up and no preferential right to be redeemed;
- are not subject to any different treatment from the treatment which applies to all shares of the same class.

The exempt or non exempt status of distributions made out of royalty income received by a company on or after 28 March 1996 depends on the source of the exempt royalty income and may be summarised as follows:

(a) Royalty income received from unconnected persons:

distributions to shareholders are fully exempt.

(b) Royalty income received from connected persons:

distributions to shareholders are exempt up to the amount of the "aggregate expenditure" on research and development incurred by the company. Aggregate expenditure includes expenditure incurred by the company, its group companies and companies under common ownership, in that accounting period and the two previous accounting periods.

The restriction on the amount of tax free distributions can be avoided, where the Revenue Commissioners are satisfied that the royalty income is from a qualifying patent in respect of an invention which:

(a) involved radical innovation; and

(b) was patented for bona fide commercial reasons and not primarily for the purposes for avoiding liability to taxation.

The Revenue Commissioners, after considering the evidence, which the recipient submits to them and after consultation (if any) as may seem to them to be necessary with such persons as in their opinion may be of assistance to them, will determine the portion of the distribution which may be exempt from tax.

The recipient will be notified of the determination in writing and will have the right of appeal to the Appeal Commissioners within 30 days.

A qualifying patent is a patent covering an invention for which the research, planning, processing, experimenting, testing, devising, designing or developing was carried out in the State.

"Income from a qualifying patent" means any royalty or other sum paid in respect of the user of the invention to which the qualifying patent relates and includes any sum paid for the grant of a licence to exercise rights under such patent.

"Resident of the State" means any person who is resident in the State for income tax or corporation tax purposes and who is not resident elsewhere.

The Finance Act 2006 introduces two anti-avoidance provisions in relation to the availability of tax-free dividends from exempt patent royalty income.

- The first provision introduces a "bona fide" test where the patent agreement is between connected parties. Dividends will only be exempt where the patent was taken out for bona fide commercial reasons and not primarily for the purpose of avoiding tax.
- The second provision introduces an "R&D test" (this test already applies to patent agreements between connected parties) for arrangements between unconnected parties that consist of a patent agreement and a franchise. Only distributions up to the level of the company's R&D expenditure incurred in a three-year period will be exempt. The bona fide test also applies in these circumstances.

The anti-avoidance provisions apply for distributions made on or after 2 February 2006.

Finance Act 2006 does not affect the availability of tax-free dividends from exempt patent royalty income between unconnected parties where no other arrangements for intellectual property exist.

Tax relief in respect of income from patent royalties is restricted with effect from 2007 in accordance with Chapter 2A TCA 1997 in the context of the limitation on the amount of certain reliefs used by certain high-income individuals (see paragraph 1.27).

1.23.3 Stallion services

TCA97 s231 The following profits on gains arising on or before 31 July 2008 are exempt from tax:

(i) profit or gain arising to the owner (or part owner) of a stallion which is ordinarily kept on land in the State from the sale of services, or the rights to such services, of mares within the State, or

(ii) profit or gain arising to the part owner of a stallion, which is ordinarily kept on land outside the State, from the sale of services (or rights to services) of mares by the stallion. However, the part owner must carry on in the State a trade which consists of or includes bloodstock breeding, and it must be shown to the satisfaction of the Inspector that the part owner acquired the stallion and held it primarily for the purpose of the service of mares owned or partly owned by the part owner of the stallion in the course of his trade.

The exemption does not apply to any profits or gains arising after 31 July 2008 (see paragraph 1.21.9).

With regard to chargeable periods commencing on or after 1 January 2004, the profits, gains and losses arising from the above activities must be included in the taxpayers annual Return of Income even though the income or gains are exempt from tax. The normal rules relating to the keeping of records and the making available of such records for inspection by the Revenue Commissioners also apply.

Tax relief in respect of income from stallion services is restricted with effect from 2007 in accordance with Chapter 2A TCA 1997 in the context of the limitation on the amount of certain reliefs used by certain high-income individuals – see paragraph 1.27.

1.23.4 Forests/woodlands

TCA97 s232 Profits or gains arising from the occupation of woodlands managed on a commercial basis and with a view to the realisation of profits are not to be taken into account for any purpose of the Income Tax Acts.

The tax-free status of income so exempted is preserved when dividends are paid out of such income.

Losses incurred in the occupation of woodlands managed on a commercial basis with a view to the realisation of profits may not be claimed under section 381.

With regard to chargeable periods commencing on or after 1 January 2004, the profits, gains and losses arising from the above activities must be included in the taxpayers annual Return of Income even though the income or gains are exempt from tax. The normal rules relating to the keeping of records and the making available of such records for inspection by the Revenue Commissioners also apply.

Tax relief in respect of income from forest/woodland services is restricted with effect from 2007 in accordance with Chapter 2A TCA 1997 in the context of the limitation on the amount of certain reliefs used by certain high-income individuals – see paragraph 1.27.

1.23.5 Greyhound stud fees

TCA97 s233 Profits or gains arising on or before 31 July 2008 from greyhound stud fees are exempt from tax on the same basis as income from stallion services outlined above.

The exemption does not apply to any profits or gains arising after 31 July 2008.

With regard to chargeable periods commencing on or after 1 January 2004, the profits, gains and losses arising from the above activities must be included in the taxpayers annual Return of Income even though the income or gains are exempt from tax. The normal rules relating to the keeping of records and the making available of such records for inspection by the Revenue Commissioners also apply.

Tax relief in respect of income from greyhound stud fees is restricted with effect from 2007 in accordance with Chapter 2A TCA 1997 in the context of the limitation on the amount of certain reliefs used by certain high-income individuals – see paragraph 1.27.

1.23.6 Payment in respect of personal injuries to permanently incapacitated individuals

TCA97 s189 Any payments made to, or in respect of, an individual by a court or under "out of court" settlements in respect of damages received for personal injury, where the individual is permanently and totally incapacitated by reason of mental or physical infirmity from maintaining himself as a result of such injury are exempt from income tax.

In addition, any income, including rental income arising from the investment of such a payment is exempt from tax and is disregarded in computing total income. However, the amount of any such income must be included in a return of total income.

The exemption only applies where the income arising from the investment of the payment is the "sole or main" income of the individual concerned. The Revenue Commissioners accept "sole or main" as being more than 50%. They also accept that an invalidity pension from the Department of Social and Family Affairs is disregarded for the purposes of calculating whether the investment income is the sole or main income of the individual, provided the injury or disability which gave rise to the payment of the Social Welfare Benefit/Pension is the same injury or disability which gave rise to the payment of the compensation.

Section 6 FA 2004 provides that with effect from 1 January 2004, compensation payments to permanently incapacitated individuals arising from claims for damages following assessment by the Personal Injuries Assessment Board will be treated in the same way as payments made following the initiation of Court proceedings, as outlined above.

Section 17 Finance Act 2004 provides that for the tax years 2004 *et seq.* the tax exemption applies to both the income and gains derived from the investment of the sums referred to. Where it was a requirement for the income exemption that the income concerned be the sole or main income of the individual, it will now be a requirement that the aggregate of the income and gains to be exempted must be in excess of 50% of the aggregate of the individual's total income and gains for the year concerned. The exemption of such income and gains does not remove the obligation to include the amounts exempted in a tax return.

Finance Act 2007 extended the exemption outlined above to income from offshore funds, which is chargeable to tax under Case IV by virtue of section 747E TCA 1997 (where a disposal of an interest in an offshore fund occurs) with effect from 2 April 2007.

1.23.7 Trusts for permanently incapacitated individuals

TCA97 s189A Income arising to the trustees of a trust which has been set up for the benefit of a permanently incapacitated individual and funded by subscriptions from the general public, is exempt from tax for the tax years 1997/98 *et seq.*

The income paid by the trustees to the incapacitated individual is also exempt from tax.

In order for the above exemptions to apply, the income arising to or being paid by the trustees, must be the sole or main income of the incapacitated individual (see paragraph 1.23.6).

The identity of the incapacitated person must be known to the subscribers and the total amount subscribed must not exceed €381,000 and no one person can make a subscription of more than 30% of the total subscriptions.

Section 17 Finance Act 2004 provides that for the tax years 2004 *et seq.* the tax exemption applies to both the income and gains derived from the investment of the sums referred to. Where it was a requirement for the income exemption that the income concerned be the sole or main income of the individual, it will now be a requirement that the aggregate of the income and gains to be exempted must be in excess of 50% of the aggregate of the individual's total income and gains for the year concerned. The exemption of such income and gains does not remove the obligation to include the amounts exempted in a tax return.

Finance Act 2007 extended the exemption outlined above to income from offshore funds, which is chargeable to tax under Case IV by virtue of section 747E TCA 1997 (where a disposal of an interest in an offshore fund occurs) with effect from 2 April 2007.

1.23.8 Payments made by the Haemophilia HIV Trust

TCA97 s190 Payments in the nature of income made by the Haemophilia HIV Trust to, or in respect of, beneficiaries under the Trust are disregarded for all purposes of the Tax Acts.

1.23.9 Hepatitis C compensation

TCA97 s191 Compensation payments made by the Tribunal set up by the Minister for Health on 15 December 1995 or received through the courts are exempt from income. Any investment income arising from the compensation is also exempt from income tax provided, that the income is the individuals sole or main income (see paragraph 1.23.6) and the person is permanently and totally incapacitated. The exemption applies to individuals who have been diagnosed positive for Hepatitis C antibodies or Hepatitis C virus where they received the blood transfusion or blood product within the State.

Section 17 Finance Act 2004 provides that for the tax years 2004 *et seq.* the tax exemption applies to both the income and gains derived from the investment of the sums referred to. Where it was a requirement for the income exemption that the income concerned be the sole or main income of the individual, it will now be a requirement that the aggregate of the income and gains to be exempted must be in excess of 50% of the aggregate of the individual's total income and gains for the year concerned. The exemption of such income and gains does not remove the obligation to include the amounts exempted in a tax return.

1.23.10 Payments in respect of thalidomide children

TCA97 s192 Compensation payments made to thalidomide children and income derived from the investments of such payments are disregarded for all purposes of the Tax Acts.

Section 17 Finance Act 2004 extends the exemption to both the income and gains derived from the investment of the sums referred to, for the tax years 2004 *et seq.*

Finance Act 2007 extended the exemption outlined above to income from offshore funds, which is chargeable to tax under Case IV by virtue of section 747E TCA 1997 (where a disposal of an interest in an offshore fund occurs) with effect from 2 April 2007.

1.23.11 Compensation payments under employment law

TCA97 s192A Section 7 FA 2004 provides that with effect from 4 February 2004, compensation awards paid following a formal hearing by a "relevant authority" under employment law in respect of infringement of employees rights and entitlements under that law are exempt from income tax. The exemption does not apply, however, to payments which are in respect of earnings, changes in functions or procedures of an employment or the termination of an employment. A "relevant authority" includes a Rights Commissioner, the Director of Equality Investigations, the Employment Appeals Tribunal, the Labour Court, the Circuit Court and the High Court.

It provides that payments under "out of court" settlements, in place of a formal hearing by a relevant authority, are also exempt from tax subject to certain conditions and restrictions. The main restriction is that the value of tax-free "out of court" settlements may not exceed those which may be awarded using the normal adjudication machinery in employment cases.

1.23.12 Payments to foster parents

TCA97 s192B Section 11 Finance Act 2005 provides for an exemption from income tax on payments made by the Health Service Executive to foster parents in respect of the care of foster children. In addition, the section exempts certain discretionary payments by the Health Service Executive to carers relating to the care of former foster children (those aged 18 or over) who suffer from a disability or until such persons reach 21 or complete their full-time education course. Corresponding payments relating to foster children made in accordance with the law of another EU Member State are also exempted under the section.

1.23.13 Payments under Scéim na bhFoghlaimeoirí Gaeilge

TCA97 s216B Section 12 Finance Act 2004 provides for an income tax exemption with effect from 1 January 2004 for income received by persons in Gaeltacht areas under the Irish language student scheme known as Scéim na bhFoghlaimeori Gaeilge. Prior to Finance Act 2004, Revenue practice was that Gaeltacht households were liable to tax on 10% of the total income earned from summer students each year.

1.23.14 Provision of childcare services

TCA97 s216C Finance Act 2006 provided for tax relief for income received from the provision of certain childcare services. The main provisions are as follows:

(i) The exemption applies if the income in the tax year 2006 does not exceed €10,000 and €15,000 in the tax years 2007 *et seq*.

Where the income exceeds €10,000/€15,000, the entire amount is taxable under self-assessment in the normal way.

(ii) The childcare service must be provided in the service provider's own home and the service cannot be provided to more than three children at any time.

(iii) In determining whether the income level exceeds €10,000/€15,000, no deductions of any kind are allowed.

(iv) The exemption must be claimed in the annual tax return and must be accompanied by evidence that the service provider has notified the appropriate person, recognised by the Health Service Executive, that they are providing childminding services. The notification can be made at any time during or after the tax year to which it relates, provided it is made by 31 October of the following year.

(v) A separate notification must be made in respect of each tax year for which the exemption is claimed.

(vi) A claim for relief under this section does not affect a person's entitlement to mortgage interest relief in respect of, nor capital gains tax relief on gains from the disposal of their principal private residence.

(vii) Income to which this section applies will not be taken into account in determining entitlement to the home carer tax credit.

1.24 Relief for Investment in Corporate Trades (BES)

TCA97 s488-s508 The relief applies to shares issued on or after 6 April 1984 and on or before 31 December 2013. The relief is only available to individuals who subscribe for new ordinary shares.

Relief is given as a deduction from total income and the maximum amount which qualifies for relief in any one tax year is €150,000 for the tax years 2007 *et seq.* (previously €31,750). Where relief cannot be obtained due to an insufficiency of income, the unrelieved amount may be carried forward and claimed as a deduction in future years, subject to the overall annual limit of €150,000.

The relief may be granted through the PAYE system. The minimum amount which can be invested in any one company during a tax year is €250. This restriction does not apply where the investment is made through a designated fund.

Where any amount raised by a designated fund between 1 January 2007 and 31 January 2007 is invested in qualifying companies on or before 31 December 2007, the individual investors who subscribed to the fund will have the option of claiming tax relief on their investment for either the tax year 2006 or 2007. Similarly, in the case of direct investment by investors in qualifying BES companies, where eligible shares are issued by 31 January 2007, the investor will have the option of claiming tax relief for either the tax year 2006 or 2007.

It should be noted that business expansion scheme relief is a "specified relief" under Chapter 2A TCA 1997 in the context of the limitation on the amount of certain reliefs used by certain high income individuals – see paragraph 1.27.

1.24.1 Qualifying individual

TCA97 s493 The individual must not be connected with the company during a period starting with the incorporation of the company (or if later, two years before the shares are issued) and ending five years after the shares are issued. In determining whether an individual is connected with the company, it is necessary to take into account any interest held by his associates. Associates do not include spouses or relatives.

In addition, an individual will be regarded as connected with the company if he, or an associate of his, is any of the following:

(a) A partner of the qualifying company or of any subsidiary of the company.

(b) A director or employee of the qualifying company or of any subsidiary of the company who, during the five years after the date the eligible shares are issued, received any "non-arm's length" payment from the company or any subsidiary. Non-arm's length payments do not include the following:

(i) Payment or reimbursement of travelling or other expenses wholly exclusively and necessarily incurred by them in the performance of their duties.

(ii) Interest at a reasonable rate on money lent to the company.

(iii) Normal dividends.

(iv) Payment for goods at arm's length.

(v) Payment for services rendered which is taken into account for the purpose of Case I or II of Schedule D.

(c) The owner of, or entitled to own, in excess of 30% of the company's issued ordinary share capital and loan capital. This restriction is removed where the issued share capital does not exceed €500,000 (previously €317,500).

(d) The individual has control of the qualifying company within the meaning of section 11.

(e) The individual has at any time in the five year relevant period had control within the meaning of section 11 of another company which has, since that time and before the end of that relevant period, become a subsidiary of the qualifying company.

(f) The individual directly or indirectly possesses or is entitled to acquire any loan capital of a subsidiary of the qualifying company.

(g) The individual, if not already connected with the qualifying company under any of the foregoing rules, subscribes for shares in the company as part of any arrangement which provides for another person to subscribe for shares in another company, but only if the individual or any other individual who is a party to the arrangement is connected with that other company.

1.24.2 Qualifying companies

In order for the individual to obtain tax relief, the investment must be made in a qualifying company. The company must for a period of three years from the date the shares are issued (or if later, three years from the company commencing to trade) satisfy a number of conditions which include the following:

(a) The company must be incorporated in the State or in any EEA State (EU, Norway, Iceland, Liechtenstein) or Irish branches of companies incorporated in EEA States that satisfy the necessary requirements.

(b) The company must be, throughout the relevant period, resident in the State or resident in an EEA State other than the State and carry on business in the State through a branch or agency.

(c) The company must not be quoted on a Stock Exchange. For this purpose a company trading on the Unlisted Securities Market is regarded as quoted.

However, with effect from 6 April 1997, companies can enter both the Irish Enterprise Exchange (IEE) of the Irish Stock Exchange and similar or corresponding markets in other EU Member States without its status as a BES qualifying company being affected, provided that it enters the IEE before or at the same time as it first enters one of the other EU unlisted markets.

(d) With effect from 1 January 2007, a company must be either:

(i) A micro or small enterprise, as defined.

(ii) A medium-sized enterprise, as defined, which is located in "an assisted area", as defined, or

(iii) A medium-sized enterprise not located in an assisted area, which is at a stage of development not beyond "start up stage" as defined.

Micro, small and medium-sized enterprises are defined in Commission Regulation 364/2004 of 25 February 2004 – OJ L63 of 28 February 2004 and may be summarised as follows:

A medium-sized enterprise is one with less than 250 employees and which has an annual turnover not exceeding €50m or an annual balance sheet total not exceeding €43m.

A small enterprise is one with less than 40 employees and which has an annual turnover and/or annual balance sheet total not exceeding €10m.

A micro enterprise is one with less than 10 employees and which has an annual turnover and/or balance sheet total not exceeding €2m.

For State Aid purposes Ireland is divided into "assisted" and "non-assisted" areas. The current "assisted" areas are all areas of Ireland excluding Dublin, Meath, Kildare and Wicklow (and with effect from 2009, Cork city and county except for Cork Docklands).

The location of a company is also clarified as the place at which the company/qualifying subsidiary carries on qualifying trading operations, or in the case of a company which is resident in another EEA State that carries on business in the state through a branch or agency, the location at which that branch or agency carries on qualifying trading operations.

Under the EU "Community Guidelines on State Aid to Promote Risk Capital Investments in Small and Medium Sized Enterprises" (OJ C194 18 August 2006), a company's stages of development are defined in terms of "seed capital", "start up capital" and "expansion capital".

"Seed capital" means financing provided to study, assess and develop an initial concept, preceding start up phase.

"Start up capital" means financing provided to companies, which have not sold their product or service commercially and are not yet generating a profit, for product development and initial marketing.

"Expansion capital" means financing provided for the growth and expansion of a company, which may or may not break even or trade profitably, for the purposes of increasing production capacity, market or product development or the provision of additional working capital.

For a "medium-sized enterprise" not located in "an assisted area", such a company must be either at "seed capital" or "start up capital" stage only.

(e) The company must not have a group connection with another company unless it has subsidiaries which would also all fulfil the required conditions.

(f) The company must be carrying on (or intend to carry on) a qualifying trade on a commercial basis, or be a company whose business consists wholly of:

 (i) The holding of shares or securities of, or the making of loans to one or more qualifying subsidiaries; or

 (ii) Both the holding of shares or securities, or the making of such loans and the carrying on principally in the State of one or more qualifying trades.

(g) Certain industry sectors are excluded from the scheme, namely shipbuilding, coal and steel sectors.

(h) Non-viable companies within the European Community Guidelines on State Aid for rescuing and restructuring firms in difficulty are excluded from the scheme.

The company will not be a qualifying company in the following circumstances:

(a) If an individual has acquired a controlling interest in the company's trade after 5 April 1984; and

(b) For a five year period beginning two years before the later of the date on which the shares were issued or the date the company began to trade, he has, or had, a controlling interest in another trade; and

(c) The trade carried on by the company or a substantial part of it:

 (i) is concerned with the same or similar types of property or provides the same or similar services as the other trade; or

 (ii) serves substantially the same or similar outlets or markets as the other trade.

(d) While the company is regarded as a firm in difficulty for the purposes of the Community Guidelines on State Aid for rescuing and restructuring firms in difficulty.

For the purpose of this prohibition, an individual has a controlling interest in a trade:

(a) In the case of a trade carried on by the company if:

  (i) He/she controls the company.

  (ii) The company is a close company and he or an associate of his is a director of the company and the beneficial owner of, or able directly or through the medium of other companies or by any other indirect means, to control more than 30% of the ordinary share capital of the company.

  (iii) Not less than 50% of the trade could be regarded as belonging to him.

(b) In any other case, if he is entitled to not less than 50% of the assets used for, or the income arising from the trade.

1.24.3 Company's limit

The maximum amount which may be raised by a company through the issue of eligible shares is €2m (previously €1m), subject to a maximum of €1.5m being raised in a twelve month period. Previous issues of eligible shares by the company or group of companies are aggregated in calculating the €2m.

Where companies are associated (within the meaning of the following paragraph), the maximum amount that can be raised under the scheme by all such associated companies is €2m. Where €2m has already been raised by the associated companies no further amounts can be raised by the applicant company under the scheme. Where the amounts previously raised by the associated companies (including the applicant company) is less than €2m, the applicant company may only raise an amount equal to the difference between the amounts so raised and €2m.

Funds previously raised under the Seed Capital Scheme (see 1.25) must be taken into account when determining the applicable limit of €2m.

A company will be associated with another company where it could reasonably be considered that:

(i) both companies act in pursuit of a common purpose, or

(ii) any person or group(s) of persons, having a reasonable commonality of identity, have or had the means or power, either directly or indirectly, to determine the trading operations carried on or to be carried on by both companies, or

(iii) both companies are under the control of any person or group(s) of persons having a reasonable commonality of identity.

The subsidiaries of companies are also taken into account for the purposes of the above rules with effect from 28 March 1996.

1.24.4 Qualifying trade

A qualifying trade is one consisting wholly or mainly of the following operations:

(a) The manufacture of goods and certain other trades within the meaning of section 443.

(b) The rendering of services in the course of a service undertaking in respect of which an employment grant was approved by the IDA, or which has received grant aid from Údarás na Gaeltachta.

(c) Tourist traffic undertakings.

(d) Qualifying shipping activities.

(e) The export sale of Irish manufactured goods by a special trading house.

(f) Construction and leasing of advance factories promoted by local community groups.

(g) The cultivation of plants in the State as defined by section 443.

(h) Certain research and development activities.

(i) The cultivation of horticultural produce in greenhouses.

(j) The production, publication, marketing and promotion of qualifying musical recordings.

(k) Trading activities on an exchange facility established in the Custom House Docks Area.

(l) Providing internationally traded services which are approved for grant aid by County Enterprise Boards.

(m) Recycling companies which have had a grant or financial assistance made available to them by an industrial development agency. However, with effect from 1 January 2008, a recycling company will qualify when it has received approval for a grant or financial assistance from an Industrial Development Agency or County Enterprise Board, or where it has obtained written confirmation from such an agency or board verifying that it has submitted a business proposal to it and that the activities carried on by the company are qualifying environmental services.

If the company is not carrying on a trade at the time the shares are issued, it will be regarded as carrying on a trade if it has expended at least 80% of the money subscribed for the shares on research and development which is connected with an undertaking with a view to the carrying on of the trade, and begins to carry on the trade within three years after that time. In all other cases, the company must commence trading within two years from the date of issue of the shares.

Where the company carries on qualifying trading operations and other trading operations, the total amount receivable from sales made and services rendered in the course of qualifying trading operations must not be less than 75% of the total amount receivable by the company from all sales made and services rendered.

1.24.5 Qualifying shares

The shares eligible for relief must be fully paid ordinary shares. During a five-year period commencing with the date on which they were issued, the shares must not carry a present or future preferential right to dividends or to the company's assets on its winding up and no present or future preferential right to be redeemed. No relief is available on shares issued after 12 April 1989 which are the subject of either a put or call option at a price other than their market value at the date at which the option is exercised.

The shares must be issued for the purpose of raising money for a qualifying trade which is being carried on by the company or which it intends to carry on.

The company must provide satisfactory evidence to the Revenue Commissioners that the money was used for any of the following purposes.

(a) Enabling the company, or enlarging its capacity, to undertake qualifying trading operations.

(b) Enabling the company to engage in research and development, the acquisition of technological information and data, the development of new or existing services or products, or the provision of new products or services.

(c) Enabling the company to identify new markets and to develop new and existing markets for the products and services.

(d) Enabling the company to increase its sale of products or provision of services.

In all cases the money must be used with a view to the creation or maintenance of employment in the company.

1.24.6 Claim for relief

The claim for relief must be made within two years of the end of the year of assessment in which the shares are issued.

A claim for relief must be accompanied by a certificate from the company certifying that the conditions for the relief have been satisfied.

1.24.7 Withdrawal of relief

Where an individual receives any value from the company during a period beginning with the incorporation of the company (or if later, two years before the issue of the shares) and ending five years after the issue of the shares, the amount of the relief granted on the shares will be reduced by the value received.

An individual receives value from the company in the following situations.

(a) (i) The company repays, redeems or repurchases, any of its share capital or securities which belong to the individual; or

(ii) It makes any payment to him for giving up his right to any of the company's share capital or any security on its cancellation or extinguishment.

(b) The company repays any debt to the individual other than a debt which was:

(i) An ordinary trade debt incurred by the company; or

(ii) Any other debt which was incurred by the company on or after the earliest date on which the subscription for the shares in respect of which the relief is claimed, otherwise than in consideration of the extinguishment of a debt incurred before that date.

(c) The company makes to the individual any payment for giving up his right to any debt or its extinguishment other than:

(i) A debt in respect of a payment of the kind mentioned earlier in connection with directors or employees.

(ii) A debt in respect of reasonable remuneration for services rendered and which are taken into account under Case I or II of Schedule D.

(iii) A debt in respect of the payment for the supply of goods which does not exceed their market value.

(d) The company releases or waives any liability of the individual to the company or discharges, or undertakes to discharge any liability of his to a third party.

(e) The company makes a loan or advance to the individual.

(f) The company provides a benefit or facility for the individual.

(g) The company transfers an asset to the individual for no consideration or for a consideration less than its market value, or acquires an asset from him for a consideration exceeding its market value.

(h) The company makes to him any other payment except a payment of the kind mentioned in connection with payments to directors or employees, or a payment in discharge of an ordinary trade debt.

An individual will also receive value from the company if any person who would be regarded as connected with the company:

(a) purchases any of its share capital or securities which belong to the individual; or

(b) makes any payment to him for giving up any right in relation to the company's share capital or securities.

The relief available to an individual may be reduced or eliminated if, at any time during the relevant period, the company repays, redeems or repurchases any of its share capital which belongs to any member, other than:

(a) the individual; or

(b) another individual whose relief is thereby reduced; or

(c) makes any payment to such member for giving up his right to any of the company's share capital on its cancellation or extinguishment.

The amount of any value received from the company is subtracted from the ordinary share capital in determining whether or not the subscribed amount exceeds the permitted 30% interest in the company.

1.24.8 Replacement capital

An individual is not entitled to relief in respect of any shares in a company where at any time in the relevant period the company or any of its subsidiaries:

(a) Begins to carry on as its trade or as part of its trade, a trade which was previously carried on at any time in the relevant period otherwise than by the company or any of its subsidiaries; or

(b) Acquires the whole or greater part of the assets used for the purposes of a trade so previously carried on.

These provisions apply where the individual is either the person who owned more than one half of the trade at any time during the relevant period or the person who has controlled another company which previously carried on the trade.

An individual is not entitled to relief in respect of any shares in the company where:

(a) The company comes to acquire all the issued share capital of another company at any time in the relevant period; and

(b) The same person controlled or controls both companies.

An individual who has been granted relief, must notify the Inspector of Taxes within 60 days of an event occurring which causes the relief to be withdrawn.

The company must give similar notification of an event occurring which causes the company to cease to be a qualifying company. Withdrawal of the relief will be by means of an assessment under Case IV of Schedule D.

1.24.9 Capital gains tax

If a gain arises on disposal, the individual will be liable to capital gains tax in the normal way, the tax relief obtained being disregarded. If the shares are sold at a loss, the loss is reduced by the amount of the relief obtained. Where relief has been granted on some shares in an individuals combined holding, the shares sold must be identified with shares for which relief has been granted on a first-in, first-out basis.

Where there has been a re-organisation of share capital and a bonus issue is made, the bonus shares are treated as also having obtained the relief.

1.24.10 Approved funds

Investment through a designated fund is permitted. The Revenue Commissioners will approve a fund as a designated fund provided certain conditions are satisfied.

1.24.11 Spouses

The relief is available to each spouse, subject to availability of income in his/her own right.

1.25 Seed Capital Investment

TCA97
s488-s508

The Business Expansion System (BES) also provides income tax relief for investment before 31 December 2013, by certain individuals in new companies.

Individuals who satisfy certain conditions may obtain income tax relief for investment in new ordinary shares in a newly incorporated company, which is engaged in a BES type activity or in certain research and development activities.

With effect from 1 January 2007, a sum of up to €600,000 (previously €190,500) subscribed for shares in the new company will be relieved against the total income of the individual for any of the six years immediately preceding the year in which the investment is made. The maximum relief in any one tax year is €100,000 for the tax years 2007 *et seq*. (previously €31,750).

The investment in the new company may be made in two stages with the second stage being made before the end of the second tax year following the tax year in which the first investment was made.

To qualify for the relief, the individual must:

(a) be a full-time employee or a full-time director with the new company at any time up to six months after the end of the tax year in which the business is established;

(b) derive not less than 75% of his total income from Schedule E sources, income from other sources not being more than €25,000 in each of the three years of assessment preceding the year of assessment immediately prior to the year of assessment in which the employment commences;

(c) not have possessed or have been entitled to acquire more than 15% of the ordinary share capital, loan capital or voting power of a company other than a seed capital company except where the individual owns more than 15% of only one other company provided:

   (i) the company's turnover in each of the three accounting periods prior to the accounting period which the investment is made in the seed capital company did not exceed €127,000 and

   (ii) the company is a trading company other than a company trading in land or financial services.

(d) acquire at least 15% of the issued ordinary share capital of the seed capital company and retain that 15% for one year (previously two years) from the date of the investment or from the date on which the company commences to trade whichever is later.

An individual will not be regarded as ceasing to comply with the employment and shareholding conditions where the company is wound up or dissolved for bona fide commercial reasons and not as part of a tax avoidance scheme.

The new company must be carrying on trading operations of a BES nature which have been certified by an industrial agency, Bord Fáilte or a County Enterprise Board, to be a bona fide new venture having the potential for the creation of employment. It must be eligible to be grant aided by the agency or Bord Fáilte as appropriate. The value of the company's interest in land and buildings (excluding fixtures and fittings) must not be greater than half the value of its total assets. It must deal on an arm's-length basis in any transactions with the individuals previous employer company during a period of three years from commencement of operations.

It should be noted that seed capital investment relief is a "specified relief" under Chapter 2A TCA 1997, in the context of the limitation on the amount of certain reliefs used by certain high income individuals — see paragraph 1.27.

1.26 Investment in Films

TCA97 s481

Relief is provided for an investment made in a qualifying film company.

The main provisions are as follows:

(i) The amount on which tax relief may be claimed is 80% of total production costs.

(ii) The overall ceiling on qualifying expenditure for any one film is €35,000,000. Finance Act 2008 increased the ceiling to €50,000,000 subject to a commencement order of the Minister for Finance after clearance with the European Commission.

(iii) Relief may be claimed on investments made between 23 January 1996 and 31 December 2008 by individuals and companies. Finance Act 2008 extended the deadline until 31 December 2012 subject to a commencement order of the Minister for Finance after clearance with the European Commission.

(iv) Individuals may claim relief at their marginal rate on 80% of investments up to €31,750 (i.e., max allowable is €25,400) in any one tax year. Where relief cannot be obtained due to an insufficiency of income, the unrelieved amount may be carried forward and claimed in the following year.

(v) There is a total annual investment limit of €10,160,000 for a company and its connected companies, in relation to any specified period of 12 months. However, a corporate investment in any one film company cannot exceed €3,810,000, and where in a twelve month period, the total of investments made by a company and its connected companies exceeds €3,810,000, the excess can only be invested in film projects with a budget of less than €5,080,000.

(vi) Where shares in a qualifying company are retained for more than one year, the relief claimed on the investment is ignored for capital gains tax purposes on a subsequent disposal of the shares. A loss on disposal is restricted by the amount of the relief.

(vii) Investments must be made directly by the investor into a qualifying company and such a company may only make one qualifying film.

(viii) Relief is only available in respect of investments in share capital.

It should be noted that film relief is a "specified relief" under Chapter 2A TCA 1997 in the context of the limitation on the amount of certain reliefs used by certain high income individuals – see paragraph 1.27.

1.26.1 Finance Act 2004 changes

The Finance Act 2004 provided for a number of amended procedures in relation to the administration of the scheme as follows:

(i) All applications for certification by a qualifying company, in relation to a film to be produced by it must be made to the Revenue Commissioners in the first instance, who will then seek authorisation from the Minister for Arts, Sport and Tourism as to whether they may, following a full examination of the company's proposal, issue a certificate that the film may be treated as a qualifying film for the purpose of this section.

The Minister for Arts, Sport and Tourism on receipt of such a request, will, in accordance with regulations made under the section, decide whether to give the authorisation having regard to the categories of films eligible for certification (as set out in the regulations) and any contribution which the film is expected to make to the development of the Irish film industry and/or the promotion and expression of Irish culture.

(ii) The Minister for Arts, Sport and Tourism will specify certain conditions in any authorisation given.

(iii) Where the Revenue Commissioners receive authorisation from the Minister for Arts, Sport and Tourism they will examine the company's proposal in full and where they issue a certificate, it will be subject to various conditions which the Revenue Commissioners consider proper, having regard to that examination and the conditions specified by the Minister in his authorisation.

(iv) New anti-abuse provisions will allow the Revenue Commissioners to refuse to issue a certificate where they have reason to believe that any item of proposed expenditure in the budget is inflated, or where they are not satisfied that there is a commercial rationale for the corporate structure proposed or that such structure would hinder them in verifying compliance with any provision governing the relief.

(v) A company will not be regarded as a qualifying company:

(a) Unless it notifies the Revenue Commissioners when principal photography, etc. commences.

(b) Unless it provides evidence to vouch each item of expenditure on a film, when requested to do so by the Revenue Commissioners for the purposes of verifying compliance with the provisions governing the relief or with any condition included in a certificate issued by them.

(c) Unless it notifies the Revenue Commissioners of the date of completion of the production of the qualifying film, provides a copy of the film and a compliance report to the

Revenue Commissioners within the time period specified in the regulations.

(vi) Where a company fails to comply with any of these provisions or any other provision governing the relief, or fails to fulfill any condition on a certificate issued to it, relief under the section may be withdrawn and the certificate issued may be revoked by the Revenue Commissioners.

1.27 Limitation on Amount of Certain Reliefs Used by High Income Individuals

TCA97 Ch2A Finance Act 2006 provides for a limit on the use of tax reliefs by certain high-income individuals for the tax years 2007 *et seq*. Basically, where a person is a high-income individual he/she is restricted in the extent to which "specified reliefs" can be applied to reduce the individual's tax bill. The provision works so that the "specified reliefs" used in any one year are limited to 50% of the individual's "adjusted income".

An individual's "adjusted income" will consist of his/her taxable income (computed on the basis of the normal income tax computation rules) but adding back the aggregate amount of the specified reliefs claimed by the individual in that year and subtracting "ring-fenced income" (e.g., Irish and European deposit interest taxable at 20%). The restriction will only apply to those individuals whose adjusted income is over €250,000 per annum. In addition, a tapering relief (that is, a graduated application of the restriction) will apply for incomes between €250,000 and €500,000. The increased taxable income amount arrived at by this computation will be taxed in accordance with the normal income tax rates.

Broadly, the reliefs to be restricted are the various property-based tax incentives and certain other reliefs such as the Business Expansion Scheme, film relief and donations. Also to be restricted are certain tax exemptions including artistic income, stallion fees and patent royalties. The normal deductible items available to the broad range of taxpayers, such as medical expenses, trade union subscriptions, the personal tax credits and exemptions such as that for child benefit, will not be restricted. Similarly, normal business expenses and deductions for capital allowances on plant and machinery, genuine business-related trading losses and losses from a rental business will not be restricted. Where an individual gets relief under a double tax agreement because the tax has been paid in another country, this relief is also not restricted.

A full list of the specified reliefs is contained in Schedule 25B TCA 1997.

A summary of the reliefs is as follows:

- All of the "area-specific tax" capital allowances incentive schemes (Urban, Rural and Town Renewal Schemes, Park-and-Ride, Living Over the Shop, Student Accommodation and University Buildings, etc).
- All properties qualifying for accelerated allowances such as hotels, holiday cottages, nursing homes, convalescent homes, qualifying hospitals, sports injury clinics, mental health care centres, qualifying units, childcare facilities, etc.
- Trading losses derived from capital allowances listed under the definition of Specified Reliefs or derived from double rent relief

(this category also extends to trading losses forward or terminal losses derived from any restricted capital allowances).

- BES relief.
- Film relief.
- Patent royalty income and patent distributions.
- Artists' Exemption.
- Interest deductions in respect of money borrowed by individuals to purchase shares in certain companies or partnerships.
- Exempt distributions and exempt profits or gains relating to income from stallion fees, stud greyhounds services, the occupation of woodlands and certain mining profits.
- Relief under section 482 – Restoration of Heritage Buildings.
- Donations to certain sports bodies.
- Donations to approved bodies such as charities.
- Any amounts carried forward to a later period as a result of the operation of the above restrictions in an earlier period.

The limitation on the use of the specified tax reliefs will work as follows:

- The taxpayer adds up the total amount of "specified reliefs" used in respect of a tax year.
- The aggregate of the specified reliefs will then be added back to the taxpayer's taxable income (as that amount is calculated under the normal income tax computation rules) to give an "adjusted income" amount.
- Where the adjusted income amount is greater than a "threshold amount" of €250,000, the restriction will apply.
- The new increased taxable income figure will be taxed at the ordinary income tax rates; and, since the top rate of 41% (previously 42%) will apply to the vast bulk of the individual's income, an effective rate of close to 20% will be achieved in respect of the adjusted income figure.
- Finally, any relief denied as a result of this section in a particular year may be carried forward to the following year (or years).

Where income subject to DIRT and certain foreign source deposit interest income treated in the same way as income subject to DIRT, is included in an individual's taxable income, such income will be excluded from the restriction calculation. In such a case, the restriction will be calculated on the basis of an adjusted income amount less DIRT income. The exclusion of DIRT from the calculation ensures that the DIRT element of taxable income is still taxed at 20% and the remainder of taxable income (as increased by the restriction) is taxed at the higher rate of 41%, giving an overall effective rate of in or around 20% on adjusted income and DIRT income.

TCA97 s485FA **Married couples**

Section 18 Finance Act 2007 introduced provisions to ensure that individuals assessed to tax as married couples will be treated as separate individuals when determining the relief available to them so that each spouse's entitlement to relief will be examined in isolation without reference to their spouse's income. In addition where one or both spouses have income below the €250,000 threshold the restriction of relief will not be applied. Therefore, where a husband and wife have income and specified reliefs separately in their own name it should be possible for both of them to maximise the relief available.

TCA97 s485FB **Requirement to provide information**

Any individual who is subject to the restriction shall be a chargeable person for tax purposes. This ensures that such individuals are within the self-assessment system and will be required to file a full tax return and are subject to the tax payment rules including preliminary tax. Even if no tax liability ultimately arises a tax return must still be filed.

The legislation also requires a statement to be supplied to Revenue by those affected by the restriction setting out the following:

(i) a calculation of their taxable income before and after the restrictions,

(ii) the tax due after the restrictions, and

(iii) details of the specified reliefs claimed in the year and included in the aggregate of the specified reliefs.

The statement is required to be submitted at the same time as and together with their income tax return. Where a husband and wife are on joint or separate assessment each spouse will be required to submit such a statement but these separate statements will be combined on one form.

Revenue also have powers to seek certain further information from individuals in relation to specified reliefs. This will ensure that the Department of Finance can quantify the level of income which is not liable to income tax.

Apportionment of relief carried forward from the tax year 2006 to the tax year 2007

As the restriction on specified reliefs applies from 1 January 2007 a new schedule, Schedule 25C has been introduced to deal with the situation where reliefs are carried forward from 2006 and prior years. The carry forward reliefs in question are capital allowances and loss reliefs under s304, s382, s305 and s384 TCA 1997. Some of the reliefs carried forward could be regarded as restricted specified reliefs while others may be regarded as unrestricted reliefs.

The new Schedule 25C sets out the basis for apportionment between restricted and unrestricted reliefs carried forward under s304, s382, s305 and s384 TCA 1997. It involves looking back at the reliefs claimed for the 2006 tax year and the three preceding tax years (i.e., tax years 2003, 2004 and 2005). For each of the carry forward reliefs in question the following formula is used to determine the restricted portion of the relief forward:

$$RF = \frac{SR}{TR}$$

In all cases RF is the relief forward. SR and TR are defined separately for the relevant sections. Broadly, the numerator is the total of the individuals restricted reliefs of that category over the previous four years and the denominator is the individual's overall use of tax reliefs of that category over the same period. The relief forward will then be classified as restricted and unrestricted on this basis.

It will be open to the taxpayer to apply to Revenue for the apportionment to operate on such longer or shorter period that, in the opinion of the taxpayer, gives a fairer apportionment. If Revenue do not accept the period put forward by the taxpayer or if some other apportionment period cannot be agreed, the taxpayer will be entitled to appeal to the Appeal Commissioners for apportionment on the basis of the period set out in his or her application.

TCA97 s485G **Calculations in other provisions of the Tax Acts**

Finance Act 2008 provided clarification in relation to the correct sequence of events where calculations in other provisions of the Tax Acts are also involved. The calculations in question are those that require total income, taxable income, tax payable or tax chargeable for a year to be taken into account, e.g., double taxation relief, top-slicing relief, etc. In general, these calculations must be carried out before the high earners restriction is applied but the benefit of a credit or reduction in tax can be given against the tax chargeable following the application of the restriction.

1.28 Residence of Individuals

1.28.1 Residence

TCA97 s819-s824 For a full tax year an individual is resident in the State in a tax year if he spends:

(a) 183 days in the State in that year, or

(b) 280 days in aggregate in that tax year and the preceding tax year.

Notwithstanding (b) above, an individual who is present in the State for 30 days or less in a tax year will not be treated as resident for that year unless he elects to be resident.

A day will only count if the individual is present in the State at the end of the day.

1.28.2 Ordinary residence

TCA97 s821 An individual is ordinarily resident in the State from commencement of the fourth tax year if he has been resident for each of the three preceding tax years.

An individual leaving the State will not cease to be ordinarily resident until he has been non-resident for three continuous tax years.

With effect from 6 April 1994 the income of an individual who is not resident but is ordinarily resident is taxable on the same basis as a resident (i.e., worldwide income) with the exception of income from:

(i) a trade or profession no part of which is carried on in Ireland,

(ii) an office or employment all of the duties of which are performed outside Ireland; (apart from "incidental duties"),

(iii) other sources which do not exceed €3,810.

The Revenue have stated that the other income not exceeding €3,810, means other "foreign" income not exceeding €3,810.

1.28.3 Split-year residence relief

TCA97 s822 With effect from 6 April 1994, for the purposes of a charge to tax on employment income, where an individual is resident in Ireland for a tax year and he was not resident in the preceding year, and he satisfies Revenue that he is in Ireland with the intention and in such circumstances that he will be resident for the following year, he will be deemed to be resident for that year only from the date of arrival.

Similarly, where an individual is resident for a tax year and he satisfies Revenue that he is leaving other than for a temporary purpose with the intention and in such circumstances that he will not be resident for the following year, he will be regarded as resident up to the date of his departure.

Where an individual is treated as resident for part of a year the employment income which arises or, in the case of an individual taxed on the remittance basis on his employment income, the amounts received in the State, will be treated as income arising or amounts received for a year of assessment in which the individual is resident in the State. Income arising, or amounts remitted in the remaining part of the year will be treated as arising or received in a year in which the individual is not resident.

1.28.4 Deduction for foreign earnings

This deduction ceased to apply on 31 December 2003.

Please see 31st or earlier editions of this book for full details.

1.28.5 Cross-border workers

Income tax payable in the State for 1998/99 *et seq*. on employment income from a country with which Ireland has a double tax treaty is reduced by the proportion which the employment income bears to total income.

The relief is not claimable where the seafarer allowance or the foreign earnings deduction is claimed.

The conditions under which the relief may be claimed are:

(a) The employment is held outside the State in a country with which Ireland has a double tax treaty;

(b) The employment is held for a continuous period of 13 weeks;

(c) The employment must not be with the Government or an authority set up by the State or under Statute;

(d) The duties of the employment must be performed wholly outside the State (incidental duties performed in the State are regarded as performed outside the State);

(e) The income must be taxed in the other country; and

(f) The employee must be at least one day per week in the State.

1.28.6 Seafarers allowance

TCA97 s472A Seafarers are entitled to a deduction of €6,350 p.a. from employment income on a sea-going ship (excluding fishing vessels) where the seafarer is at sea on a voyage to or from a foreign port for at least 161 days in a tax year. A mobile or fixed installation in foreign waters may be treated as a foreign port for this purpose.

The allowance may not be claimed in any year in which a seafarer claims the foreign earnings deduction or the remittance basis or split year rules apply.

The foreign earnings deduction has been amended for seafarers to provide that where a seafarer is outside Ireland for a continuous period of 14 days and during that period visits a port in the United Kingdom and also visits a port other than in the United Kingdom or Ireland, the foreign earnings deduction may be claimed as if the UK visit were a qualifying period.

1.28.7 Domicile

TCA97 s71 The principle of domicile is a matter of international law and broadly refers to the country which an individual considers as his natural home. It is not therefore determinable in the same manner as residence or ordinary residence.

An individual acquires a domicile of origin at his birth and this is normally that of the father. This domicile of origin is retained unless the individual takes steps to acquire a domicile of choice. Such steps would normally entail a positive indication of a change of citizenship, the making of a will under the laws of the place adopted as the new domicile, disposing of property in the place where the domicile of origin arises, etc.

The Domicile and Recognition of Foreign Divorces Act 1985 provides, that the domicile of married women is to be determined in the same way as that of any other adult.

In the case where the individual is not domiciled in the State or being a citizen of the State not ordinarily resident in the State, he is liable to tax only on so much of his foreign income as is remitted to or enjoyed in any form in the State unless otherwise chargeable to tax in full. In this connection there are anti-avoidance provisions to prevent the use of "back to back" loans. (These provisions apply only to individuals ordinarily resident in the State.) Income arising in the UK does not qualify for the remittance basis regardless of whether it is remitted into the State or not.

1.28.8 Remittance basis of taxation

TCA97 Ch4 s71-75 Up to 31 December 2007, an individual who is resident in Ireland but not domiciled in Ireland was liable to Irish income tax in full on his income arising in Ireland and the UK, and on "foreign income" only to the extent that it is remitted to Ireland. This is known as the remittance basis of taxation and it also applies to an individual who is a citizen of Ireland but who is not ordinarily resident in Ireland (e.g., an Irish citizen who has been living abroad for many years and who returns to Ireland and has not become ordinarily resident, as they have not been resident in Ireland for three consecutive tax years).

With effect from 1 January 2008, the remittance basis has been extended to UK source income.

Finance Act 2006 provided for the discontinuance with effect from 2006 of the remittance basis of taxation in respect of income from an office or employment insofar as that income relates to the performance in the State of the duties of that office or employment.

TCA97 s985 Finance Act 2006 also contains a number of provisions, which are designed to ensure that tax that should be deducted under the PAYE system is in fact deducted. These provisions, which have effect from 31 March 2006, are as follows:

Intermediaries: Where a payment of emoluments is made by an intermediary on behalf of an employer, the employer is to be treated for the purposes of the PAYE regulations as having made the payment if the intermediary does not operate PAYE.

Non-resident employer: Where an employee works for someone based in the State (the relevant person), but is employed by a non-resident employer and PAYE is not applied by the employer (or a non-resident intermediary), the relevant person will be liable to account for PAYE on the amount that the employee receives, grossed up where the employee is entitled to a net sum, free of tax.

Employment not wholly exercised in the State: In circumstances where part only of an employee's earnings are chargeable to tax under Schedule E (because duties of the employment, as well as being performed in the State, are also performed outside it), and the part which is not chargeable is unknown at the time, Revenue may, on application from the employer, give a direction as to the proportion of pay on which PAYE is to be operated. In the absence of a direction, the employer must operate PAYE on the whole amount (see e-Brief No. 28/2006).

Mobile workers: This provision deals with the case where the employees of one person work for another person who is not their employer. Where it appears likely to Revenue that the employer will not operate PAYE, they can issue a direction requiring the other person to deduct tax under PAYE from any payments made by that person to the employer.

1.29 Securitisation of Assets

TCA97 s110 Securitisation is an arrangement under which an originator, such as a bank or asset finance company sells off a portfolio of its assets to investors. It is provided that the company acquiring the qualifying assets is brought into charge under Case III of Schedule D but the taxable profits are calculated using Case I rules. The provisions ensure that the existing tax treatment is continued in the event of securitisation, that is, normal trade expenses are deductible and the treatment of bad and doubtful debts and the recovery of debts already deducted is the same as for the originator.

TCA97 s110 A securitisation vehicle which is an IFSC certified company is brought into charge under Case I of Schedule D.

A company must notify the Revenue Commissioners in advance of its intention to fall within the scope of section 110 TCA 1997.

The minimum deal size for any qualifying securitisation is €10m.

1.30 Trusts and Settlements

TCA97 s791 Where a settlor has power to enjoy the income of his settlement, or where the settlor or his wife has power of revocation, all the income of the settlement will be deemed to be his income for tax purposes.

TCA97 s792 Where the settlor divests himself absolutely of his capital into a settlement he will not be charged to tax on any income arising to the settlement.

TCA97 s795-s746 The income of a settlement created by a living parent in favour of his children, who are under 18 and unmarried, is deemed to be the income of the parent for tax purposes, unless the settlement is irrevocable and accumulating.

1.30.1 Surcharge on undistributed income

TCA97 s805 Trustees are liable to tax at the standard rate on settlement income. Where there is undistributed settlement income, there is an additional 20% surcharge. If the distributable income of the settlement is distributed within the year of assessment, or within 18 months of the end of the year of assessment, the surcharge does not apply. In computing the distributable income the expenses of the trustees, which are properly chargeable to income are allowable deductions. Undistributed income of a charity or of an approved pension scheme is not liable to the surcharge.

CHAPTER 2 CORPORATION TAX

2.1 Administration and Fundamental Concepts

2.1.1 Scope of corporation tax

TCA97 s4 All companies resident in the State and all non-resident companies which carry on a trade in the State through a branch or agency, subject to specific exceptions, are liable to corporation tax.

TCA97 s882 A company which commences to carry on a trade, profession or business is obliged to deliver a written statement within thirty days of commencement to the Revenue Commissioners containing such information as the name of the company, its registered office, the name of the secretary and the nature of the trade, profession or business.

The penalty for not submitting such a statement is €630 on the company and €125 on the secretary. If judgement is given and a statement is still outstanding then a further penalty of €60 per day is payable.

An Inspector of Taxes has the power to make corporation tax assessments on any company whether it is resident in the State or not.

The appeal provisions that exist for income tax purposes also apply for corporation tax purposes (see 1.1.12).

2.1.2 Corporation tax rates

TCA97 s22 With effect from 1 January 2003 the following rates of corporation tax apply:

(i) **10%** Applicable to the trading profits of manufacturing companies and certain IFSC and Shannon Airport Zone companies

(ii) **12½%** Applicable to Schedule D Case I and II profits

(iii) **20%** Applicable to profits arising from certain residential land transactions

(iv) **25%** Applicable to Schedule D, Case III, IV and V profits, certain land dealing activities and income from working minerals and petroleum activities.

The 10% rate will continue to apply to manufacturing income until such time as title to that rate expires, at which stage such income will be taxable at 12½%.

2.1.3 Foreign dividends

Section 43, Finance Act 2008 made a number of changes to the taxation of foreign dividends received by companies within the charge to Irish tax from companies that are resident for tax purposes in EU Member States or in countries with which Ireland has a tax treaty. Such dividends that are paid out of trading profits will be chargeable to tax here at the 12.5% rate of corporation tax instead of at the 25% rate. Where dividends do not qualify to be charged at the 12.5% rate, they continue to be charged at the 25% rate. Where a dividend is paid partly out of trading profits and partly out of other profits, the part of the dividend that is paid out of trading profits of the dividend paying company will be taxable at the 12.5% rate.

Trading profits of such foreign companies will be allowed to pass up through tiers of companies by way of dividend payments so that, when ultimately paid to a company within the charge to corporation tax in the State, that company will be taxed on the dividends received by it at the 12.5% rate.

The full amount of a foreign dividend received by a company will be chargeable at the 12.5% rate where certain conditions are met, notwithstanding that a part of the dividend may not be paid out of trading profits. The conditions are:

- That 75% or more of the dividend-paying company's profits must be trading profits, either trading profits of that company or dividends received by it out of trading profits of lower tier companies that are resident in EU Member States or in countries with which Ireland has a double tax treaty.
- That an asset condition must be satisfied on a consolidated basis by the company that receives the dividend and all of its subsidiaries. The aggregate value of the trading assets of those companies must not be less than 75% of the aggregate value of all of their assets.

Companies that are portfolio investors and that receive a dividend from a company resident in an EU Member State or a country with which Ireland has a double tax treaty will be taxed on the dividends at the 12.5% rate. A portfolio investor in a company is an investor with a holding of not more than 5% in the company.

The new rules are deemed to have applied as respects dividends received by a company on or after 1 January 2007.

2.1.4 Development land

TCA97 s21A

(i) 25% Rate – Non-Residential Land

Profits arising from dealing in undeveloped non-residential land (but not profits from construction operations) are taxable at 25%.

(ii) 12.5% Fully Developed Land

Profits arising from dealing in land which has been fully developed by a company are liable at the standard rate. Fully developed land is defined as land:

(i) On which a building or structure has been constructed by or for the company before that time, and

(ii) Which has been developed by the company to such an extent that it could be reasonably expected at that time that no further development of the land would be carried out in the 20 years beginning at the time of disposal. Development which is not material and which is intended to facilitate the occupation of and the use or enjoyment of the structure for the purposes for which it was constructed may be ignored.

Material Development

A development will not be material if it consists of one or more of the following:

(i) An exempt development (see below), or

(ii) A development, where the total floor area of the building or buildings on the land *after* such development is not greater than 120% of the total floor area of the building or buildings on the land calculated without regard to that development.

An "exempt development" refers to a development within Class 1 of Part I of the Second Schedule to the Local Government Planning and Development Regulations 1994, which complies with the conditions and limitations specified for that class.

TCA97 s644B *(iii) 20% Rate – Residential Land*

An effective corporation tax rate of 20% applies to profits or gains derived from dealing in or developing residential land. This 20% rate is arrived at by taxing the profits at 25% (i.e. the excepted trade rate) and claiming a 1/5th relief under section 664B which reduces the effective rate to 20%.

The 20% rate also applies to profits from certain construction operations referred to as preparatory measures which include:

(i) the demolition or dismantling of any building or structure on the land,

(ii) the construction or demolition of any works forming part of the land, being roadworks, water mains, wells, sewers or installations for the purposes of land drainage, or

(iii) any other operations which are preparatory to residential development on the land other than the laying of foundations for such development.

"Residential development land" means land

(a) disposed of to:

- a housing authority,
- the National Building Agency Limited, or
- a body approved of for the purposes of section 6 of the Housing (Miscellaneous Provisions) Act, 1992,

where the land is specified in a certificate in writing given by a housing authority or the National Building Agency Limited, (as appropriate) to be land required for the purposes of the Housing Acts, 1966 to 1998;

(b) which has permission for residential development under section 26 of the Local Government (Planning and Development) Act, 1963, and such permission has not ceased to exist; or

(c) which is, in accordance with a development objective (as indicated in the development plan of the planning authority) concerned), for use solely or primarily for residential purposes.

See 1.7.11 re: income tax rate applying to residential development land.

2.1.5 Residence

TCA97 s24-s25 Prior to the Finance Act 1999, the residence of a company was determined not by the place of incorporation but by where the central management and control actually resides. The key factors to be considered in determining where the central management and control resides are:

(a) Location of Directors' Meetings;

(b) Location of Shareholders' Meetings;

(c) Location of Head Office of the Company;

(d) Location of Statutory Books, Company Seal;

(e) Where major contracts are negotiated and policy determined.

All companies incorporated in the State after 11 February 1999 are resident for tax purposes and all companies incorporated prior to that date, are resident for tax purposes from 1 October 1999. However the link between incorporation and residence will not apply where:

(I) the company or a related company carries on a trade in the State, and either the company is ultimately controlled by persons resident in EU Member States or countries with which Ireland has a tax treaty, or the company or a related company are quoted companies.

or

(ii) the company is regarded as not resident in the State under a tax treaty between Ireland and another country.

2.1.6 Accounting periods

TCA97 s27

Corporation Tax is chargeable in respect of the taxable profits of a company for an accounting period. An accounting period commences whenever a company:

(a) commences to carry on a trade,

(b) becomes resident in the State,

(c) acquires its first source of income, or

(d) is being wound up.

An accounting period ends on the occasion of any of the following:

(a) On the expiration of twelve months from the beginning of the accounting period.

(b) On an accounting date of the company, or, if there is a period for which the company does not make up accounts, the end of that period.

(c) On the company beginning or ceasing to trade or to be, in respect of the trade or (if more than one) of all the trades carried on by it, within the charge to corporation tax.

(d) On the company beginning or ceasing to be resident in the State.

(e) On the company being wound up.

2.1.7 Self-assessment

TCA97 s951

The self-assessment system applies to companies with effect from 1 October 1989.

2.1.8 Returns

TCA97 s951

A company must submit a return of profits, chargeable gains and other particulars to the Inspector of Taxes as follows:

Accounting Period Ending	Due Date
Before 1st January 2003	9 months after the end of the accounting period.
On or after 1st January 2003	On a date, 9 months after the end of the accounting period but no later than the 21st day of that month.

2.1.9 Late returns

TCA97 s1084

Where a company's tax return is not submitted to the Inspector of Taxes on or before the return filing date, the company is penalised by way of a surcharge and a restriction on the use the company may make of certain reliefs and allowances, as outlined below:

(a) Surcharge

Where a company's return is not submitted on or before the filing date, the tax liability for that period is increased by a surcharge on the amount of the tax assessed. The rate of surcharge applicable is 10% for accounting periods ending on or before 5 April 1995.

For accounting periods ending on or after 6 April 1995, the surcharge is as follows:

(a) 5% of the amount of tax subject to a maximum of €12,695, where the return is submitted before the expiry of two months after the specified date, and

(b) 10% of the amount of tax subject to a maximum of €63,485 where the return is not submitted within two months after the specified date.

Finance Act 2004 provided for the application of a surcharge where a company which is claiming certain specified reliefs fails to give the additional information which will now be required to be included on the annual tax return forms with effect for chargeable periods commencing on or after 1 January 2004. The surcharge will only arise where, after the filing of the tax return, the taxpayer becomes aware, or it is brought to their attention that the additional information has not been included on the return and the taxpayer fails to provide the required information without undue delay. Where a surcharge applies in these circumstances it will be the 5% surcharge which is subject to the normal maximum of €12,695.

Where a surcharge is applied, it must be included in an assessment so that the taxpayer can appeal against the surcharge to the Appeal Commissioners if the taxpayer is aggrieved with it.

(b) Restriction of Allowances and Reliefs

TCA97 s1085 Where a company failed to submit a tax return for accounting periods ended between 1 April 1992 and 5 April 1995 on time, there was an effective 50% restriction on the use the company could make of certain reliefs and allowances. With regard to accounting periods ending on or after 6 April 1995 the restrictions are graded and capped as follows:

(i) Where the delay in filing is less than two months, reliefs and allowances are restricted by 25% subject to a maximum in each case of €31,740.

(ii) Where the delay is two months or more, reliefs and allowances are restricted by 50%, subject to a maximum in each case of €158,715.

The following are the reliefs and allowances which are restricted:

- set off for excess Schedule D Case IV and Schedule D Case V capital allowances against total profits;
- set off for trading losses against total profits in current year and carry back to prior year;
- carry back of Schedule D Case V deficiency against Schedule D Case V income of previous accounting period;
- refund of tax credit on franked investment income;
- entitlement to reverse claim for refund under section 25 (1);
- entitlement to reverse claim under section 26 (1) (refund of tax credit on franked investment income by use of trading losses and terminal losses in case of financial concerns);
- relief for ring-fenced trading losses against ring-fenced trading income;
- relief for ring-fenced trading losses on a value basis;
- entitlement to group relief. This includes: entitlement to make group payments without withholding tax;
- group loss relief;
- consortium relief;
- relief for ring-fenced trading losses and charges against other ring-fenced income within a corporate group;
- relief for excess ring-fenced trading losses and charges on a value basis within a corporate group.

In the case of any of the reliefs which involve groups of companies (e.g. loss relief) it is a condition that both the surrendering company and the claimant company should each have submitted their tax returns on time.

2.1.10 Expression of doubt

TCA97 s955 Where a taxpayer is in doubt as regards a matter to be included in a return, his obligations with regard to the matter will be fulfilled if he draws the Inspector's attention to the matter in question. The provision does not apply where the Inspector or the Appeal Commissioners are of the opinion that the doubt was not genuine and the taxpayer was acting with an avoidance or evasion of tax motive.

2.1.11 Payment of corporation tax

(i) Accounting periods ending on or before 31 December 2005.

Please see the 31st or earlier editions of this book for details.

(ii) Accounting periods ending on or after 1 January 2006.

For accounting periods ending on or after 1 January 2006, preliminary tax will be due and payable on a day 31 days prior to the end of the accounting period, but no later than the 21st day of the month in which that day falls.

Where the accounting period is less than one month and one day, preliminary tax is due and payable on the last day of the accounting period, but no later than the 21st day of the month in which that day falls.

Where there is tax payable by a company and any of the following occur:

- The company has defaulted in the payment of preliminary tax,
- The preliminary tax paid by a 'small company' is less than 90% of the actual liability, or 100% of the corporation tax liability for the preceding period,
- Where the company is not a small company and the preliminary tax is less than 90% of the actual tax for the period; or
- the preliminary tax is not paid by the date on which it is due and payable,

then the tax shall be deemed to have been due and payable on the date on which the preliminary tax for the chargeable period was due.

Where a company pays its preliminary tax by the appropriate due date, but:

- the preliminary tax paid is less than 90% of the tax payable for the chargeable period; or
- the preliminary tax is not less than 90% of the tax payable for the chargeable period if it excluded any amount in respect of a chargeable gain arising in the last month of the accounting period; and,
- the company makes a further payment of preliminary tax within one month of the accounting period and this payment and the first instalment equals 90% of the actual tax liability,

then the preliminary tax payable by the company shall be deemed to have been paid by the date on which it was due and payable.

(iii) Small Companies

"Small companies" (i.e., companies where the tax liability of the preceeding chargeable period does not exceed a relevant limit) may base their preliminary tax payment on 100% of the prior year's corresponding corporation tax liability. The relevant limits are as follows:

Due date for preliminary tax	Limit
On or before 06/12/2006	€50,000
Between 07/12/2006 - 05/12/2007	€150,000
On or after 06/12/2007	€200,000

(iv) Start up Companies

New companies which do not expect their tax liability for the first year to exceed a relevant limit are not required to pay preliminary tax in their first year. The relevant limits are as follows:

Due date for preliminary tax	Limit
Between 07/12/2006 - 05/12/2007	€150,000
On or after 06/12/2007	€200,000

(v) IFRS Companies

A transitional rule, which related to preliminary tax for the first three accounting periods in respect of which a company applied International Financial Reporting Standards (IFRS) or equivalent Irish Generally Accepted Accounting Practice (GAAP) to gains and losses from financial instruments, has been made permanent. This rule provides that the amount of preliminary tax to be paid one month before the end of the accounting period does not have to take account of unrealised gains or losses on financial instruments that arise from movements in the fair value of those instruments in the last two months of the accounting period. The company makes a top-up payment one month after the end of the accounting period, to bring the amount of preliminary tax up to 90% of the final tax liability for that accounting period.

(vi) Pay and file for corporation tax

In respect of accounting periods ending on or after 1 January 2003 a pay-and-file system operates for corporation tax purposes. Corporation tax returns for relevant periods must be submitted to the Collector General's office as opposed to the relevant Inspector of Taxes. The submission date for corporation tax returns has been advanced. Previously the return filing was nine months after the end of the accounting period. Where this date fell on a calendar date later than the 21st day of the month, section 950 TCA 1997 provides that the filing date is now brought back to the earlier 21st day of the month. Section 950 TCA 1997 was amended as regards companies where a winding up has commenced - the requirement to file a return within three months of the commencement of the winding up is now amended to provide that where this date would fall later than the 21st day of the calendar month, the filing date is now the 21st day of the calendar month. Section 958 TCA 1997 provides that the due date for the balance of corporation tax due in respect of an accounting period is the same date as the filing date for the return - that is within nine months of the end of the accounting period subject to the 21 day rule referred to above. The balance of corporation tax is payable by the return filing date even if the return is filed early.

2.1.12 Calculation of taxable profits and allowable losses

TCA97 s76 Corporation tax is charged on the profits of a company, i.e. income and chargeable gains.

Except as otherwise provided in the Corporation Tax Act income must be calculated in accordance with income tax principles. Income is calculated under the different Schedules and Cases appropriate to income tax.

Finance Act 2005 provides for the tax implications of the move by companies to the new International Financial Reporting Standards.

All EU companies listed on a stock exchange will, for any period of account commencing on or after 1 January 2005, be required to prepare their consolidated financial statements for the group in accordance with a common set of accounting standards entitled – International Financial Reporting Standards (IFRS) instead of the Irish generally accepted accounting practice (GAAP). Individual accounts of companies may be prepared in accordance with IFRS. However, once a company moves to IFRS, it will be required to use IFRS for the future except in exceptional circumstances.

The starting point for calculating taxable trading income of a company is the profit of the company according to its accounts. Where a company prepares its individual company accounts on the basis of IFRS, the section provides that such IFRS accounts will be used as the starting point for the calculation of taxable trading profits.

The legislation also provides for specific treatment of certain items for tax purposes and for some transitional arrangements.

The purpose of the transitional rules is to ensure against double taxation or no taxation of certain income on the move to IFRS – profits, losses and expenses that could otherwise fall out of the charge to tax are taxed or allowed as appropriate over a five-year period. The transitional provisions cover situations where companies make a "piecemeal" move to IFRS – this can arise, for example, where Irish generally accepted accounting practice (GAAP) moves gradually towards IFRS.

The current computation of income from finance leasing for tax purposes is retained.

Payments such as annuities, patent royalties, rents, and (to a limited extent) interest paid by a company, which are known as charges on income, are not deductible if they are charged to capital in the accounts. Finance Act 2006 provides that any royalty payments that are revenue in nature are not denied a deduction solely because they are included in the cost of an asset under IFRS treatment.

The provisions of the Capital Gains Tax Act 1975 apply to chargeable gains of companies. Gains or losses are calculated in the normal way.

Where "Development Land" is disposed of any gain arising is assessed to Capital Gains Tax.

TCA97 s83A Section 83A TCA 97 is a response to the OECD recommendation to prohibit a deduction for tax purposes of illegal payments made to a foreign official. The section explicitly denies a tax deduction in computing the amount of any income chargeable to tax under Schedule D for any payment, the making of which constitutes a criminal offence or, in the case of a payment made outside the State, where the payment, if made in the State would constitute a criminal offence.

2.1.13 Pre-trading expenses

TCA97 s82 An allowance may be claimed in respect of pre-trading expenses in the case of a trade or profession which is set up and commenced on or after 22 January 1997, provided that the expenses:

(i) were incurred for the purpose of the trade or profession, and

(ii) were incurred within three years of commencement, and

(iii) are not otherwise allowable in computing profits.

Where an allowance is granted for pre-trading expenses, it is treated as if the expenditure was incurred on the date on which the trade/ profession commenced.

A deduction may also be claimed in respect of certain pre-trading charges.

The pre-trading expenditure which is allowed cannot be used for the purpose of set off against income of the company other than that arising from the trade of profession in respect of which the expenditure was incurred.

2.1.14 Losses/management expenses

TCA97 s396 Trading losses are computed in the same manner as trading profits. A trading loss can be:

(a) Set off against other profits before charges in the same accounting period.

(b) Set off against profits before charges of the preceding accounting period of corresponding length, if the company carried on the trade in that period.

(c) Set off against future profits of the same trade unless the loss has been otherwise utilised.

TCA97 s396A New provisions in the Finance Act, 2001 place a ring fence on the offset of losses in the context of the new corporation tax rate structure. Two new rules apply as follows:

(i) losses incurred in a trade, the income from which is taxable at the standard corporation tax rate, may be set sideways in the current accounting period or backwards to the previous accounting period but only against "relevant" trading income, i.e. trading income other than income taxable at the 25% rate such as investment income.

(ii) for the financial years 2001 and 2002, losses incurred in a trade, the income from which is taxable at 10%, may be set sideways in the current accounting period or backwards to the previous accounting period but only against income which is taxable at the 10% rate.

TCA97 396B The Finance Act, 2002 introduced new provisions effective from 6 March 2001, that where there are unutilised losses they may be set off on a value basis against income for the current year and the previous accounting period. The value of the losses is computed by applying the tax rate in the year the loss arises and not the rate applicable in the year in which the losses are used. A company or group must first of all use available losses against other ring-fenced income before utilising the excess on the value basis for claims made on or after 6 February 2003.

Unused losses may be carried forward for offset against all trading income of the trade in which the loss is incurred.

Losses under the other Cases of Schedule D and capital losses may be utilised as follows:

TCA97 s396	CASE III (Trading)	Carry forward only against future Case III profits.
TCA97 s399	CASE IV	Carry forward only against Case IV profits.
TCA97 s399	CASE V (Rents)	Carry back to previous accounting period of same length and source and forward against future Case V profits.
TCA97 s308	CASE V (Excess Capital Allowances)	Same as trading losses.
TCA97 s78	CAPITAL LOSSES	Carry forward only against future capital profits.
TCA97 s653	CAPITAL LOSSES (Development Land)	Set against other capital profits of same accounting period or forward against future capital profits or development land profits.

TCA97 s397 Terminal loss relief arises where a company incurs a loss in its last twelve months trading and claims to carry back against income from the same trade in the preceding three years the loss incurred in the last twelve months. Terminal loss relief will be given only where all other claims for loss relief have been made.

TCA97 s83 If management expenses exceed the profits of a resident investment company the excess may be carried forward for set off against profits of a subsequent period.

TCA97 s157 Trading losses can be off set against franked investment income received in the current accounting period or in the preceding accounting period of equal length, resulting in a repayment of the tax credit.

If the company subsequently decides to avail of these losses, which were relieved at the standard rate, against future profits liable at a higher rate, it can do so under the provisions of section 157. The Revenue will clawback the income tax repaid by an assessment under Case IV of Schedule D.

TCA97 s663 Relief for losses incurred by a company in farming or market gardening is restricted in that the farming must be carried on a commercial basis. To enable losses to be set off against other income, it would be necessary for the company to make a profit every fourth year, or, in exceptional circumstances, every fifth year.

TCA97 s400 In a company reconstruction, the successor company can take over the accumulated trading losses of the predecessor company provided 75% of the shareholders in the successor company were shareholders in the predecessor company in the three-year period, one year before and two years after the reconstruction.

TCA97 s401 The carry forward of accumulated trading losses of a company will be disallowed where there has been both a change of ownership of the company and a major change in the nature or conduct of the trade carried on.

TCA97 s396B The corporation tax attributable to a life assurance business where the corporation tax is referable to profits of policyholders is excluded from eligibility for loss relief on a value basis. This limitation of loss relief applies to claims made on or after 4 February 2004.

2.1.15 Charges on income

TCA97 s243 Income tax at the standard rate should be deducted by companies from certain interest payments, patent royalties, annuities and other annual payments. These payments are known as charges and are not allowable as an expense in computing income for corporation tax purposes; they are, however, deductible from the corporation tax profit figure (i.e. the income plus chargeable gains figure). There are some exceptions to the general rule that income tax must be deducted from a payment if it is to qualify as a charge on income. Under current rules, payments of interest only qualify if they are paid to lending institution in the State. Finance Act 2005 provides that interest paid to similar institutions in the EU also come within the scope of the relief. Where there is an excess of charges in any year, the excess can be carried forward and set off against future profits of the same trade. Excess charges can, however, be utilised to augment a terminal loss.

TCA97s243A The ring fence provisions introduced in Finance Act, 2001 in relation to losses (see 2.1.14 above) apply in a similar manner to charges.

TCA97 s243B The further provisions introduced in Finance Act 2002 in relation to losses (see 2.1.14 above) apply in a similar manner to charges except that excess charges can only be utilised against other profits of the same accounting period. The requirement that a company or group must first of all use losses against other ring-fenced income before utilising the excess on the value basis also applies in a similar manner to the use of ring-fenced charges against other ring-fenced income.

TCA97 s239 Any income tax deducted from charges must be paid over to the Revenue within six months of the end of the company's accounting period. However where the company has received income under deduction of tax it may deduct the income tax suffered from the income tax owed and pay the balance to the Collector General. Where the income tax suffered exceeds the income tax owed, the excess is allowed as a deduction from the corporation tax payable.

2.1.16 Interest relief on borrowings to make an investment

TCA97 s247, s249 Interest relief is granted as a charge against a company's total profits for the year of payment when the interest arises on borrowings used to make an investment in a company. There is no ring-fencing of this charge.

There are anti-avoidance rules relating to recovery of capital and replacement loans. If there is a recovery of capital under these rules, then the borrower loses tax relief on the interest paid on the loan corresponding to the amount of interest paid which would be referable to the amount recovered.

The interpretation of the rules is complex and may require clarification from Revenue in many cases.

In relation to loans made on or after 2 February 2006, interest relief under section 247 will not be available when interest is paid by an investing company on a loan made to it by a company which is connected with it, where the loan is used to acquire ordinary share capital of a company from a company that is also connected with the investing company, or on lend to another company which uses the funds directly or indirectly to acquire capital of a company from a company that is connected with the investing company.

Interest relief will continue to apply:

- where the loan is used to acquire shares on their issue by a company, where the share capital is used to increase the capital available to that company for use in its trade or business, and not as part of any arrangement involving a circular flow of funds to the lending company or a connected company, or
- where the interest in respect of which relief under section 247 is being claimed by the investing company is matched by interest received or receivable by that company, or by dividends received by the company which are chargeable to corporation tax. There are

further provisions easing the new restrictions where such matching income arises in other companies that are connected with the investing companies.

2.1.17 Section 239 assessments

TCA97 s239 In respect of accounting periods ending on or after 6 April 1990, the requirement on companies to make a return and pay over to the Revenue, any income tax deducted from certain payments within six months of the end of the accounting period, was changed as follows:

(a) A return of payments must be made at the same time as the return of profits, and

(b) the income tax due is treated as corporation tax payable for the company's accounting period.

TCA97 s240 Where a company makes payments under deduction of tax in a period which is not an accounting period of the company, both the return of such payments and the tax deducted must be made within six months of the end of the accounting period.

TCA97 s241 Companies not resident in the State, but which carry on trade in the State are subject to the same conditions as are set out under section 239 above for accounting periods ending on or after 6 April 1990.

The income tax payments which are deemed to be payments of corporation tax by virtue of section 239 are not to be taken into account in calculating relief under the 10% corporation tax rules.

TCA97 s884 When required by notice, a company must furnish a return within the time limit stipulated in the notice, of the following:

(i) The profits of the company, specifying the sources of income, any capital gains or losses and particulars of all charges on income.

(ii) Distributions received with related tax credits.

(iii) Payments made under deduction of income tax.

(iv) A list of loans to participators.

2.2 Manufacturing Companies - Reduced Rate of 10%

TCA97
s442-s457

A reduced rate of corporation tax applies to manufacturing companies in respect of income arising from the sale of goods manufactured in the State. The corporation tax rate applicable to the sale of manufactured goods is:

Period	*Normal CT Rate*	*Reduction Factor*	*Manufacturing Rate*
1/4/1991 to 31/3/1995	40%	3/4	10%
1/4/1995 to 31/3/1997	38%	28/38	10%
1/4/1997 to 31/12/1997	36%	26/36	10%
1/1/1998 to 31/12/1998	32%	22/32	10%
1/1/1999 to 31/12/1999	28%	18/28	10%
1/1/2000 to 31/12/2000	24%	14/24	10%
1/1/2001 to 31/12/2001	20%	10/20	10%
1/1/2002 to 31/12/2002	10%	6/16	10%
1/1/2003 - onwards	12.5%	25/125	10%

Agreement has been reached between the Irish Government and the EU Commission with regard to the phasing out of the 10% manufacturing rate and profits which were taxed at 10% will be taxed at 12½% from 1 January 2003, with the following exceptions:

(i) Companies which carried on a manufacturing trade at 23 July 1998 continue to be taxed at 10% until 31 December 2010.

(ii) Companies which were not carrying on a manufacturing trade at 23 July 1998, but which were approved by a government grant agency on or before 31 July 1998 continue to be taxed at 10% until 31 December 2010.

(iii) IFSC Companies

Where certified operations were approved, on or before 31 July 1998, the 10% rate applied until 31 December 2005 and where certified operations were approved after 31 July 1998, the 10% rate applied until 31 December 2002.

(iv) Shannon Airport Zone

Where certified operations were approved on or before 31 May 1998, the 10% rate applied until 31 December 2005 and where certified operations were approved after 31 May 1998, the 10% rate applied until 31 December 2002.

TCA97 s448 The reduced rate applies to profits derived from goods manufactured and sold by the company. Other goods sold by the company are referred to as merchandise. The corporation tax payable is reduced by the formula:

$$\text{Corporation Tax} \times \frac{\text{Sales of Goods}}{\text{Sales of Goods and Merchandise}} \times \frac{\text{Income from Goods* and Merchandise}}{\text{Total Income*}} \times \text{Reduction Factor}$$

* Income less charges as deducted against 10% manufacturing income.

Finance Act 2008 amends section 448 TCA1997, which deals with the calculation of manufacturing relief by reducing the tax charged at the 12.5% rate of corporation tax on income from manufacturing to an effective 10% rate. This is a technical amendment which permits the offset of losses, charges and group relief on a euro-for-euro basis against certain foreign dividends liable to corporation tax at 12.5%.

TCA97 s443 "Goods" are defined in section 443 and mean goods manufactured in the State in the course of a trade by a company which, for the relevant accounting period, is the company claiming relief in relation to the trade. However, where:

(a) there are two companies one of which manufactures goods and the other of which sells them in the course of its trade, and

(b) one of the companies is a 90% subsidiary of the other or both companies are 90% subsidiaries of a third company, any goods manufactured within the State by one of the companies shall, when sold in the course of its trade by the other company, be deemed to have been manufactured within the State by the other company. 90% means where the parent company must be entitled to 90% of any distribution of profits and 90% of the assets on a winding up.

The definition of goods does not include goods sold by retail unless they are sold:

(a) to a person who carries on a trade of selling goods of a class to which the goods sold to him belong, or

(b) to a person who uses goods of that class for the purposes of a trade carried on by him, or

(c) to a person, other than an individual, who uses goods of that class for the purposes of an undertaking carried on by him.

The term manufacturing is extended to include the subjecting of commodities or materials belonging to another person to a process of manufacture within the State. Such services are regarded as manufacture of goods and the amount receivable from them is treated as an amount receivable from the sale of goods.

In addition to conventional manufacturing the following activities also qualify for the 10% manufacturing relief:

(a) Fish produced on a fish farm within the State.

(b) Mushrooms cultivated within the State. This activity ceases to come within the scope of the 10% rate in respect of accounting periods beginning on or after 1 June 1994.

(c) Repairing of ships carried out within the State.

(d) Design and planning services the work on the rendering of which is carried out in the State in connection with chemical, civil, electrical or mechanical engineering works executed outside the territories of the Member States of the European Communities.

(e) From 13 April 1984, Computer Services i.e., data processing services and/or software development services, the work on the rendering of which is carried out in the State in the course of a service undertaking in respect of which an employment grant was made by the IDA under S2 of the Industrial Development (No.2) Act 1981.

From 6 April 1989 the definition of "Computer Services" is extended to include technical or consultancy services which relate to data processing services and/or software development services, the work on the rendering of which is carried out in the State in the course of a service undertaking for which an employment grant was made by the Industrial Development Authority.

Where a grant for such Computer Services is made by the Shannon Free Airport Development Company Ltd or by Údarás na Gaeltachta, such services will be regarded as the manufacture of goods with effect from 1 January 1988.

(f) Qualifying shipping activities, i.e., the carriage of cargo and passengers on sea going ships which are Irish owned and registered or which are leased from foreign lessors without a crew. Losses and capital allowances arising from qualifying shipping trades cannot be offset against profits and income other than against another qualifying shipping trade. The 10% manufacturing relief applies for the period 1 January 1987 to 31 December 2000.

Manufacturing relief is granted to fishing vessels where the fish are subjected to a manufacturing process on board the qualifying ship, and to the letting or charter of a qualifying ship for qualifying purposes. It is also granted where a qualifying ship is used for transporting supplies or personnel to a mobile or fixed rig, platform vessel or installation of any kind at sea involved in hydrocarbon exploration and development - where

(i) the operation of the ship

and

(ii) the crew of the ship remain under the direction and control of the company.

Such companies do not qualify for investment in corporate trades relief and are subject to the leasing restrictions under S40 FA 1984.

Finance Act, 2001 provided for the early application of the 12.5% to qualifying shipping activities for the financial year 2001 and 2002. Thereafter, the standard rate of corporation tax was reduced to 12.5% for all trading activities. The ring-fence on capital allowances of a shipping trade remained in place until 31 December 2002.

(g) Income of Trading Houses.

A trading house is a company carrying on a trade which consists solely of the sale by wholesale on the export market of goods manufactured in the State.

(h) Cultivation of plants by the process known as micro propagation or plant cloning.

(i) Repair or maintenance of aircraft, aircraft engines or components within the State.

(j) The production of a film for exhibition to the public in cinemas or on television or for training or documentary purposes provided that not less than 75 per cent of the work on its production is carried out in the State.

(k) Meat processed within the State, including that owned by the Intervention Agency, in an establishment approved and inspected in accordance with the European Communities (Fresh Meat) Regulations 1987. For any accounting period beginning on or after 1 April 1990 there shall be excluded from the definition of manufacture any goods sold into an intervention agency and shall exclude from the definition of manufacture any goods sold to a person which are subsequently sold to the intervention agency.

(l) Fish processing carried on in the State.

(m) The remanufacture or repair of computer equipment or of subassemblies within the State, where such equipment or subassemblies were originally manufactured by that company or a connected company.

(n) Activities carried on by an agricultural or fishery society where:

– its trade consists wholly or mainly of the selling by wholesale of goods which have been acquired from its members;

– its members have already qualified for manufacturing relief in respect of the processing of these goods; and

– all, or the majority of its members are themselves agricultural or fishery societies.

(o) The purchase of milk by an agricultural society from its members and the subsequent sale of that milk to a certified qualifying company.

A qualifying company is one carrying on a trade which consists wholly or mainly of the manufacture of specified milk products, or is certified by the Minister for Agriculture, Food and Forestry as a qualifying company for the purposes of the section, notwithstanding that the trade does not consist wholly or mainly of the manufacture of milk products. In the latter case, the milk manufacturing activity will be regarded as a separate trade. This treatment will not apply, however, if the company's trade consists mainly of the application of a process of pasteurisation of milk. The Minister may issue a qualifying certificate where he is satisfied that a company has carried on or is intending to carry on the milk manufacturing trade for a period of at least three years.

Certificates remain in force for two years but may be revoked by the Minister at any time.

(p) The production of a newspaper, which is published at least fortnightly for sale to the public, regardless of whether the production company prints the newspaper or not. The relief applies to both the income from the sale of the newspaper and to the income from advertising services provided in the course of the production of the newspaper.

(q) Certain trading operations carried out in the Customs House Docks Area as follows:

TCA97 s446

The Customs House Docks Area is as defined in section 322. To qualify for the relief the company must obtain a certificate from the Minister for Finance. The Minister has to certify that such trading operations as specified in the certificate are relevant trading operations for the purpose of the section. The relief applies from the date specified in the certificate until 31 December 2005 unless the certificate is revoked because the company fails to set up in the Customs House Docks Area, or where it fails to comply with any of the conditions set out in the certificate. The Minister must give notice of the revocation in writing.

The Minister will not certify that a trading operation is a relevant trading operation unless:

(a) it is carried on within the Customs House Docks Area,

(b) the Minister is satisfied that it will contribute to the development of the area as an international financial business area,

(c) it falls within one or more of the following classes of trading operations

(i) the provision for persons not ordinarily resident in the State of services, in relation to transactions in foreign currencies, which are of a type normally provided by a bank in the ordinary course of its trade,

(ii) the carrying on behalf of persons not ordinarily resident in the State of international financial activities including, in particular,

(1) global money management

(2) international dealings in foreign currencies and in futures, options and similar financial assets which are denominated in foreign currencies

(3) dealings in bonds, equities and similar instruments which are denominated in foreign currencies, and

(4) insurance and related activities

(iii) the provision for persons not ordinarily resident in the State of services of, or facilities for processing, control, accountancy, communication, clearing, settlement, or information storage in relation to financial activities,

(iv) the development or supply of computer software for use in the provision of the services at (iii) above or for the reprocessing, analysing or similar treatment of information in relation to financial services, or

(v) the carrying on of operations which are similar to, or ancillary to, any of the operations described in the foregoing paragraphs, in regard to which the Minister is of the opinion that they will contribute to the use of the area as an international financial services centre,

(vi) dealing in commodity futures or commodity options on behalf of persons not ordinarily resident in the State,

(vii) the income and gains arising to a Foreign Life Assurance company or Foreign Unit Trust business located in the IFSC on investments located outside the State.

(viii) The provision of management services to collective investment undertakings, the investors in which are non-resident and the provision of services ancillary to such management services.

Any reference to a service or facility provided for an activity carried on, on behalf of a person not ordinarily resident in the State will not qualify to the extent that it is provided for any part of the non resident's trade which is carried on in the State.

Where a company, because of circumstances, cannot immediately locate in the Custom House Docks Area a certificate will be granted provided the company within a certain time limit moves into the area.

2.2.1 Losses

TCA97 s455 Section 455 imposes a restriction or "ring fence" on losses and allowances attributable to "10 per cent" trading activities. From 1 April 1992 such losses and allowances may only be set against "10 per cent" income in the current and previous accounting periods and carried forward for set-off against trading income in subsequent accounting periods. There are certain exceptions to this rule in the case of an IFSC company or where the loss is created by capital allowances due under certain projects approved by the IDA in the two-year period ended 31 December 1988.

Similarly where a company incurs a charge (e.g., royalties, interest etc.) in the course of a 10 per cent activity the amount of relief available for that charge is restricted to the income arising from the 10 per cent activity.

Additional ring fence provisions are contained in Finance Act, 2001 in relation to the new corporation tax rate structure. (See 2.1.14, 2.1.15 and 2.4.)

Section 455 ceased to have effect from 1 January 2003.

The Finance Act 2002 introduced provisions for the set off of losses on a value basis (see 2.1.14, 2.1.15 and 2.4).

2.2.2 Exclusions

TCA97 s443 Sales of manufactured goods to the Intervention Agency are specifically excluded from the 10% relief, and for the purpose of this exclusion the sale of goods to a person other than the Intervention Agency shall be deemed to be a sale to the Intervention Agency if, and to the extent that, these goods are ultimately sold to the Intervention Agency.

Sales of goods from mining and construction operations are specifically excluded from the 10% relief. However, companies carrying on such activities which also manufacture goods in course of the same trade may be entitled to relief on a just and reasonable basis.

For any relevant accounting period beginning on or after the 1 April 1990 the following activities are not regarded as manufacturing:

(i) Processes applied to any product, produce or material acquired in bulk for sale or distribution such as: dividing, cutting, drying, mixing, sorting, packaging, branding, testing or purifying.

(ii) The application of methods of preservation, pasteurisation or maturation to any foodstuffs.

(iii) The preparation of food or drink for human consumption where it is intended to be consumed at or about the time it is prepared.

(iv) Improving or altering any articles or materials without imposing on them a change in their character.

(v) Repairing, refurbishing, reconditioning or restoring articles or materials.

(vi) Except where a company sells goods manufactured by a closely connected company, no company will be entitled to manufacturing relief if it does not carry out the process for which the relief is being claimed.

2.2.3 Time limit

TCA97 s448 A claim for manufacturing relief must be lodged before the date on which the assessment for the accounting period becomes final and conclusive.

2.2.4 Anti-avoidance provisions

TCA97 s453 Section 453 deals with transactions between associated persons and effectively substitutes arm's length prices for artificial prices in respect of dealings between connected persons. These rules apply in the following cases:

(1) If a buying company is making a claim and buys from another person (the seller) and:

  (a) the seller has control over the buyer, or the seller being a body corporate or partnership, the buyer has control over the seller or some other person has control over both the seller and the buyer, and

  (b) the price in the transaction is less than that which might have been expected to obtain if the parties to the transaction had been independent parties dealing at arm's length,

  the income or losses of the buyer and the seller are computed for any purpose of the Taxes Acts as if the price in the transaction had been that which would have obtained if the transaction had been a transaction between independent persons dealing as aforesaid.

(2) Where a company claiming relief sells goods to another person (the buyer) and

(a) the buyer has control over the seller or, the buyer being a body corporate or partnership, the seller has control over the buyer or some other person has control over both the seller and the buyer, and

(b) the goods are sold at a price greater than the price which they might have been expected to fetch if the parties to the transaction had been independent parties dealing at arm's length,

the income or losses of the buyer and the seller are computed, for any purpose of the Taxes Acts, as if the goods had been sold by the seller to the buyer for the price which they would have fetched if the transaction had been a transaction between independent persons dealing as aforesaid.

Control is defined as having the meaning assigned to it by section 11.

2.2.5 Shannon airport

TCA97 s445

Certain trading operations of a qualified company carried on within the airport qualify for the manufacturing companies' tax rate of 10%. This expired on 31 December 2005. The Minister for Finance gave a certificate certifying that such operations qualify for this rate if they fell within one or more of the following classes of trading operations.

(a) Repair or maintenance of aircraft.

(b) Trading operations in regard to which the Minister is of the opinion, after consultation with the Minister for Transport, that they contribute to the use or development of the airport.

(c) Trading operations which are ancillary to any of those operations described in the foregoing paragraphs or to any operation consisting, apart from this section, of the manufacture of goods.

A condition of the relief was that the operations must be derived from an "initial investment" within the principles of Articles 92/94 of the EU Treaty.

2.3 Research and Development

TCA97 s766 Finance Act 2004 introduced a new incentive to companies to carry on Research and Development (R&D) in Ireland. These new incentives are subject to EU approval before they come into effect.

2.3.1 Credit for R&D expenditure

A credit of 20% of the incremental expenditure on revenue items, royalties, plant and machinery related to R&D can be offset against a company's corporation tax liability in the year in which it is incurred. A credit of 20% of the cost of a building used for the purposes of R&D and in respect of which capital allowances are granted is available on a straight line basis over four years. The computation of credit is made by reference to expenditure incurred in a group as opposed to on a company by company basis.

R&D credit can effectively be group relieved. Any unused credit can be carried forward indefinitely against the corporation tax liability for subsequent periods until it is used.

2.3.2 Definition of R&D

R&D for the purposes of the relief includes basic research, applied research or experimental development. These activities must seek to achieve scientific or technological advancement and involve the resolution of scientific or technological uncertainty.

In relation to accounting periods ending on or after 2 February 2006, the Revenue Commissioners or a Revenue-authorised officer may consult with experts to determine whether the expenditure incurred by a company was incurred in the carrying on by it of research and development activities. Where the company shows to the satisfaction of the Revenue Commissioners or their authorised officer, or on appeal to the Appeal Commissioners, that disclosure of information to such person could prejudice the company's business, then the Revenue Commissioners or their authorised officer will not make such disclosure.

2.3.3 Entitlement to R&D relief

A company which carries on a trade in Ireland, undertakes R&D activities in Ireland or within the EEA and incurs the expenditure shall be entitled to the credit. Where the R&D company does not trade, the company may nevertheless qualify for the credit if it is a 51% subsidiary of a trading company or of a holding company of trading companies. This will allow expenditure incurred by a dedicated R&D company of a trading group to qualify for the relief.

Also, where the company is not a member of a trading group and is in its pre-trading phase, provision is made to allow R&D carried out by that company to qualify for the credit at a later date - the credit can be used when the company commences to trade and has a corporation tax liability. This facilitates the claiming of credits by campus companies when they commence trading.

Irish R&D credit is denied for R&D activities undertaken in EEA countries that also grant relief to the company for that expenditure.

2.3.4 Base/incremental expenditure

The section introduces the concept of a base year for calculating qualifying expenditure. The section as amended by Finance Act 2008 changes the base year rules so that for the future the position will be as follows:.

(a) as respects accounting periods commencing before 2014, the base year is 2003,

(b) as respects later accounting periods, the base year is a corresponding year ending 10 years before the end of the year of claim (e.g., for 2014 the base year will be 2004).

Expenditure on revenue items, royalties, plant and machinery, which qualifies for credit in any year is the incremental expenditure over the expenditure incurred in the base year.

There is no calculation of a base for expenditure on buildings. However, there is provision for full claw back of the credit where the building is sold/used for non-R&D purposes within a 10-year period.

2.3.5 Qualifying expenditure

In general, credit is given for all R&D related expenditure that consists of:

- royalties
- expenses deductible for trading purposes
- plant and machinery entitled to capital allowances,
- revenue and capital expenditure on scientific research, and
- buildings entitled to capital allowances.

The credit is not available for a royalty that is exempt royalty income in the hands of the recipient or is not arm's length. Further, no credit is available for expenditure that is State funded.

In relation to accounting periods ending on or after 2 February 2006 where machinery or plant will not be used wholly and exclusively for research and development activities, there will be a proportionate allocation, as appears just and reasonable, of the expenditure on plant and machinery for the purposes of determining the amount that will be treated as wholly and exclusively incurred on research and development activities. A subsequent apportionment is to be made where the earlier apportionment requires to be revised in the light of actual events, and any resulting assessments or repayments of tax as are necessary will be made.

2.3.6 Use of universities and subcontractors

Where a company subcontracts the R&D, neither the company nor the sub-contractor is entitled to the credit except where the R&D is sub-contracted to universities or third level institutions in the EEA. Where this exception applies, the payment to the university, up to an amount that does not exceed 5% of the expenditure incurred on R&D activities carried out by the company, will qualify for R&D credit in the company bearing the cost.

Finance Act 2007 provides that expenditure by companies on sub-contracting research and development work to unconnected parties will qualify under the tax credit scheme up to a limit of 10 per cent qualifying research and development expenditure incurred by the company in any one year. This will apply where the sub-contractor carrying out the research and development does not claim a tax credit in respect of such expenditure. This measure is in addition to the existing provision in the scheme in respect of research and development work carried out for companies by universities.

The Finance Act 2007 provision in relation to sub-contracting research and development work applies for accounting periods ending on or after 1 January 2007 in respect of expenditure incurred on or after 1 January 2007.

2.4 Group Relief

TCA97
s410-s429

Group relief may be claimed where one member of a group of companies is entitled to surrender its trading loss to another member of the same group. To be a member of a group of companies, the following conditions have to be satisfied:

(a) Both companies must be resident in the State or in one of the Member States of the European Economic Area with which Ireland has a tax treaty and one company must be a 75% subsidiary of the other company, or both companies must be 75% subsidiaries of a third company which is also resident in the State or in one of the Member States of the European Economic Area with which Ireland has a tax treaty.

Loss relief however, is restricted to losses incurred in a trade in respect of which the company is within the charge to corporation tax in the State.

(b) The parent company must be beneficially entitled to not less than 75% of the profits available for distribution to the equity holders.

(c) The parent company must be beneficially entitled to not less than 75% of the assets available for distribution to the equity holders on a winding up.

It is not necessary for the claimant company to make a claim for the full amount of trading losses available and therefore two or more group or consortium companies may make a claim in respect of the same surrendering company for the same accounting period.

Similarly, an investment company which has an excess of management expenses for an accounting period may surrender the excess to a fellow group member. Excess charges may also be surrendered within a group of companies. Claims for group relief must be made by the claimant company within two years from the end of the surrendering company's accounting period to which the claim relates.

The surrendering company must also notify the Inspector of Taxes of its consent to surrender the relief.

Group relief is also available to members of a consortium where the loss making company is owned by a consortium. A consortium is one where five or fewer companies own between them all the ordinary share capital of a trading company or of a holding company whose business consists wholly or mainly in the holding of shares in trading companies which are its 90 per cent subsidiaries. The loss making company cannot be more than a 75% subsidiary of any member of the consortium.

Inter-group charges are paid gross but with the condition that both the paying company and the receiving company must be resident in the State. Finance Act 2005 relaxes this condition in certain circumstances. It provides that companies in other EU Member States or in countries outside the EU which are in the European Economic Area and with which Ireland has a double taxation treaty may also benefit from the withholding tax exemption, provided that the payment is taken into account in computing income subject to tax in the recipient's country. All the other conditions in relation to the exemption from the obligation to deduct withholding tax in respect of group payments remain.

TCA97 s420 Losses, excess capital allowances or excess charges on income of a company liable at a 10% rate of tax can only be surrendered to another group or consortium company which is also liable at a 10% rate of tax.

The two exceptions to this rule are:

(i) surrenders to or from companies carrying on a trade within the IFSC area, and

(ii) for the duration of export relief, this restriction will not apply where the last claim to relief from CT by a company in respect of manufacturing income was a claim for ESR.

TCA97 s420A The ring-fence provisions introduced in Finance Act 2001 in relation to losses and charges on income (see 2.1.14 and 2.1.15 above) apply in a similar manner to group relief.

TCA97 s420B The provisions introduced in Finance Act, 2002 in relation to losses and charges (see 2.1.14 and 2.1.15 above) apply in a similar manner to group relief. It should be noted that group relief can only be utilised against the profits of the corresponding accounting period.

With effect from 4 February 2004 section 420B excludes from eligibility for group loss relief on a value basis the corporation tax attributable to a life assurance business where that corporation tax is referable to profits of the policyholders.

TCA97 s617 Sales of assets between companies within a Group are treated as if the transaction gives rise to a no profit/no loss situation. See paragraph 2.4.1 re: a company leaving a group, having received an asset by way of inter-group transfer.

Finance Act, 2002 allows transfers of assets involving Irish branches of companies resident in a Member State of the European Economic Area with which Ireland has a tax treaty to be treated on a tax neutral basis. To benefit from the treatment each of the companies involved must either be resident in the State or be an EU resident company carrying on a trade in the State through a branch and in respect of which the transferred asset is a chargeable asset for capital gains tax purposes in the State.

The principal changes made are:

- A company resident in a Member State of the European Economic Area with which Ireland has a tax treaty which is not resident in the State but which carries on a trade in the State through a branch or agency may be a party to a reconstruction or amalgamation involving the transfer of a business on a tax neutral basis. No tax is paid at the time of transfer but the company receiving the assets is treated as having acquired them at the cost to the transferring company. The assets must be chargeable assets in relation to the non-resident company.

- A company resident in a Member State of the European Economic Area with which Ireland has a tax treaty (which is not resident in the State) but which carries on a trade in the State through a branch or agency may be a party to a transfer of assets between members of a group on a tax neutral basis. The assets are treated as being transferred at a consideration which gives rise to neither a gain nor a loss for capital gains tax purposes. The assets must be chargeable assets in relation to the non-resident company.
- A company resident in a Member State of the European Economic Area with which Ireland has a tax treaty (which is not resident in the State) but which carries on trade here through a branch or agency can avail of rollover relief in a group context. This allows deferral of capital gains tax where the group disposes of an asset used in a trade and reinvests the proceeds in new assets for use in the trade. All trades carried on in the State by group members are regarded as a single trade.
- A charge to capital gains tax will crystallise where a company acquires an asset in a transaction and the asset subsequently ceases in certain circumstances to be a chargeable assets in relation to the company.

Anti-avoidance measures have been amended to protect the Irish tax base following this extension of tax neutral treatment of transfers involving non-resident companies.

2.4.1 Anti-avoidance

(i) Company leaving a Group

TCA97 s423 Where a company leaves a group, after having received an asset by way of inter-group transfer, it incurs a chargeable gain on the asset. The gain is calculated by reference to the date at which the original owner company acquired the asset.

These provisions do not apply where:

(i) the asset was acquired by the company leaving the group prior to 6 April 1974, or

(ii) the asset has been held by the company leaving the group for more than 10 years, or

(iii) the company leaves the group by reason of it or any other company being wound up. This exclusion applies only where a company ceases to be a member of a group on or after 28 March

1996 by way of a winding up or dissolution, which is for bona fide commercial reasons and must not be part of a scheme or arrangement the main purpose or one of the main purposes of which is the avoidance of tax, or

(iv) two or more companies which themselves form a sub group, leave together and the asset had earlier been transferred between them. However, where the companies leave the group on or after 23 April 1996, and

a dividend has been paid or a distribution made by one of those companies to a company which is not one of those now leaving the group; and

this dividend or distribution has been paid wholly or partially out of profits which derive from the disposal of an asset by one of the companies to another, then

the amount of the dividend paid, or distribution made, to the extent that it comes out of those profits, shall be deemed for capital gains tax purposes to be part of the consideration received by the member of the group making the disposal. Thus the amount which the company receives together with such a dividend constitutes the proceeds of the disposal.

(ii) Company entering a Group

TCA97 s626A The "pre-entry losses" of a company joining a group on or after 1 March 1999 cannot be used to offset subsequent capital gains within the group. The company entering the group will, however, be able to use such losses in the same way that it could have, had it never joined the group.

(iii) Depreciatory Transactions

TCA97 s621 Certain anti-avoidance provisions may be invoked where a loss arises on the disposal of a group company and the loss has arisen as a result of a depreciatory transaction. Such transactions may include the movement of assets or the payment of dividends.

Any loss arising under these circumstances will be reduced by such an extent as appears to the Inspector of Taxes to be just and reasonable.

(iv) "Loss Buying" of trading losses

TCA97 s401 Trading losses cannot be carried forward where there is a change in ownership and a major change in the nature or conduct of the trade.

2.4.2 European Court of Justice ruling on foreign losses

TCA97 Pt12 Ch5

Finance Act 2007 amends the provisions in relation to group relief to comply with a ruling of the European Court of Justice (ECJ) on foreign losses. The ruling was that the UK model of group relief (which the Irish model broadly matched) contravened EU law where a parent company resident in the UK was precluded from getting relief for the losses of a subsidiary company resident elsewhere in the EU, in circumstances where the subsidiary's losses could not otherwise be relieved.

Finance Act 2007 gives relief to Irish companies in respect of trading losses incurred by their non-Irish subsidiary companies that are resident in EU Member States and EEA States with which Ireland has a double tax treaty. The losses will be available for relief "vertically upwards" from the non-resident subsidiary to the Irish-resident parent but will only be available when certain conditions – for example, in relation to the way the loss is computed and the type of loss involved – are met. Losses that are available for offset against profits in another territory, or that can be used at any time by setting them against any company's profits in the country where the loss is incurred, are not covered by the new rule.

Where the new rule is applicable, it will allow an Irish-resident parent company to offset against its taxable income the losses of an EU/EEA resident subsidiary. The legislation includes an anti-avoidance provision to disallow losses where arrangements are entered into primarily to secure an amount that would qualify for the new group relief.

2.5 Mining Taxation

TCA97 s670-s683

The main features of mining taxation are:

- Scheduled minerals
- Mine Development Allowance
- Exploration Expenditure
- Allowance for expenditure on abortive exploration
- Expenditure incurred by one member of a group of companies may, by election, be deemed to be the expenditure of another member
- Investment allowance of 20% on new plant purchased on or after 6 April 1974 (with the exception of cars, lorries, etc.)
- Annual mineral depletion allowance on capital expenditure in acquiring after 31 March 1974, a scheduled mineral asset entitling one to work deposits of schedule minerals.

Where after 31 March 1974 a person sells any scheduled mineral asset the net proceeds are to be brought into charge to tax.
In respect of a marginal mine, the tax chargeable on the profits of that mine may be reduced to such amount (including nil) as the Minister for Finance may specify.

2.5.1 Exploration expenditure

An "Exploration Company" is one whose business consists primarily of exploring for scheduled minerals.

Exploring for scheduled minerals means the carrying on in the State of any of the following activities in relation to scheduled minerals:

(i) Searching for deposits,

(ii) Testing deposits,

(iii) Winning access to deposits,

(iv) The systematic searching for areas containing scheduled minerals,

(v) Searching by drilling or other means,

but the definition excludes operations for developing or working a qualifying mine.

For as long as a company is an exploration company which does not carry on a trade of working a qualifying mine and incurs expenditure on exploring for scheduled minerals, it shall be deemed to be carrying on a trade of working a qualifying mine coming within the charge to corporation tax when it first incurs capital expenditure.

Where such companies incur expenditure on or after 1 April, 1990 the following provisions apply:

(i) Unsuccessful exploration expenditure can be carried forward for set-off against mining income indefinitely.

(ii) Allowances due to an exploration company may be transferred to its 100 per cent parent or subsidiary company. If such a transfer is made a claim for Group Relief cannot also be made.

(iii) Should an exploration company which is deemed to be carrying on a trade of working a qualifying mine commence to actually work a qualifying mine it may carry forward any unused losses of the deemed trade against income of the actual trade providing there is no change in ownership about the time actual trading begins.

2.5.2 Rehabilitation expenditure

An allowance is available for expenditure incurred on the rehabilitation of the site of a qualifying mine following the closure of the mine. Where the rehabilitation expenditure is incurred after cessation of the trade of working a qualifying mine it will be treated as incurred on the date of cessation of the trade and, accordingly, an allowance will be made in respect of that expenditure in the chargeable period in which the trade ceases.

2.5.3 Petroleum companies

Corporation Tax

TCA97 s684-s697

A special rate of corporation tax of 25% applies to income arising from petroleum leases. Special features are:

- Separation of trading activities
- 25% rate of corporation tax
- Ring fence on losses arising in a petroleum activity as well as losses from another trade
- Ring fence on group relief for losses
- Ring fence on capital gains tax losses
- Restrictions on relief for interest
- Restrictions on set-off of advance corporation tax
- Capital allowances on development and exploration expenditure
- Surrender of the benefit of the deduction for exploration expenditure to an associated company
- Relief for additional expenditure on abandonment of exhausted oil fields
- Rules for valuation of petroleum in certain circumstances
- Deferral of capital gains tax on certain disposals and exchanges

Where the holder of a lease or licence under the Petroleum and other Minerals Act, 1960 engages another person to carry out the actual work, such holder is deemed to be the agent of the other person and can be assessed to tax accordingly.

A dividend or other distribution by a company in respect of shares in that company will not be regarded as "investment income" for the purposes of the close company surcharge if the close company to which it is paid would be exempt from capital gains tax on any gain on the disposal of these shares under the new exemption as an "investor company" in section 626B, that is, the new holding company participation exemption regime.

Profit Resource Rent Tax

TCA97 Ch3 Pt24 Finance Act 2008 introduces a new Chapter, Chapter 3, into Part 24 of the Taxes Consolidation Act 1997. The new Chapter gives effect to the Government decision of 30 July 2007 that a Profit Resource Rent Tax will apply in the case of any petroleum lease entered into following on from an exploration licence or a reserved area licence awarded by the Minister for Communications, Energy and Natural Resources after 1 January 2007 or from a licensing option. The tax which will apply when profits exceed certain defined levels, is in addition to the corporation tax rate of 25% that currently applies to profits from petroleum activities.

A key feature of the new tax is that it is based on the profit ratio of a petroleum field, which is defined as the rate of profits (net of 25% corporation tax) for the field, divided by the accumulated level of capital investment in the field. Different rates of Profit Resource Rent Tax will apply, depending on the ratio, as follows:

Profit Ratio	Profit Resources Rent Tax Rate
4.5 or more	15%
3 or more and less than 4.5	10%
1.5 or more and less than 3	5%
Less than 1.5	Nil

2.6 Close Companies

TCA97 s430 Broadly speaking, a close company is a company which is under the control of five or fewer participators or under the control of its directors. Companies owned by the State are excluded from the definition of a close company and this exclusion is extended to companies owned by EU Member States and countries with which Ireland has a double tax treaty from 1 January 2003.

2.6.1 Participators and associates

TCA97 s433 A participator in a company is a person having a share or interest in the company's capital or income, whilst an individual's associates include his spouse, his partners and direct relatives.

2.6.2 Certain expenses for participators and associates

TCA97 s436 Where a close company incurs expense in providing a benefit of any kind for a participator or an associate of a participator of the company, who is not a director or employee of the company, and without that person paying for it, the company will be deemed to have made a distribution (See Schedule F and Company Distributions) equal to the amount of that expense. The expense will therefore not be allowed in computing the company's profits for tax purposes. The recipient of the benefit will be deemed to have received a dividend of the grossed up amount which will be liable to higher rates of income tax if applicable.

2.6.3 Interest paid to directors and directors' associates

TCA97 s437 Interest paid to directors and directors' associates in excess of a specified limit (13%) will in certain circumstances be treated as a distribution with the same consequences as outlined above for section 436.

2.6.4 Loans to participators, etc.

TCA97 s438 Most loans to participators or their associates are deemed to be annual payments made under deduction of income tax but are not considered as charges under section 243. The company is obliged to pay over income tax at a rate of 20/80ths (income tax year 2001 *et seq.*) of the loan to the Revenue Commissioners. If the loan or part of it is repaid the company is entitled to reclaim the proportionate part of the tax originally paid over. If such a loan is released or written off the grossed up amount of the loan will be regarded as income of the borrower in the year in which the loan is written off and the tax paid over will cease to be recoverable by the company.

There is an exception to these provisions where a loan of not more than €19,050 is made to a participator or his associate who is a director or employee of the close company or of an associated company. The loan must satisfy the following conditions:

(a) the aggregate of the loans made to the borrower or his spouse by the close company or its associated companies must not exceed €19,050 and

(b) the borrower works full time in the close company or in an associated company, and

(c) the borrower together with his associates must not directly or indirectly control more than 5% of the ordinary share capital of the company.

If the borrower together with his associates acquires more than 5% of the ordinary share capital of the company the loan outstanding at that time will be regarded as an annual payment with the usual implications.

TCA97 s438A *Use of Non-Resident Companies*

The charge to income tax at the standard rate on the grossed-up equivalent of a loan or advance made by the company to a participator or an associate of the participator also extends to a loan made by a close company to a non-resident company so as to counter avoidance opportunities. With effect from 6 February 2003 the application of the anti-avoidance legislation is limited to non-resident companies outside the EC. One of the effects of this change is that avoidance opportunities which were previously closed-off are now re-opened in the case of non-resident companies resident in other EC countries. To counter this, a new provision was introduced which brings within the scope of section 438 a case where a close company does not itself make the loan, but sets up or acquires a subsidiary which then makes the loan to the participators in the parent close company. This provision applies regardless of the residence status of the various companies

2.6.5 Surcharge on certain undistributed income

TCA97 s440-s441 A surcharge of 20% is chargeable on a close company which does not distribute its after tax investment income or rental income within 18 months of the end of the accounting period. However where the undistributed income figure is €635 or less the surcharge is not applied and for amounts slightly over €635 there is marginal figure. There is no surcharge on undistributed trading income.

The 20% surcharge also applies to service companies and in respect of accounting periods ending on or after 1 April 1995 is calculated as 20% of:

- ½ of distributable income, plus
- ½ of distributable investment and estate income, less
- any distributions made for the period.

With regard to accounting periods ending on or after 1 April 1996, the 20% surcharge has been reduced to 15% in respect of the trading or professional income but investment and rental income is still subject to the 20%.

The same €635 exemption and marginal relief referred to above also apply in the case of service companies.

With effect from 14 March 2001 new rules apply in calculating the surcharges which take account of the changes in the corporation tax rate structure. The previous formulae which were based on a single rate of corporation tax, no longer produce the correct amounts of distributable income used in the calculation of the surcharges. As part of the changes a 7½% reduction applies to both undistributed investment and estate income in the case of trading companies only.

A dividend or other distribution by a company in respect of shares in that company will not regarded as "investment income" for the purposes of the close company surcharge if the close company to which it is paid would be exempt from capital gains tax on any gain on the disposal of these shares under the new exemption as an "investor company" in section 626B, that is, the new holding company participation exemption regime.

Finance Act 2008 amended the close company surcharge rules to allow a company making a distribution and the company receiving it to jointly elect that the distribution will not be treated as a distribution for the purposes of section 440.

Prior to Finance Act 2008, in calculating the distributable estate and investment income of a holding company that is a close company, distributions received from a non-resident company were not taken into account while distributions received from an Irish-resident company (being franked investment income) were.

Finance Act 2008 allows an Irish-resident holding company and an Irish-resident company that pays or makes a distribution to the holding company to elect that the distribution be afforded the same treatment as distributions received from a non-resident subsidiary. If such an election is made, the distribution will be treated as not being a distribution received by the holding company and as not being a distribution made by the subsidiary.

2.7 Schedule F and Company Distributions

TCA97 s136 Schedule F charges to income tax on an actual basis dividends and other liable distributions received by individuals. Dividends paid between 6 April 1976 and 5 April 1999 were paid net but attracted a tax credit (See Chart 10). An individual was liable to income tax on both the net dividend and the related tax credit at his marginal rate less a deduction for the tax credit. Tax credits were abolished with effect from 6 April 1999 at which time a dividend withholding tax was introduced (see 2.8).

2.7.1 Matters to be treated as distributions

TCA97 s130 The following are some of the matters which constitute distributions under corporation tax legislation.

(a) Dividends paid by a company including a capital dividend.

(b) Any distribution out of assets in respect of shares, except any part of it which represents a repayment of capital. Acquisition by a company of its own shares in certain circumstances is excluded (see 6.7.1).

(c) Redemption of bonus shares and bonus debentures.

(d) The transfer by a company of assets to its members at undervalue is treated as a distribution. However, that treatment does not apply to such a transfer between certain related companies where both are resident in the State. In determining whether the appropriate relationship exists, holdings by companies resident in Member States of the European Economic Area with which Ireland has a tax treaty are taken into account for that purpose. However, the relief continues to apply only to transfers between companies which are resident in the State.

(e) Interest on loans with rights of conversion into shares or securities.

(f) Interest the rate of which depends on the results of the company. Such interest will not be treated as a distribution where it is paid on a "Rachet Loan" which provides higher levels of interest where the borrower's profits fall and lower levels of interest where the borrower's profits rise.

(g) Interest paid to a non resident parent or associate company where there is at least a 75% ordinary shareholding relationship.

Prior to Finance Act, 2001 IFSC/Shannon companies could elect to treat such interest as interest rather than distribution thereby ensuring a deduction for a trade expense.

The election to treat interest as deductible interest rather than distribution in these circumstances now applies to interest paid by all companies in the ordinary course of their trade to companies resident in another EU Member State or in a tax treaty country. Finance Act 2007 provides that a company paying yearly interest to a non-resident (irrespective of the location) 75 per cent parent or associated company may treat such interest as a deductible trading expense.

The section as drafted does not avoid withholding tax for non-treaty territories and does not deal with short interest.

Banks subject to certain conditions can elect to take a deduction for interest paid to a non-resident parent/associated company irrespective of the place of residence of the parent/associated company.

Non-trading interest (e.g., charges) paid to a 75% related company in an EU Member State other than Ireland is not treated as a distribution with effect from 6 February 2003.

Distributions made in a winding up are not chargeable under Schedule F.

2.7.2 "Section 84 loans"

TCA97 s133 There are exceptions in the case of certain loans of a type mentioned at (e) (i) and (ii).

All new loans made after 19 December 1991 must satisfy the following conditions:

(i) the borrower commenced to trade after 31 January 1990 or the trade is one in relation to which the borrower was committed to the creation of additional employment under a business plan approved by one of the grant-giving bodies;

(ii) the trade of the borrower was included in a list prepared by the IDA and approved by the Minister for Industry and Commerce and Minister for Finance before 25 March 1992 specifying the amount of borrowing considered essential for the success of the trade. The amount specified is to be treated as reduced (with certain exceptions) by the amount of any relevant principal advanced or treated as advanced, to a borrower and the reduced amount is then treated as the amount specified on the list.

(iii) the borrower does not carry on relevant trading operations in the IFSC.

Where on or after 6 May 1993 the repayment period of an existing "section 84" loan is extended, the lender will be treated as having received repayment of the "section 84" loan and as having advanced a new non-"section 84" loan in its place.

Currency exchange gains which are connected with "section 84" loans denominated in a foreign currency are taxed as income from the sale of manufactured goods. In addition, gains and losses on such "section 84" loan are treated as profits or gains or losses of the borrowers trade in the course of which the loans are used.

No domestic sourced loans in a foreign currency will qualify from 30 January 1991, where the interest rate on the loan exceeds 80% of DIBOR. This limit will not apply to:

(i) Loans drawn down before 30 January 1991, where the rate of interest on that date exceeded 80% of DIBOR, provided that the rate does not exceed that which would apply if the loan was in the same currency, both at the time the interest is paid and on 30 January 1991.

(ii) Loans on the IDA list made on or after 30 January 1991, but before 20 December 1991, provided that the rate does not exceed a rate approved by the Minister for Finance or, if lower, the rate applicable to the currency in which the loan was advanced.

(iii) Loans on the IDA list made on or after 20 December 1991, provided that the rate does not exceed a rate approved by the Minister for Finance.

"Section 84" loans drawn down on or after 11 April 1994 have a time limit of seven years, while loans drawn down before that date will cease to qualify as "section 84" loans on 11 April 2001. Where certain "section 84" loans were repaid prematurely before 7 December 1993 a replacement loan for such a loan will only be a qualifying loan up to the scheduled repayment date of the original loan.

2.7.3 Distributions from manufacturing profits

TCA97 s147-s151

The formula below sets out the amount of the manufacturing dividend paid by a company. The formula determines the manufacturing dividend paid for an accounting period in the proportion which the company's manufacturing distributable income for the period bears to its total distributable income for the period. The formula is:

$$Y \times \frac{(A - B) + E - U}{(R - S) + T - W}$$

where:

Y – the distribution made by the company.

A = the amount of the company's 10% manufacturing relieved income for the accounting period.

B = the reduced corporation tax attaching to the income at "A".

E = the amount of any manufacturing dividends received in the accounting period.

R = the total amount of the company's income finally charged to corporation tax for the period excluding chargeable gains but including exempt income.

S = the corporation tax attributable to the income at "R", after manufacturing relief and export sales relief.

T = the total of all distributions received in the accounting period.

U = the amount of 10% distributions included in W.

W = the amount of all distributions made before 6 April 1989 treated as made for an accounting period for which the distribution Y is to be treated as made.

The formula to determine the distributable income of the company is

$$(R - S) + T - W$$

The distributable manufacturing income is determined by the formula

$$(A - B) + E$$

A company which makes a distribution out of manufacturing profits on or after 6 April 1989 may by notice in writing to the Inspector within 6 months from the end of the accounting period in which the distribution is made nominate the accounting period for which it is paid. This is provided:

(i) the nominated accounting period is within nine years of the payment date

and

(ii) the distribution or part thereof does not exceed the undistributed income of the company for that accounting period at the date of payment.

The company will not be entitled to state that the distribution was made for the accounting period in which it was actually paid unless it is one of the following:

(a) An interim dividend paid before 6 April 2002.

(b) A "section 84" distribution.

(c) A preference share funding distribution.

(d) A distribution of the accounting period in which the company commences or ceases to be within the charge to corporation tax.

(e) It should be noted that where a company pays an interim dividend it is not entitled to claim that it is a distribution made for the accounting period in which it is made where:

  (i) the company would have to use estimation in order to determine the amount of the dividend which was a specified dividend under the provisions of section 147, or

  (ii) the payment of the interim dividend would assist the company in arrangements whereby the company could attach different rates of tax credit to dividends paid on similar shareholdings.

The above election applies to dividends paid on or after 1 June 1994 out of income, regardless of whether it is 10%, export sales relief, Shannon exempt or other income.

2.8 Dividend Withholding Tax

2.8.1 General

In his budget speech of 2 December 1998 the Minister for Finance stated the following:

> *"since owners of capital in the form of shares would benefit from the reduced corporation tax rate on profits, I believe it right that the government should accordingly take action to ensure that the tax due on dividends is paid to the Exchequer. The existing tax credit on dividends will be abolished as and from 6 April next under measures taken in my first Budget. In effect this means that after 5 April the onus of payment of tax on dividends received by individuals will rest on self assessment and income declaration by shareholders.*
>
> *I propose, therefore, to introduce on and from 6 April 1999 a withholding tax at the standard rate of income tax on dividends paid to individuals resident in the State and certain non residents. This tax will have to be deducted from dividends before they are paid out. Those individual shareholders liable to tax at the higher rate will be required as before to declare their dividend income in their tax returns and to pay the balance of income tax due to the Exchequer".*

As stated by the Minister this change was introduced in the context of the phasing in of the reduced rates of corporation tax and is intended to claw back some of the revenue foregone through the introduction of the reduced rates. The imputation system of corporation tax which was designed to prevent, in some degree, the payment of double taxation on the same profits was abandoned and income tax is payable on the gross amount of the dividend declared with a deduction against tax liability being granted in respect of the tax withheld on payment of the dividend.

The new provisions can be summarised as follows:

TCA97
Pt 6, Ch 8A

(a) Tax at the standard rate applies to distributions (including scrip dividends and non cash distributions) made by an Irish resident company on or after 6 April, 1999.

(b) This applied to all distributions including those payable out of exempt or disregarded income for the tax year 1999/00. It no longer applies to payment out of such income with effect from 6 April 2000. However companies making such payments must continue to make a return of the distributions in their Dividend Withholding Tax returns.

(c) A recipient who is liable to tax on a distribution, such as an Irish resident individual, can claim an off-set for the tax withheld against his tax liability. Where the withholding tax exceeds the tax liability, the balance will be refunded. The general four year time limit that applies to other tax repayments also applies to refunds of DWT.

(d) Exemption is granted to an Irish resident company, a pension scheme, a personal retirement savings account (PRSA), the trustees of minimum retirement funds and approved retirement funds, a qualifying employee share ownership trust, a collective investment undertaking, a charity, exempt unit trusts, certain amateur and athletic sports bodies, certain persons who would be entitled to exemption from income tax (mainly related to permanent incapacity) in respect of distributions made and distributions made to designated brokers for the benefit of the holders of SPIAs.

(e) Exemption is also granted to residents of tax treaty countries, residents of EU Member States, companies not resident in the State which are ultimately controlled by residents of tax treaty countries or EU Member States and companies the principal class of shares of which are substantially and regularly traded on a recognised stock exchange in such countries or Member States.

With effect from 6 April 2000, exemption has been extended to

(i) all companies resident in another EU Member State or a tax treaty country and which are not controlled by Irish residents. Qualification for the exemption is conditional on the production of a certificate of tax residence from the tax authority of the relevant territory concerned and a certificate from the auditor of the non-resident company certifying that it is not controlled by Irish residents and

(ii) non resident companies which are wholly owned by two or more companies each of whose principal class of shares is substantially and regularly traded on one or more recognised stock exchanges in a "relevant territory or territories". Qualification for the exemption is conditional on the production of a certificate from the auditor of the non-resident company certifying that it is wholly owned by two or more such companies.

Section 38 Finance Act 2007 extended the exemption to cases where the parent company trades only on the Irish Stock Exchange.

(f) A declaration in the prescribed form and any other evidence required must be provided to establish entitlement to the exemption.

(g) Where exempt status is established payment can be made in full directly to the shareholder or through an "authorised intermediary".

(h) There are provisions for a "withholding agent" to pay distributions and withhold tax on behalf of the company.

(i) Qualifying intermediaries who receive distributions on behalf of clients are required to submit a full annual report only on request from the Revenue.

(j) The withholding tax must be paid over to the Revenue on or before the 14th day of the month following the month in which the distribution was made.

(k) Shares in lieu of dividends

With effect from 6 April 1999 the treatment of shares received in lieu of cash dividends is amended in line with the introduction of the dividend withholding tax. The effect of the amendment is that the company issues a number of shares which has a value, at the date of distribution, equal to the cash foregone, reduced by an amount equal to income tax at the standard rate on the amount of cash foregone. The distributing company must pay over the notional income tax deducted to the Collector General in the normal way. Where the distributing company is quoted the shareholder is taxed on this type of distribution under Schedule F and, where the company is unquoted, under Schedule D, Case IV. The taxable amount is the full amount of the cash foregone and credit is given for the withholding tax paid by the company.

(l) A statement showing the tax withheld must be supplied to the shareholder in all cases. These details can be supplied on the dividend counterfoil.

(m) Penalties and fines are imposed for the non operation or incorrect operation of the withholding tax provision.

(n) Section 153 TCA 1997 currently provides for an effective exemption from the charge to Irish income tax for all non-resident persons in respect of distributions made by Irish resident companies. With effect from 6 April 1999 this exemption will apply only to a person (other than a company) who is resident for tax purposes in another EU Member State or in any tax treaty country and who is neither resident nor ordinarily resident in the State and certain other non-resident companies.

With effect from 6 April 2000, the following categories of non-residents are exempt:

(i) non-resident companies which are resident in another EU or Tax Treaty country and which are controlled directly or indirectly by non-Irish residents; and

(ii) a non resident company who itself (or its 75% parent) is wholly owned by two or more companies both of which are quoted on a stock exchange in another EU Member State or tax treaty country.

(o) Individuals resident outside the EU or tax treaty countries are subject to Dividend Withholding Tax. The tax charge on such individuals in respect of distributions will be confined to the standard rate of income tax. Thus, in effect the Dividend Withholding Tax will discharge the full liability of such individuals.

2.9 Foreign Aspects

2.9.1 Foreign exchange transactions

TCA97
s79, s79B
s402

As the taxation of international financial transactions is beyond the scope of this summary the authors would refer readers to the Institute's publication - *Taxing Financial Transactions.* However the following sets out the major changes for corporation tax purposes, of the treatment of foreign exchange gains and losses related to corporate borrowings for the purposes of a trade.

Prior to the passing of the 1994 Finance Act, tax law effectively ignored foreign exchange gains and losses arising in respect of long term borrowings. Such borrowings were deemed to be capital liabilities and therefore the exchange gains or losses arising on them were ignored in the computation of trading profits. Since the borrowings are not regarded as assets for capital gains tax purposes, gains or losses arising did not give rise to chargeable gains or losses. However, the matching losses and gains on hedging instruments were charged to tax, thereby producing anomalous tax results.

Section 56 Finance Act 1994 brought the foreign exchange gains and losses on both trade borrowings and related hedging contracts into the computation of a company's trading income for tax purposes to the extent that those gains and losses have been properly credited or debited to the company's profit and loss account.

These accounting entries are brought into the computation of income for tax purposes regardless of whether they represent realised or unrealised gains and losses and also regardless of whether the trade borrowing is characterised as a "revenue" or "capital" item for tax purposes.

Hedging gains and losses are to be excluded in the computation of the company's chargeable gains. In addition, since gains and losses arising on holdings of foreign currency for trade purposes are also brought into the computation of income, they too are excluded from the computation of chargeable gains.

The above provisions apply in respect of accounting periods beginning on or after 1 January 1995.

The treatment of hedging instruments in respect of trade borrowings outlined above, was extended to hedging instruments designed to remove exchange rate risks in relation to the corporation tax liability of a company in respect of accounting periods ending on or after 1 April 1996. Accordingly gains or losses which arise on such instruments are not chargeable gains or allowable losses

Certain provisions also exist to deal with the computation of capital allowances and loss relief due to a trading company which has a "functional currency" other than Irish pounds. For accounting periods commencing on or after 1 January 1994, such a company may compute its capital allowances in that foreign currency. Where the company incurs capital expenditure in a currency other than its functional currency, it must translate that expenditure into the functional currency equivalent at the rate of exchange at the time the expenditure was incurred and must compute the capital allowances due by reference to that functional currency amount.

In the case of a company which has losses in the functional currency it may carry them forward in that currency and convert them into Irish Pounds as and when they are used.

Section 79B TCA 1997 allows a company to elect to match for tax purposes a trading asset denominated in a foreign currency with redeemable share capital denominated in that currency. Where the option is exercised, any foreign exchange gain or loss on the share capital is to be taken into account in calculating taxable income of the company so as to match a corresponding foreign exchange loss or gain on the asset. (See also paragraph 6.2.18.)

Finance Act 2007 amended section 79B of TCA 1997 to ensure that the original provision as amended by Finance Act 2006 operates as intended. Companies are allowed to elect to match for tax purposes a trading asset denominated in a foreign currency with redeemable share capital denominated in that currency. Where the option is exercised, any foreign exchange gain or loss on the share capital is to be taken into account in calculating taxable income of the company so to match a corresponding exchange loss or gain on the asset. In exercising this option a company achieves tax neutrality in relation to such exchange movements. The two amendments are:

- The first amendment ensures that unrealized foreign currency movements on the share capital can be taken into account for tax purposes over the period of the loan on a "mark to market" basis. This achieves a better timing of the matching allowed under the section so as to achieve full neutrality.
- The second amendment provides that the tax neutrality provided for under section 79B, which currently assumes a euro functional currency, is also available to a company whose functional currency is other than the euro. This could arise, for example, where a company whose functional currency is the US$ gives loans denominated in sterling.

As Finance Act 2007 clarifies the original intention of the legislation as amended by Finance Act 2006, it is intended that it takes effect from 1 January 2006 – the original commencement date.

2.9.2 The Euro

Section 47 and Schedule 2 of the 1998 Finance Act provide amendments to cater for the change in currency of the State to the Euro on 1 January 1999.

2.9.3 Double taxation relief

Finance Act 2006 introduced two amendments to the way that foreign taxes on foreign income are dealt with.

The first amendment concerns the way that the income doubly taxed is computed. Previously, the income was computed as the gross income from overseas less the expenses that might be directly attributed or apportioned to that income. The foreign taxes were then given as a credit against that income and, to the extent that credit could not be given, the foreign tax was effectively given by way of deduction.

Under Finance Act 2006, the income on which the relief for foreign taxes is computed is a proportion of the total profits of the trade. The proportion is the amount of the income as a percentage of the total amount receivable from the trade.

Secondly, Finance Act 2006 sets out the mechanism for relieving double taxation where a dividend is received from a foreign company that is a member of a group which is taxed on a consolidation basis. The new provision treats the group of companies as a single company and applies Schedule 24 on the basis of dividends received from that single company.

This change is relevant for jurisdictions taxing groups of companies rather than single entities. Consolidated returns are made, for example, in the US, the Netherlands and Luxembourg, and the computation of relief for foreign taxes has been an issue for such entities.

Finance Act 2008 clarified that the formula introduced in 2006 to calculate the amount of doubly taxed trading income that arises from a payment from which foreign tax is deducted, does not apply to foreign branch profits with effect from 31 January 2008. The 2006 rules continue to apply to foreign branch profits up to 31 January 2008 unless an election in writing is made to the Revenue Commissioners to use the new 2008 rules with effect from 1 January 2006.

2.9.4 Unilateral relief – dividends

TCA97 Sch24 A company resident in the State or an Irish branch of a company resident in a Member State of the European Economic Area with which Ireland has tax treaty which receives a dividend from a "25% subsidiary" which is resident in a territory with which Ireland does not have a double tax treaty will be entitled to reduce Irish tax on the dividend by any withholding tax paid in that territory on the dividend and by an appropriate part of the foreign tax on the income underlying the dividend.

A company resident in the State or an Irish branch of an a company resident in a Member State of the European Economic Area with which Ireland has tax treaty which receives a dividend from its "25% subsidiary" resident in a country with which Ireland has a double tax treaty or otherwise, which subsidiary has itself subsidiaries, will be entitled to reduce the Irish tax by an appropriate amount of withholding tax and underlying tax borne by those subsidiaries and their subsidiaries. This is conditional on the company paying the dividend being a 25% subsidiary of the company to which it pays the dividend and being connected with the ultimate Irish parent company.

The Finance Act 1999 introduced new measures on double tax relief as follows:

(a) Where an Irish resident company receives a dividend from a subsidiary in a tax treaty country and the double tax relief available to it under the treaty is less generous than unilateral relief the company may claim the unilateral relief.

(b) Tests on whether companies are "related" or "connected" are based with effect from 6 April 1999 on voting rights rather than ordinary share capital for the purposes of unilateral relief and double tax relief.

The Finance Act, 2002 ensures that credit is given for foreign tax suffered on income of an Irish branch of a company resident in a member state of the European Economic Area with which Ireland has a tax treaty such as Norway.

Finance Act 2004 amended Schedule 24 TCA 1997 in a number of respects as it relates to unilateral credit relief.

The provisions are as follows:

The shareholding threshold to qualify for unilateral credit relief in the case of dividends received from certain foreign subsidiaries is reduced from 25% of the subsidiary to 5%. In addition, credit may now be allowed for local income taxes where these are paid in addition to state taxes on income but are not covered by the relevant tax treaty.

Changes have also been made to a provision that gives credit against Irish tax on dividends received by an Irish company from its foreign subsidiaries for foreign tax paid by lower tiers of subsidiaries, as follows:

(i) Tax which may be credited now includes foreign tax paid by such subsidiaries on their branch profits.

(ii) A reduction in the shareholding threshold from 25% to 5% also applies. The new requirement will be that a subsidiary must be owned to the extent of at least 5% by the company immediately above it, and also to the extent of at least 5% indirectly by the Irish parent company.

Finance Act 2008 introduced a new paragraph to Schedule 24, to extend the circumstances under which a double tax relief credit is made available to Irish companies in receipt of dividends from foreign companies. The legislation up to Finance Act 2008 provided that, where a foreign company pays a dividend to another foreign company which then pays a dividend to an Irish company, the Irish company is entitled to a credit against Irish tax on the dividend for the foreign tax paid by the first company on the profits out of which the dividend is paid.

Under the Finance Act 2008 amendment, credit relief will also be available when the profits of the first company become profits of the second foreign company other than by way of a dividend, such as, for example, where there is a merger of companies. In future, credit relief will be given on a dividend paid by a company following a merger, in respect of the underlying tax paid by its predecessor companies. The relief will be limited, where appropriate, to the amount that would have been due had the profits been transferred instead by way of a dividend, and will not apply where the profits transfer is a result of a tax avoidance scheme.

2.9.5 Onshore pooling – taxation of foreign dividends

Finance Act 2004 introduced a form of onshore pooling that will provide a more effective mechanism for Irish companies to obtain foreign tax credit relief for double tax.

Up to 2004, a 25% tax on foreign dividends coupled with credit for foreign direct and underlying tax results in no Irish tax where subsidiaries of an Irish company are taxed at rates in excess of 25%. However, when the subsidiaries were located in both low and high tax jurisdictions, Ireland's mechanism for relieving tax on an item-by-item basis meant that eligible foreign tax on high-taxed dividends was effectively wasted as it could be credited against Irish tax on low taxed dividends.

Finance Act 2004 introduced onshore pooling as a means of dealing with the situation where the foreign tax on dividends exceeds the Irish tax and allows any excess to be offset against Irish tax on other foreign dividends received in the accounting period concerned, and any unused balance to be carried forward and offset in subsequent accounting periods. Offshore pooling is not impacted by the legislation.

New rules for pooling of foreign tax relief apply in respect of dividends received by a company on or after 1 January 2008. From that date, pooling arrangements will apply separately to dividends that are taxable at the 12.5% rate and to dividends that are taxable at the 25% rate. Any surplus of foreign tax arising on dividends taxable at the 12.5% rate will not be available for offset against tax on dividends taxable at the 25% rate. However, there will not be a similar restriction in the case of dividends taxable at the 25% rate.

2.9.6 Unilateral relief – interest

TCA97 Sch24 Finance Act, 2002 provides for unilateral credit relief in respect of withholding tax, suffered in countries with which Ireland does not have a tax treaty, on interest received by a company where the interest falls to be included in the company's trading income. The method of calculation for the relief is clarified in Finance Act 2003 for accounting periods ending on or after 6 February 2003.

2.9.7 Additional credit – interest

Finance Act 2006 provided for an additional credit that applies only to interest income ("relevant income") of a trade received from a 25% subsidiary resident in a country with which Ireland has a double taxation treaty. Where part of the foreign tax suffered is deducted in arriving at the taxable income, a further amount can be deducted as a credit from any tax payable on other relevant income. This additional amount is 87.5% of the foreign tax deducted (assuming a 12.5% tax rate). Where the deduction is not used because of insufficient income, the relief is lost – it is not carried forward to future years.

2.9.8 Unilateral relief – foreign branch profits

Finance Act 2007 provided unilateral credit relief for foreign tax suffered by a company that has a branch or agency in a country with which Ireland does not have a tax treaty. This allows such a company to reduce its Irish corporation tax liability by the foreign tax suffered on the profits of the branch or agency. In the absence of such relief, the company would only be entitled to a deduction for the foreign tax in computing its taxable income.

The section also allows pooling in the case of foreign branch profits. Where the foreign tax on branch profits in one country exceeds the Irish tax on those profits, the credit is limited under existing law to the amount of the Irish tax on those profits and no credit can be given for the balance of the foreign tax. Pooling allows such surplus foreign tax to be credited against tax on branch profits in other countries.

2.9.9 Branch profits

TCA97 s847 Section 847 TCA 1997 provides for the exemption from corporation tax and capital gains tax of income and gains from a foreign branch in the case of a company meeting certain conditions in relation to capital investment and employment creation. No company can avail of the relief unless it holds a certificate issued by the Minister for Finance before 15 February 2001.

The relief terminates on 31 December 2010 in accordance with an amendment in Finance Act 2004.

2.9.10 Companies changing residence

TCA97 s627-s629 Where a company ceases to be resident in the State on or after 21 April 1997, it is deemed to have disposed of and reacquired all of its assets immediately before the event of changing residence, at their market value at that time, even though no actual disposal has taken place. However, assets which continue to be used in Ireland by a branch or agency of the company are not subject to the above provision.

In addition, the above provision will not apply where the company is ultimately owned by a foreign company, i.e., a company controlled by persons resident in a country with which Ireland has a double taxation treaty.

Roll-over relief will only apply to assets disposed of prior to changing residence if their replacements acquired after that time are similarly used in Ireland by a branch or agency of the company.

Where a company which transfers residence is a 75% subsidiary of an Irish resident company, then both companies may elect in writing within two years of the change of residence, to have the deemed disposal and its resulting tax charge deferred.

A charge to capital gains will in those circumstances crystallise only if:

(i) within 10 years the assets are actually disposed of, or

(ii) the company ceases to be a 75% subsidiary of the other, or

(iii) the Irish resident parent itself changes its residence.

In the event of non payment of tax arising under provisions as outlined above, the Revenue Commissioners may collect the tax due from any Irish resident group company or controlling director of the company.

2.9.11 Tax status of foreign person with Irish investment manager

TCA97 s1035A Under general legislation a non-resident person could be liable to tax in the State in respect of a trade carried on in the State through an agent. The right to charge such a non-resident to tax in the State can be taken away under the provisions of Double Taxation Agreements where the agent is independent of the non-resident. Section 1035A removes the potential tax charge on all non-residents carrying on a financial trade in the State through an agent in certain circumstances. The agent must be a person whose activities are regulated by the Central Bank of Ireland (or the competent authority in another Member State of the EU). It is a requirement that such an agent act independently of the non-resident and certain other conditions must be met in the arrangements between the Irish agent and the foreign person.

2.9.12 Ireland as a holding company location

TCA97 s626B Finance Act 2004 introduced a number of new measures designed to enhance Ireland's position as a holding company location. Ireland's taxation regime now contains the following key features:

- Interest deduction is available to Irish companies borrowing funds which are used to acquire shares in trading subsidiaries or to make loans to such subsidiaries.
- No thin capitalisation rules providing for specific debt to equity ratios or interest cover ratios, in order to obtain a full tax deduction for interest expense.
- Currently, no transfer pricing rules.
- Participation exemption from capital gains tax on disposal of shares in certain foreign and domestic subsidiaries which exempts such disposals from capital gains tax (new measure - described in further detail below).
- Favourable treatment of dividend income received from foreign subsidiaries resulting from an expansion of foreign tax credit relief in Finance Act 2004. Furthermore, with the introduction of onshore pooling in Finance Act 2004, an Irish resident company will have no further tax to pay in Ireland on dividends it receives from foreign subsidiaries provided that the effective rate of foreign tax paid on those dividends (mixed together) in a particular year is 25%. If the mixed effective foreign tax rate is greater than 25%, the excess foreign tax credit can be carried forward and utilised in future years.

The combination of these measures makes Ireland competitive as a holding company location and Ireland compares favourably to traditional holding company locations such as The Netherlands and Luxembourg.

The Finance Act 2004 new measures were subject to EU approval before they could be commenced and some changes were agreed with the EU before implementing the final arrangements in Finance Act 2005.

Participation exemption

Finance Act 2005 removed the valuation thresholds proposed in the original 2004 legislation and replaced them with a flat 5% share holding requirement to qualify for the participation exemption.

Conditions of the exemption

In essence, the relief will apply to certain disposals of shares or assets "related to" shares in EU/DTA resident companies (for example, put/call options over shares and convertible/exchangeable instruments). With the EU increasing in size to include 25 countries with effect from May 2004, in addition to Ireland's tax treaty network which continues to expand, this should result in exemption for disposals of subsidiaries in approximately 70 countries.

In essence, there are two main conditions which must be met for the relief to apply:

- The holding must be a "substantial shareholding" of shares that do not derive their value from Irish land or buildings.
- The company being disposed of (in the legislation referred to as the investee) must be a company resident for tax purposes in an EU/DTA resident country and a trading company/ a member of a "trading group".

The relief applies automatically where the necessary conditions are satisfied, and the selling company will not be liable to tax on gains (nor will it get relief for losses) on disposal of <u>*any*</u> shares in the EU/ DTA resident investee or an asset "related to" shares of the investee.

Substantial shareholding condition

A shareholding is substantial if the selling company is beneficially entitled, directly or indirectly, to an economic interest of at least 5% of the investee company.

The economic interest held in a company will be determined based on the percentage entitlement to the company's ordinary share capital, distributable profits and distributable assets. Where the shareholding is split between several companies in the selling group (wherever resident), the group shareholdings are aggregated in determining whether the 5% holding test is satisfied (with the exception of shares held by the long-term insurance fund of an insurance company).

In addition, the substantial shareholding must have been held for a continuous 12-month period ending within the two years prior to the date of disposal. One consequence of this provision is that part disposals out of a shareholding greater than 5% can qualify for exemption for up to 24 months after the 5% test ceases to be satisfied.

Intra-group changes of ownership are generally ignored when computing the 12-month period. In particular, where a company acquires the shares in the investee from another company as a result of a transfer which is treated as a no gain/no loss transfer for the purposes of the Tax Acts, the period for which the shares were held by the transferor is taken into account in determining whether the transferee satisfies the 12-month holding test. The most common form of such transfer would be a transfer of shares in the investee between two members of a capital gains tax group that are both within the charge to Irish corporate tax. Also, where shares in one company are exchanged for shares in another company and the transaction is treated as a tax-neutral reconstruction/reorganisation, the vendor can satisfy the 12-month holding period test by virtue of its holding of shares in the second company plus the period for which it held shares in the first company.

The relief permits a company to be treated as continuing to hold shares in the investee where it transfers those shares to another person under the terms of a stock-lending arrangement or sale and repurchase agreement. Also, provision is made to ensure that companies in liquidation will not be excluded from benefiting from the relief.

As noted above, the shares must not derive the greater part of their value from Irish land or buildings nor must they be held as part of the long-term insurance fund of an insurance company.

Investee company conditions

The investee company must be a company resident for tax purposes in an EU/DTA resident country. In addition, the company must be a trading company or a member of a "trading group" consisting of the selling company, the investee and all companies in which the selling company and investee company has a substantial interest as defined above.

Therefore, in general the relief is aimed at exempting from tax:

a) gains arising on sale of trading companies, or

b) gains arising on sale of non-trading companies by trading groups.

2.10 Advance Corporation Tax

(Abolished from 6 April 1999)

TCA97 s159-s172

Where an Irish resident company made a distribution in the period 9 February 1983 and 5 April 1999 it was liable to pay advance corporation tax (ACT). The amount of the ACT was equal to the tax credit attaching to the distribution.

(See 2001 edition (or earlier) of this book).

2.11 Special Companies for Corporation Tax

2.11.1 Agricultural and fishery co-operatives

TCA97 s443

Co-operatives were largely exempt from corporation tax prior to 1992.

The exemption ceased from 1 April 1992 and the co-operatives concerned are subject to corporation tax in the same manner as any other company. From 1 April 1992 the activities of agricultural and fishery co-operatives can be divided into three separate categories:

(i) manufacturing activities which qualify for the 10% rate under the definition of manufacturing as existed prior to 1992;

(ii) the two categories of activity for which manufacturing relief has been specifically introduced in the case of agricultural and fishery co-operatives as dealt with in section 443.

(iii) other categories of activity which would have been exempt under the previous regime but which do not qualify for manufacturing relief.

Losses incurred prior to 1 April 1992 are available for set-off against future trading income under section 396 to the same extent as they would have been available if the co-operative had been subject to tax at all times. The co-operative is deemed to have made any claims which it could have made under section 396 in the period prior to 1 April 1992. This means that it is assumed to have already used up any losses which it could have used against exempt income but it will not be assumed to have claimed such "exempt losses" against other income or gains prior to 1 April 1992.

2.11.2 Building societies

TCA97 s703
Sch16

Where a building society converts to a company the following taxation provisions apply:

A. Commencement/Cessation

(i) The trade of the society is not treated as permanently discontinued and the trade of the successor company is not treated as having commenced.

(ii) Financial assets and financial trading stock are shown in the accounts of the successor company at their cost to the society.

B. Capital Allowances

The conversion does not give rise to a balancing allowance or charge.

C. Capital Gains

(i) The conversion of the society into the successor company does not give rise to a charge to capital gains tax. Assets acquired by the company are deemed to have been acquired at the date and cost at which they were acquired by the Society.

(ii) Where members of the society receive shares in priority to others or for no consideration or at a reduced value they are regarded as having obtained an option.

(iii) Where a member of the Society receives shares in the successor company, he is treated as having acquired the shares for the actual consideration given or for no consideration.

The Revenue Commissioners can obtain information for capital gains tax purposes in relation to the issue of shares to the members of a mutual building society in the event of that entity ceasing to be a mutual company.

2.11.3 Trustee savings banks

TCA97 s704 Sch17

Provision is made to deal with the taxation consequences of mergers under the Trustee Savings Banks Act, 1989. These main provisions are:

(a) Amalgamation
On the amalgamation of two or more Trustee Savings Banks, the merged bank and the former banks will be treated as the same person.

(b) Reorganisation

(i) Unused trading losses of a company controlled by the Minister cannot be set off against profits of a company not controlled by the Minister.

(ii) The acquisition of Financial Assets and Financial Trading Stock from the Trustee Savings Banks by the successor will be treated as having been acquired at their cost to the original bank.

(iii) The reorganisation from Trustee Savings Banks to Companies will not give rise to a Balancing Allowance or Charge.

(iv) Unused Capital Allowances, carried forward by the Trustee Savings Banks, cannot be utilised by the successor company.

(v) Trustee Savings Banks will not be liable to Capital Gains Tax, as the transfer will be deemed to give rise to neither a gain nor a loss.

(vi) For subsequent disposals by the successor company, it will be deemed to have acquired the assets at the same time and at the same cost at which it was acquired by the Trustee Savings Banks.

2.11.4 General exemptions

TCA97 s220

Profits arising to the following are exempt from corporation tax:

- An Bord Pinsean
- Dublin Docklands Development Authority
- Horse Racing Ireland
- Housing Finance Agency plc
- National Development Finance Agency
- National Lottery
- National Treasury Management Agency
- Nítrigin Éireann Teoranta (NET)
- Investor Compensation Company Limited
- Commission for Electricity Regulation
- Personal Injuries Assessment Board (PIAB)

2.11.5 Non-Commercial State Sponsored Bodies

TCA97 s227

Section 227 provides an exemption from tax in respect of non-trading income for certain non-commercial State sponsored bodies, which would otherwise be chargeable to income tax or corporation tax. Schedule 4 TCA 97 lists the non-commercial State sponsored bodies and is added to from time to time.

2.12 Special Employment Related Receipts and Payments

2.12.1 Scheme payments

TCA97 s226 Payments to employers under the following schemes are disregarded for all purposes of the Taxes Acts:

(a) Employment Incentive Scheme.

(b) Employment Maintenance Scheme.

(c) Employers' Temporary Subvention Fund.

(d) Employers' Employment Contributions Scheme.

(e) Employment grants under section 2, Industrial Development (No. 2) Act 1981.

(f) Enterprise Allowance Scheme of Minister of Labour.

(g) The Enterprise Scheme of An Foras Aiseanna Saothair.

(h) Employment grants under section 10(5)(a), Údarás na Gaeltachta Act 1979 (paid on or after 1 April 1993).

(i) Employment grants under section 21(5)(a) Industrial Development Act 1986, as amended (paid on or after 1 April 1993).

(j) An Bord Tráchtála under the Market Development Fund, and

(k) An Foras Áiseanna Saothair (FÁS) under the Employment Subsidy Scheme.

(l) From 1 April 1995, certain employment grants made by Údarás na Gaeltachta, IDA Ireland and Forbairt to medium/large industrial undertakings under the schemes known, respectively, as:

- "Deontais Fhostaíochta ó Údarás na Gaeltachta do Ghnothais Mhóra/ Mheánmhéide Thionsclaíochta", and
- "Scheme Governing the Making of Employment Grants to Medium/Large Industrial Undertakings"

(m) From 6 April 1996, the following payments made to employers in respect of new employment provided by them:

The Back to Work Allowance Scheme,

- A scheme to be established by the Minister for Enterprise and Employment and administered by FÁS for the purpose of promoting the employment of individuals who have been unemployed for three years or more,
- Operating Agreements between the Minister for Enterprise and Employment and the County Enterprise Boards,
- The EU Leader II Community Initiative (1994 to 1999),

– The Area Partnerships Scheme administered by Area Development Management Limited under the EU Operational Programme for Local, Urban and Rural Development,

– The Special European Union Programme for Peace and Reconciliation in Northern Ireland and the Border Counties of Ireland,

– The Joint Northern Ireland/Ireland INTERREG Programme 1994 to 1999, or

– Initiatives of the International Fund for Ireland.

– The Shannon Free Airport Development Limited (Amendment) Act, 1970.

(n) From 6 April 1997 payment made to employers under:

– The employment support scheme which is administered by the National Rehabilitation board, and

– The Pilot Programme for the Employment of People with Disabilities which is administered by the Rehab Group.

2.12.2 Long-term unemployed

TCA97 s88A Employers may claim a double deduction in respect of certain emoluments paid to employees who were long-term unemployed.

The employment must be a "qualifying employment" and the emoluments must be payable to a "qualifying individual".

The double deduction may be claimed against trading or professional profits in respect of:

1. Emoluments paid to the qualifying employee in the first 36 months of the employment, and
2. The employer's PRSI contribution on those emoluments.

See paragraph 1.3.14 for allowances available to employee under Revenue Job Assist.

2.13 Renewable Energy Generation

TCA97 s486B A company investing in a renewable energy project may, subject to certain conditions, obtain a deduction in computing taxable profits.

The relief operates as follows:

- A deduction from company profits may be obtained for an investment in new ordinary shares in a company setting up a renewable energy project.
- Such renewable schemes are in wind, hydro and biomass technology.
- The maximum amount which may be funded under this project is 50% of the capital expenditure. This figure excludes land and is net of grants. There is an overall limit of €9,525,00 on any project.
- An individual company or group of companies may not invest more than €12,700,000 per annum in such projects.

The shares when issued must be held for a period of 5 years, otherwise the relief will be withdrawn.

The original scheme came into effect on 18 March 1999 for three years. The scheme currently applies to 31 December 2006 and is to be extended to 31 December 2011 subject to EU approval.

2.14 Accelerated Capital Allowances for Energy Efficient Equipment

TCA97 s285A Finance Act 2008 introduced a new section into the TCA 1997 to provide for accelerated capital allowances in respect of expenditure by companies on certain energy-efficient equipment bought for the purposes of the trade. The scheme, which will run for a trial period of three years, will apply to new equipment in designated classes of technology. Equipment eligible under the scheme will be published in a list established by the Minister for Communications, Energy and Natural Resources (with the approval of the Minister for Finance) and maintained by the Sustainable Energy Authority of Ireland.

The main features of the new scheme are as follows:

- Capital allowances of 100% will be available in the first year in which the expenditure is incurred on the equipment covered by the scheme.
- To qualify, the equipment that is purchased must meet certain energy-efficiency criteria (laid down by the Minister for Communication, Energy and Natural Resources) and be specified on a list of approved products.
- Energy-efficient equipment on the list will fall into one of three classes of technology and expenditure must be above a certain minimum amount to qualify for the increased allowance. The technology classes (and minimum expenditure amounts) are: motors and drives (€1,000), lighting (€3,000) and building energy management systems (€5,000).
- The list will be established, and may be amended, by order of the Minister for Communications, Energy and Natural Resources. Sustainable Energy Ireland (SEI) will be responsible for maintaining the list.
- The scheme will be confined to new energy-efficient equipment purchased by companies, and it will not apply to equipment that is leased, let or hired. It will run for a period of three years from the date that the first order establishing the list of energy efficient equipment is made. Energy-efficient equipment purchased in the period between 31 January 2008 and the date of the first order will qualify under the scheme, provided the equipment purchased in that period is on the list established by that first order.

The new scheme is subject to clearance by the European Commission from a State Aid perspective and will come into operation by way of commencement order to be made by the Minister for Finance following such clearance.

Chapter 3 Double Taxation Agreements and EU Directives

3.1 Existing Double Taxation Agreements

Finance Act 2006 changed the procedures that apply to give the force of Irish law to double taxation treaties, and treaties concerned with exchange of information between tax authorities, entered into by the Government. Previously, such a treaty had the force of law once the Government made an Order that it had entered into the treaty and the Order had been approved by the Dáil. An additional step was introduced so that a treaty will have the force of law only after the Government has made an Order that has been approved by the Dáil and law has been enacted by the Oireachtas that inserts a reference to the Order into a new Schedule that has been inserted into the Taxes Consolidation Act 1997. The position of existing Double Taxation Agreements in Irish Law is secured by listing them in Schedule 24A.

Australia	Greece	Norway
Austria	Hungary	Pakistan
Belgium	Iceland	Poland
Bulgaria	India	Portugal
Canada	Israel	Romania
Chile	Italy	Russia
China	Japan	Slovak Republic
Croatia	Korea (Rep of)	Slovenia
Cyprus	Latvia	South Africa
Czech Republic	Lithuania	Spain
Denmark	Luxembourg	Sweden
Estonia	Malaysia	Switzerland
Finland	Mexico	United Kingdom
France	Netherlands	United States of America
Germany	New Zealand	Zambia

New treaties with Argentina, Egypt, Kuwait, Malta, Macedonia, Moldova, Morocco, Thailand, Tunisia, Turkey, Ukraine and Vietnam are being negotiated. Negotiations have also taken place with Singapore but some matters remain to be agreed. Existing treaties with Cyprus, France, Italy and Korea are in the process of re-negotiation.

3.2 Double Taxation Agreement Republic of Ireland - United Kingdom

(As applicable to residents of Republic of Ireland)

A double taxation agreement based on the model OECD Agreement was ratified in June 1976. This has been amended by protocols signed in October 1976, November 1994 and November 1998.

The agreement is based on the "credit" method of allowance for tax payable in the country of non residence. The main features of the agreement are:

3.2.1 Residence of individuals

Article 4 To determine in which of the two countries an individual is resident for the purposes of the treaty the following series of tests is applied:

(a) where has the individual his permanent home or the centre of his vital interest, or

(b) where has the individual his habitual abode, or

(c) of which State is the individual a national.

If any one of the foregoing tests can be positively applied, the residence of the individual is determined as being in the particular country.

Should all these tests fail to produce a positive answer, the final decision is left to be agreed between the Revenues of each country.

The concept of "double residence" is effectively removed by the operation of these provisions.

3.2.2 UK dividends

Article 11 Dividends are taxed both in the country in which the recipient individual is resident and in the country of payment, i.e. the country in which the company paying the dividend is resident.

For all tax years up to and including 1998/99, relief was afforded by:

(i) providing that the tax to be charged in the country of payment is not to exceed 15% of the gross amount of the dividend (i.e. the dividend paid and the associated tax credit), the balance of the tax credit can be reclaimed directly in the case of Irish residents, from the UK Revenue authorities and

(ii) allowing a credit against the tax payable in the country of residence in respect of tax payable in the other.

However, due to changes in domestic rules relating to tax credits in both Ireland and the UK, the terms of the treaty were altered by a provision in the protocol, and with effect from 6 April 1999, dividends paid by UK corporations to an Irish resident will not carry an entitlement to the tax credit and neither will there be an entitlement to any credit against Irish tax on the dividend income. As a result the Form/Individual/Credit is redundant.

3.2.3 Interest

Article 12

Taxable only in Ireland for individuals resident in Ireland. United Kingdom tax deducted from interest is repayable in full.

3.2.4 Rents

Article 7

Taxable in the United Kingdom with a right to set off the United Kingdom tax against the tax payable in Ireland on the same income.

3.2.5 Business profits

Article 8

Taxable only in Ireland unless there is a permanent establishment in the United Kingdom when the profits applicable to the permanent establishment will be taxed in the United Kingdom. Any tax payable in the United Kingdom will be available as a credit against the tax payable in Ireland on the same profits.

3.2.6 Royalties

Article 13

Taxable only in Ireland.

3.2.7 Capital gains

Article 14

An Irish resident earning capital gains in the United Kingdom is normally taxable in Ireland alone. There are some exceptions to this

(a) Gains derived by an Irish resident from the alienation of immovable property in the United Kingdom or from certain shares deriving the greater part of their value from such shares may also be taxed in the United Kingdom.

(b) Gains from the alienation of business property of a permanent establishment may also be taxed in the United Kingdom.

3.2.8 Salaries, wages and directors fees

Articles 15 and 16

Salaries, wages and directors fees paid from the United Kingdom are liable to tax under PAYE in the United Kingdom. Any tax so paid is available as a credit against the tax paid on the same income in Ireland (there are circumstances where the remuneration may be taxable in the state of residence only).

3.2.9 Pensions

Article 17

(a) Other than Government pensions: Taxable only in Ireland.

(b) State pensions and remuneration: Taxable only in the United Kingdom unless the recipient is a sole national of Ireland when tax is payable also in Ireland with a right to set off the United Kingdom tax paid against the Irish tax payable on the same income.

3.2.10 Charities and superannuation schemes

Article 14A Such bodies continue to be exempt from tax in appropriate circumstances.

3.2.11 Government service

Article 18 Salaries, wages and other similar remuneration, other than a pension, are taxable only in Ireland. They may, however, be taxable in the United Kingdom if the services are rendered there by a resident of the United Kingdom who is also a United Kingdom national.

3.2.12 Exchange of information

Article 25 Provision is made for the exchange of information as is necessary for the carrying out of the convention which is expressed to be for the avoidance of double taxation and the prevention of fiscal evasion with respect to taxes on income and capital gains.

3.3 EU Directives

3.3.1 Parent / Subsidaries Directive No 90/435/EEC

TCA97 s831 The provisions of this Directive known as the Parent/Subsidaries Directive on dividends and distributions paid by subsidiary companies are applied by section 831. The directive applies to the distributions between companies with a 25% shareholding relationship. Member States may alternatively by means of bilateral agreements apply a 25% holding of voting rights criterion for parent/subsidiary status. The purpose of these provisions is to grant credit for tax paid on profits in EU Member States out of which distributions are made to companies in other Member States. To qualify for this treatment the foreign company must be resident in an EU country and at least 25% of its share capital must be owned directly by a company from another Member State.

Where a parent/subsidiary relationship exists and the subsidiary pays a distribution other than a distribution in a winding up to the parent the Directive requires the following reliefs to be given:

1. The parent company's State must either exempt the distribution received from the charge to tax (the exemption method) or else give credit against tax charged for any foreign withholding tax deducted from the distribution and for underlying tax suffered by the subsidiary on the profits out of which the distribution was paid (the credit method).
2. The subsidiary's State must not deduct withholding tax from the distribution.
3. The parent company's State must not deduct withholding tax from the distribution.

Parent / Subsidiaries Directive No 2003/123/EC

Finance Act 2004 implements EU Council Directive 2003/123/EC which amends earlier Directive 90/435/EEC on the common system of taxation applicable in the case of parent companies and their subsidiaries of different Member States. Finance Act 2005 extends the benefits to Swiss companies.

The Parent /Subsidiaries Directive which was concerned with eliminating double taxation on dividends across borders within the EU from subsidiaries to their parents, was implemented by section 831 TCA 1997. Finance Act 2004 makes a number of changes to section 831 to give effect to the new Directive as follows:

- The shareholding threshold for a company to be considered as a parent company is reduced from 25% to 5%;

- Irish branches of companies of other Member States will be entitled to the same reliefs as Irish resident companies where they receive dividends from their subsidiaries;
- References to Irish unlimited companies are deleted from section 831. Unlimited companies are not covered by the earlier Parent/ Subsidiaries Directive but are now covered following its amendment by the new Directive. Consequently, a specific reference to them in section 831 is no longer necessary;
- Tax paid by lower tiers of subsidiaries may be taken into account for the purpose of giving credit relief to an Irish company that receives dividends from its subsidiaries in EU Member States subject to a shareholding of 5% at each tier;
- Relief from double taxation under the Directive is specifically provided for in the unusual scenario where a subsidiary is regarded as a company in its home Member State but is considered to be transparent for tax purposes in the Member State of its parent company;
- Finally, provisions relating to allowing a credit against Irish tax on dividends received by a parent company for withholding tax applied to those dividends pursuant to derogations from the 1990 Parent/Subsidiaries Directive are modified. References to Germany, Portugal and Greece are removed as the Directive now prohibits withholding tax on relevant dividends in those Member Sates.

3.3.2 Interest and Royalty Directive No 2003/49/EC

Finance Act 2004 enacts provisions of the statutory instrument which was passed in 2003 giving effect to the EU Directive on interest and royalties. Finance Act 2005 extends the benefits to Swiss companies.

Much of the detail on the Interest and Royalty Directive and its application within Irish tax law is outlined in Schedule 1 of the Finance Act 2004.

The purpose of the Directive is the total elimination of double taxation on cross border payments of interest and royalties between 25% associated companies. This means an exemption from withholding tax in the source State on those interest or royalty payments. The provisions are effective from 1 January 2004.

Conditions Applicable

In order that an interest or royalty payment falls within the terms of the legislation and is exempt from withholding tax, the following conditions must apply:

- The payment must be between one EU Member State and another.
- The recipient must be the beneficial owner (not the intermediary) of the interest or royalties.

- The rules only apply to companies and permanent establishments ("PE") in the relevant Member State.
- Both the payer and recipient company must be "associated" (see below) with the payer and recipient companies being associated for a minimum of a two-year period (uninterrupted).

In order that the exemption apply to a payment of interest or royalty by or to a PE;

- The interest or royalty must be a tax deductible expense of the PE.
- The PE must be considered the beneficial owner of the interest or royalty. This can only be the case if the interest or royalty is effectively connected with the PE and if the receipt is subject to corporation tax/or foreign equivalent tax.
- In relation to any payments to branches, the "head office" company must also be resident in an EU Member State (for example, a UK branch of a French company).

Definition of interest and royalties

Interest

Interest is very widely defined and includes debt claims of every kind. It includes interest on securities, bonds and debentures but specifically excludes penalty charges for late payment.

Royalty

Royalties also include payments of any kind, with the wording of the Finance Act being very similar to the OECD model treaty definition. An important point to mention in relation to the definition of royalties is that it specifically includes payments in respect of leasing or software, which is very helpful.

Exclusions from interest/royalty definitions

Certain payments are not considered to fall within the definition of interest or royalties for the purposes of the legislation. Examples of these exclusions are:

- Debt claims without provision for repayment, namely perpetual debt.
- Non EU companies/branches - (for example, payment from an Irish company to a Russian branch of a French company).
- Non "arms length" payments, where the excess does not qualify for exemption.

Associated test

To be associated, there must be a 25% direct shareholding relationship, i.e. one company controls 25% or more of the voting power of another or both are controlled 25% by a third company (triangular test). The legislation focuses on a direct rather than an indirect relationship, which in practice is a problem for many groups.

In the case of a company, the company must be:

(i) Tax resident in a relevant EU Member State,

(ii) Established in one of the forms outlined in the legislation (which includes a limited company, industrial and provident societies, building societies etc.), and

(iii) Subject to Irish corporation tax or a foreign equivalent type tax.

In the case of a PE, the PE must have a fixed place of business in an EU Member State through which business of a company of another Member State is wholly/partly carried on (for example a UK branch of French company).

Transitional provisions

There are a number of countries with transitional provisions. Specifically, Spain is permitted to apply withholding tax to royalties only whilst Greece and Portugal are permitted to apply withholding tax to interest and royalties, providing they gradually reduce their tax rate over a eight-year transition period. The transition period for Spain is six years. During this transition period, credit should be allowed in Ireland for any such withholding tax suffered, subject to domestic tax rules, which in practice creates a substantial cost.

In summary, section 41 and Schedule 1 removes the obligation to operate withholding tax in respect of qualifying interest and royalty payments. It also removes any potential for an income tax or corporation tax liability derived in the payer country. Although the implementation of the Directive in the Finance Act 2004 is helpful, it should be noted that section 246 TCA 1997 permits certain interest paid to companies resident in EU/DTA countries to be made gross. Both of these options should be considered when looking to make payments of interest gross.

3.3.3 Savings Directive No. 2003/48/EC

Savings directive

The EU Savings Directive was brought into legislation in December 2003 and is now enshrined in our tax legislation in sections 898B to 898R TCA 1997. The purpose of the Directive is to ensure reporting/ withholding of cross-EC border interest arising to a beneficial owner who is an EC resident individual or a residual entity in an another EC Member State. It is important to note that it does not apply to payments of interest to companies, neither does it apply to interest payments within the same country. Most countries, including

Ireland, are following the exchange of information route. Luxembourg, Austria and Belgium are applying withholding tax in respect of cross border interest payments within the scope of the Directive.

Finance Act 2005 amended the legislation to recognise the agreements reached between the EU and Andorra, Liechtenstein, Monaco, San Marino and the Swiss Confederation, respectively, under which those countries will introduce measures equivalent to the Savings Directive.

There is a detailed timeframe in relation to the full implementation of the Directive and although some of the legislation is effective 1 January 2004 (specifically new account information requirements), the reporting obligations and collection of information only applies from 1 July 2005.

Savings Directive - timeframe

3 Jun 2003	Final Directive
1 Jan 2004	New account information requirement
1 July 2005	Directive applies
31 Mar 2006	Date by which information on 2005 activity to be provided to Irish Revenue
30 Jun 2006	Ireland exchanges information with other EU tax authorities

Interest payments within the scope of the Directive

Essentially, two categories of interest are caught within the scope of the Directive. Firstly, interest paid relating to debt claims and interest accrued/capitalised on the sale/redemption of the debt claims. Secondly, income deriving from interest payments distributed by certain funds and income realised on the sale/redemption of shares or units of certain funds are also within the scope of the Directive.

"Debt claims" is very widely defined and includes all possible connotations of interest. There are a number of exemptions in relation to certain government issues and issues by Member States. In the case of funds, there are very specific rules outlining whether a payment of interest falls within the scope of the Directive, depending on whether more than 15% of the assets of the fund are in debt claims (in the case of EU funds). In the case of income realised on the sale or redemption of fund units, there is a 40% test (which applies to EU and non EU funds). The rules are reasonably complex and the Revenue have issued draft guidelines on the application of the Directive.

Key considerations

Key considerations in respect of the Directive include:

- The definition of the paying agent
- The definition of interest
- Identification of the beneficial owner
- Reporting obligations

The financial services industry is affected by these new rules. Many banks and other forms of paying agent continue to address the practical and systems issues in relation to the application of the Directive.

With effect from 31 March 2006, a penalty of €1,520 will apply for non-compliance with the requirements under the Savings Directive as enacted into Irish legislation. In the case of a body of persons, the secretary will also be liable to a separate penalty of €950.

3.3.4 Mergers Directive No 90/434/EU

The purpose of this directive is to remove tax barriers to mergers, divisions, transfers of assets and exchanges of shares between companies from different Member States. In general terms it achieves this by deferring any capital gains tax which would arise at the time of the merger, etc. sections 583-584 contain the necessary legislation to deal with exchanges of shares.

Mergers and divisions (as defined in the Directive) cannot occur under Irish company law and accordingly no tax legislation is possible.

The chapter, therefore, deals with transfers of assets in the main and, broadly speaking, allows the following transactions to take place without corporation tax or capital gains tax implications:

(a) The transfer of a trade or part of a trade by one company to another in exchange for shares in the latter company which then carries on that trade as a branch of its activity. Both companies must be EU Member States companies.

(b) The transfer of trading assets by an Irish subsidiary to its 100% parent within the EU.

(c) The transfer of development land in the course of a scheme of reconstruction or amalgamation.

(d) The transfer of development land within a group.

The relevance of (c) and (d) is that previously transactions in development land gave rise to a tax charge in these situations as Irish tax law did not allow a deferral of gains on development land or similar transactions between Irish resident companies.

3.3.5 European company ("SE") and European co-operative society ("SCE") (EU Directive No. 2005/19/EC)

Finance Act 2006 introduced new provisions to deal with the existence of both the European Company (SE) and European Co-operative Society (SCE) under Irish tax law.

It has been possible to create an SE by merger of two companies in different Member States by conversion into an SE where, for two years, the company has had a subsidiary or branch in another Member State, or by creating a subsidiary SE in conjunction with a company resident in another Member State since October 2004.

It will be possible to create an SCE under similar conditions from August 2006.

Without the new provisions, the creation of either an SE or SCE could have had adverse Irish tax consequences.

Measures introduced in Finance Act 2006 include:

- Inserting a definition of both SE and SCE in the tax legislation.
- Provision that, where the principal company in a group becomes an SE or SCE, this will not change the group for Irish tax purposes.
- Where a company ceases to be resident by means of a merger into an SE or SCE, Irish tax rules will continue to apply to it as though it was resident in relation to any matter preceding the merger.
- Expansion of the Mergers Directive provisions to apply equally to SEs and SCEs.
- The expansion of the pre-entry loss rules to deal with the creation of an SE or SCE by merger.

There are also anti-avoidance rules to disapply the above reliefs in the case where the SE or SCE was not created for bone fide commercial reasons.

3.4 Tax Information Exchange Agreements

TCA97 s826, s912A

Tax Information Exchange Agreements are arrangements to be entered into between the State and other jurisdictions (typically the jurisdictions with which Ireland does not have a Double Tax Agreement) to enable the exchange of information regarding tax matters between the State and the other territory.

3.4.1 Background

Double Tax Agreements entered into between Ireland and other territories typically have an exchange of information clause. These clauses typically allow Revenue Authorities of either State to share information – this information can be gathered using the domestic powers available to the Revenue authority. Arising from revelations concerning tax evasion, the Revenue Commissioners have had discussions with territories with which Ireland does not have Double Tax Agreements with a view to entering into formal Exchange of Information Agreements.

3.4.2 Exchange of information provisions

Amendments to section 826 TCA 1997 and a new section 912A TCA 1997 provide a statutory framework for exchange of information arrangements with territories with which Ireland does not have Double Tax Agreement. The State can use a number of existing domestic powers to obtain information regarding potential tax liabilities owed in other territories. It should be noted that these powers can only be used and information can only be shared, for the purposes of the prevention and detection of tax evasion. The taxes concerned are income tax, corporation tax, tax on chargeable gains and any other taxes of a similar nature. Finance Act 2004 extends the powers of the Revenue Commissioners to include gift tax and inheritance tax and taxes of a similar nature. Finance Act 2004 extends the powers of the Revenue Commissioners to include gift tax and inheritance tax and taxes of a similar nature. "Tax evasion" is not defined in this section or indeed anywhere else in the Tax Acts so it takes its "everyday" meaning.

3.4.3 Relevant powers for exchange of information

The relevant powers, which the Revenue Commissioners can use for the purposes of exchange of information arrangements, are as follows:

- Section 900 TCA 1991 – request for production of books, information and explanations
- Section 901 TCA 1997 – High Court application for information under section 900

- Section 902 TCA 1997 – request for information from a third party
- Section 902A TCA 1997 – High Court application for order to obtain information from third party (however the provision in section 902A that the order can be in respect of persons whose individual identities are not known to Revenue is excluded for the purposes of this section)
- Section 906A TCA 1997 – information to be furnished by financial institutions
- Section 907 TCA 1997 – application to Appeal Commissioners for information from financial institutions (however the provision in section 907 that the order can be in respect of persons whose individual identities are not known to Revenue is excluded for the purposes of this section)
- Section 908 TCA1997 – application to High Court seeking order to obtain information from financial institutions (however the provision in section 908 that the order can be in respect of persons whose individual identities are not know to Revenue is excluded for the purposes of this section).

During the course of the passage of Finance Act 2003 through the Dáil, a structure which circumvented to a significant extent the new anti-avoidance legislation came into the public domain.

This new structure involved establishing a company to acquire the property with the individuals financing that company by way of debt finance. The interest arising on the funds borrowed by the individuals would have been available as a tax write-off. At the time, the Minister announced, by way of press release, that such structures were prohibited with effect from 1 January 2003 and announced that the legislation giving effect to his statement would be introduced in Finance Act 2004. Broadly, this legislation is now set out in section 22 Finance Act 2004.

This section restricts the availability of interest relief on loans in the following situations:

1. where money borrowed by an individual and invested in, or loaned to, a company is used after 1 January 2003 by the company involved, in whole or in part, directly or indirectly, to acquire a specified building (essentially an industrial or commercial building with a remaining tax life) from a company, to replace money used to so acquire, or to pay off a loan used to so acquire.

2. where the individual uses borrowed money to pay off another loan or part of a loan where money under the earlier loan was used after the 1 January 2003 by the company involved for any of these purposes.

3. to other situations where an individual acquires share capital in a certain type of rental company on or after 20 February 2004

and the company acquires or had acquired a specified building, on or after 1 January 2003 from another company, without the use of money borrowed by the individual.

Where the above situations apply, interest relief for a year of assessment in relation to interest paid by an individual on a loan or part of a loan may not exceed the individuals return from the company in that year in relation to the specified amount of the loan involved. An individuals return from a company is broadly the amount of dividends or interest received by the individual from the company.

CHAPTER 4 ANTI-AVOIDANCE/ REVENUE POWERS

4.1 Anti-Avoidance Legislation

The principal anti-avoidance provisions are:

4.1.1 Friendly societies

TCA97 s211

Restriction of exemption for Friendly Societies to those which satisfy the Revenue Commissioners that they are "bona fide" societies.

4.1.2 Transfer of assets abroad

TCA97 s806

Prevention of tax avoidance by an individual ordinarily resident in the State of liability to tax by means of transfers of assets by virtue or in consequence of which either alone or in conjunction with associated operations income becomes payable to persons, e.g. a tax haven company, resident or domiciled outside the State.

The legislation provides that the income of the non-resident or non-domiciled person is to be treated as the income of the resident individual unless he proves that the transfer was not for the purpose of avoiding liability to tax and was a bona fide commercial transaction.

Finance Act 1998 amends the provision by extending it to transfers made by individuals resident in the State. It also applies irrespective of when the transfer was made but only to income arising after 12 February 1998.

Finance Act 2007 made a number of changes in the legislation relating to transfer of assets abroad. The main change relates to an exemption from the charge that is available if the individual concerned can satisfy the Revenue Commissioners that the purpose of the assets transfer was not to avoid tax or that the transactions concerned were bona fide commercial transactions and were not designed for tax avoidance reasons. The rules used to ascertain whether or not the purpose of the transfer of assets was to avoid tax are strengthened. The changes are designed to ensure that all relevant factors, relating both to the subjective intentions of the individual and the authenticity of the transaction itself, are to be taken into account in determining whether or not a transaction has an avoidance purpose. The Finance Act 2007 also closes a possible loophole by confirming that all operations associated with the initial transfer of assets are taken into account in determining whether or not liability arises under the provisions. Transnational arrangements are also included to ensure that asset transfers related to the existing rules and/or to the new rules are treated appropriately.

The Revenue Commissioners have substantial powers to obtain information in connection with any transfer of assets abroad.

4.1.3 Property transactions

TCA97 s639-s647

Prevention of avoidance involving gains from (real) property transactions or transactions in shares deriving value from real property.

4.1.4 Industrial and provident societies

TCA97 s438

Loans or advances made on or after 23 May 1983 to participators or their associates by a registered industrial or provident society are deemed to be annual payments made under the deduction of tax. The society is therefore obliged to pay over income tax at a rate of 20/80ths of the loan to the Revenue Commissioners (see loans to participators etc., 2.6.4).

4.1.5 Exchequer bills

TCA97 s45-s48

Exemption does not apply in respect of the excess of the amount received on redemption over the issue price of Exchequer Bills and Agricultural Commodity Intervention Bills issued after 25 January 1984 unless a tender for them was submitted on or before that date.

4.1.6 Bond washing

TCA97 s815

A person who transfers or sells certain securities is to be treated for taxation purposes as having received the interest which has accrued to the date of sale. The securities referred to are those exempted from capital gains tax under the provisions of section 607, and stocks, bonds and obligations of any government, municipal corporation, or other body corporate. Shares of a company within the meaning of the Companies Act 1963, or similar body, are excluded.

The provisions do not apply:

(a) where the security has been held by the same owner for a continuous period of at least two years, or

(b) where the vendor is a dealer in securities, the profits of whose trade are assessed to tax under Case I Schedule D, or

(c) where the transfer or sale is between a husband and wife at a time when they are treated as living together for income tax purposes. (The combined period of ownership of the spouses is taken into account for the purpose of the two year rule), or

(d) where the security is one, the interest on which is treated as a distribution under the Tax Acts.

4.1.7 Partnerships – limited and general

TCA97 s1013 In respect of limited partnerships set up after 22 May 1985, the right of the limited partners to set off losses and capital allowances arising out of the partnership trade against their other income is restricted to the amount of their contribution to the limited partnership trade.

Losses and capital allowances arising from contributions to limited partnerships by limited partners on or after 24 April 1992 will only be available for setoff against profits or gains arising from the partnership trade and will not be available against the total income of the limited partner.

Similar restrictions apply in the case of partnerships whose activities include producing, distributing or holding films or video tapes or exploring for or exploiting oil and/or gas resources. A partner in such a partnership who does not work for the greater part of his/her time on the day-to-day management or conduct of the partnership trade will be subject to restrictions in respect of the use of losses, capital allowances and certain interest payments.

The definition of limited partner in relation to claims for the income tax years 2005 *et seq.* includes individuals in partnerships or similar arrangements registered outside the State where the individuals are not involved in the day-to-day management or conduct of the trade.

With effect from 29 February 2000 non-active partners in all partnerships, limited or general, are restricted as to the offset of:

(i) Interest paid after 29 February 2000;

(ii) Capital allowance in respect of expenditure after 29 February 2000; and

(iii) Losses arising in a trade after 29 February 2000.

Such losses and allowances are available only against profits from that trade and then only up to the limit of the partners' contribution to the partnership.

The following losses and allowances are covered by transitional measures effective up to the specified date:

(i) Double Rent Relief, interest paid, capital allowances or losses in double rent seaside resort holiday home schemes up to 5 April 2004.

(ii) Other double rent deductions until the entitlement to such a deduction ends.

(iii) Accelerated Capital Allowances on the BIM approved scheme for the extension of the white fish fleet up until the year 2000/01 and interest on a loan for such expenditure taken out before 4 September 2000 (this covers the life of this scheme)

(iv) Any allowances on the leasing of equipment for renewable energy projects such as windmills in respect of expenditure incurred on obligations entered into before 1 March 2001.

The following are wholly excluded from the operation of these provisions:

(i) Partnerships where the €31,750 ceiling on Capital Allowances claim on buildings apply i.e., Rural, Urban and Town Renewal Schemes.

(ii) Hotel allowances in the 7 north-western counties: Cavan, Donegal, Leitrim, Mayo, Monaghan, Roscommon and Sligo (excluding seaside resort areas).

(iii) Transitional provisions relating to the above two at section 409A and 409B.

4.1.8 Transactions to avoid liability to tax

TCA97 s811 If the Revenue Commissioners form an opinion that a transaction is a "tax-avoidance transaction", they will notify each person, undertaking such a transaction, of this, state the amount of tax that they consider the person is attempting to avoid and how they propose to recharacterise the transactions for tax purposes to counteract the avoidance. In examining the transaction, the Revenue Commissioners may look at both the substance and outcome of the transaction and of related transactions and not merely the form.

The Revenue Commissioners will not regard a transaction as a tax-avoidance transaction if it was made with a view to the realisation of profits in the course of business and was not primarily to avoid tax, or if the transaction was undertaken to obtain the benefit of a tax incentive, provided that the transaction would not result in a misuse or abuse of the incentive.

Anyone receiving such a notice from the Revenue Commissioners may lodge an appeal within 30 days. The appeal procedure will be in the form normally applying to Income Tax appeals.

The section applies to any transaction completed on or after 25 January 1989. It also applies to transactions carried out on or before that date if the transaction would reduce any charge or assessment to tax which could not fall due earlier than 25 January 1989 and to transactions which would generate a refund which would not be payable earlier than that date.

Finance Act 2006 ensures that, where the opinion of the Revenue Commissioners, that a transaction is a tax-avoidance transaction becomes final, interest and a 20% (previously 10%) surcharge will be payable on the tax that that taxpayer unsuccessfully attempted to avoid paying. Finance Act 2006 also provides that, by making a protective notification to Revenue in respect of a transaction within 90 days of beginning a transaction, the taxpayer can, on a wholly non-prejudicial basis, obtain protection from the possibility of such interest or surcharge arising in the event of Revenue successfully challenging the transaction.

An appeal against Revenue's opinion, that a transaction is a tax-avoidance transaction will be deemed to be finally determined where it is settled by agreement between the taxpayer and Revenue.

Refunds by a taxpayer of tax repayments received on foot of avoidance will be treated as additional tax payable for the purposes of the surcharge.

Interest will be applied by reference to when tax would have been payable if there had been no avoidance.

Interest in respect of periods (of delay in payment) beginning when Revenue's opinion has become final is not covered by a protective notification. The new section 811A requires Revenue to specify, for the purpose of charging interest, the dates from which tax would have been due and payable if there had been no attempted avoidance. It also provides a right of appeal to the taxpayer against Revenue's specification of those dates. The surcharge is payable when Revenue's opinion becomes final (unless a protective notification has been made).

The protective notification must be delivered in a prescribed form to Revenue offices specified on the form. The notifications must contain full details of the transaction, full reference to relevant tax law, and details of how that tax law is considered to apply to the transaction. The use of the expression of doubt procedure will not be regarded as representing a protective notification. Protective notifications do not involve or imply any doubt on the part of the taxpayer. They are a provision of information to Revenue to protect against any possibility of surcharge and interest. The taxpayer has the right to appeal in the event of Revenue contending that a full and timely notification was not made.

The provisions in Finance Act 2006 apply to transactions wholly or partly undertaken after 2 February 2006. They also apply to transactions wholly undertaken before that date where they have the effect of reducing liabilities or causing repayments after that date.

Section 140, Finance Act 2008 amends s811A TCA97 as follows:

1. A new s811A(1A) is inserted to provide the four year enquiry period in s955(2)(a) (time period to issue assessments) and s956(1)(c) (time period to make enquiries) will not prevent Revenue making any enquiry or taking any action under s811A or s811.
2. Where a valid protective notification is received, and is in full compliance with the terms of s811A, Revenue will not be permitted to form an opinion that the transaction (the subject of the protective notification) is a tax avoidance transaction after

the expiry of two years from the date on which the protective notification was due to be filed or, if earlier, the date the notification was received by Revenue. However, this limitation only extends to the ability of Revenue to form an opinion as they are still entitled to make enquiries for an unlimited period;

3. In the event of a protective notification not being filed (or being invalid where filed), s811A(1C) provides that s811(9) is amended to allow an appeal against an opinion issued under s811 to be determined on the basis that the transaction or any part of it could reasonably be considered to be a tax avoidance transaction. This is a fundamental change to the standard proof under which appeals are determined under s811. In contrast, where a valid protective notification is filed, the standard of proof remains that there is a requirement on the appellate body to find that there was a tax avoidance transaction for the opinion to be upheld;
4. The surcharge levied under s811A(2)(a) (where a valid protection notification is not filed with Revenue) is increased to 20% from 10%;
5. The new provisions, as outlined below, are intended to apply to transactions arranged or undertaken wholly or partly on or after 19 February 2008. In relation to the filing deadlines for a protective notification filed in relation to a transaction wholly or partly arranged or undertaken on or after 19 February 2008, these should be filed by the later of 90 days after the date on which the transaction commenced or 19 May 2008. This is reflected in an amendment to s811A(3).
6. Other technical amendments are made to confirm:-
   (i) that the protective notification will protect against the new provisions of s811(1C) applying as well as surcharge and interest and
   (ii) that an 'expression of doubt' filed under the general tax filing heads will not constitute a protective notification to avoid the impact of subsection 811A(1C).
7. If a valid protective notification has been made prior to 19 February 2008, s811A will only apply to that transaction as if s140 FA08 had not been enacted.

4.1.9 Capital distribution treated as dividend

TCA97 s817 Where a shareholder disposes of shares in a close company without significantly reducing his percentage shareholding in the company, the proceeds of sale will be treated as a receipt assessable under Schedule F. The close company will be regarded as having made a distribution of an equivalent amount.

Amendments in Finance Act 2005 refine the provisions relating to the description of arrangements coming within the scope of the legislation.

An exemption applies in the case of bona fide disposals of shares which are not part of any scheme or arrangement to avoid tax.

Finance Act 2006 reinforces the original premise of the section to apply the 20% capital gains tax rate to capital receipts.

4.1.10 "Specified Trade" schemes

Finance Act 2003 introduced an anti-avoidance measure designed to counter schemes whereby tax reliefs available to a trading company (and relievable at the general corporation tax rate) are transferred to individuals (in which case the tax reliefs are set against income taxable at up to 42%).

The schemes (referred to in the section as "specified trades") are in the area of electricity generation, the film and music industries and oil and gas exploration. The effect of the section is to ringfence the tax reliefs available to a specified trade carried on by an individual in a passive way to the actual income arising to the individual from that trade.

4.1.11 Transfer of capital allowances

Finance Act 2003 gave legislative effect to the announcement made by the Minister for Finance in his press release of 20 January 2003 to close off a loophole relating to the effective transfer of capital allowances on buildings from companies to individual investors. The legislation will operate where three criteria are met. These are:

- a company must, at any time on or after 1 January 2003, hold the relevant interest in relation to capital expenditure incurred on the construction or refurbishment of a building in respect of which expenditure a company (not necessarily the company currently holding that relevant interest) has claimed capital allowances;
- subsequent to 1 January 2003, an individual becomes entitled to that relevant interest, whether or not subsequent to that time (i.e. on or after 1 January 2003) any other person or persons had in the interim become entitled to that relevant interest; and
- the individual concerned is entitled to set off the capital allowances in respect of the capital expenditure concerned or the residue of that expenditure against his or her Irish rental income (i.e. the individual must be a lessor of the building).

Where these three criteria are met, then, any capital allowance to be made to such an individual for the tax year 2003 or any subsequent tax year in respect of the capital expenditure concerned or the residue of that expenditure may only be set off against the individual's profit rent from the relevant building for that tax year. If the capital allowance for that year exceeds that profit rent, the excess may be carried forward for set-off against the profit rent of the individual from the relevant building for the next tax year, and so on for subsequent tax years.

During the course of the passage of Finance Act 2003 through the Dáil, a structure which circumvented to a significant extent the new anti-avoidance legislation came into the public domain.

This new structure involved establishing a company to acquire the property with the individuals financing that company by way of debt finance. The interest arising on the funds borrowed by the individuals would have been available as a tax write-off. At the time, the Minister announced, by way of press release, that such structures were prohibited with effect from 1 January 2003 and announced that the legislation giving effect to his statement would be introduced in Finance Act 2004. Broadly, this legislation is now set out in section 22 Finance Act 2004.

This section restricts the availability of interest relief on loans in the following situations:

(i) Where money borrowed by an individual and invested in, or loaned to, a company is used after 1 January 2003 by the company involved, in whole or in part, directly or indirectly, to acquire a specified building (essentially an industrial or commercial building with a remaining tax life) from a company, to replace money used to so acquire, or to pay off a loan used to so acquire.

(ii) Where the individual uses borrowed money to pay off another loan or part of a loan where money under the earlier loan was used after the 1 January 2003 by the company involved for any of these purposes.

(iii) To other situations where an individual acquires share capital in a certain type of rental company on or after 20 February 2004 and the company acquires or had acquired a specified building, on or after 1 January 2003 from another company, without the use of money borrowed by the individual.

Where the above situations apply, interest relief for a year of assessment in relation to interest paid by an individual on a loan or part of a loan may not exceed the individuals return from the company in that year in relation to the specified amount of the loan involved. An individual's return from a company is broadly the amount of dividends or interest received by the individual from the company.

4.1.12 Transfer of right to interest (including dividends)

TCA97 s812

Section 812 TCA 1997 deems the owner of securities to have received income where the owner sells or transfers a right to receive interest (including dividends) without selling or transferring the actual securities.

Scope for the use of two of the provisions of section 812 in unintended ways was identified by Revenue. The first provides that the interest, which the owner of the securities is deemed to receive, shall not be deemed to be the income of any other person; the second provides that, where there is a subsequent disposal of the right to receive the interest, the proceeds of the sale, transfer or other realisation shall not be deemed to be income of the person who effects that subsequent disposal.

Finance Act 2006 deleted these two provisions, and the changes apply to a sale, transfer or other realisation that takes place on or after 7 March 2006.

4.2 Revenue Powers

4.2.1 General

Chapter 4, Part 38 of the TCA 1997 provides for certain Revenue Powers. The Finance Act 1999 substituted existing powers under sections 900, 901, 902, 907 and 908 by new powers and it provided for additional powers contained in sections 902A, 904A, 906A and 908A. In addition, it also amended the provisions of sections 905 and 909.

Given the exceptional nature of these extended powers, the Revenue have issued a Statement of Practice (SP-Gen 1/99) setting out the approach that they will adopt in using these powers and they have also published Guidance Notes and Instructions for Revenue staff, which are available to taxpayers and their advisers.

A brief summary of Revenue powers is as follows:

4.2.2 Inspector's right to make enquiries

TCA97 s899 This section enables an inspector to verify the accuracy of information provided by:

- persons acting as agents in respect of rents
- Ministers, health boards, local authorities, etc. in respect of rents paid
- fees or commissions paid for services
- persons in receipt of income on behalf of others
- nominee holders of securities
- intermediaries in relation to UCITS
- persons in relation to third party returns
- interest paid gross by financial institutions
- intermediaries in returns of details of persons they have assisted in establishing foreign bank accounts or in purchasing certain foreign investment products.

4.2.3 Power to require production of accounts and books

TCA97 s900 This section gives power to an authorised officer to require a person to produce, or make available books, etc. and furnish information etc. relevant to the person's tax liability.

An "authorised officer" is an inspector or other Revenue officer authorised in writing for the purpose of this section by the Revenue Commissioners.

A person carrying on a profession cannot be required to disclose any information or professional advice of a confidential nature given to a client.

4.2.4 Production of books and records – Application to High Court

TCA97 s901 This section gives power to an authorised officer to apply to a judge of the High Court for an order seeking production or availability of books, etc. and information, etc. from a person, which are relevant to the person's tax liability. A person carrying on a profession shall not be required to disclose any information or professional advice of a confidential nature given to a client.

4.2.5 Power to obtain from certain persons particulars of transactions with and documents concerning tax liability of taxpayer

TCA97 s902 This section gives power to an authorised officer, when enquiring into the tax liability of any person, to seek from a third party books, etc. or information, etc. relevant to the tax liability of the person subject to enquiry (who will be given a copy of the notice served on the third party).

4.2.6 Information from third parties – Application to High Court

TCA97 s902A An authorised officer can apply to a judge of the High Court for an order seeking books, etc. and information from a third party that are relevant to the tax liability of a person, including a group or class of persons. Before such an application is made the authorised officer must have the consent of a Revenue Commissioner. A person carrying on a profession shall not be required to disclose any information or professional advice of a confidential nature given to a client.

4.2.7 Power of inspection: life policies

TCA97 s902B An authorised officer of the Revenue Commissioners can sample the information (other than medical records) held by a life assurance company in respect of a class or classes of policies and their policyholders. The use of this power is subject to a Revenue Commissioner being satisfied that there are circumstances suggesting that such class or classes of policies have been used as an investment vehicle for untaxed funds. The information obtained by use of this sampling power can only be used to assist in making an application to a judge of the High Court for an order to have wider access to the information held by the life assurance company in relation to that class or those classes of policies and their policyholders.

4.2.8 PAYE

TCA97 s903 Similar powers, as outlined above, exist in relation to the operation of PAYE. These include the power:

- to enter and search any premises which is connected with the operation of PAYE; other than a premises or part of a premises used as a private residence, unless the consent of the occupier is given or the officer has obtained a warrant from a judge of the district court for that purpose,
- to examine, remove and retain records, and
- to seek explanations from all persons on the premises other than customers or clients.

4.2.9 Sub-contractors

TCA97 s904 The Revenue Commissioners also have extended powers in relation to the supervision and monitoring of the sub-contractors legislation.

An authorised officer may, at all reasonable times, enter any premises where he has reason to believe:

(a) that relevant operations are being carried on;

(b) that any person is making or has made payments to a sub-contractor in connection with the performance by the sub-contractor of a relevant contract in relation to which that person is principal;

(c) that any person is or was in receipt of such payments;

(d) that records are or may be kept in those premises.

An officer is prevented from entering a premises or part of a premises occupied as a private residence, unless the consent of the occupier is given or the officer has obtained a warrant from a judge of the district court for that purpose.

He may require the principal or sub-contractor or any employee or any other person providing bookkeeping, clerical or other administrative services to the principal or sub-contractor who is on that premises to produce any records which he requires for the purpose of that enquiry

If he has reason to believe that any of the records which have not been produced to him are on those premises, he can search the premises.

He can examine, copy, take extracts from, remove or retain any records for a reasonable period for the further examination thereof or for legal or criminal proceedings.

The authorised officer may require the principal or sub-contractor or any employee or any other person providing bookkeeping, clerical or other administrative services to the principal or sub-contractor to give all reasonable assistance including providing information, explanations and furnishing documents.

4.2.10 DIRT

TCA97 s904A s904B, s904C, s904D This section gives power to an authorised officer to audit the DIRT returns of a relevant deposit taker i.e. banks, etc. The Finance Act 2000 allows the Revenue Commissioners to appoint any person as an authorised officer where they consider that the person has suitable experience.

The Revenue Commissioners were also empowered to report the results of a "look back" audit of financial institutions in relation to DIRT. The existing powers in relation to DIRT are also extended to the audit of returns of appropriate tax in the case of life assurance companies and investment undertakings.

4.2.11 Inspection of documents and records

TCA97 s905 This section gives power to an authorised officer to enter premises where any trade or profession is carried on at a reasonable time and to request, search for and inspect records. An amendment to the definition of records in Finance Act, 2002 gives the authorised officer access to a wide range of documents apart from financial records. The authorised officer is empowered to remove the records for examination and to require certain persons at the premises to render all reasonable assistance. A search may be conducted at a private residence only where the officer has been invited to enter the house by the occupier or on foot of a warrant by the District Court.

TCA97 s905 This section also gives power to an authorised officer to carry out an on-site audit of a financial institution.

Furthermore under this section, as amended, application can be made to a judge of the District Court for the issue of a search warrant in relation to any premises. The judge can issue such a warrant if satisfied on information given on oath, that there are reasonable grounds for suspecting that there has been a failure to comply with the tax legislation, which failure is seriously prejudicial to the proper assessment or collection of tax and that records that are material to such assessment or collection are likely to be kept at the premises concerned.

Finance Act 2007 separates the powers of the Revenue to investigate for the purposes of establishing a tax liability from an investigation with a view to initiating criminal proceedings. (See 4.2.17.)

4.2.12 Authorised officers and Garda Síochána

TCA97 s906 This section gives power to an authorised officer who is authorised to enter premises to carry out inspection duties to bring with him/her a member or members of the Garda Síochána. If the Revenue officer is obstructed or interfered with, the Gardaí have the power of arrest without warrant.

Section 134 Finance Act 2008 provides for an authorised officer of the Revenue Commissioners to question suspects in Garda custody who have been arrested and detained by the Gardai in respect of serious indictable offences under Revenue law.

4.2.13 Information to be furnished by financial institutions

TCA97 s906A This section gives power to an authorised officer to issue a notice to a financial institution requiring it to make available for inspection books etc. or to furnish information relevant to a person's tax liability. The person subject to inquiry will be given a copy of the notice. Before such a notice is issued by an authorised officer the consent of a Revenue Commissioner is required.

4.2.14 Application to Appeal Commissioners seeking determination that authorised officer is justified in requiring information to be furnished by financial institutions

TCA97 s907 This section gives power to an authorised officer to apply to the Appeal Commissioners for consent to issue a notice to a financial institution requiring it to make available for inspection books, etc., or to furnish information relevant to a person's tax liability (including a group or class of persons and a person who is claiming exemption from DIRT on the basis of non-residence in the State). Before such an application is made the authorised officer must have the consent of a Revenue Commissioner.

4.2.15 Application to High Court seeking order requiring information to be furnished by financial institutions

TCA97 s908 This section gives power to an authorised officer to apply to a judge of the High Court for an order seeking from a financial institution access to books, etc. or information relevant to a person's tax liability (including a group or class of persons and a person who is claiming exemption from DIRT on the basis of non-residence in the State.) Application can also be made by the authorised officer for an order of the Court to freeze assets of a person in the custody of the financial institution. Before an application to the High Court is made by an authorised officer under this section, he or she must have obtained the consent of a Revenue Commissioner.

4.2.16 Application to Circuit Court or District Court seeking order requiring information to be furnished by financial institutions

TCA97 s908A, s908B

This section gives power to an authorised officer to apply to a judge of the Circuit Court or of the District Court for an order authorising the officer to inspect and take copies of bank records for the purpose of investigating a Revenue offence. A judge may make such an order if he or she is satisfied that on information given on oath that there are reasonable grounds for suspecting that an offence which would result in serious prejudice to the proper assessment or collection of tax is being, has been, or is about to be committed and that there is material in the possession of the financial institution which is likely to be of substantial value in the investigation of that offence. Before an application is made by an authorised officer under this section, he or she must have obtained the consent of a Revenue Commissioner.

Finance Act 2004 empowers the Revenue Commissioners to make an application to the High Court to seek an order requiring a financial institution to supply documents and information held by a non-resident entity over which it has control.

4.2.17 Search warrants in criminal proceedings

TCA97 s908C-D

Section 124 amends Chapter 4 of Part 38 of the Taxes Consolidation Act 1997 that sets out various investigation powers that are available to the Revenue Commissioners. The purpose is to help make a person, under investigation by the Revenue Commissioners, aware as to whether that investigation is for the purposes of establishing a tax liability or with a view to criminal proceedings. A new power enables Revenue, when investigating with a view to initiating criminal proceedings, to apply to a judge of the District Court for a search warrant. As a consequence of the introduction of this power specifically targeted at criminal investigations, consequential amendments are made to the existing power to apply for a search warrant under s905(2A).

In addition, in order to avoid the necessity to apply for a search warrant in inappropriate circumstances (e.g. when seeking information from an unconnected third party) the section introduces a power to apply to a judge of the District Court for an order requiring the person named therein to supply specified information to the Revenue Commissioners, when they are carrying out an investigation with a view to initiating criminal proceedings.

4.2.18 Statement of affairs

TCA97 s909

An Inspector of Taxes may by notice in writing, require a person who has delivered a return of income tax or capital gains tax and his spouse if they are living together, to provide a statement of affairs within a specified period. The statement of affairs should include all assets wherever situated to which the taxpayer and his spouse are beneficially entitled and all liabilities for which they are liable on a specified date.

Where a person is chargeable to tax in a representative capacity, he may be required to provide a statement of all the assets and liabilities of the person in respect of which he is chargeable. Similarly a person chargeable as a trustee may be required to provide a statement of all the assets and liabilities comprised in the trust.

Assets acquired otherwise than at arm's length must be identified and the name and address of the disponer provided.

4.3 Reporting Requirements

4.3.1 Returns of certain information

TCA97 s894 The self assessment system applies to "third party" returns. These are returns:

(a) by letting agents and managers of premises. The return must contain the following:

- (i) the full address of all such premises;
- (ii) the name and address of every person to whom such premises belong;
- (iii) a statement of all rents and other such payments arising from such premises, and
- (iv) such other particulars relating to all such premises as may be specified in the notice.

(b) of fees and commissions paid. With regard to these returns it should be noted:

- (i) Government departments and State bodies are included in the category of persons who must make returns under the section;
- (ii) in addition to other particulars the tax reference number of the payee must be included on the return. This means that the administrative burden of ascertaining each person's tax number will be transferred from the Revenue to the "third party";
- (iii) the return is to include details of payments made on behalf of any other person;
- (iv) no return will be required in respect of payments totalling less than €635 to any one person.

(c) of interest paid or credited without deduction of tax,

(d) of income received belonging to others. No return is required where the income received in respect of any one person does not exceed €635.

(e) by nominee holders of securities.

(f) by certain intermediaries in relation to UCITS.

The onus is on the "third party" concerned to make the return without any notice being served by the Inspector of Taxes.

The return must be submitted by the normal filing date i.e. within nine months of the end of the accounting period for a company or by 31 October following the year of assessment in the case of an individual.

The returns mentioned above with the exception of returns of interest paid and credited, may be subject to audit by the Inspector of Taxes.

4.3.2 Off-shore funds

TCA97 s896

Financial institutions, consultants and other intermediaries who assist Irish residents in acquiring a material interest in certain off-shore funds are obliged to report the matter to the Revenue Commissioners on an automatic basis. The Irish resident investors are also obliged to report such acquisitions on their annual returns of income. Section 743 lists the off-shore funds to which these reporting requirements apply.

4.3.3 Foreign accounts

TCA97 s896

Reporting requirements are imposed on Irish intermediaries who assist or act in opening such accounts and on the taxpayer concerned.

An intermediary, who assists or acts for an Irish resident in relation to the opening of a foreign account is obliged to supply to the Inspector of Taxes the following information:

(i) the full name and permanent address of the resident;

(ii) the resident's tax reference number;

(iii) the name and address of the person with whom the account was opened;

(iv) the date on which the account was opened.

A resident who requests an intermediary to provide him with a service in relation to the opening of a foreign bank account must furnish to the intermediary the details which the intermediary is required to include in the above return. The intermediary is also obliged to take all reasonable care (including, where necessary, the requesting of documentary evidence) to confirm that the details furnished are true and correct.

The intermediary must supply the above information to the Inspector of Taxes on or before the normal return filing date, i.e. 31 October following the end of the year of assessment for an individual or within nine months of the end of the accounting period in the case of a company.

TCA97 s895

Irish residents are obliged to report the opening of foreign bank accounts on their annual returns of income. Non-compliance attracts the surcharge for late submission of returns. The surcharge applies for the year in which the undeclared account was opened. A PAYE taxpayer is deemed to be a chargeable person for the purposes of this section.

4.3.4 Non-resident companies

TCA97 s882

Companies which are incorporated in the State but not resident for tax purposes (see page) and companies which are neither incorporated nor resident in the State but carry on a trade there must supply the Revenue Commissioners with the following information:

Incorporated but not resident

(i) the territory in which it is resident

(ii) if treated as being non-resident by virtue of the fact that it is ultimately controlled by residents of the EU or a tax treaty country and the company or a related company is trading in the State, to identify the company trading in the State.

(iii) if treated as being non-resident under the terms of a tax treaty, to identify

(a) where the company is controlled by a quoted company, the name and address of the quoted company, and

(b) in any other case the ultimate beneficial owners of the company.

Neither incorporated or resident but carrying on a trade

(i) The address of the company's principal place of business in the State.

(ii) The name and address of the agent, manager, factor or the representative of the company; and

(iii) The date of commencement of the company's trade, profession or business.

The above requirements apply to new companies incorporated on or after 11 February 1999 and to companies incorporated before that date from 1 October 1999.

Where a company fails to make a return of the information outlined above or to pay any penalty arising, the penalty can be recovered from the company secretary or where the company secretary is not an Irish resident individual from an Irish resident director of the company.

The information must be supplied within 30 days of:

- the company commencing to carry on a trade, profession or business, wherever carried on, or
- any time at which there is a material change in information previously delivered by the company, or
- when requested to do so by an Inspector of Taxes.

4.3.5 Show tax reference

TCA97 s885

Persons carrying on a profession, or a trade consisting solely of the supply of services, must show one of their tax reference numbers on invoices, credit notes, debit notes, receipts, accounts, vouchers and estimates relating to amounts of €7 or more. "Tax reference number" means either a tax serial number or a VAT registration number.

4.3.6 Information from Ministers

TCA97 s910 The Revenue Commissioners have power to request any Minister to provide them with such information in the possession of the Minister in relation to payments made by the Minister to such persons or classes of persons as the Revenue Commissioners may specify in the notice. The 1999 Finance Act extended this power to payments made by statutory bodies.

4.3.7 Information related to pension products

TCA97 s897A Finance Act 2004 obliges employers to provide additional information with the end of year "P35" returns in respect of the overall amount of employee tax deductible contributions to pension products deducted from the wages and salaries of employees. The total number of employees in respect of whom the employer is making such tax deductible contributions will be required as well as information in respect of tax deductible contributions made by employers to pension products. The information will be required for the tax year 2005 and subsequent years. The first returns will be due in February 2006.

4.3.8 Information in relation to certain tax expenditures

TCA97 s1052, s1054 Finance Act 2004 amends the penalty and surcharge provision to provide for the application of penalties and a surcharge where a taxpayer who is claiming certain specified reliefs fails to give the additional information required to be included on the annual tax return forms: that is, the Form 11 for self employed persons, the Form 12 for persons subject to PAYE and the Form CT1 for companies. The additional information will be required to be included in the 2004 tax returns to be submitted by the end of October 2005.

The provisions imposing a penalty for non-compliance with the requirement to supply this additional information are such that the penalty, under section 1052 TCA 1997, will only apply in a case where, after the filing of the tax return, the taxpayer becomes aware or it is brought to the taxpayer's attention that the additional information has not been included on the return and the taxpayer fails to provide the required information without undue delay.

Similarly, the surcharge for the failure to supply the additional information, under section 1054 TCA 1997, will only arise where, after the filing of the tax return, the taxpayer becomes aware, or it is brought to the taxpayer's attention, that the additional information has not been included on the return and the taxpayer fails to provide the required information without undue delay. Where a surcharge applies in these circumstances, it will be the 5 per cent surcharge. This surcharge is subject to the normal maximum of €12,695.

TCA97 s1084 Where the surcharge is to apply, it must be included in an assessment so that the taxpayer can appeal against the surcharge to the Appeal Commissioners if the taxpayer is aggrieved with it.

4.3.9 Reporting requirements for financial institutions

TCA97 s891B Section 891B TCA 1997 provides an enabling provision to allow the Revenue Commissioners to make regulations with the consent of the Minister for Finance, requiring financial institutions and State bodies to make an annual return of the names and addresses of customers and others resident in the State to whom interest or other profit payments are made.

The enabling provision facilitates the phasing in of reporting requirements for financial institutions. The phased introduction of the measure in a series of regulations specific to particular classes of financial institutions, etc., is intended to allow for a systematic evaluation of the cost/benefits arising from automatic reporting. This approach is intended to facilitate detailed consultation with the financial institutions on the logistics of implementing a reporting system in the different sectors.

Section 133 FA08 amends s891B by ensuring that s4 of the Post Office Savings Bank Act (which restricts the disclosure of information relating to deposits) will not prohibit the disclosure to Revenue of certain information in relation to payments made by financial institutions.

Statutory Instrument No. 136 of 2008 provided that the first phase payments made by banks, building societies, credit unions and the Post Office Savings Bank, from which DIRT was deducted for the year 2005 and 2006 must be reported to Revenue by 15 September 2008 and for the year 2007 by 31 October 2008. Accounts and investments that pay interest of more than €635 in a year will be reported. Anti-account splitting provisions will apply.

4.4 Revenue Offences

TCA97 s1078 Section 1078 contains very wide provisions relating to the topic of revenue offences, the main details of which are set out below.

(1) A person shall, without prejudice to any other penalty to which he may be liable, be guilty of an offence under this section if, after the date of the passing of this Act, he:

(a) knowingly or wilfully delivers any incorrect return, statement or accounts or knowingly or wilfully furnishes any incorrect information in connection with any tax

(b) knowingly aids, abets, assists, incites or induces another person to make or deliver knowingly or wilfully any incorrect return, statement or accounts in connection with any tax

(c) claims or obtains relief or exemption from, or repayment of, any tax, being a relief, exemption or repayment to which, to his knowledge, he is not entitled

(d) knowingly or wilfully issues or produces, any incorrect invoice, receipt, instrument or other document in connection with tax,

(e) fails to make any deduction of dividend withholding tax and related matters,

(f) fails to make any deduction of DIRT required by section 257,

(g) fails to pay to the Collector General appropriate tax within the meaning of section 739E in relation to collective funds,

(h) fails without reasonable excuse to comply with any provision of the Acts requiring:

(i) the furnishing of a return of income, profits or gains, or of sources of income, profits or gains, for the purposes of any tax,

(ii) the furnishing of any other return, certificate, notification, particulars, or any statement or evidence, for the purposes of any tax,

(iii) the keeping or retention of books, records, accounts or other documents for the purposes of any tax, or

(iv) the production of books, records, accounts or other documents, when so requested, for the purposes of any tax,

(i) knowingly or wilfully, and within the time limits specified for their retention, destroys, defaces, or conceals from an authorised officer -

(i) any documents, or

(ii) any other written or printed material in any form, including any information stored, maintained or preserved by means of any mechanical or electronic device, whether or not stored, maintained or preserved in a legible form, which a person is obliged by any provision of the Acts to keep, to issue or to produce for inspection.

(j) knowingly or wilfully falsifies, conceals, destroys or otherwise disposes of, or causes or permits the falsification, concealment, destruction or disposal of, any books, records etc in certain circumstances.

(i) fails to remit certain income tax or value-added tax,

(ii) fails to deduct and remit relevant contracts tax

(k) obstructs or interferes with any officer of the Revenue Commissioners, or any other person, in the exercise or performance of powers or duties under the Acts for the purposes of any tax.

(2) A person guilty of an offence under this section shall be liable

(a) on summary conviction to a maximum fine of €3,000 which may be mitigated to not less than one fourth part thereof or, at the discretion of the court, to imprisonment for a term not exceeding 12 months or to both the fine and the imprisonment, or

(b) on conviction on indictment, to a fine not exceeding €126,970 or at the discretion of the court, to imprisonment for a term not exceeding five years or to both the fine and the imprisonment.

(3) Notwithstanding the provisions of any other enactment, proceedings in respect of an offence under this section may be instituted within 10 years from the date of the commission of the offence or incurring of the penalty (as the case may be).

4.4.1 Facilitating fraudulent evasion of tax

Finance Act 2005 amends section 1078 to create new offences of being knowingly concerned in the fraudulent evasion of tax or being knowingly concerned in, or being reckless as to whether or not one is concerned in, facilitating the fraudulent evasion of tax (or other Revenue offences under section 1078). Section 1078 is also amended so that where a body corporate has committed a revenue offence, and the offence is shown to be attributable to any recklessness on the part of certain officers of the body corporate, those officers will be deemed to be guilty of that offence and may be proceeded against accordingly.

4.4.2 Creation of new Revenue offences and procedures in relation to Court hearings

TCA97 s1078A-C

New criminal offences and procedures in respect of Court hearings into civil and criminal matters regarding tax were provided for in Finance Act 2003 as follows:

(i) Concealing facts disclosed by documents

Section 1078A TCA1997 creates a new criminal offence where material is falsified, concealed or destroyed by a person. "Material" is not defined in this section. The material which appears to be relevant for the section is material which has been falsified, concealed or destroyed by a person who knows or suspects that the material would be relevant to an investigation which is being carried out or is likely to be carried out by Revenue into a tax offence. The person concerned either knows or suspects that Revenue is carrying out an investigation or are likely to carry out an investigation.

There is no time restriction imposed in relation to the creation date of material dealt with in this section.

A person found guilty of an offence under this section faces the following penalties:

- on summary conviction, a monetary fine not exceeding €3,000 and/or imprisonment not exceeding 6 months
- on conviction on indictment, a monetary fine not exceeding €127,000 and/or imprisonment not exceeding 5 years

(ii) Presumptions to be made in Court proceedings

Section 1078B TCA 1997 sets out a number of presumptions that can be made in the course of Court proceedings in relation to civil or criminal offences under the tax code. These presumptions can be summarised as follows:

- documents and statements which purport to have been created or made by a person will be taken to have been so made or created unless the contrary can be shown.
- a document which purports to have been created by one person and sent to another shall be taken to have been so created and received and any statements made in that document shall be taken to have been made by the person sending it and noted by the person receiving it unless the contrary can be demonstrated.
- a document received from an electronic storage system will be taken to have been created by the person who ordinarily uses that system in the course of their business.
- where an official of Revenue authorised for that purpose gives evidence in Court that to the best of his/her knowledge and belief records presented to the Court as being records removed by that authorised officer from a specific taxpayers premises are the

property of a taxpayer, they shall be held to be property of that taxpayer unless the contrary can be shown. Where the authorised officer gives further evidence that to the best of his/her knowledge and belief those records relate to a trade, profession or other activity carried on by the person, this shall be taken to be the case unless the contrary can be shown.

- a certificate provided in Court proceedings from an authorised officer of Revenue certifying that a return, statement or declaration was received by Revenue shall be taken as evidence of that fact unless the contrary can be proven. The Revenue official must sign this certificate evidencing this fact. The Court will take that signature to be made by the relevant official without the need for further evidence.

(iii) Provision of information to juries

Section 1078C TCA 1997 authorises a Judge, in the course of a trial on indictment of a tax offence, to order that copies of certain documents may be given to the jury in whatever form the Judge considers appropriate including:

(a) any document admitted in evidence at the trial or any charts, diagrams, graphics, schedules or agreed summaries of evidence produced at the trial.

(b) the transcripts of counsels' opening and closing speeches, the whole or any part of the evidence given at the trial and the Judge's charge to the jury.

(c) any other document that the Judge considers to be of help to the jury's deliberations. Included in this category is an affidavit by an accountant or other suitably qualified person summarising in a form that the jury is likely to understand any transactions entered into by the accused or other persons relevant to the tax offence. Where such an affidavit is to be provided to the jury the accused is entitled to receive a copy of the affidavit prior to the trial and may make representations in respect of its proposed provision. If an affidavit is to be provided to the jury, the accountant or other qualified person may be summoned to attend the trial as a prosecution witness and may be required to give evidence in relation to any relevant procedures or principles within her/her area of expertise.

4.4.3 Revenue offences made public

TCA97 s1086 The Revenue Commissioners may publish any number of lists of persons or companies who have been convicted of tax offences or who have made back duty settlements with the Revenue Commissioners during a year. Publication of back duty settlements is confined to those cases where the amount of the settlement exceeds €30,000 including a penalty, for settlements relating to the tax years 2005 *et seq.* (previously €12,700) and where a full voluntary disclosure had not been made. However, where the penalty is 15% or less of the tax, details will not be published. Following initial publication in Iris Oifigiuil the Revenue may reproduce the list in any other manner or format, e.g., on its website. The limit of €30,000 can be increased by Ministerial Order every five years by reference to the Consumer Price Index.

4.4.4 Recovery of civil penalties

TCA97 s978, s1061

The Finance Act 2003 allows the Revenue Commissioners to instigate proceedings for the recovery of civil penalties at District or Circuit Court level.

4.4.5 Penalties involving deceased taxpayers and personal representatives

(i) Penalties agreed (or awarded in proceedings) prior to the deceased's death

With effect from 18 March 2008 where a settlement that includes a penalty element has been agreed between Revenue and a deceased taxpayer prior to his/her death (or where a penalty has been awarded in proceedings finalised prior to the taxpayer's death), and that penalty remains unpaid or not fully paid as at the date of death, Revenue will continue to proceed against the personal representatives of the deceased for the recovery of that unpaid penalty. There is no change to existing Revenue practice in these particular circumstances.

(ii) Agreements (or proceedings) not finalised at the date of death

Where the taxpayer dies before a settlement has been agreed with Revenue, Revenue will not seek recovery of any penalty element from the deceased's personal representatives (and will discontinue proceedings for recovery of such penalty if they have been initiated).

(iii) Publication under section 1086 of the Taxes Consolidation Act 1997

Cases falling under (i) above will continue to be published where the publication criteria in section 1086 TCA 1997 are met. Cases falling under (ii) above will not be published under section 1086 – because there is no tax-geared penalty as part of an agreed settlement and no court-imposed penalty.

(iv) Cases currently open

Where a case is ongoing and has not been finalised at 18 March 2008, Revenue will follow the procedures set out above in any such case.

(v) Settled Cases

Settled cases will not be reopened.

4.5 Resignation of Professional Advisers

TCA97 s1079 Auditors and tax advisers are obliged to cease to act for a company in certain circumstances. The features of these provisions are as follows:

(1) An auditor or tax adviser (referred to as a relevant person), who in the course of his or her normal work for a client company becomes aware of certain material tax offences committed by the company, is obliged to communicate particulars of the offences to the company and request it to either rectify the situation or report the offences to the Revenue Commissioners within six months after the communication. If the company does not do so the relevant person is obliged to cease to act for the company as auditor or as tax adviser and not to so act for a period of three years or until the matter has been rectified, if that is earlier. An auditor who is required to resign under the section must notify the company of his or her resignation and send a copy of the notification to the Revenue Commissioners.

(2) The main offences are making an incorrect return, failure to make a return (except where a return has been made in one of the last three years), false claims to relief and issuing false documents.

(3) Penalties for failure to comply with the section consist of, in the case of summary conviction, a fine of €1,265 which can be mitigated to one fourth of that amount and, in the case of conviction on indictment, a fine not exceeding €6,345 or imprisonment of up to two years, or both.

(4) The requirement to cease to act for the company will not prevent a person from acting in the preparation for, or conduct of, legal proceedings which are extant or pending six months after the time at which the offences are required to be communicated to the company.

(5) The measure provides that it will be a good defence against a prosecution under the section for a relevant person to show that he or she would not have been aware of the offences by the company if the person had not been assisting or advising the company in preparing for legal proceedings. It also provides indemnity for a relevant person who complies with his or her obligations under the section.

4.6 Tax Clearance Certificates

4.6.1 Liquor licences, etc.

TCA97 s1094

A licensee or permit holder or a prospective licensee or permit holder must obtain a tax clearance certificate from the Collector General before certain licences or permits can be obtained or renewed (see below). A clearance certificate will be issued where the applicant has complied with all obligations imposed by the Tax Acts, and the Value-Added Tax Act 1972 in relation to:

(i) the payment or remittance of taxes, interest and penalties required to be paid or remitted under the Acts, and

(ii) the delivery of returns.

It is necessary for the beneficial holder of the licence to apply for the tax clearance certificate. This means that a nominee holder of a licence cannot apply for it.

Where a licence is transferred and the predecessor is connected with the successor then the affairs of both the predecessor and the successor must be in order before a certificate will be issued. This provision also applies in the case of licences which had elapsed within the previous five years when they had been beneficially held by a person other than the current applicant.

Connected persons in the case of a partnership means the other partners and in the case of a company any shareholder who owns or controls (directly or indirectly) more than 50% of the ordinary share capital of the company.

An applicant has a right of appeal against the Collector General's refusal to issue a clearance certificate. However, this right does not apply where tax arrears are the reason for the refusal.

4.6.2 List of licences and permits

The tax clearance procedure outlined above applies to the following activities:

- All liquor licence holders;
- Vendors of hydrocarbon oil and liquid petroleum gas;
- Wholesalers of spirits, beer and wine;
- Bookmakers;
- Gaming licence holders;
- Auctioneers (in respect of their licence, auction permits or house agent permits);
- The holder of permits for public places in which amusement machines are located.

4.6.3 Other tax clearance certificates

TCA97 s1095

Finance Act 2002 converts the provisions of section 1095 into a generally applicable tax clearance procedure covering applications for tax clearance for whatever reason other than those catered for in:

(a) Section 1094, dealing with certain licences

(b) sports bodies within section 847A,

(c) the Standards in Public Office Act, 2001 and

(d) the Free Legal Aid Board.

As a result of the changes made by Finance Act 2002, it will be possible to apply for and obtain tax clearance certificates through electronic means (e.g. The Revenue ROS system). Revenue will also be permitted, subject to the applicant's agreement, to publish the certificate, for example, on a website where he/she may authorise persons to view it for verification purposes.

CHAPTER 5 CAPITAL ACQUISITIONS TAX

5.1 Capital Acquisitions Tax

The Capital Acquisitions Tax Act 1976 introduced a gift tax in respect of every taxable gift taken on or after the 24th February 1974 and also an inheritance tax in respect of every taxable inheritance taken on or after the 1 of April 1975. The legislation in relation to Capital Acquisitions Tax was consolidated in the Capital Acquisitions Tax Consolidation Act 2003, (CATCA) which became law on 21 February 2003.

5.1.1 Rate of CAT

The current rate of CAT is 20% (see Chart 25 for earlier rates).

5.1.2 Territorial Limits

In the period from the date of introduction of capital acquisitions tax up to 30 November 1999 the domicile of the disponer was the dominant factor in determining whether liability arose. While special rules continue to apply to non-domiciled disponers and beneficiaries, the liability on gifts and inheritances take on or after 1 December 1999 is determined primarily by whether the donor or donee is resident or ordinarily resident in the State. If neither the doner nor donee is resident or ordinarily resident in the State, the tax charge is confined to gifts or inheritances situated in the State. (Please see the 31st or earlier editions of this book for previous treatments).

5.1.3 Calculation of CAT

The aggregate of gifts and inheritances take on or after 5 December 1991 from disponers, to which the same tax-free group thresholds (see below) apply, is taken into account when calculating CAT. This aggregate is then reduced by the tax-free amount and the balance is taxed at 20%

5.1.4 Tax-free Group Thresholds

The tax-free thresholds applicable for gifts and inheritances are set out below. There are three categories which are based on the relationship between the disponer and the beneficiary:

Group A: Applies where the beneficiary is a child or minor child of a deceased child of the disponer, or a foster child or the disponer, subject to certain conditions. This threshold also applies to inheritances taken by a parent from a deceased child, subject to certain exceptions.

Group B: Applies where the beneficiary is a lineal ancestor, lineal descendant (other than a child, or minor child or a deceased child), a brother, sister, or a child of a brother or sister of the disponer.

Group C: Applies where the beneficiary does not fall within group A or B.

The thresholds for gifts and inheritances taken in 2008 are:

Group A:	€521,208
Group B:	€52,121
Group C:	€26,060

See Chart 26 for earlier thresholds.

5.1.5 Surviving spouses

CATA76 Para8 Sch2 ; CATCA Para6 Sch2

Surviving spouses are deemed to have the same relationship as their deceased spouses where benefits are received from a relation of the deceased person. For example, the normal group threshold between a father in law and his daughter in law is Group C. However, if her husband dies before the disponer, the group threshold is Group A as she becomes a child of the disponer for CAT purposes.

5.1.6 Capital gains tax set-off/same event allowance

FA85 s63; FA88 s66 CATCA s104

Capital gains tax payable by reference to an event which gives rise to a charge to capital acquisitions tax is available for credit against such capital acquisitions tax. This applies from 30 January 1985. If on or after 6 April 1988 gift tax or inheritance tax is charged on a property and the same event constitutes a disposal for capital gains tax purposes, the CGT in so far as it has been paid, shall be deducted from the net gift tax or inheritance tax as a credit against same, provided that the amounts deducted shall be equal to the lesser of the net gift tax or inheritance tax or CGT.

FA06 s119 CATCA s104

On and from 21 February 2006, the credit for capital gains tax against capital acquisitions tax will cease to apply to the extent that the property the subject matter of the gift or inheritance is subsequently disposed of by the beneficiary within two years of its acquisition.

FA85 s62 CATCA s105

Where capital acquisitions tax is chargeable more than once in respect of the same property on the same event, the net tax payable on an earlier event will be allowable as a credit against tax on the later event.

5.1.7 Nephew or niece of the disponer

FA89 s83 Para9 Sch2; CATCA Para7 Sch 2

If a nephew or niece of the disponer has worked substantially on a full time basis for the period of five years ending on the date of the gift or the date of the inheritance in carrying on, or assisting in the carrying on of the trade, business or profession or the work of or connected with the office or employment of the disponer, and the gift or inheritance consists of property used in connection with the trade, business or profession, or of shares in a company owning such property, then the nephew or niece will enjoy a Group I threshold (previously Class (a)) as if he or she was a child of the disponer. In relation to gifts or inheritances taken on or after 1 May 1989 except gifts or inheritances taken under a discretionary trust, the following conditions apply:

Where the gift or inheritance consists of property used in connection with the business, trade or profession of the disponer and the donee or successor works

(i) more than 24 hours per week for the disponer at a place where the business etc is carried on, or

(ii) more than 15 hours as above where the business etc is carried on exclusively by the disponer, spouse of the disponer, and the donee or successor.

Where the gift or inheritance consists of shares in a private trading company controlled by the disponer of which he is a director, and the donee or successor works

(i) more than 24 hours per week at a place where the business etc of the company is carried on, or

(ii) more than 15 hours per week for the company as above where the business etc is carried on exclusively by the disponer, any spouse of the disponer and the donee or successor.

5.1.8 Relief in respect of certain marriage settlements

FA81 s46 CATCA Para8 Sch 2

This was introduced to give relief in the case of marriage settlements satisfying the following conditions:

(a) There must have been a disposition made prior to 1 April 1975, and

(b) the settlor must be a grandparent of the donee or successor, and

(c) the expressed consideration for the disposition must have been the marriage of the parents of the donee or successor.

If the above conditions are satisfied and there is a termination of the parents interest and the donee or successor becomes entitled in possession, then the donee or successor will enjoy the Group I threshold as if he or she was a child of the disponer.

5.1.9 Agricultural relief

FA80 s19, s83; FA82 s100; FA91 s114; FA93 s128; FA94 s141; FA95 s158; FA96 s122; FA97 s134 CATCA s89

Normally the tax is based on the market value of the property comprised in the gift or inheritance and allowance is given for all liabilities, costs and expenses that are properly payable out of the taxable gift or inheritance. However, where the donee or successor is a farmer within the meaning of the Act, the market value of all agricultural property passing on or after 23 January 1997 is reduced by 90%. Relief available in respect of earlier gifts and inheritances is as follows:

Date of Gift or Inheritance	*Agricultural Property*	*Threshold*	*Relief*	
			Gifts	*Inheritance*
11.4.94 to 7.2.95	Farm land & buildings	£300,000	80%	65%
		Balance	30%	30%
	Other farm assets	All	25%	25%
8.2.95 to 22.1.96	Farm land & buildings	£300,000	80%	65%
		Balance	50%	50%
	Other farm assets	All	50%	50%
23.1.96 to 22.1.97	All farm assets	All	75%	75%

It should be noted that where the reliefs applying between 8.2.95 and 22.1.96 are more beneficial, they may be claimed instead of the 75% reduction.

FA91 s114; FA94 s141; FA95 s158; FA96 s122; FA97 s134; FA00 s140 CATCA s89(1)

A "farmer" means an individual in respect of whom not less than 80 per cent of his or her assets, after taking a gift or inheritance consist of agricultural property, as defined, on the valuation date of the gift or inheritance. For the purposes of the 80 per cent test, in the case of gifts or inheritances taken before 1 February 2007, no deduction was allowed from the market value of property for borrowings in respect of that property. In the case of gifts or inheritances taken on or after 1 February 2007, borrowings can be deducted against the value of off-farm principal private residences for the purposes of the 80 per cent test.

Prior to 31 March 2006, an individual needed to be of Irish domicile to qualify for the relief.

FA00 s140 CATCA s89(1)

In respect of gifts or inheritances taken on or after 10 February 2000, an individual is deemed to be beneficially entitled in possession to an interest in expectancy and to property which is subject to a discretionary trust made by the individual where the individual is an object of the trust. This provision ensures that a person who would not otherwise come within the relief cannot do so by transferring his or her non-agricultural assets into a trust shortly before the relevant date.

Agricultural property is defined as meaning agricultural land, pasture and woodland in the State and crops and timber grown thereon, together with houses and other buildings appropriate to the property. It includes with effect from 11 April 1994, livestock, bloodstock and farm machinery. Also included with effect from 31 March 2006 is the EU Single Farm Payment Entitlement.

For gifts or inheritances taken on or after 23 January 1996, the relief claimed in respect of agricultural property was clawed back if the property was sold or compulsorily acquired within ten years of the date of the gift or inheritance (previously six years), and not replaced within one year by other agricultural property. Finance Act, 2002 extended this reinvestment period to six years in the case of compulsory acquisitions made on or after 25 March 2002. If a beneficiary ceases to be resident for the three years of assessment immediately following the year of gift/inheritance, a claw-back will arise.

Finance Act 2000, reduced the clawback period from 10 years to 6 years where the sale or compulsory acquisition which causes the agricultural value to cease to be applicable occurs on or after 10 February 2000. However, as and from 2 February 2006, where land that qualified for either agricultural or business relief is disposed of between 6 to 10 years after the date of the gift/inheritance, the relief granted will be clawed back in respect of any development value relating to the land at the time of the gift/inheritance. Where the event that gives rise to the clawback occurs on or after 1 February 2007, interest will only be charged from the date the land is disposed of (previously interest was charged from the valuation date of the relevant gift or inheritance).

Finance Act 2005 clarifies in respect of any clawback, followed by a partial reinvestment within the appropriate time limit that the extent of the clawback will relate to the amount of the proceeds not being reinvested.

5.1.10 Business relief

FA94 PtVI Ch1
CATCA s90-101

Provision is made for relief from CAT for business property acquired by gift or inheritance or on the termination of a life interest. The features of this relief are as follows:

FA95 s162-163

(i) The relief available in respect of all qualifying assets is as follows:

Date of Gift or Inheritance	*Threshold*	*Relief*
11.4.94 to 7.2.95	£250,000	50%
	Balance	25%
8.2.95 to 22.1.96	All	50%
23.1.96 – 22.1.97	All	75%
23.1.97 – onwards	All	90%

FA96 s125, 126 FA01 s228 (ii) For gifts and inheritances taken between 11 April 1994 and 14 February 2001, there was a requirement that the business must be carried on wholly or mainly in the State. For gifts or inheritances taken on or after 15 February 2001, this condition has been removed.

FA97 s140, s141; FA98 s128; FA00 s148 FA01 s228 CATCA s93 (iii) The relief applies to business property as follows:

(a) property consisting of a business or an interest in a business;

(b) unquoted shares or securities of a company subject to certain conditions;

(c) land, buildings, machinery or plant owned by the disponer but used by a company controlled by the disponer or by a partnership in which the disponer was a partner;

(d) quoted shares or securities of a company which were owned by the disponer prior to their becoming quoted.

For gifts and inheritances taken prior to 15 February 2001, there was a requirement that the company in question must be incorporated in the State or that the land or buildings, plant or machinery in question must be situate in the State.

(iv) The business carried on must not consist wholly or mainly of dealing in land, shares, securities or currencies or of making or holding investments. This restriction shall not apply to gifts or inheritances of shares of securities in a holding company if:

(a) the business of the holding company consists wholly or mainly in being a holding company of one or more companies whose business does not fall within the restrictions above, or

(b) the value of the shares or securities in a holding company (determined without reference to section 99) is wholly or mainly attributable, directly or indirectly, to business that does not fall within the restrictions above.

(v) The relevant business property must have been owned by the disponer, or by the disponer and his spouse, for at least five years prior to the transfer, or for at least two years where the transfer gives rise to an inheritance taken on the disponer's death. There are provisions for modifying the five-year and two-year periods where business property is replaced by other business property.

(vi) Assets not used wholly or mainly for the business concerned are ignored in valuing relevant business property.

(vii) Agricultural property was initially excluded from business relief. However, with effect from 12 April 1995, agricultural property owned by a company could be taken into account for the purposes of calculating relief on the shares in that company, provided the conditions outlined at 1 to 6 above could be satisfied.

On or after 10 February 2000, agricultural property is not specifically addressed and accordingly will qualify for relief whether held by a company or an individual, provided all the above conditions can be satisfied and provided agricultural relief does not apply.

(viii) For gifts or inheritances taken before 23 January 1996, the relief was clawed back if, at any time within a period of six years commencing on the date of the gift or inheritance, the business property was sold or otherwise disposed of and was not replaced by other qualifying business property or ceased to be a qualifying business property.
In the case of gifts or inheritances taken on or after 23 January 1996, the clawback period was extended from 6 to 10 years.

The Finance Act 2000 reduced the clawback period from 10 years to 6 years where the event giving rise to the clawback occurs on or after 10 February 2000.

Finance Act 2005 clarifies that where business property is replaced in the clawback period by other business property, the value of which is less than that of the original property, the clawback shall be in proportion to the difference between the market value of the replacement property to the market value of the original property.

However, as and from 2 February 2006, where land that qualified for either agricultural or business relief is disposed of between 6 to 10 years after the date of the gift/inheritance, the relief granted will be clawed back in respect of any development value relating to the land at the time of the gift/inheritance.

The death of the donee or successor does not give rise to a clawback.

5.1.11 Exemptions

CATCA Pt 9 The following are some of the main exemptions from CAT:

s70-71 ***Exemptions for spouses***

An inheritance taken on or after 30 January 1985 by a successor, who is at the date of the inheritance the spouse of the disponer.

A gift taken on or after 31 January 1990 by a donee who is at the date of the gift the spouse of the disponer.

Inheritances taken by parents

CATCA s79 An inheritance taken by a parent from a child on the death of the child. This exemption applies where the child had taken a non-exempt gift or inheritance from either or both of its parents within the period of five years immediately prior to the death of the child.

First €3,000 exempt for gifts

CATCA s69 With effect from 1 January 2003, the first €3,000 of the total value of all gifts received from any one disponer in any year to 31 December. This exemption does not apply to inheritances, except in the case of a gift which becomes an inheritance on the death of the disponer within two years of the relevant disposition. The exemption applicable from 1 January 1999 to 31 December 2002 was €1,270.

Certain dwellings

CATCA s86 A gift or inheritance taken on or after 1 December 1999 of a dwelling house including an area of up to one acre occupied by the donee/successor as his only or main residence for a period of three years immediately preceding the date of the gift or inheritance (or in the case where the property replaced other qualifying property, the donee/successor resided in both properties for 3 out of the 4 years prior to the gift/inheritance).

The donee/successor must not be beneficially entitled to any other dwelling house and, if under the age of 55 years, must retain and continue to occupy the dwelling house as his only or main residence for a period of six years thereafter. There are replacement provisions and exceptions to the clawback, where the property is sold to fund medical care or the dwelling ceases to be occupied because of residence in a nursing home or because the donee/successor is working abroad or obliged by his employer to live elsewhere.

For gifts (not inheritances) taken on or after 1 February 2007, any period during which a child of a disponer occupied a house that was during that period the disponer's only or main residence, will not be treated as a period of occupation in the three-year period prior to the date of the gift. Accordingly, a parent can no longer gift free of CAT the family home they share with their child unless the parent has moved out of the home at least three years prior to the gift, while the child remained in occupation of it as its principal residence.

Where replacement property is the subject of a gift on or after 1 February 2007, the period of occupancy of the replaced property by the recipient will only be taken into account where the replaced property was also owned by the disponer prior to the date of the gift. (Previously where a parent gifted a property to a child to replace the child's own property, the child could count the period of occupation in their own house for the purpose of the 3 out of 4 year occupancy rule).

Where this exemption is claimed and subsequent events give rise to a clawback, interest on the tax due will run from the date of the event giving rise to the clawback and not the original date of the inheritance or the gift.

S60 Policies

CATCA s72
CATCA s73 The proceeds of a qualifying insurance policy effected by the insured person are exempt from inheritance tax in so far as such proceeds are

used to pay such tax arising on the insured person's death or within a year of his death under dispositions made by him. Initially the "section 60" policy was restricted to a policy effected on the life of a single individual.

The Finance Act 1989 extended the section 60 policy concept to a policy effected for the joint lives of spouses and the life of the survivor.

The Finance Act 1991 extended cover to exposure to gift tax or inheritance tax arising under an inter vivos disposition made by the insured within one year after the appointed day. The appointed day is defined as meaning a date occurring not earlier than eight years after the date on which the relevant insurance policy is effected, or a date on which the proceeds of a relevant insurance policy become payable either on the critical illness or the death of the insured.

The Finance Act 1996 extended the scope of the exemption granted to cover a policy effected by a life tenant for the purpose of paying an inheritance tax liability arising on the life tenant's death under a disposition made by someone other than the life tenant.

Finance Act 2005 further extends the scope of the relief to include proceeds of an insurance policy effected for the purpose of discharging approved retirement fund tax (income tax) arising on the death of the beneficial owner of the approved retirement fund.

Gift tax or inheritance tax payable on an appointment out of an inter vivos discretionary trust set up by the insured are not covered by a relevant insurance policy.

Benefits to charities and public bodies

CATCA s76 Gifts or inheritances taken for public or charitable purposes are exempt where the Revenue Commissioners are satisfied that they have been, or will be, applied to purposes which are, in accordance with the law of the State. This exemption covers political subscriptions, subject to certain conditions e.g. the subscriptions are within the terms of the Electoral (Amendment) Act, 2001, they are not anonymous and they are expended for political purposes.

Works of art, stately houses, gardens, etc.

CATCA s77 Works of art, scientific collections, libraries, houses or gardens, etc. provided that they are of national, scientific, historic or artistic interest, are kept permanently in the State and are open to public viewing. The exemption may be lost if the objects are sold within six years after the valuation date. But, the exemption will still be granted where the sale is a sale by private treaty to:

- The National Gallery of Ireland,
- The National Museum of Science and Art,
- Any other similar national institution,
- Any university in the State (or any constituent college thereof),

- A local authority,
- The Friends of the National Collection of Ireland, or
- The Irish Heritage Trust (as proposed).

Superannuation benefits

CATCA s80 Superannuation benefits payable to an employee.

Compensation, damages, winnings, etc.

CATCA s82(1) Certain compensation payments or damages, winnings from lotteries or prizes.

Companies owning heritage property

CATCA s78 A gift or inheritance of shares in a company holding heritage property - see (e) above. The relief will be clawed back in certain circumstances.

Support, maintenance or education

CATCA s82(2)
s82(4) Certain normal and reasonable payments received in the disponer's lifetime by members of his family or after the death of both parents by a minor child, for support, maintenance or education, or by a dependent relative for support or maintenance.

Government and other securities

CATCA s81 Government securities and unit trusts holding Government securities where any such security forms part of a gift/ inheritance on condition that the donee/successor is neither domiciled nor ordinarily resident in the State at the date of the gift/inheritance and the disponer was the beneficial owner from 14 April 1978 to the date of the gift/inheritance, or for the three years prior to the gift or inheritance. Finance Act 2001 extended the period of ownership from three to six years for gifts or inheritances taken on or after 15 February 2001. The Finance Act 2003 further extended the period of ownership from 6 years to 15 years with effect from 24 February 2003.

Unit trusts, UCITs and common contractual funds

CATCA s75 With effect from the passing of the 1989 Finance Act any gift or inheritance which comprises units of specified investment undertakings at the date of the gift or inheritance and at the valuation date shall be exempt from tax and shall not be taken into account in computing tax on any gift or inheritance taken by the donee or successor provided at the date of the disposition:

- the disponer is neither domiciled nor ordinarily resident in the State or the proper law of the disposition is not the law of the State, and
- at the date of the gift or inheritance the donee or successor is neither domiciled nor ordinarily resident in the State.

Finance Act 2001 extended this exemption to investment undertakings which qualify for the new collective funds regime introduced by section 58 Finance Act 2000

Finance Act 2005 also extends the exemption to units in an investment vehicle which qualifies as a common contractual fund (CCF).

Certain life assurance policies

CATCA s74 Certain life assurance policies issued to non ordinarily resident and non domiciled persons or where the "proper law" is Irish by companies located in the International Financial Services Centre. Finance Act 2002 extended this exemption to life policies issued by domestic life assurance companies on or after 1 January 2001.

Certain medical expenses

CATCA s84 A gift or inheritance taken exclusively for the purpose of discharging the medical expenses of a permanently, incapacitated individual.

Trusts for incapacitated individuals

CATCA s82(3) Moneys raised by public subscription for permanently incapacitated individuals provided that these moneys are held in a qualifying trust. This applies with effect from 6 April 1997.

Retirement benefits

CATCA s85 Any balance in an "approved retirement fund" or in an "approved minimum retirement fund" which passes on the death of a pensioner or of his spouse will be exempt from inheritance tax in certain circumstances; see 1.3.25(f).

Heritage property

Finance Act 2006 introduced a new scheme of tax relief for heritage property donated to the proposed Irish Heritage Trust. "Heritage property" will include buildings, gardens and contents of buildings insofar as they are historically associated with the buildings. The new relief will apply to a person who makes a gift of heritage property to the Trust and will take the form of a payment on account of an amount equal to the value of the property against the person's tax liabilities.

The taxes to which the measure will apply are income tax, corporation tax, capital gains tax, gift tax and inheritance tax, and may relate to past, current and future liabilities.

Divorced spouses

CATCA s88 All transfers of property from one former spouse to another are exempt where those spouses have divorced and the transfer is made pursuant to certain court orders.

5.1.12 Disclaimer

CATA76 s13
CATCA s12

A successor is entitled to disclaim his or her right to an inheritance, or his or her legal rights under Part IX of the Succession Acts. Such disclaimer is not a disposition for the purpose of the CAT Act and therefore does not give rise to a claim for inheritance tax on the original inheritance nor to a claim for gift tax on the benefit conferred by the disclaimer. The ultimate beneficiary however, takes a taxable inheritance from the deceased.

A legacy or specific devise which is disclaimed falls into the residue of a testator's estate and if not effectively disposed of by will goes on intestacy. If a residuary gift is disclaimed the residuary estate goes on intestacy.

5.1.13 Joint tenants

CATA76 s14
CATCA s13

The liability to inheritance tax in respect of an inheritance taken by persons as joint tenants is the same in all respects as if they took the inheritance as tenants in common in equal shares.

5.1.14 Free use of property

CATA76 s31
CATCA s40

Where a person is allowed to have the use, occupation or enjoyment of another person's property free or for less than market value, this constitutes a gift for CAT purposes.

5.1.15 Companies

FA93 s34, s129
CATCA s43

A disposition by or to a private controlled company may give rise to a gift or inheritance which will be received by or disposed of by the beneficial owners of the shares of the company in the same proportions as the market value of each person's shareholding. All acts, omissions and receipts of the company are deemed to be as those of the beneficial owners of the shares.

5.1.16 Discretionary trusts

FA90 s129;
FA92 s224;
FA94 s143
FA01 s229
CATCA s15-18

Chapter 1, Part V Finance Act 1984 imposed a once off charge on the property of new and existing discretionary trusts. It is provided that where, on or after 25 January 1984, property is or becomes subject to a discretionary trust, the trust will be deemed to have taken an inheritance. A charge to tax will not arise, however, until:

(a) the disponer is deceased, and

(b) none of the principal objects of the trust is under the age of 21 years (see below).

Section 143 Finance Act 1994 increased the initial once-off charge from 3% to 6% with effect from 11 April 1994. It also provided for a full refund of the increase in the charge, if, within 5 years of the death of the disponer or, in the case of a trust with principal objects, within 5 years of the youngest reaching 21 years of age, all property within the trust has been transferred absolutely to the beneficiaries.

Section 229 Finance Act, 2001 extended this relief to a discretionary trust which comes into existence on the death of a life tenant and provides that the five-year period commences on the date of death of the life tenant.

Following a High Court decision in 2006, section 113 Finance Act 2007 clarified that, when assets become subject to a discretionary trust created under a deceased person's will, the five-year period commences on the date when property becomes subject to the discretionary trust, i.e. when it is transferred to the discretionary trust by the executors of the estate. This provision applies to inheritances deemed to be taken on or after 1 February 2007.

Principal Objects - These are defined as such objects of the trust as are for the time being:

(a) The spouse of the disponer.

(b) The children of the disponer.

(c) The children of a child of the disponer where such child predeceased the disponer.

Exemptions - Exemption from this tax is granted to any discretionary trust which has been created exclusively for any of the following purposes:

(a) For public or charitable purposes in the State or Northern Ireland.

(b) (i) For the purposes of certain superannuation schemes.

(ii) From 5 April 1990 a sponsored superannuation scheme will only qualify where it contains no object other than to benefit employees.

FA85 s65 (c) For the purposes of a registered Unit Trust Scheme.

(d) For the benefit of an individual for the reason that such individual is because of age, improvidence or physical, mental or legal capacity, incapable of managing his own affairs.

(e) For the purposes of providing for the upkeep of a house or garden referred to in section 39, Finance Act 1978.

General - Apart from the above provisions, the transfer of property into a discretionary trust is not a taxable disposition for gift or inheritance tax purposes. When, however, a beneficiary receives a distribution of either income or capital from a discretionary trust, CAT may become payable depending on the relationship between the disponer and the beneficiary.

The following are exempt from the 6% discretionary trust tax:

(a) Property which on the termination of the discretionary trust is taken by the State.

(b) The notional interest on interest free loans deemed to be benefits under the provisions of section 31 of Capital Acquisitions Tax Act 1976.

FA86 s102-s108; FA92 s225 CATCA s19-28 The Finance Act, 1986 as amended introduced an annual levy of 1% on the assets held by discretionary trusts which were affected by the provisions of the Finance Act, 1984, i.e. where:

(a) the disponer is dead, and

(b) none of the principal objects of the trust is under the age of 21 years (previously 25 years).

The 1% levy applies to property which has become subject to a discretionary trust on 5 April in any year from 5 April 1986 onwards. The 1% levy is not payable in the same year as the 6% charge. In order to facilitate compliance and collection costs, the values of real property and non quoted shares agreed for one chargeable date may, subject to certain limitations, apply to the following two chargeable dates.

Section 225 Finance Act, 1992 provides that on and from 5 April 1994 the 1% levy applies as soon as the last of the principal objects of the trust attains the age of 21 years (reduced from 25 years).

Section 116 Finance Act 2006 changed the date on which the 1% levy becomes chargeable from 5 April to 31 December for years commencing with the year 2007. For the year 2006 there were two chargeable dates, i.e., 5 April and 31 December. The tax chargeable on 31 December 2006 was 73.97% of the tax due on that date to take account of the fact that there are two chargeable dates for the year 2006. In addition, the market value agreed with Revenue for the valuation date 5 Aril 2006 will be treated as the market value of the property on 31 December 2006.

CATCA s25 With effect from 1 October 2003 where Trustees who fail to comply with the requirement to deliver a return, the penalty imposed is the lesser of €1,265 and the difference between the tax paid and the tax that would have been payable if the return had been delivered and had been correct.

5.1.17 Self assessment

FA84 s36, s41, s43, s45, s106, s107; FA89 s74; FA95 s164; FA96 s129; FA00 s141 In order to introduce a self-assessment system for Capital Acquisitions Tax a number of important changes were required in the Principal Act dealing particularly with returns, assessments, payment of tax, interest and penalties, etc. The self-assessment system took effect from 1 September 1989.

CATCA Part 6 s45-50 A person who is primarily accountable for CAT is obliged to deliver a return within four months of the valuation date where the aggregate of all taxable gifts exceeds 80% of the Group threshold. The following must be shown on the Return:

(a) The gift or inheritance.

(b) The property comprised in the gift or inheritance.

(c) An estimate of the market value of the property.

(d) Any other particulars which may be relevant to the assessment of tax.

The taxpayer is obliged to make an assessment of the tax which to the best of his knowledge, information and belief ought to be paid and to pay that amount.

Provision is made for the payment of CAT by instalments and by the transfer of certain Government Securities.

Persons who are secondarily accountable for CAT are obliged, if required in writing by the Revenue, to comply with the self assessment procedures.

An accountable person must, if required in writing by the Revenue, deliver a statement stating such particulars relating to the property and such evidence as they require as may be relevant to the assessment of tax.

The Revenue may authorise a person to inspect any property comprised in a gift or any books, accounts, etc relating to any property as may be relevant to the assessment of tax. Any person having the custody or possession of property, books, records, etc. must permit the authorised person to make the inspection at all reasonable times. The Revenue has power to require additional returns from the accountable person if the return made was materially defective and to make any consequent additional assessments.

If an accountable person who has made a return or additional return becomes aware that the return was defective in a material respect, he shall within three months of becoming aware of the defect in the original return make a new return, amend the assessment and pay the outstanding tax.

The tax due must accompany the return.

FA89 s75 Notwithstanding the introduction of the self assessment system, the Revenue Commissioners retain the right to raise assessments, additional assessments and to correct assessments.

FA89 s76 If an accountable person pays the self assessed tax within four months of the valuation date no interest will be charged.

If an accountable person makes a conditional or an incorrect tax payment, such payment will be treated as a payment on account.

CATCA s45A With effect from 1 October 2003 an accountable person is required to retain records for six years from the valuation date or the date of filing of returns if these were not filed by the due date.

5.1.18 Penalties

FA89 s77
CATCA s58

The following penalties are payable:

Self Assessment: Failure to make returns	€2,535
Obstruction of person inspecting property	€1,265
Fraudulent or Negligent Returns or Valuation Statements	*€6,345
Assisting or inducing incorrect returns	€1,265
If Court Judgement obtained for failure to make returns, a further penalty for each day the failure continues of	€30

CATCA s58 *The penalty for failure to deliver a return is €2,535 and for a fraudulent/negligent return or valuation statement is €6,345 plus in each case an amount equal to the difference between the amount of tax paid and the amount of tax that would have been payable had the return been correct.

FA89 s78 Accountable persons and persons with secondary accountability are obliged to comply with the self-assessment provisions in relation to Discretionary Trust Tax.

5.1.19 Surcharge

FA89 s79
CATCA s53

Where an accountable person delivers a return which contains an estimate of the market value of a gift or inheritance which, when expressed as a percentage of the agreed value of that asset is within any of the percentages set out below, a surcharge will be applied as follows:

Percentage of Agreed Value Estimated on Return	*Surcharge*
67% – 100%	nil
50% – 66%	10%
40% – 49%	20%
0% – 39%	30%

Interest will be charged on any surcharge raised as per the provisions of section 41 of the Principal Act.

An accountable person aggrieved by the imposition on him of a surcharge can appeal the imposition of the surcharge within 30 days of notification to him on the grounds that having regard to all the circumstances there were sufficient grounds on which he might reasonably have based his estimate of the market value of the asset. This is the only grounds for an appeal. The usual rights for the rehearing of the appeal by the Circuit Court and on a point of law by the High Court apply.

5.1.20 Delivery of returns

FA82 s36, s37, s38, s101;

The donee of a gift or the successor of an inheritance may deliver a return in a form delivered by electronic, photographic or other

FA89 s82 process where the form is approved by the Revenue Commissioners.

CATCA s46 Affidavits and accounts must be made on a form provided by or approved by the Revenue Commissioners.

No return is required where 80% of the threshold amount has not been exceeded.

Additional requirements arise on the occasion of inheritance. The Inland Revenue affidavit must be lodged with the Revenue Commissioners. In addition to giving details of all the chargeable assets, wherever situate, the affidavit should also provide the following information:

(a) Details of all gifts made by the deceased within two years of his death.

(b) Details of the inheritances under the deceased's will, together with a copy of the will.

(c) Details of all other inheritances arising on his death.

(d) The names and addresses of the beneficiaries.

(e) Such other particulars as may be required for the purposes of the tax.

FA99 s200; FA00 s141 CATCA s46(12) The Finance Act 1999 imposes an obligation on a person to deliver a capital acquisitions tax return if requested to do so by the Revenue Commissioners even if no benefit has been received. This Act also imposes an obligation on the donor of a gift or a disponer in relation to a discretionary trust to make a return.

CATCA s46 From 1 January 2005 any enquiries, inspections and amendments to assessments must be made within four years of the date of receipt of the return save in the case of fraud or neglect.

CATCA s46A From 1 October 2003 an expression of doubt can be made in relation to any matter to be included in a return. No interest charge will arise under CATCA section 51(2) in respect of any additional liability arising as a result of the doubt being determined by the Commissioners provided the doubt is genuine.

5.1.21 Interest on tax underpaid/overpaid

FA98 s133 CATCA s51 From 1 April 1998 to 31 August 2002 interest on tax underpaid is payable at a rate of 1% per month or part of a month and interest on tax overpaid is payable at 0.5% per month or part of a month.

From 1 September 2002 to 31 October 2003 the rate is 0.0322% per day or part of a day in respect of tax underpaid and 0.0161% per day or part of a day in respect of tax overpaid.

From 1 November 2003 to 31 March 2005 tax repayments will carry interest at a rate of 0.011% per day from six months after the repayment claim is made, unless paid before that date.

From 1 April 2005 the rate has been reduced to a rate of 0.0273% per day or part of a day in respect of tax overpaid. Finance Act 2005 also provided that in respect of any tax overpaid after 1 April 2005 interest will be calculated by reference to a daily rate for all periods of delay whether before or after 1 April 2005 instead of a monthly basis for periods up to 31 August 2002 and a daily basis thereafter.

From 31 October 2003, repayment claims must be made within four years of the later of the valuation date or the date on which the tax is paid. This time limit does not apply to claims made by 31 December 2004 in respect of repayments arising on or before 28 March 2003.

For claims for repayment of tax made on or after 31 January 2008, the repayment claims must be made within 4 years from the date of payment of the tax, where the tax has been paid within the 4-month period after the valuation date of the gift/inheritance. Where the tax has not been paid within the 4-month period after the valuation date of the gift/inheritance, the repayment claims must be made within 4 years of the valuation date of the gift/inheritance.

5.1.22 Accountable persons

FA89 s81
CATCA s45

In the majority of cases, the donee or successor will be primarily accountable.

The disponer and every trustee, personal representative, guardian, agent or other person in whose care the property is placed on or after the date of the gift or inheritance is secondarily accountable.

The 1989 FA extends the definition of accountable persons by making a disponer a secondarily accountable person for inheritance tax purposes, where:

(a) the inheritance is taken on or before the date of death of the disponer and

(b) the date of the disposition is on or after 1 May 1989.

The limitation of liability to the value of the property is not applicable to disponers who are accountable persons.

5.1.23 Appeals

FA95 s51, s52, s159; CATCA s66 s68

There is the right to appeal to the Property Arbitrator where the taxpayer does not agree with the Revenue's valuation of real property. The normal appeal procedures which apply for income tax, broadly apply for CAT in relation to matters other than the valuation of real property. The Revenue Commissioners have the right however, to request the re-hearing of an appeal by the Circuit Court.

In relation to gifts or inheritances taken after 11 February 1998 an appeal may only be lodged against a decision or assessment of the Revenue Commissioners if the taxpayer has lodged a self-assessed return and paid the tax in accordance with that return.

5.1.24 Certificate of discharge

FA84 s48, s113;
FA00 s142
CATCA s61

The Revenue Commissioners may issue a certificate of discharge from liability for CAT on property to an accountable person. Such a certificate will discharge the property from liability to CAT in respect of the particular gift or inheritance to the extent specified in the certificate. The Finance Act 1984 enables the Revenue Commissioners to issue a certificate which will discharge from tax a person who is accountable but not primarily accountable for payment of CAT or who is a personal representative.

5.1.25 Clearance certificate

FA94 s146;
FA96 s128
CATCA s62

With effect from 23 May 1994, a CAT clearance certificate must be obtained in respect of applications for registration of title to land which are based on possession. Such applications will not be dealt with by the Land Registry unless the Revenue Commissioners have issued a certificate to the effect that they are satisfied that any liability to gift tax, inheritance tax and probate tax charged on the land, has been, or will be paid within a reasonable time.

The 1996 Finance Act relaxes the clearance certificate requirement by providing self-certification as an option for solicitors dealing with applications for registration of title to land which are based on possession. The relaxation may be availed of in cases where the solicitor is satisfied that the property in respect of which the application is being made is not part of a larger holding of property and that its market value does not exceed the following limits:

- €19,050 in a case where the area occupied by the property does not exceed five hectares, or
- €127,000 in a case where the applicant is a statutory authority.

There are two exceptions to the rule that the property being registered should not be part of a larger property. The first exception is where the larger property is itself within the prescribed limit. The other exception is where the sole purpose of the application for registration is the rectification of the Register to take account of small mapping errors not exceeding 500 square metres in area or €2,540 in value.

5.1.26 Joint accounts

FA86 s61, s110
FA01 s223
CATCA s109

In the case of deaths occurring on or after 26 January 2001 and before 1 January 2002, where a sum of money in excess of £25,000 (previously £5,000) was lodged or deposited (other than in a current account) in the joint names of two or more persons and one of such person dies, the banker concerned cannot make payments to the survivor(s) until he is furnished with a certificate by the Commissioners that there is no outstanding claim for inheritance tax in connection with the deceased. In the case of deaths occurring on or after 1 January 2002, the amount is €31,750.

5.1.27 Valuation of shares in private companies

FA93 s125; FA96 s121 CATCA s27

Shares in private companies, regardless of whether they are trading or non-trading companies, are, with effect from 24 February 1993 valued on a market value basis for CAT purposes. There are also certain specific valuation rules set down in respect of controlling interests as follows:

(a) The valuation of shares in private companies is to be determined on the basis of an apportioned part of the market value of each class of share;

(b) Apportionment as between shares of a particular class is to be by reference to the nominal amount (i.e. the total value is spread equally over each single share with no regard being had to the size of a particular holding);

(c) Apportionment as between different classes of share is to have due regard to the rights attaching to each of the different classes (i.e. discounting the market value for entitlement or otherwise to voting rights).

5.1.28 Anti-avoidance

FA89 s90; FA93 s126 CATCA s44

Capital acquisitions tax is payable where arrangements result in a shift of value from one class of share to another even though no actual transfer of shares has taken place. The tax payable is calculated based on the amount by which the value of shares has been reduced. These provisions are extended to situations where a benefit is conferred by the redemption of shares in a private company and no consideration is paid for the redemption.

FA00 s138 s139 CATCA s6, s11

Where a disponer is domiciled in the State the proportion of the market value of any share in a private company incorporated outside the State, controlled by the donee/successor which is derived from assets located in the State, is deemed to be situate in the State.

5.1.29 Valuation of limited interests

CATA76 Sch1 CATCA Sch 1

Limited interests in property are taxed by reference to the capital in which the interest subsists but the taxable value is arrived at by taking the appropriate percentage as provided in the First Schedule. The percentage takes into account the age and sex of the donee or successor or the period of time for which the interest is to last.

5.1.30 Arrangements for relief from double taxation

FA03 s79
CATCA s106

The Government has the power to make arrangements with the government of any territory outside the State in relation to double taxation relief on gift tax or inheritance tax and in relation to the exchange of information for the purpose of prevention and detection of tax evasion in respect of these taxes.

5.1.31 Unilateral credit relief

CATA76 s67
CATCA s107

A credit is in certain circumstances given for foreign estate taxes/ inheritance taxes against capital acquisitions tax where there is no double tax treaty with the foreign territory in respect of estate taxes. Credit is given for foreign tax on a property where the property is situated in the territory in which the foreign tax is chargeable.

Finance Act 2005 provides that as and from 1 December 2004 credit will also apply for foreign tax levied in a country other than where the property is situate.

5.2 The CAT/Inheritance Tax Double Tax Agreement with the United Kingdom

All references are to the Ireland-United Kingdom Double Taxation Agreement.

The Double Tax Treaty between Ireland and the United Kingdom (SI 279 of 1978) provides relief from double taxation in respect of taxes on estates of deceased persons and inheritances and on gifts and it came into force on 2 October 1978. Its provisions are retrospective to the introduction of CAT in Ireland and capital transfer tax (CTT) in the United Kingdom.

Inheritance Tax (IHT) was introduced by the UK Finance Act 1986 to replace CTT. The Treaty now applies to IHT in place of CTT.

5.2.1 Elimination of double taxation

Article 8
CATCA s106
CATCA s107(2)

(1) If tax is paid in Ireland and in the United Kingdom on property which is situated in one country only, the country in which the property is not situated must give a credit for the tax paid in the other State where the property is situated. If both the Irish and the United Kingdom tax authorities disagree regarding the situation of property the country with subsidiary taxing rights must give the credit for the attributable tax paid in the other country.

(2) Where both Ireland and the United Kingdom tax property situated in a third territory, the country with subsidiary taxing rights gives a credit for the attributable tax paid in the other country, on the third territory doubly taxed property.

(3) Any credit given in Ireland under the above provisions will only be allowed if the gift/inheritance on which Irish tax is due, has been reduced by the payment of United Kingdom IHT.

(4) The tax attributable to any property is the United Kingdom or Ireland tax less any tax paid in a foreign territory on that property.

5.2.2 Time limit for credit or repayment

Article 9

Any claim for a credit or a repayment under the Double Taxation Agreement shall be made within six years from the date of the event in respect of which the claim is made.

5.2.3 How to determine the country with subsidiary rights

Article 4(2)

The necessity to determine the country with subsidiary taxing rights generally only arises if both countries claim the domicile of the donor.

To determine in which of the two countries an individual is or was domiciled for the purposes of the treaty the following series of tests is applied:

(a) Where has or had the individual his permanent home or the centre of his vital interest, or

(b) where has or had the individual his habitual abode, or

(c) of which State is or was the individual a national.

If any one of the foregoing tests can be positively applied, then the domicile of the individual is determined as being in the particular country.

Should all these tests fail to produce a positive answer, the final decision is left to be agreed between the Revenues of each country.

Article 5(2) Having settled the question of domicile the rules for determining the country with subsidiary taxing rights are as follows:

(a) In relation to property, (other than settlement property) the State where he is not regarded as domiciled has subsidiary taxing rights.

(b) For settlement property:

(i) If at the date it was made the law of the settlement was the law of Ireland and the settlor's domicile (only United Kingdom claiming) was in the United Kingdom the country with subsidiary taxing rights will be the United Kingdom.

(ii) If the proper law of the settlement was not the law of Ireland and the undisputed domicile is the United Kingdom at the date the settlement was made, but at some time later the proper law of the settlement becomes Irish or the settlor's domicile becomes indisputably Irish then Ireland will have the subsidiary taxing rights.

(iii) If the proper law of the settlement was not the law of Ireland and the settlor's domicile is disputed and determined at the time the settlement was made under Article 4(2) the State where he is not domiciled will have subsidiary taxing rights.

6.1 Capital Gains Tax

TCA97 s28 Capital gains tax is payable on chargeable gains arising on the disposal of assets after 5 April 1974.

6.1.1 Disposal

TCA97 s534 A disposal takes place whenever the ownership of an asset changes and includes a part disposal. A disposal occurs even where no capital sum is derived from the change in ownership, e.g., gift or exchange.

6.1.2 Death

TCA97 s573 Death is not an occasion when disposal occurs. A person becoming entitled to an asset by reason of death is treated for capital gains tax purposes as having acquired the asset on the date of death and at its market value on that date.

6.1.3 Part disposals

In computing the chargeable gain or allowable loss on the disposal of part of an asset, the amount to be deducted from the proceeds of sale is restricted to the proportion of the original cost, or 6 April 1974 value of the asset, which the proceeds of sale bear to the value of what remains. The proportion is given by the following fraction:

$$\frac{A}{A+B}$$

where

A = The amount or value of the consideration for the part disposal.

B = The market value of that part of the asset which remains undisposed of.

6.1.4 Assets

TCA97 s532 All forms of property are assets for the purpose of the Capital Gains Tax Acts, whether situated in the State or not, including options, debts and currency other than Irish currency.

6.2 Computation of Chargeable Gains and Allowable Losses

Up to and including 5 April 1978 the computation of chargeable gains and allowable losses was made by comparing the proceeds of disposal with the original cost of the asset or its market value at 6 April 1974 where it was owned at that date.

6.2.1 Indexation

TCA97 s556

Relief is provided for the inflation content of chargeable gains accruing on the disposal, on or after 6 April 1978, of assets owned for more than twelve months prior to the date of disposal. Certain restrictions apply to the disposal of development land on or after 28 January 1982.

Inflation is measured by the increase in the Consumer Price Index, as compiled by the Central Statistics Office, in the period from mid-February in the year preceding the year of acquisition or in the year preceding the year in which further allowable expenditure was incurred to mid-February in the year preceding the year in which disposal takes place. All chargeable assets held on 6 April 1974 are deemed to have been acquired at their market value on that date with the result that the relief for inflation is calculated by reference to the level of the Consumer Price Index at mid-February 1974.

The relief is granted by allowing the cost and, if applicable, additional expenditure on the asset to be adjusted by multiplying it by a figure as specified in section 556. For disposals of assets taking place since 6 April 1987, the "multiplier" to be applied is shown at Chart 23.

While indexation was abolished in respect of expenditure incurred on or after 1 January 2003, the indexation factors to be applied to expenditure incurred before that date are shown in Chart 23.

Development land

The relief for inflation applies to all assets but certain restrictions apply to disposals of development land or shares deriving their value from such land on or after 28 January 1982.

TCA97 s650, s651

The application of the relief for inflation to the computation of chargeable gains arising on the disposal of development land or shares deriving their value from such land is as follows:

(i) Where the land or shares were acquired after 5 April 1974, the adjustment for inflation will only apply to that portion of the purchase price as reflects the current use value of the land at the date of purchase. The remainder of the purchase price is allowed as a deduction.

(ii) Where the land or shares were owned at 6 April 1974 the adjustment for inflation will only apply to that portion of the market value at that date as reflects the current use value of the land at that date. The remainder of the market value will be allowed as a deduction.

Development land is land in the State, the consideration for the disposal of which, or the market value of which at the date of disposal exceeds the current use value of that land at the date of disposal. Current use value means the open market value of the land at a particular time, calculated on the assumption that it was at that time, and would remain, unlawful to carry out development, other than development of a minor nature.

Where the total consideration received by an individual from the sale of development land in a year of assessment does not exceed €19,050 no liability to "development land" capital gains tax will arise. The normal capital gains tax will apply.

As outlined above, indexation will not apply to expenditure incurred on or after 1 January 2003.

6.2.2 Deductions

TCA97 s552 In computing chargeable gains or allowable losses the amounts to be deducted from the consideration received for an asset, excluding development land, include the following:

(a) The cost of acquisition as increased by the relief for inflation (indexation).

(b) Additional expenditure on the asset for the purpose of enhancing the value of the asset, as increased by the relief for inflation, calculated by reference to the date on which such expenditure is incurred.

(c) Incidental costs of acquisition and disposal.

No deduction is allowed for expenditure which is allowable for income tax purposes.

Where any of the expenditure, which is allowable as a deduction from the consideration received for an asset was incurred after the date of acquisition of the asset, and a chargeable gain arises to which tapering relief applies, the chargeable gain is attributed to the original and additional expenditure in the relative proportions of that expenditure as adjusted for inflation. The tapering relief is then applied to the chargeable gain by reference to the dates on which the expenditure was incurred.

6.2.3 Interest

TCA97 s552 Interest is not an allowable deduction for capital gain tax purposes except in certain circumstances where a company borrows money to defray expenditure on the construction of any building, structure or works.

6.2.4 Losses

TCA97 s546 Chargeable gains of a year of assessment are aggregated with allowable losses of the year for the purpose of computing the net amount assessable to capital gains tax. Losses brought forward from earlier years are also deductible. Losses are set off against gains chargeable at the highest rate of capital tax and so on in order. Allowable losses which remain unrelieved may be carried forward indefinitely.

TCA97 s651 Gains on development land may only be off set by losses on development land. Losses on development land may be set off against gains on disposals of other assets.

Inflation relief (indexation) cannot convert a monetary gain to an allowable loss.

6.2.5 Assets which have qualified for capital allowances

TCA97 s561 The majority of such assets would be wasting assets and but for express provision would be exempt from capital gains tax under the provisions of section 603. Section 561 provides that where a gain arises on such assets, the computation disregards the fact that capital allowances have been granted. This is because the capital allowances will have been recovered by means of a balancing charge. The chargeable gain is computed by comparing cost with proceeds of sale. The indexation and, if applicable, tapering reliefs are granted in the normal way.

Where a loss arises on the disposal of such assets, that loss will not be allowed to the extent that it has been covered by capital allowances.

6.2.6 Grants

TCA97 s565 Where any part of the cost of an asset has been met directly or indirectly by any Government, by any Board established by statute or by any public or local authority, whether in the State or elsewhere, the grant or subsidy must be deducted in arriving at the cost of the asset for capital gains tax purposes. If the asset was owned on 6 April 1974 the cost will be the market value at that date and any grant or subsidy received before that date must be deducted from the market value. By this means the indexation is applied to the net amount after deducting the grant or subsidy.

6.2.7 Leases

TCA97 s566 A disposal of an interest in a lease which has more than 50 years to run is a normal disposal for capital gains tax purposes. Where a lease which has less than 50 years to run is disposed of, it is treated as a wasting asset and special rules apply as to the amount of the cost which is allowable as a deduction on disposal from the proceeds of sale. The rate at which the cost is assumed to be written off is in accordance with the table set out on page .

On disposal of a lease which has less than 50 years to run, the amount of the costs to be allowed is:

$$C - C \times \frac{P(1) - P(3)}{P(1)}$$

where

C = *Cost*

P(1) = *the percentage derived from the table overleaf for the duration of the lease at the beginning of the period of ownership.*

P(3) = *the percentage derived from the same table for the duration of the lease at the time of the disposal.*

Where additional expenditure is incurred during the currency of the lease the amount of that expenditure allowable as a deduction is:

$$C - C \times \frac{P(2) - P(3)}{P(3)}$$

where

C = *Cost*

P(2) = *the percentage derived from the table overleaf at the date the additional expenditure was incurred.*

P(3) = *the percentage derived from the same table for the duration of the lease at the time of the disposal.*

Where payment of a premium is required under a lease, there is a part disposal of the freehold or other asset out of which the lease is granted. Any part of the premium which is taxed under Case V of Schedule D is excluded from the consideration to be taken into account for capital gains purposes.

Table

Disposal of Short Lease

Years	Percentage	Years	Percentage
50 (or more)	100.00	25	81.1
49	99.7	24	79.6
48	99.3	23	78.1
47	98.9	22	76.4
46	98.5	21	74.6
45	98.1	20	72.8
44	97.6	19	70.8
43	97.1	18	68.7
42	96.6	17	66.5
41	96.0	16	64.1
40	95.5	15	61.6
39	94.8	14	59.0
38	94.2	13	56.2
37	93.5	12	53.2
36	92.8	11	50.0
35	92.0	10	46.7
34	91.2	9	43.2
33	90.3	8	39.4
32	89.4	7	35.4
31	88.4	6	31.2
30	87.3	5	26.7
29	86.2	4	22.0
28	85.1	3	17.0
27	83.8	2	11.6
26	82.5	1	6.0
		0	0.0

6.2.8 Time of disposal

TCA97 s542

The time of disposal is the time at which the contract is made. If the contract is conditional the time of disposal is the time when the condition is fulfilled. There are also provisions covering the time of disposal in the case of compulsory acquisition, hire purchase, capital sums derived from assets and certain life assurance policies and contracts for deferred annuities.

6.2.9 Identification of shares disposed of with shares purchased

Shares of the same class disposed of on or after 6 April 1978 are identified with purchases on a first in, first out basis. There are special problems, however, in relation to shares held at 6 April 1978, and acquired on or after 6 April 1974. Where some of these shares have been disposed of they have, up to and including 5 April 1978, been treated on a pool basis, i.e. treated as a single asset growing or diminishing on the occasion when shares were acquired or disposed of. The continuation of the pooling system for disposal of these shares on or after 6 April 1978 would not permit the inflation and tapering reliefs to be correctly applied. In order that the reliefs may be applied, it is provided that pools of shares existing at 6 April 1978 are to be unravelled by matching acquisitions and disposals in the period from 6 April 1974 to 5 April 1978 in the proportion which the number of shares disposed of bears to the total number of shares in the pool immediately prior to the disposal. The shares remaining at 6 April 1978 will then be identifiable by reference to both date of acquisition and cost.

The unravelling procedure will not affect computations of chargeable gains or allowable losses for periods up to 5 April 1978.

6.2.10 Options

TCA97 s540 Options are assets for capital gains tax purposes.

The granting of an option is a disposal separate from the asset to which it relates. If the option is exercised, the grant of the option ceases to be a separate transaction and becomes part of the overall transaction in which the asset is sold and acquired.

The abandonment of an option is a disposal but no allowable loss can occur.

6.2.11 Restrictive covenants

TCA97 s541BA A charge to capital gains arises where:

(i) A person who (whether under a legally binding arrangement or not) gives an undertaking to curtail their conduct or activities and in exchange for that undertaking, consideration is obtained by them or any other person, and

(ii) Where such amount is not liable to income tax or not otherwise liable to capital gains tax by virtue of it not being consideration for the disposal, in whole or in part, of an asset.

The above provision applies in respect of undertakings given on or after 6 February 2003.

6.2.12 Liquidations

TCA97 s571 The appointment of a liquidator does not give rise to a disposal for capital gains tax purposes. Any disposal of assets by a liquidator during the course of the liquidation or a distribution in specie of assets to the shareholders is a disposal by the company.

When the shareholders receive a distribution, either in cash or in specie, this is a disposal for capital gains tax purposes.

Capital gains tax arising on chargeable gains on disposals made by a liquidator, receiver, mortgagee or chargee ("accountable persons") is recoverable by means of an income tax assessment under Case IV of Schedule D, raised on the accountable person.

6.2.13 Reorganisations and amalgamations or reconstructions

TCA97 s584-s587

Sections 584 to 587 of the TCA 1997 deal with share re-organisation on the amalgamation or reconstruction of companies by way of exchange of shares or securities. All of these sections provide that where, subject to certain conditions, a shareholder, either an individual or a company, receives in exchange for the shares which they hold, a new form of share or security in the company being re-organised or in a new company in the case of amalgamations or reconstructions, no capital gains tax charge will arise at that point. The gain is deferred until such time as the new shares/securities are disposed of by the holder. The new shares/securities are deemed to have been acquired at the cost and on the date on which the original shares/securities were acquired. These deferrals are commonly referred to as "paper for paper".

The definition of securities in the sections referred to is very wide and includes debentures, loan stock or other similar securities.

If there is any payment of cash on either a takeover or a capital reorganisation, a part disposal will occur.

The relief will only apply where it is shown that the exchange was effected for bona fide commercial reasons and does not form part of any arrangement or scheme of which the main purpose or one of the main purposes is avoidance of liability to tax.

Finance Act 2003 removed the facility to defer capital gains tax by the issue of debentures, loan stock or other similar securities under the provision of section 584 – 587 TCA 1997 as described above.

Subject to two transitional provisions, the change takes effect in relation to an issue or allotment of debentures, etc. on or after 4 December 2002, unless such an issue or allotment is made pursuant to a written binding agreement made before that date. However, capital gains tax deferral will still apply where debentures are issued on or after that date by one company to another company under a company amalgamation by exchange of shares (section 586) or under a company reconstruction and amalgamation (section 587) where both companies are members of the same group for the purposes of section 616 of the Taxes Consolidation Act 1997.

6.2.14 Inheritances and gifts

TCA97 s573

Assets acquired by inheritance or gift are deemed to have been acquired at market value at the date of death or gift.

6.2.15 Rights issues

TCA97 s584

Expenditure on a rights issue is deemed to have been incurred when the consideration was given. The relief for inflation is applied accordingly.

6.2.16 Calls on shares

TCA97 s582 Where there has been an issue of shares or debentures and a person gives any consideration on a date which is more than 12 months after the allotment of the shares or debentures, the consideration will be deemed to have been incurred on the date on which it was given. As a result, the relief for inflation applies from the later date.

6.2.17 Matching of foreign currency assets and foreign currency liabilities

TCA97 s79A In computing any chargeable gain or loss on the disposal of a relevant foreign currency asset it is possible to match such assets with relevant foreign currency liabilities for accounting periods ending on or after 6 February 2003. The legislation deals with a company acquiring share capital denominated in a foreign currency (i.e., other than the Euro). It applies where after the investment of share capital the relevant company owns at least 25% of the target's share capital and the target is either a trading company or a holding company of a trading company. Within three weeks of the acquisition of the share capital, the company may give notice to the Revenue Commissioners that it wishes to match the shares held in a foreign currency with a corresponding foreign currency liability. When this election is made any gain arising in relation to the disposal of the share capital as a result of exchange rate movements can be adjusted so that the deemed proceeds is reduced by any corresponding loss arising in respect of the foreign currency liability due to exchange rate movements. Conversely if the company realised a gain on the repayment of a liability due to exchange rate movements the gain is added to the deemed proceeds arising in respect of the foreign currency asset, provided the increase does not exceed the amount of a capital gains tax loss arising on the disposal of the shares due to exchange rate movements. The effect of the section is to match the relevant foreign currency asset with the related foreign currency liability for tax purposes. (See also paragraph 2.9.1)

Finance Act 2007 amended section 79B of the Taxes Consolidation Act 1997 to ensure that the original provision as amended by Finance Act 2006 operates as intended. Companies are allowed to elect to match for tax purposes a trading asset denominated in a foreign currency with redeemable share capital denominated in that currency. Where the option is exercised, any foreign exchange gain or loss on the share capital is to be taken into account in calculating taxable income of the company so to match a corresponding exchange loss or gain on the asset. In exercising this option a company achieves tax neutrality in relation to such exchange movements. The two amendments are:

- The first amendment ensures that unrealized foreign currency movements on the share capital can be taken into account for tax purposes over the period of the loan on a "mark to market" basis. This achieves a better timing of the matching allowed under the section so as to achieve full neutrality.
- The second amendment provides that the tax neutrality provided for under section 79B, which currently assumes a euro functional currency, is also available to a company whose functional currency is other than the euro. This could arise, for example, where a company whose functional currency is the US$ gives loans denominated in sterling.

As Finance Act 2007 clarifies the original intention of the legislation as amended by Finance Act 2006, it is intended that it takes effect from 1 January 2006 – the original commencement date.

6.3 Persons Chargeable

TCA97 s29 Individuals, trusts, unincorporated bodies, etc. are chargeable to capital gains tax. Capital gains of companies are chargeable to corporation tax.

6.3.1 Residence

An individual who is resident or ordinarily resident in the State for a year of assessment is chargeable to capital gains tax on chargeable gains made on the disposal of assets wherever situated. An individual who is neither resident nor ordinarily resident in the State for a year of assessment is chargeable to capital gains tax only on chargeable gains made on the disposal of:

(a) Land or buildings in the State.

(b) Assets of a business carried on in the State.

(c) Minerals in the State.

(d) Exploration or exploitation rights in the continental shelf

(e) Unquoted shares deriving the greater part of their value from such assets as mentioned above at (a), (c) and (d).

An individual who is resident or ordinarily resident, but not domiciled in the State, is liable to capital gains tax on chargeable gains on the disposal of assets situate outside the State and the United Kingdom, only to the extent that the chargeable gains are remitted to the State. Losses accruing on the disposal of such assets are not allowable losses for capital gains tax purposes.

6.3.2 Temporary non-residents

TCA97 s541(b) Finance Act 2003 imposes a capital gains tax charge in respect of a deemed disposal of certain assets (relevant assets) that an individual owns on the last day of the last year of assessment for which the individual is taxable in the State, prior to becoming taxable elsewhere. However, the capital gains tax charge will only arise:

(i) If the individual is not taxable in the State for a period of five years or less before again becoming so taxable, and

(ii) To the extent that the individual disposes of those assets during that period.

Relevant assets are shares in a company, or rights to acquire shares in a company, being shares or rights which he or she beneficially owned on the last day of the year of his or her departure and the market value of which on that day;

(i) is equal to, or exceeds, 5% of the value of the issued share capital of the company, or

(ii) exceeds €500,000.

Whereas the gain on the deemed disposal arises before the individual ceases to be taxable in the State, the gain is required to be included in the individuals return and the tax in respect of it accounted for in the year in which the individual is again taxable in the State. Credit will be given in respect of any foreign tax payable on an actual disposal of the assets where such tax is payable in a territory with which Ireland has a double taxation treaty.

The above provisions apply to individuals who cease to be resident in the Sate on or after 4 December 2002.

Disposals to a spouse, separated spouse or former spouse are exempt from capital gains tax – see below. However, the exemption does not apply to disposals on or after 7 December 2005 where the spouse acquiring the asset would not be liable to Irish capital gains tax if he/ she disposed of it in the year in which he/she acquired it (i.e., if he/ she disposed of the asset abroad while being non-resident in the State for tax purposes).

6.3.3 Husbands and wives

TCA97 s1028 The chargeable gains of a married woman are assessed on the husband unless separate assessment is claimed.

Any unallowed loss of one spouse is deductible in computing the chargeable gains of the other.

A transfer of assets between husband and wife does not give rise to a disposal for capital gains tax purposes. The spouse who receives the asset is deemed to have acquired it on the date and at the cost at which the other acquired it.

See paragraph 6.3.2 re: subsequent disposals by a non-resident spouse.

6.3.4 Separated spouses

TCA97 s1030 A charge to capital gains tax will not arise where a person disposes of an asset to his or her spouse and both spouses:

(a) have been granted, or are treated as having been granted a judicial separation under the Family Law Act, 1995, or

(b) are parties to an order made under Part II of the Judicial Separation and Family Law Reform Act, 1989, on or following the granting of a decree of judicial separation where such order is treated, by virtue of section 3 of the Family Law Act, 1995 as if made under the corresponding provisions of the Family Law Act 1995, or

(c) are parties to a deed of separation, or

(d) are the subject of a relief order within the meaning of the Family Law Act, 1995, made following the dissolution of marriage.

The spouse to whom the disposal is made will be treated as having acquired the asset on the same day and at the same cost as the spouse who had made the disposal.

See paragraph 6.3.2 re: subsequent disposals by a non-resident spouse.

6.3.5 Divorced persons

TCA97 s1031 With effect from 10 May 1997, a charge to capital gains tax will not arise when a person who has obtained a Decree of Divorce under the Family Law (Divorce) Act, 1996 disposes of assets pursuant to a Court Order under that Act to his or her former spouse.

The spouse acquiring the asset is deemed to have acquired it at the same time and the same cost as the other spouse.

With effect from 10 February 2000, a charge to capital gains tax will not arise in respect of disposals where:

(i) an order for the disposition of property between spouses is made by an Irish Court on foot of a foreign judicial separation; and

(ii) property disposition orders are made by foreign courts, which are analogous to those made by Irish courts in similar circumstances, on foot of foreign divorces and foreign judicial separations which are recognised in the State.

See paragraph 6.3.2 re: subsequent disposals by a non-resident spouse.

6.4 Exemptions, Reliefs and Allowances

6.4.1 Personal exemptions and reliefs

TCA97 s601 For the tax years 1998/99 *et seq.*, the first £1,000/€1,270 of chargeable gains of an individual is exempt. The exemption is not transferable between spouses.

TCA97 s593 Disposals of life assurance policies and deferred annuities by the original beneficial owner in respect of policies issued by an Irish life assurance company.

TCA97 s602 A gain accruing to an individual on the disposal of an asset which is tangible moveable property and not a wasting asset where the consideration does not exceed €2,540 is exempt. Where the consideration exceeds €2,540 marginal relief applies to restrict the tax payable to one half of the excess of the consideration over €2,540. Losses accruing on the disposal of such assets are restricted to the difference between cost and deemed proceeds of sale of €2,540.

This exemption does not apply to a disposal of commodities by a person dealing on a terminal market or to the disposal of currency of any description.

TCA97 s603 The disposal of an asset which is tangible moveable property and which is a wasting asset (a wasting asset means an asset with a predictable life not exceeding 50 years) is exempt.

The exemption does not apply to assets which have been exclusively used for the purpose of a trade or profession and have or could have qualified for capital allowances. Part use for the purpose of a trade or profession will cause part of the exemption to be lost.

The exemption does not apply to a disposal of commodities by a person dealing on a terminal market.

TCA97 s606 A gain on the disposal a work of art, valued at not less than €31,740 where it has been loaned to an approved gallery or the proposed Irish Heritage Trust for a period of not less than 10 years for display to the public.

TCA97 s607 Irish Government securities and certain others.

TCA97 s608 Gains accruing on the disposal of investments held as part of an approved superannuation fund or the assets of a personal retirement savings account (PRSA) to the extent that the income from the investment funds is exempt from tax, or investments held as assets of certain occupational pension schemes in situations where the trustees are exempt from income tax.

TCA97 s609 A gain accruing to a charity exempt from income tax, subject to certain conditions.

TCA97 s610 Gains accruing to the list of bodies contained in Schedule 15 TCA 1997, which include:

(a) A registered trade union to the extent that the proceeds of the disposal giving rise to the gain or, if greater, the consideration for the disposal under the Capital Gains Tax Acts have been, or will be, applied solely for the purposes of its registered trade union activities.

(b) Registered and unregistered friendly societies whose income is exempt from income tax.

(c) A local authority.

(d) The Central Bank of Ireland.

(e) The Health Service Executive.

(f) A vocation education committee established under the Vocational Educational Act 1930.

(g) A committee of agriculture established under the Agricultural Act 1931.

(h) Bord Fáilte and certain regional tourism authorities.

(i) Disposals on or after 5 December 1994 of assets by the Cork and Dublin District Milk Boards and their associated companies to an Interim Board and any subsequent disposal of the assets by the Interim Board.

(j) The National Rehabilitation Board.

(k) National Development Finance Agency.

(l) Tourism Ireland Limited.

(m) An approved body, within the meaning of section 235(1) TCA 1997, to the extent that the proceeds of the disposal giving rise to the gain or, if greater, the consideration for the disposal under the Capital Gains Tax Acts have been, or will be, applied for the sole purpose of promoting athletic or amateur games or sports.

(n) Any body established by statute for the principal purpose of promoting games or sports, and any company wholly owned by such a body, to the extent that the proceeds of the disposal giving rise to the gain or, if greater, the consideration for the disposal under the Capital Gains Tax Acts have been, or will be, applied for that purpose.

(o) The Courts Service (from 02/02/2006).

(p) The Irish Auditing and Accounting Supervisory Authority (from 02/02/2006).

TCA97 s613 Gains on:

(a) National savings schemes.

(b) Prize bonds.

(c) Compensation or damages for personal injury or wrong.

(d) Betting winnings.

(e) Payments under pension schemes.

(f) The disposal of a life interest under a settlement by the person for whose benefit the settlement was created or by any other person except where the interest was acquired for a consideration in moneys worth.

6.4.2 Private residence

TCA97 s604

A gain accruing to an individual on the disposal of an interest in a private residence and grounds of up to one acre which has been occupied by him throughout the period of ownership as his only or main residence. Certain periods of absence are regarded as periods of occupation. These are:

(a) The last 12 months of ownership.

(b) Any period of absence throughout which the individual worked in a foreign employment.

(c) Any period of absence, not exceeding four years, during which the individual was prevented from occupying the residence because of local employment conditions.

Periods of foreign or local employment will only qualify as periods of occupation if the individual occupies the residence both before and after the periods.

The gain arising on any portion of a private residence used exclusively for business purposes is not exempted.

For the purpose of the relief, an individual may not have more than one main residence at any one time. If an individual has more than one residence, he may agree with the Inspector of Taxes which is to be treated as his main residence by giving notice to the Inspector within two years of the beginning of the period of acquisition of the second residence. Spouses living together may only have one main residence for both.

The relief applies to a chargeable gain arising on the disposal by a trustee of an asset which was settled property and occupied as his only or main residence by an individual entitled to occupy it under the terms of the settlement.

The relief is extended to disposals on or after 6 April 1979 of a dwellinghouse which, during the period of ownership, was the sole residence rent free of a dependent relative. No more than one residence may qualify at any one time.

In the case of a married couple living together, relief may be claimed separately by each spouse in respect of a dwelling house owned by that spouse and occupied by a dependent relative.

The relief given to an individual on the sale of his/her residence does not apply to the part of the gain reflecting "development value". The relief is calculated only by reference to the gain that would have arisen if the property was both bought and sold for its value solely as a residence.

This restriction on the relief is contained in s604(12) TCA 1997 and applies where the disposal takes place on or after 25 January 1984.

The gain on the disposal of the property is calculated in the normal way (as development land; see 6.2.1), and the resulting gain is reduced by the restricted residence relief. The balance of the gain is chargeable in full as a development land gain.

6.4.3 Transfer of land to children for construction of residences

TCA97 s603A An exemption from capital gains tax arises where a parent transfers land, valued at:

- not more than €254,000 during the period 6 December 2000 and 4 December 2007, and
- not more than €500,000 on or after 5 December 2007.

to his or her child, to enable the child to build a principal private residence.

The above thresholds apply where both parents make a simultaneous disposal of a site to their child.

For disposals made on or after 1 February 2007, the area of the land must not exceed 0.4047 hectare, i.e., 1 acre (exclusive of the area on which the house is to be built).

If the child subsequently disposes of the land (other than to their spouse) and the land does not:

(i) contain a dwelling house which was constructed by the child since the acquisition of the land; and

(ii) which had been occupied for a period of at least three years;

then the chargeable gain which would have accrued to the parent shall accrue to the child. This is in addition to any gain arising to the child on the land itself. Where a child suffers such a claw-back, they may subsequently receive a further exempt land transfer.

With regard to disposals made on or after 31 March 2006, a child also includes a foster child who resided with and was under the care of and maintained at the expense of the individual making the disposal for a period of five years, or periods, which together amounted to five years up to the time that such foster child reached 18 years of age. However, the claim for relief must not be based on the uncorroborated testimony of one witness.

6.4.4 Retirement relief

(a) Disposal of business or farm or shares in family company

TCA97 s598 A gain arising to an individual who has attained the age of 55 on the disposal of his business or farm or shares in his family company or holding company is disregarded where the consideration is less than €750,000, in respect of disposals made on or after 1 January 2007 (previously €500,000 in respect of disposals made between 6 February 2003 and 3 December 2006). Where the consideration is more than the limit, there is marginal relief which restricts the tax payable to one half of the difference between the consideration and the limit.

To qualify for the relief, the individual must have owned the assets for a minimum period of 10 years ending with the disposal and where the farm or business is disposed of through shares in the family company, the individual must have been a working director of the relevant company for a period of not less than 10 years during which period he or she has been a full-time working director of the relevant company for a period of not less than five years.

With effect from 1 January 2002, a taxpayer claiming retirement relief in respect of the disposal of shares in a family company, may also claim the relief in respect of land and buildings and machinery and plant which the individual has owned for a period of at least 10 years ending on the date of the disposal provided that:

(i) the assets were used by the company throughout the taxpayers period of ownership, and

(ii) the assets are disposed of at the same time and to the same person as the shares in the family company.

With effect from 6 February 2003, the use of an asset by a deceased spouse of an individual will be taken into account for the purposes of determining whether the individual qualifies for the relief. In addition, the period that an individual was a director of a company will be deemed to include the period during which the individual was a director of another company where, under a scheme of reconstruction or amalgamation, shares in that other company were exchanged for shares in the first-mentioned company.

The relief is also available to farmers transferring land into the early retirement scheme provided that the farmer used the land for the purposes of farming for a period of at least 10 years ending on the date of the transfer.

Subsequent disposals of such land which had been leased under the scheme will also qualify for the relief with effect from 27 November 2000.

With effect from 1 January 2002, retirement relief is extended to include the compulsory purchase of a farmer's land by a local authority for the purposes of road widening when, at the time of purchase, or in the preceding five years, the farmer had let the land and provided that immediately before the time the farmer let the land he or she used it for the purposes of farming for a period of at least 10 years.

With regard to disposals made on or after 31 January 2008, the relief will not apply to a disposal of qualifying assets unless it is shown that a disposal is made for bona fide commercial reasons and does not form part of any arrangement or scheme of which the main purpose, or one of the main purposes, is the avoidance of tax.

The EU Single Farm Payment Entitlement will qualify as an asset for the purposes of the relief for disposals made on or after 1 January 2005 provided the farmer fulfils the 10 year rule in relation to the ownership and usage of the land, which is disposed of at the same time as the Entitlement.

In the case of a husband and wife who are co-owners of land but only one of them becomes a partner in a Milk Production Partnership, an exemption can be sought from the requirement for both of them to become partners in such partnerships by obtaining a certificate from the Minister for Agriculture and Food. Accordingly, retirement relief will apply equally to both spouses in respect of disposals on or after 1 January 2005.

With regard to disposals on or after 14 May 2004 (see Revenue e-Brief No. 14/2005), the Revenue Commissioners will consider claims for retirement relief from taxpayers who at the time of the disposal are within 12 months of their 55th birthday, providing the following conditions are met:

(i) The taxpayer is, due to severe or chronic ill health, unable to continue farming, or in his/her trade, profession, office or employment, or as a working director in a relevant company.

(ii) On cessation, the taxpayer disposes of the qualifying assets and all the other conditions of the relief are satisfied, other than the age requirement.

(iii) The taxpayer provides medical evidence of the illness and outlines the circumstances in which the relief is being claimed.

With effect from 2 April 2007, the relief is extended in certain circumstances, to disposals of land that had been let prior to its disposal.

The land in question must have been let for a period of not longer than 15 years ending with the date of the disposal, it must have been owned and used for farming by the individual making the disposal for a period of not less than 10 years prior to the initial letting and it must be disposed of to a child within the meaning of section 599 TCA 1997.

TCA97 s598a The relief also applies on the dissolution of farming partnerships and the disposal of qualifying assets in the period 13 March 2008 to

31 December 2013. The asset being disposed of must have been owned and used by the farming partnership for 10 years prior to the dissolution of the partnership. Where one of the partners has acquired a share of the partnership by way of inheritance, the period of ownership and use of the farm will run from the date that the donor originally entered the partnership. The relief provides that a gain will not be treated as accruing in respect of a relevant partnership asset and that asset will be treated as having been acquired at the same time and for the same consideration as it was originally acquired by the partner who disposed of that asset. The relief does not apply to the disposal of trading stock.

Subject to a Ministerial Order, the relief will apply to compensation payments made under the scheme for the decommissioning of white fish vessels, in accordance with Council Regulation (EC) No. 1198/2006 of 27 July 2006. In order for the relief to apply, the person who receives the compensation payment must have owned and used the fishing vessel for the period of six years prior to the receipt of that payment (rather than the normal 10-year period) and must be at least 45 years of age at that time (rather than the normal 55 years of age).

6.4.5 (b) Disposal within the family of business or farm or shares in family company

TCA97 s599 For disposals on or after 6 April 1978, of assets as mentioned above at section 598, an individual, meeting the conditions as for section 598 and making the disposal to his children, is exempt from capital gains tax irrespective of the consideration. If the assets upon which exemption has been granted are disposed of within six years of having been acquired by the child, the capital gains tax which would have become payable, but for the exemption, becomes payable as well as any other capital gains tax which may be due on the disposal by the child.

For the purpose of the exemption "a child" includes:

(i) a child of a deceased child (with effect from 02 April 2007), and
(ii) a nephew or niece who has worked in the business substantially on a full time basis for the period of five years ending with the disposal, and
(iii) in respect of disposals made on or after 31 March 2006, a foster child who resided with and was under the care of and maintained at the expense of the individual making the disposal for a period of five years, or periods, which together amounted to five years up to the time that such foster child reached 18 years of age. However, the claim for relief must not be based on the uncorroborated testimony of one witness.

Where a parent disposes of land used for farming, on or after 2 April 2007, to his or her child and the consideration for its disposal consists of other land, no gain will arise on the disposal by the child. The parent acquiring the land will be treated as having acquired the land at the date and for the consideration that the child originally acquired it and he or she will be deemed to have farmed that land for the same period that the child farmed it.

The reliefs under section 598 and section 599 are not mutually exclusive.

6.4.6 Replacement of business and other assets

TCA97 s597 Abolished in respect of disposals on or after 04/12/2002. See the 31st or earlier editions of this book for details.

6.4.7 Replacement of certain residential properties

TCA97 s600A Abolished in respect of disposals on or after 04/12/2002. See the 31st or earlier editions of this book for details.

6.4.8 Sale of shares - unquoted company

TCA97 s591 Abolished in respect of disposals on or after 04/12/2002. See the 31st or earlier editions of this book for details.

6.4.9 Compulsory purchase

TCA97 s605 Abolished in respect of disposals on or after 04/12/2002. See the 31st or earlier editions of this book for details.

6.4.10 Compensation and insurance money

TCA97 s536 A person may claim that an amount received for compensation or damage to an asset which is not lost or destroyed may be treated as reducing the cost of the asset for capital gains tax purposes. To qualify for the relief, the amount received must be applied wholly or substantially in restoring the asset.

Any amount received as compensation or damages, and applied in restoring the asset, is to be deducted from the expenditure on restoration. Indexation is then applied to the net amount.

Where the asset is lost or destroyed, and the amount received in compensation is used within one year in replacing the asset, a person may claim that neither a gain nor a loss arises on the receipt of the compensation and as if the cost of the replacement asset were reduced by whatever amount which gives rise to no gain on the disposal of the old asset. The Revenue Commissioners have power to extend the time limit of one year.

If part only of the proceeds of the compensation is reinvested in a replacement asset, partial deferment will be allowed but only so long as the amount not reinvested is less than the monetary gain.

The relief under this section does not apply to amounts received for wasting assets and thus excludes amounts received for plant and machinery.

6.4.11 Scheme for retirement of farmers

TCA97 s612

Any premium paid under the European Communities (Retirement of Farmers) Regulations 1974 is excluded from the consideration for the disposal of the farm.

6.4.12 Transfer of a business to a company

TCA97 s596-s600

Where an individual transfers a business to a company, together with the whole of the assets of the business, or the whole of the assets other than cash and the business is transferred in exchange for shares issued by the company to the individual, the chargeable gain arising is deferred until such time as the shares are disposed of.

Should the consideration for the transfer consist partly of shares and partly of cash, the gain is calculated on the basis of the total disposal of the business. The proportion referable to the shares is deducted from the cost of the shares and the balance, applicable to the proportion in which the consideration has been taken other than in shares, is taxable in the normal manner.

Transfers made on or after 24 January 1992 must be for bona fide commercial reasons and not form part of any arrangement or scheme for an avoidance of liability to tax.

6.4.13 Disposal of shares in certain foreign and domestic subsidiaries

TCA97 s626B

Certain exemptions exist in relation to the disposal of shares in foreign and domestic subsidiaries which were primarily introduced to enhance Ireland's position as a holding company location – see paragraph 2.9.12.

6.5 Rates of Capital Gains Tax

6.5.1 General

The rate of capital gains tax is 20% in respect of the disposal of all assets on or after 1 December 1999, (with the exception of foreign life assurance policies and off-shore funds where the rate is 40%). (See Chart 24 for the rates applying to earlier disposals.)

6.5.2 Development land

In recent years the rate applying to gains on development land varied depending on the "residential" status of the land and can be summarised as follows:

Period	Land	Rate
Before 23/04/98	All development land	40%
23/04/98 – 30/11/99	Development land sold for residential development	20%
	Development land other than for residential development	40%
	Development land between connected parties	40%
	Shares deriving value from development land	40%
01/12/99 – onwards	All development land	20%

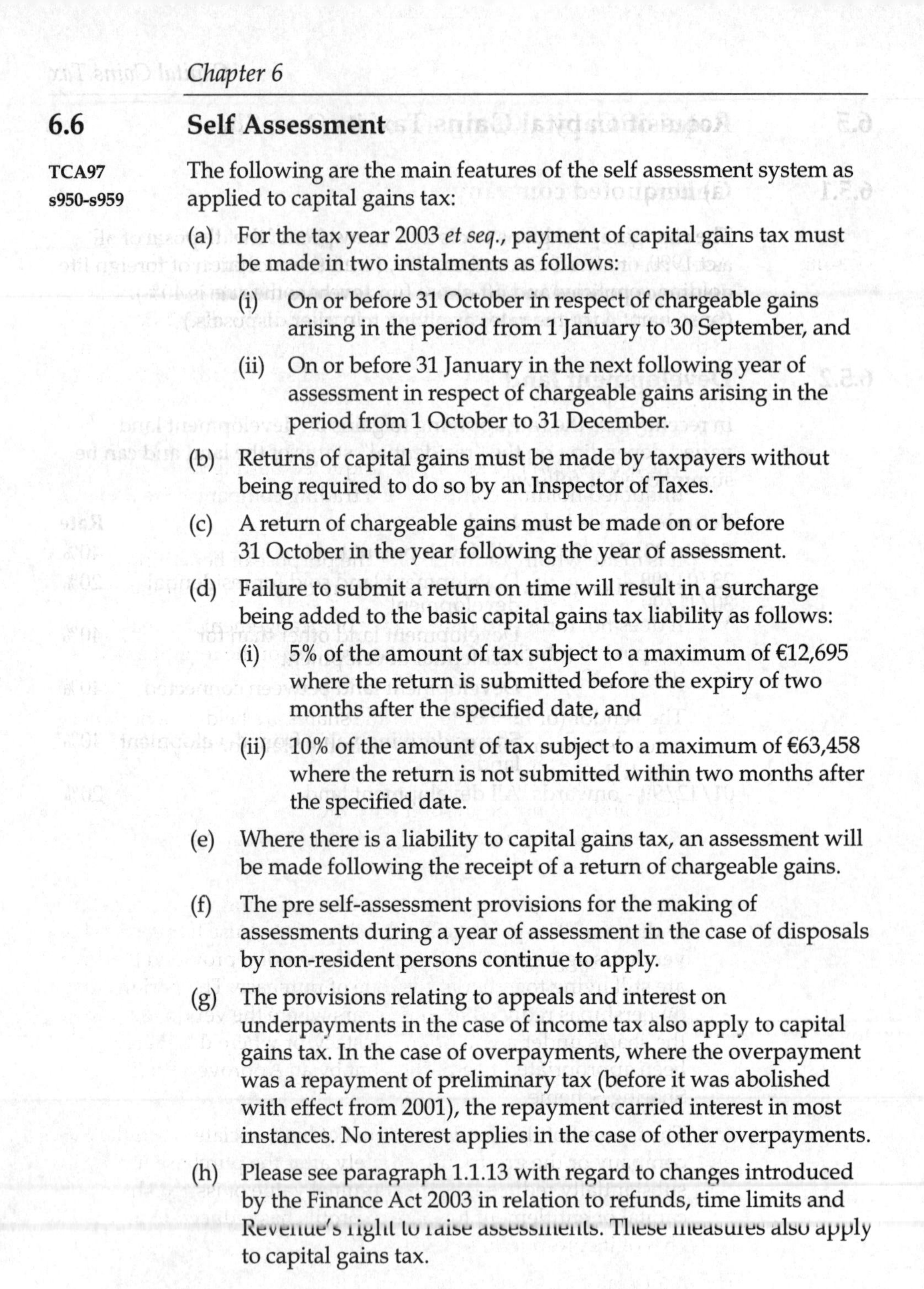

6.6 Self Assessment

TCA97 s950-s959

The following are the main features of the self assessment system as applied to capital gains tax:

(a) For the tax year 2003 *et seq.*, payment of capital gains tax must be made in two instalments as follows:

(i) On or before 31 October in respect of chargeable gains arising in the period from 1 January to 30 September, and

(ii) On or before 31 January in the next following year of assessment in respect of chargeable gains arising in the period from 1 October to 31 December.

(b) Returns of capital gains must be made by taxpayers without being required to do so by an Inspector of Taxes.

(c) A return of chargeable gains must be made on or before 31 October in the year following the year of assessment.

(d) Failure to submit a return on time will result in a surcharge being added to the basic capital gains tax liability as follows:

(i) 5% of the amount of tax subject to a maximum of €12,695 where the return is submitted before the expiry of two months after the specified date, and

(ii) 10% of the amount of tax subject to a maximum of €63,458 where the return is not submitted within two months after the specified date.

(e) Where there is a liability to capital gains tax, an assessment will be made following the receipt of a return of chargeable gains.

(f) The pre self-assessment provisions for the making of assessments during a year of assessment in the case of disposals by non-resident persons continue to apply.

(g) The provisions relating to appeals and interest on underpayments in the case of income tax also apply to capital gains tax. In the case of overpayments, where the overpayment was a repayment of preliminary tax (before it was abolished with effect from 2001), the repayment carried interest in most instances. No interest applies in the case of other overpayments.

(h) Please see paragraph 1.1.13 with regard to changes introduced by the Finance Act 2003 in relation to refunds, time limits and Revenue's right to raise assessments. These measures also apply to capital gains tax.

6.7 Acquisition by a Company of its Own Shares

6.7.1 (a) Unquoted company

TCA97 s173-s186

The changes introduced to company law (Part XI of the Companies Act 1990 – to enable a company acquire its own shares or those of its holding company) would have very severe consequences without consequent changes to tax legislation in view of the distribution rules in the Tax Acts. Section 130 provides that a premium payable on the redemption of a share shall be treated as a distribution. Under the provisions of section 173–186 a person is liable to capital gains tax where the following conditions are satisfied:

1. The acquisition is made by an unquoted trading company or an unquoted holding company of a trading company. (See quoted companies below).
2. It is made wholly or mainly for the purpose of benefiting a trade carried on by the company or by any of its 51% subsidiaries.
3. It does not form part of a scheme or arrangement the main purpose of which is to avoid the treating of the receipt as a dividend.
4. The vendor (or his nominee if the shares are held by a nominee) is resident or ordinarily resident in the State for the period in which the purchase occurs.
5. The vendor is not connected with the purchaser, or any company which is a member of the same group as the purchaser, after the sale.
6. The shares have been owned by the vendor for five years prior to disposal. The period of ownership of a spouse living with the vendor is aggregated with that of the vendor, provided that they are still living together at the date of purchase. The period of ownership is reduced to three years where the vendor acquired the shares under a will or an intestacy, or where the shares have been appropriated to a participant by an Approved Profit Sharing Scheme.
7. The interest of the vendor and that of his associates if any in the company or the group immediately after the purchase has substantially reduced, i.e. the nominal value of issued share capital or entitlement to share of profits has reduced to at least 75% of its pre-purchase level.

The other major provisions are:

(a) Where a company acquires shares from one of its shareholders such shares, where they are not cancelled, are deemed to be Treasury Shares. Treasury shares held by a company are deemed to be cancelled upon acquisition by the company. Such cancellation does not give rise to a chargeable gain or allowable loss. The re-issue by the company of Treasury shares is not treated as an issue of new shares.

(b) Dealers in shares will continue to be subject to tax under Case I and II of Schedule D on profits realised on the disposal of shares in this manner.

(c) For the purpose of this chapter associates include:

   (i) Husband and wife living together.

   (ii) A person under the age of 18 years and his parents.

   (iii) A person having a controlling interest in a company and that company.

   (iv) Two companies under common control.

(d) A person is connected with the company if he directly or indirectly possesses or is entitled to acquire more than 30% of the issued share capital or loan capital and voting rights of the company or is entitled to more than 30% of the assets of the company on a winding up.

(e) Any advance corporation tax payable on the purchase, redemption or repayment of shares which does not qualify for capital gains tax treatment is to be treated as though it was payable on a dividend.

(f) A group is defined as a company with its 51% subsidiaries. A company which has succeeded to a business previously carried on by a member of a group shall, together with this group of companies, be included as part of the group where that company commenced to carry on a business within three years.

(g) A company which makes a payment for shares is required to make a return on a prescribed form to the Inspector within nine months of the end of the accounting period in which the purchase occurs. This requirement is amended to take account of the situation where an inspector requests in writing such a form; then the time limit in which the company must comply is not less than 30 days from the issue of such notice.

(h) Cost incurred by a company in buying back its own shares (including legal costs, etc.) are not allowed as a deduction for tax purposes.

6.7.2 (b) Quoted company

The redemption, repayment or purchase by a quoted company or a subsidiary of a quoted company of its own shares is not to be treated as a distribution received by the shareholders but instead will be treated as a capital gains tax disposal by the shareholder. This treatment is not subject to the numerous conditions for unquoted companies outlined above.

6.8 Trusts

TCA97 s574 The creation of a trust is a disposal by the settlor who will be charged to tax by reference to the market value of the assets placed in the trust.

Changes in investments effected by the trustees during the life of the trust will give rise to a charge to tax either by reference to the market value at the date the assets were placed in the trust or the cost of the assets where acquired by the trustees.

Where an asset leaves the trust by reason of a person becoming absolutely entitled as against the trustees, a charge to tax arises by reference to the market value of the asset at the date on which the person becomes absolutely entitled to the asset.

A charge to tax will not occur where the event which gives rise to the person becoming absolutely entitled is the termination of a life interest by the death of the person entitled to that interest. In these circumstances, the person becoming absolutely entitled acquires the asset at its market value at the date of death of the life tenant. This treatment only applies where no event giving rise to a charge has occurred since 5 April 1974.

Where a life interest terminates with the property remaining in the trust a charge to tax arises based on the market value of the assets at the date of termination.

A charge to tax does not arise where the asset in question is comprised in an inheritance taken on the death and is exempt from tax in relation to the inheritance under section 55, Capital Acquisitions Tax Act, 1976. The charge to tax will crystallise should the assets cease to qualify for exemption from inheritance tax.

Where a trust is wound up either wholly or partly, any unallowed losses which have accrued on the property leaving the trust are treated as losses accruing to the beneficiary.

TCA97 s579 This section deals with the attribution of off-shore trust gains to Irish resident beneficiaries as and when the gains arise. It applies where the settlor or one of the settlors is domiciled and either resident or ordinarily resident in the State, or was domiciled and either resident or ordinarily resident in the State when such settlor made the settlement.

Section 88, Finance Act 1999 as amended by section 47, Finance Act 2002 contains detailed provisions on the following:

TCA97 s579A (a) The attribution of chargeable gains of off-shore trusts, to beneficiaries who are resident or ordinarily resident in the State on a receipts basis.

TCA97 s579B (b) The imposition of a charge to tax where the trustees of a trust cease to be resident and ordinarily resident in the State.

TCA97 s579C (c) The migration of a trust off shore because of the death of a trustee and the coming on shore of a trust for a similar reason.

TCA97 s579D (d) The imposition of a secondary liability on certain trustees where as a result of the trustees of a trust migrating off shore a capital gains tax charge arises, as at (b) above.

TCA97 s579E (e) The imposition of a charge where a trust ceases to be liable to Irish capital gains tax because of the provisions of any double taxation agreement.

TCA97 s613-s613A Section 90, Finance Act 1999 removes the exemption from capital gains tax for the disposal of an interest in a trust where the trust is or ever was an off shore trust or the trust is or ever was outside the charge to Irish capital gains tax by virtue of a double taxation agreement.

6.9 Clearance Certificates

TCA97 s980 Where any of the following assets is disposed of, the person by whom or through whom the consideration is paid must deduct capital gains tax at 15% from the payment:

(a) Land in the State.

(b) Minerals in the State.

(c) Exploration rights in a designated area.

(d) Unquoted shares deriving their value or the greater part of their value from assets at (a), (b) or (c).

(e) Unquoted shares accepted in exchange for shares deriving their value or the greater part of their value from assets at (a), (b) or (c).

(f) Goodwill of a trade carried on in the State.

The deduction is not required where the consideration does not exceed €500,000 in respect of disposals on or after 1 January 2002 (previously £300,000 for disposals between 23 March 2000 and 31 December 01) or where the person disposing of the asset produces a certificate from the Revenue Commissioners authorising payment in full. A clearance certificate may be obtained by making application on form CG50 to the Revenue Commissioners supported by a copy of the agreement or contract for sale.

The clearance certificate will be issued on the basis that:

(a) the vendor is resident in the State, or

(b) no amount of capital gains tax is payable in respect of the disposal, or

(c) the capital gains tax chargeable in respect of the disposal of the asset has been paid.

Clearance must be obtained before the consideration is paid. There is no exemption from the clearance procedure where the asset is held as trading stock or where the transaction is intra group and a capital gains tax liability does not arise. Failure to obtain the certificate will lead to the purchaser being assessed to capital gains tax for an amount of 15% of the consideration.

In the case of disposals made on or after 2 April 2007, the purchaser must, within 30 days of the date of payment, deliver an account to the Revenue Commissioners of the payment made and of the amount deducted from the payment and pay over the amount deducted. If the purchaser fails to do so, the Revenue Commissioners can raise an assessment for the amount deducted, including any interest due because of late payment. The amount deducted will, in due course, be allowed as a credit in computing the capital gains tax liability of the vendor.

Where the consideration is of a kind from which the 15% deduction cannot be made and the vendor does not produce a clearance certificate the person acquiring the asset must within seven days of the time at which the acquisition is made:

(i) notify the Revenue Commissioners of the acquisition by providing particulars of:

   (a) the asset acquired

   (b) the consideration for acquiring the asset

   (c) the market value of that consideration

   (d) the name and address of the person making the disposal

(ii) pay to the Collector General, an amount of capital gains tax equal to 15% of the market value. This tax is payable without the making of an assessment. Any tax so paid is recoverable from the seller of the asset. Where the seller can prove that payment was made to the purchaser, credit for the tax will be granted to him or her.

If the vendor obtains a clearance certificate in respect of the disposal, the capital gains tax withheld will be repaid to the purchaser.

Disposals of assets which do not involve the purchaser acquiring an asset are within the scope of these provisions.

TCA97 s980(9) The clearance procedures do not apply to the payment of insurance claims in respect of damage to property.

In the case of newly constructed houses, a builder may produce either a clearance certificate or one of the following, in respect of disposals made on or after 23 March 2000.

(i) a current Certificate of Authorisation issued under section 531, Taxes Consolidation Act, 1995. (C2 Clearance Certificate);

(ii) a current tax clearance certificate issued under section 1094 (certain licences including auctioneers licences);

(iii) a current tax clearance certificate issued under section 1095 (public sector contracts);

The builder may use the above certificate for the sale of any number of houses during the period of that certificate.

6.10 Anti-avoidance

There are provisions to prevent avoidance by means of the following:

TCA97 s549 Sales to connected persons.

TCA97 s550 Assets disposed of in a series of transactions.

TCA97 s579 Dealings through non-resident trusts (see paragraph 6.8).

TCA97 s589 Controlled companies transferring assets at undervalue.

TCA97 s590 Dealings through non-resident companies.

TCA97 s590 Abnormal dividends paid in connection with the disposal of shares or securities.

6.10.1 Miscellaneous

TCA97 s914 The administration of the tax is under the care of the Revenue Commissioners. Returns must be made by those persons liable to capital gains tax.

Issuing houses, stockbrokers, auctioneers etc may be required to give particulars of transactions carried out on behalf of clients. In the case of transactions effected on or after 6 April 1995, involving assets which are tangible, movable property, only transactions with a disposal consideration in excess of €19,050 need be returned.

7.1 Residential Property Tax

Abolished with effect from 5 April 1997. See the 31st or earlier editions of this book for more details.

7.1.1 Clearance on sale of certain residential property

FA93 s107
FA07 s118

A person selling a residential property after 11 February 2000, which had been acquired prior to 6 April 1996, and with a value in excess of the general exemption limit, must provide the purchaser with a certificate issued by the Revenue Commissioners, certifying that all residential property tax has been paid. If the certificate is not produced, the purchaser must make a deduction from the purchase price and remit the amount to the Revenue Commissioners. The amount to be deducted is 1.5% of the value in excess of the general exemption limit multiplied by the number of years that the previous owner has owned the property subject to a maximum five.

For disposals between 5 April 2006 and 31 January 2007, a clearance certificate must have been obtained where the sale proceeds exceed €1,389,000 (see Chart 55 for previous limits).

A clearance certificate was required:

(i) Where the property was acquired after 5 April 1996 and sold after 10 February 2000, or

(ii) For contracts dated on or after 1 February 2007, or

(iii) For contracts dated before 1 February 2007, where the sale was completed on or after 1 February 2007.

8.1 Stamp Duties

The legislation on stamp duties is contained in the Stamp Duties Consolidation Act, 1999 – SDCA 99.

Stamp duty is charged on instruments, i.e., written documents. Before the Finance Act 1991 stamp duty was unique among taxes in that, apart from a few exceptions, there were no statutory enforcement provisions. Taxpayer compliance was achieved in many indirect ways mainly by reason of conveyancing or commercial practice. However, under Finance Act 1991 in respect of instruments executed on or after 1 November 1991, stamp duty is compulsory and specific persons are made accountable for the duty. For example, in a sale, the accountable person is the purchaser, in a lease the accountable person is the lessee and in an instrument which operates as a gift, both the donor and donee are accountable persons.

The SDCA 99 is drafted on the assumption that documents are stamped before execution. It is normal practice however to stamp after execution, and if a document is presented for stamping within 30 days of execution no penalty is payable. If a document is submitted for adjudication (formal system whereby the Revenue Commissioners give their opinion on the amount of stamp duty payable on a particular document), stamp duty does not have to be paid until 14 days after the notice of assessment by the Revenue Commissioners is received. Furthermore, if a document was executed outside the State and retained abroad, penalties would not run until the expiration of 30 days after the document was brought into the State. The new system makes no distinction between documents executed inside the State or outside the State. If the documents are not stamped within 30 days of execution, penalties are chargeable, and these new penalties apply also to all documents whenever executed which are unstamped or insufficiently stamped on 1 November 1991.

8.1.1 Amnesty

Where an instrument which was executed prior to 1 November 1991 remained unstamped on 30 January 1992 it could be stamped free of interest and penalties if the duty was paid on or before 30 June 1992. If the instrument was stamped between 1 July 1992 and 30 September 1992 interest and penalties were charged only as if it had been executed on 1 June 1992.

8.2 Charge To Stamp Duty

SDCA99 Pt2

Stamp duty is chargeable on certain instruments and on certain transactions. Stamps are impressed on or affixed to the instruments. Stamp duty may be divided into two categories as follows:

(1) Duty based on the value of the transaction (*ad valorem* duty).

(2) Duty of a fixed amount regardless of the value of the transaction. In the vast majority of such cases the amount of duty is minimal.

The following are examples of the main items to which *ad valorem* duty applies and the rates applicable.

8.2.1 Conveyance or transfer on sale of

SDCA99 Pt7 Ch2

(a) Stocks or marketable securities

€1 per €100 or part of €100 of the consideration. Where a computation of the 1% duty on the transfer of shares falls under €1, a minimum duty of €1 will now be payable in respect of instruments executed on or after 6 February 2003.

(b) Non-Residential Property

The current rate structure, applicable to transfers of non-residential property executed on or after 4 December 2002 is summarised in Chart 27.

(c) Residential Property

Residential property was distinguished from other land and buildings with effect from 23 January 1997. The current rate structure is summarised for all categories of purchasers in Chart 27.

A transfer of property which includes both residential and non-residential elements is treated as that of two properties. The consideration is apportioned on a just and reasonable basis and the residential portion attracts the new rates while the existing rates apply to the non-residential portion.

There is provision for surcharges in the case of both over-valuation and under-valuation of the residential element in the case of a mixed property.

SDCA99 Pt3 Ch3

(d) Leases

Ad valorem duty is payable on the granting of a lease on the amount of the consideration (other than rent) moving to the lessor. The rates are similar to those charged under the head of charge "conveyance or transfer on the sale of any property other than stocks or marketable securities", including the higher rates on residential property, except that there is no consanguinity relief as given in the latter head of charge. Duty is also payable on that part of the consideration which consists of rent and the rates of duty in this case depend on the length of the term of the lease in question. Under section 75, Stamp Act 1891, an agreement for a lease for any term not exceeding 35 years is to be charged the same duty as if it were an actual lease made for the term and consideration mentioned in the agreement.

The duty on rent is:

(i) 1% of the average annual rent where term does not exceed 35 years or is indefinite.

(ii) 6% of the average annual rent where term exceeds 35 years but does not exceed 100 years.

(iii) 12% of the average annual rent where term exceeds 100 years.

These rates apply to instruments executed on or after 1 September 1990.

Domestic leases executed on or after 13 March 2008 with annual rent of less than €30,000 (previously €19,050) and where the term is indefinite or is less than 35 years are not liable to stamp duty.

8.2.2 Payment of consideration without conveyance (resting in contract)

SDCA99 s31A Section 110 Finance Act 2007 provides (subject to Ministerial Order) that a charge to stamp duty will arise in respect of a contract or agreement for the sale of an estate or interest in land in the State where 25 per cent or more of the consideration has been paid under that contract or agreement. The charge will arise where a conveyance of the lands has not been presented for stamping within 30 days after the relevant amount of consideration has been paid. The section also provides that where stamp duty has been paid in respect of a contract or agreement, in accordance with the new section, a conveyance or transfer made in conformity with that contract or agreement will not be liable to stamp duty and the Revenue Commissioners will, on application made to them, either denote the payment of the duty on the conveyance or transfer or will transfer the duty to the conveyance or transfer on production to them of a stamped contract or agreement.

8.2.3 Payment of consideration to carry out development on land

SDCA99 s31B Section 110 Finance Act 2007 provides (subject to Ministerial Order) that a charge to stamp duty will arise where the holder of an estate or interest in land in the State enters into an agreement with another person under which that other person is allowed to carry out development on that land and 25 per cent or more of the market value of the land is paid to the holder of the land, other than as consideration for the sale of all or part of the land. The charge will arise within 30 days after the relevant amount of the consideration has been paid.

8.2.4 Payment of consideration for an agreement to lease

SDCA99 s50A Section 110 Finance Act 2007 provides (subject to Ministerial Order) that an agreement for a lease for more than 35 years will be liable to the same duty as if it were an actual lease made for the term and consideration mentioned in the agreement where 25 per cent or more of that consideration has been paid. The duty will be payable by the person who has paid the consideration.

8.2.5 The CREST system

SDCA99 Pt6 The Finance Act 1996 imposes a stamp duty charge of 1% on the electronic transfer of shares. It adapts the stamp duty code to ensure that existing provisions apply notwithstanding the fact that there is no instrument which can be physically stamped.

8.2.6 Letters of renunciation

SDCA99 Pt5 Ch7 Statutory Instrument No. 152 of 1985 provided for the charging to stamp duty of a renunciation of a right under a letter of allotment to stocks or shares which are not quoted on the Stock Exchange. Such renunciations are charged at the rate applicable to securities. This provision came into effect on 11 June 1985 and was continued on by section 95 Finance Act 1986.

8.2.7 Voluntary dispositions *inter vivos*

SDCA99 Pt5 Ch2 These are liable to the same rate of duty as conveyances or transfers on sale with substitution of the market value of the property in place of the consideration on sale. Up to 9 June 1983, however, where the disposition was in consideration of marriage it was exempt from duty provided it was for the benefit of a party to the marriage or of a party to and the issue of the marriage. This relief was abolished by section 92 Finance Act 1983.

8.2.8 Where consideration cannot be ascertained

SDCA99 Pt5 Ch2 In the case of an instrument where the amount or value of the Ch2 consideration cannot be ascertained at the date of the execution of the instrument, the Revenue Commissioners may charge *ad valorem* duty on the value of the property conveyed or transferred.

8.2.9 Valuation of property chargeable with stamp duty

SDCA99 sPt3 The provisions of sections 15, 16 and 17 CAT Act 1976 in respect of the market value of property are applied to stamp duty in respect of instruments executed on or after 1 November 1991. With effect from 23 May 1994 only the provisions of section 15 CAT Act 1976 apply.

8.2.10 Fixed rate of duty

SDCA99 Sch1 The following are examples of the main items to which a fixed rate of duty applies:

Cheques, drafts and orders drawn on an account in the State	€0.30
Duplicate or counterpart of any instrument chargeable (max)	€12.50
Credit/Charge cards	€30 per a/c p.y.
Debit cards	€5 per a/c p.y.
Cash ATM cards	€5 per a/c p.y.
Combined cards	€10 per a/c p.y*.

The rates for ATM/debit/combined cards took effect for the year ending 31 December 2007 and for charge/credit card accounts for the year ending 1 April 2008.

*With effect from 1 January 2006, the stamp duty charged on combined cards is based on the function of the combined card used in a year. If only one function is used in a year (i.e., as an ATM card only or a Laser card only), the current charge of €10 will be reduced to €5.

Finance Act 2005 provides for an exemption from a second or subsequent charge to stamp duty for financial cards such as credit cards, charge cards, ATM cards, Laser cards and combined cards arising from the switching of accounts within a financial institution, or from one financial institution to another, in the same year of charge. The change in relation to credit cards and charge cards took place with effect form 2 April 2005, while the change in relation to ATM cards, Laser cards and combined cards took effect from 1 January 2006.

8.3 Deductions, Reliefs and Exemptions

8.3.1 Deductions in relation to certain conveyances and transfers

SDCA99 Pt7 Section 34, Finance Act 1978 restricts the deductions which can be made from the value of a property in relation to a conveyance or transfer operating as a voluntary disposition and in relation to a conveyance in contemplation of sale made with a view to a possible later sale to the transferee. Following the passing of the 1993 Finance Act duty must be determined without regard to the following deductions:

(a) any power on the exercise of which the property may be revested in the person from whom it was conveyed or transferred;

(b) any annuity or other periodic payment reserved out of the property or any part of it, or any life or other interest so reserved, being an interest which is subject to forfeiture;

(c) any right of residence, support, maintenance, or other right of a similar nature which the property is subject to or charged with, except where such rights are reserved in favour of the transferor or the spouse of the transferor and in any such case regard shall be had to such rights only to the extent that their value does not exceed 10% of the unencumbered value of the property.

8.3.2 Transactions between related persons

In the case of a conveyance or transfer on sale or in the case of a conveyance or transfer operating as a voluntary disposition inter vivos where the instrument contains a certificate to the effect that the parties to the transaction are related, the duty payable thereon is restricted to 50% of the duty that would otherwise be payable. A person is related to another if he is his lineal descendant, parent, grandparent, step parent, brother or sister of a parent or brother or sister, or lineal descendant of a parent, husband or wife or brother or sister. Transactions between spouses are exempt.

With effect from 31 March 2006, a child includes a foster child who is defined as a person who, prior to the date of execution of the instrument has resided with, was under the care of, and was maintained at the expense of the transferor or lessor throughout a period of five years, or periods which together comprised at least, five years, prior to the person attaining 18 years of age, but only if such claim is not based on the uncorroborated testimony of only one witness.

8.3.3 Transfer on divorce

As stated above there is a total stamp duty exemption for transfers between spouses. This section incorporates into the Finance Act, provisions already included in the Family Law Act 1995 and the Family Law (Divorce) Act 1996. These provide that where under any order of the Family Law or Family Law Divorce Acts, property is transferred on the dissolution of a marriage, the stamp duty exemption applies.

However, this exemption will not apply where the property, although transferred under a Family Law Order, is conveyed to a person other than one of the parties to the marriage. Thus transfers to children are not exempt.

With effect from 10 February 2000, the exemption is extended to transfers between former spouses executed on foot of a foreign court order or other similar determination made under or in consequence of the dissolution of a marriage where the dissolution is entitled to be recognised as valid in the State (see 8.2.1 (c) Residential Property).

8.3.4 Young farmers

SDCA99 s81, 81AA

Transfers of land between 1 January 2000 and 31 December 2008 to young trained farmers are exempt from stamp duty. The features of this exemption are as follows:

(a) The relief applies in respect of stamp duty on the transfer of agricultural land (including buildings) to young trained farmers.

(b) The relief applies to sales and gifts where no power of revocation exists.

(c) A young trained farmer is a person under 35 years of age at the date of transfer who meets certain educational attainments. While these educational attainments must still be met, the requirement for specific minimum education attainments at the date of transfer of the land was abolished by Finance Act 2007.

(d) The instrument of transfer must contain a certificate stating that the provisions of the section apply.

(e) The young trained farmer must furnish a written declaration to the Revenue Commissioners confirming that for a period of five years after the date of transfer he intends to spend not less than 50% of his normal working time in farming the land and that he will retain ownership of the land. The five-year period commences from the date the claim for repayment of duty is made to Revenue.

(f) Where all the training conditions have not been satisfied at the date of transfer it is possible to apply for a refund of stamp duty paid provided the conditions are satisfied within four years (previously three years) of the date of execution of the instrument.

(g) The Revenue Commissioners must adjudicate all instruments where relief is claimed.

(h) The Revenue Commissioners have power to claw back the relief if the land is disposed of within the five-year period and is not replaced within one year with other agricultural land.

(i) The timeframe in which a refund claim can be made was extended by Finance Act 2007 from within six months to within four years of attaining the educational qualifications.

Sections 119 and 120 Finance Act 2005 provide a formula which calculates the amount of the claw-back of stamp duty by way of penalty in respect of disposals or part disposals of land on or after 3 February 2005. The extent of the penalty will relate to the amount of the proceeds not re-invested.

8.3.5 Farm consolidation relief

(a) Exchange of Lands

SDCA99 s81B Section 121 Finance Act 2005 provides for a relief from stamp duty on an exchange of farm land between two farmers for the purposes of consolidating each farmer's holding where the lands exchanged are of equal value. In a case where the lands exchanged are not of equal value, stamp duty will be charged on the amount of the difference in the values of the land concerned. Where consideration is paid for the difference, it must be payable in cash.

The following main conditions must be satisfied before the relief will be granted by the Revenue Commissioners under the section:

(i) There must be a valid consolidation certificate issued by Teagasc in existence at the date of the exchange of lands which must be submitted to the Revenue Commissioners in support of an application for relief.

(ii) The farmers involved in the exchange of land must each sign a declaration, for submission to the Revenue Commissioners, to the effect that each of them will remain a farmer (i.e., will spend not less than 50% of that persons normal working time farming) and will farm the land exchanged for a period of at least five years from the date of the exchange.

(iii) All the joint owners of the land exchanged including the farmers must make a declaration, for submission to the Revenue Commissioners, to the effect that it is the intention of each of them to retain ownership of their interest in the land and to use the land for the purpose of farming, for at least five years from the date of the exchange.

(iv) The instruments effecting the exchange of land must be submitted at the same time to the Revenue Commissioners for adjudication.

The section provides that the Minister for Agriculture and Food with the consent of the Minister for Finance may make the necessary guidelines in relation to how applications for consolidation certificates are to be made to Teagasc and setting out, inter alia, the conditions of such consolidation.

The section also provides for a claw-back of the relief where the land or part of the land included in the exchange is disposed of or partly disposed of before the end of the five-year holding period. A claw-back of the relief will not occur where such land is compulsorily acquired or is the subject of another exchange of farmland to which section 81B applies. In addition, the section provides for penalties to apply where a false declaration is made or where an invalid consolidation certificate is used to obtain the relief. The section applies to instruments executed on or after 1 July 2005 and on or before 30 June 2007.

(b) Sale and Purchase of Farm Lands within 18 months

SDCA99 s81C Section 104 Finance Act 2007 provides for a relief from stamp duty where a farmer sells farm land and purchases farm land, in order to consolidate his holding, where both the sale and purchase of farm land occur within 18 months of each other.

Where there is a purchase and sale of farm land within 18 months of each other that satisfy the "conditions of consolidation", then stamp duty will only be paid on the purchase to the extent that the value of the farm land that is purchased exceeds the value of the farm land that is sold. If the sale takes place before the purchase, then relief will be given at the time of purchase. However, if the purchase takes place first, then stamp duty will have to be paid but on the subsequent sale a claim for repayment can be made to the Revenue Commissioners.

Whether a claim for relief for stamp duty arises on a purchase of farm land where a sale of farm land has already taken place or where relief is claimed in relation to a purchase where the sale of farm land occurs after the purchase, the following main conditions must be satisfied before relief will be granted:

(i) There must be a valid consolidation certificate issued by Teagasc in relation to the purchase and sale of land, occurring within 18 months of each other. This certificate must be submitted to the Revenue Commissioners in support of an application for relief together with the instrument giving effect to the purchase of the land and a certified copy of the instrument giving effect to the sale of the land.

(ii) The farmer, or each of them if there is more than one, involved in the purchase of the land must each sign a declaration, for submission to the Revenue Commissioners, to the effect that the farmer will remain a farmer (i.e., will spend not less than 50% of that person's normal working time farming) and will farm the land purchased for at least five years from the date on which the first claim for relief in respect of the purchase of land is made to the Revenue Commissioners.

(iii) All the joint owners of the land purchased, including the farmers, must make a declaration, for submission to the Revenue Commissioners, to the effect that it is the intention of each of them to retain ownership of their interest in the land and to use the land for the purpose of farming, for at least five years from the date the first claim for relief in respect of the purchase of land is made to the Revenue Commissioners.

(iv) The instrument giving effect to the purchase of the land must be submitted to the Revenue Commissioners for adjudication.

The section provides that The Minister for Agriculture and Food with the consent of the Minister for Finance, will make the necessary guidelines detailing how applications for consolidation certificates are to be made to Teagasc under the new section and also setting out the conditions of consolidation.

Finally, the section also provides for a claw-back of the relief where the land or part of the land purchased is disposed of or partly disposed of before the end of the five year holding period. Such a claw-back will not occur where the land purchased is compulsorily acquired. The section provides for penalties to apply where a false declaration is made or where an invalid consolidation certificate is used to obtain the relief.

The relief applies to instruments executed on or after 1 July 2007 and on or before 30 June 2009. However, the commencement of the section is the subject of a Ministerial Order and is dependent on State Aid approval from the European Commission.

8.3.6 Exemptions/exceptions

First time buyers

SDCA 99 s93B (A) General

With regard to instruments executed on or after 31 March 2007, owner occupying, first-time buyers of residential property, whether new or second hand are exempt from stamp duty

A first-time buyer is a person (or, where there is more than one buyer, each of such persons):

(i) who has not on any previous occasion, either individually or jointly, purchased or built on his/her own behalf a house (in Ireland or abroad), and

(ii) where the property purchased is occupied by the purchaser, or a person on his behalf, as his/her only or principal place of residence, and

(iii) where no rent, other than rent under the rent-a-room-scheme, is derived from the property within five years of the date of transfer giving effect to the purchase. For instruments executed before 5 December 2007, to the extent that a dwelling-house or apartment is rented out on or after 5 December 2007, it will not involve a claw-back of the relief where this occurs in the third, fourth or fifth year of ownership. For instruments executed on or after 5 December 2007, the claw-back period is reduced from five to two years.

(B) Separated/Divorced Spouse

A person whose marriage is the subject of a decree of divorce, judicial separation, nullity or a deed of separation may be treated as a first-time purchaser once and only once where the person buys another house to live in. The conditions for this are that the person no longer retains an interest in the former marital home and that at the time of the new purchase, the spouse (or former spouse) of that person continues to occupy the former marital home, which was occupied by both of them prior to the decree or prior to the deed of separation being made.

This latter condition was relaxed by section 108 Finance Act 2007 to provide that the spouse (or former spouse), must occupy the former marital home, as his or her only or main residence, following the granting of the decree or the making of the deed of separation, but does not necessarily have to still be occupying it at a time when the person, who originally left the marital home, purchases a new home. However, first-time purchaser relief will be denied to that person, where at the date of the decree or at the date the deed of separation is made, the person has an interest in another house/apartment apart from the former marital home.

Finally, in a case where the person, leaving the former marital home, would be denied first-time purchaser relief on the purchase of a new home, for the sole reason, that he or she goes ahead and purchases a new home in anticipation of, but prior to, the actual grant of the decree or the making of the deed of separation, that person can apply to the Revenue Commissioners for a repayment of the stamp duty paid on the purchase of the new home, where, subject to complying with certain conditions, the purchase is made in connection with, and within six months of, the granting of the decree or the making of the deed of separation. The above changes apply to instruments executed on or after 1 February 2007.

SDCA99 s92b (C) Anti-Avoidance

Finance Act 2008 introduced an anti-avoidance provision to prevent abuse of the "first-time purchaser relief" and to ensure that the relief is restricted to genuine first-time purchasers. The provision deals with a situation where part of the consideration is derived from an unconditional gift or a bona fide loan evidenced in writing made to the individual for the purposes of the purchase of the property.

To be a bona fide unconditional gift it is essential that:

(i) the donor is not a party to the instrument giving effect to the purchase of the dwelling-house or apartment, or

(ii) that the donor cannot intend to or in fact occupy the dwelling-house or apartment with the purchaser, as the only or principal residence of each of them, or

(iii) there is no arrangement for the transfer of the dwelling-house or apartment or an interest in the dwelling-house or apartment to the donor at same time in the future.

Similar rules are introduced in relation to the definition of a bona fide loan.

These restrictions do not apply where the donor of the gift or the individual making the loan to the purchaser is a parent or the purchaser.

New property – owner-occupier other than first-time buyer

SDCA99 s91A Section 91A SDCA 1999 provides that certain smaller new residential properties may avail of full exemption from stamp duty. This provision applies to new residential properties only. The size of the property is fundamental to the operation of the relief, and there is a requirement for certification of the property. The certification includes certification of the tax clearance status of the builder also. It is necessary for the purchaser to occupy the property as an owner-occupier and not to receive rent in relation to the property other than rent derived from the provision of furnished residential accommodation while occupying the property (rent-a-room scheme). It is not necessary for the purchaser to be a first-time buyer.

SDCA99 s92 Section 92 SDCA 1999 provides that certain larger new residential properties may avail of a significant reduction in the consideration chargeable to stamp duty (up to 75%). This provision applies to new residential properties only. There are also certain certification requirements in relation to this relief. It is necessary for the purchaser to occupy the property as an owner-occupier and not to receive rent in relation to the property other than rent derived from the provision of furnished residential accommodation while occupying the property (rent-a-room scheme). It is not necessary for the purchaser to be a first-time buyer.

Transfer of site to a child

SDCA99 s83A The transfer or lease of a site to a child, the purpose of which is for the child to build their own home. The market value of the site must not exceed €500,000 in respect of instruments executed on or after 5 December 2007 (previously €254,000). The exemption is subject to a number of conditions and applies to instruments executed on or after 6 December 2000.

The size of the site is limited to 0.4047 hectare (i.e., 1 acre) exclusive of the area of land on which the child's principal private residence is to be constructed, in respect of instruments executed on or after 1 February 2007.

Transfer of farmland from child to parent

SDCA99 s83B Certain transfers of farmland from a child to a parent as consideration for land received from their parents where retirement relief under S599 TCA 1997 is being claimed, in respect of instruments executed on or after 2 April 2007.

Transfer on delivery

The property in chattels, e.g., stock in trade, plant and machinery (other than fixed plant and machinery), motor vehicles, cash, bank balances, generally passes by delivery without documentation. Accordingly no liability to stamp duty arises if there is no documentation. If the chattels, however, form part of a larger transaction with other property which is liable to duty on conveyance it is aggregated with the other property for the purpose of determining the rate of duty which applies to the conveyance of that other property. If the chattels are included in the conveyance, they are liable to stamp duty. Under section 59, Stamp Act 1891, certain chattels are liable to stamp duty at contract stage if included in a contract for sale.

Liquidations

Transfers on liquidation of a company where the shareholders receive distributions in specie of the property of the company.

Reconstructions and amalgamations

Certain reconstructions and amalgamations of companies involving the transfer of shares in one company to another attract a zero rate of duty. The conditions to be satisfied are:

(i) There must be a scheme of reconstruction or amalgamation effected for bona fide commercial reasons and not having as a main purpose the avoidance of tax.

(ii) The acquiring company must be a limited company.

(iii) The acquiring company must issue new shares in exchange for 90% or more of the shares in the target company.

(iv) The shares being issued in the acquiring company must represent at least 90% of the value of the shares in the target company.

(v) The acquiring company must retain its beneficial ownership of the shares in the target company for at least two years unless it loses this as a result of a reconstruction, amalgamation or liquidation.

(vi) The relief applies where the acquiring company is registered in the State or in another EU State, while the target company may be registered anywhere in the world.

(vii) Adjudication by the Revenue Commissioners is necessary within 12 months of the transaction.

The same relief from duty applies where the undertaking of one company is transferred to another provided that, in general, similar conditions are fulfilled.

Transfers between associated companies

Duty on such transactions was abolished with effect from 8 February 1995. To qualify for this relief certain conditions must be satisfied as follows:

(a) The transferor was entitled to the entire beneficial interest in the relevant property and this becomes vested in the transferee.

(b) At the time of the transfer one of the companies owns directly or indirectly at least 90% of the issued share capital of the other, or at least 90% of the issued share capital of each is owned directly or indirectly by a third company. The provisions of section 156 Corporation Tax Act 1976 apply in determining indirect ownership. The 1990 Finance Act extends the 90% relationship to being entitled to not less than 90% of the profits and not less than 90% of the assets on distribution, in the event of the company being wound up. The 90% share capital test was changed to exclude fixed rate preference shares in respect of instruments executed on or after 6 February 2003.

(c) There is no arrangement whereunder the consideration is provided directly or indirectly by a person outside the prescribed 90% relationship.

(d) Without prejudice to the generality of the previous condition an arrangement shall be treated as being in existence if it is one whereunder the transferor or the transferee, or a body corporate associated with either is to be enabled to provide any of the consideration, or is to part with it, by or in consequence of the carrying out of transactions involving, or any or them involving, a payment or other disposition by a person other than the body corporate so associated.

(e) There is no arrangement whereunder the property was previously transferred directly or indirectly by a person outside the prescribed 90% relationship.

(f) The transfer must not be made in pursuance of or in connection with an arrangement whereby the transferor and the transferee are to cease to be associated in the prescribed 90% relationship.

(g) The relief will be lost where the prescribed 90% relationship ceases to exist within a period of two years from the date of the conveyance or transfer.

(h) Adjudication by the Revenue Commissioners is necessary. The relief will also be granted to foreign bodies corporate with effect from 6 February 2003 which do not have a capital structure based on share capital, provided that they have a capital structure which is equivalent to a share capital structure and comply with all the other conditions of the relief.

General exemptions

(a) Transfer of shares in:

(i) Irish Government or Oireachtas stocks, the payment of the interest on which is guaranteed by the Minister for Finance, or any loan stock of the ESB, RTE or Bord Gáis Éireann, where the interest is not so guaranteed. Irish Telecommunications Investments plc continues to benefit from the exemption but only in relation to loan stock issued before 15 February 2001.

(ii) UK Government stocks which are registered in the books of the Bank of Ireland in Dublin.

(iii) Transfers of stocks or securities to which s92 FA 1973 applies.

(b) Instruments for the sale or transfer either absolutely or by way of mortgages of ships or aircraft.

(c) Wills.

(d) Bills of exchange (including cheques) and promissory notes drawn outside the State.

(e) Conveyances, transfers or leases of land and houses for charitable purposes in Ireland to bodies of persons or trusts which have been established for charitable purposes only.

(f) Transfers between spouses whether separately or jointly except in sub-sale situations.

(g) Any instrument under which any land, easement, way-leave, water right or other right whatsoever over or in respect of the land or water is acquired by the Dublin Docklands Development Authority or any of its 100% subsidiaries.

(h) Instruments securing the advancement of moneys by the Housing Finance Agency plc to housing authorities.

(i) Leases for an indefinite period or any term not exceeding 35 years, of any dwelling-house, part of a dwelling-house or apartment at a rent not exceeding €19,050 per annum.

(j) Commercial woodlands where such woodlands are sold or leased with land. (stamp duty applies to the land.)

(k) A licence or a lease granted by the Minister for Energy in respect of oil exploration or the sale, assignment or transfer of any such licence or lease or any right or interest therein.

(l) Conveyance or transfer of units in investment undertakings and units in certain unit trusts.

(m) Conveyance or transfer of stocks or marketable securities of a company which is not registered in the State provided that such conveyance does not relate to:

  (i) any immovable property situated in the State, or any right over or interest in such property, or

  (ii) any stocks or marketable securities of a company having a register in the State.

(n) Certain instruments used predominantly in the financial services industry including the following:

  (i) a debt factoring agreement.

  (ii) a swap agreement.

  (iii) a forward agreement.

  (iv) a financial futures agreement.

  (v) an option agreement.

  (vi) a combination of any two or more of the instruments specified under (i) to (v) above.

  (vii) a transfer of, or agreement to transfer, any instruments specified under (i) to (v) above or a combination of any two or more such instruments or an American depositary receipt.

(o) Foreign immovable property provided the instrument of transfer does not relate to Irish immovable property or shares.

(p) Instruments executed by or on behalf of the National Treasury Management Agency and similar instruments executed by or on behalf of the Minister for Finance.

(q) Instruments relating to the acquisition of property in the Temple Bar area by Temple Bar Properties Limited or any of its subsidiaries.

(r) Shared ownership leases of houses and for any subsequent instrument whereby the lessee acquires the remaining interest of the lessor in the property. The shared ownership lease must have been granted by an "appropriate person" as defined.

(s) The issue and transfer of specified categories of marketable debt instruments including certain types of corporate bonds and mortgage-backed securities.

(t) Transfers of foreign national and local government securities.

(u) Certain transfers of unquoted loan stock.

(v) Certain stock borrowing, stock return and stock repro transactions.

(w) The transfer, sale or assignment of mortgages by a housing authority to a designated body or the transfer of securities issued by a designated body.

(x) Transfers or leases of land to a voluntary body approved by the Minister for the Environment and Local Government under section 6 of the Housing (Miscellaneous Provisions) Act, 1992 for the purposes of the Housing Acts, 1966 to 1998. The exemption applies to instruments executed on or after 15 February 2001.

(y) Transfers or leases of land to the National Building Agency Limited, for the purposes of the Housing Acts, 1966 to 1998. The exemption applies to instruments executed on or after 26 January 2001.

(z) A policy of life assurance issued or varied after 1 January 2001.

(aa) With effect from 1 January 2003, all instruments executed by or on behalf of the National Development Finance Agency in respect of any property being acquired by the Agency and any acquisitions of land by a company set up by the Agency under section 5 of the National Development Finance Agency Act 2002, from the Agency, from another company set up under section 5 of the Act or from a State authority referred to in Schedule 1 of the Act.

(bb) The sale, transfer or other disposition of intellectual property as defined. Intellectual property includes any patent, trademark, copyright, registered design, design right, invention, domain name, supplementary protection certificate or plant breeders' rights.

SDCA99 s82A (cc) With effect from 31 March 2006, donations of publicly quoted securities to approved bodies who come within the scheme of tax relief for donations to approved charities, schools and third-level colleges, as well as to other approved bodies under section 848A TCA 1997.

SDCA99 s88B (dd) With effect from 31 March 2006, any instrument made for the purposes of or in connection with a scheme of reconstruction or amalgamation under which a foreign fund transfers its assets to a domestic fund in return for the domestic fund issuing units in the domestic fund to the holders of units in the foreign fund.

SDCA99 s88C (ee) With effect from 31 March 2006, any instrument made for the purposes of or in connection with the reconstruction or amalgamation of a common contractual fund to which section 739H(3) TCA 1997 applies.

SDCA99 s99A (ff) With effect from 31 March 2006, any instrument under which any land, easement, way-leave, etc. is acquired by the Courts Service.

SDCA99 s101A (gg) With effect from 1 January 2005, the sale, transfer or other disposition of any EU Single Farm Payment Entitlement.

SDCA99 s82B (hh) The acquisition of land by a sporting body approved under section 235 TCA 1997, where the land will be used for the sole purpose of promoting athletic or amateur games or sports – in respect of instruments executed on or after 7 December 2006.

SDCA99 s88D (ii) With effect from 13 March 2008, instruments made for the purpose of or in connection with the reconstruction or amalgamation of certain investment undertakings to which section 739H TCA 1997 applies.

SDCA99 s90A (jj) With effect from 5 December 2007, the sale, transfer or other disposition of a "greenhouse gas emissions allowance" as defined.

SDCA99 s106B (kk) With effect from 13 March 2008, the conveyance, transfer or lease of a house, building or land by or to a housing authority in connection with any of its functions under the Housing Acts 1966 to 2004 or by or to the Affordable Homes Partnership in connection with the services specified in Article 4(2) of the Affordable Homes Partnership (Establishment) Order 2005, as amended.

8.4 Companies' Capital Duty

SDCA99 Pt8 Abolished for transactions effected on or after 7 December 2005. See the 31st or earlier editions for details.

8.5 Miscellaneous

8.5.1 Management provisions

SDCA 99 Pt11 Ch7 The Finance Act 2003 inserted a new Chapter 7 into the Stamp Duties Consolidation Act 1999, containing three new sections:

(i) Repayments

Section 159A restricts the repayment of stamp duty to valid claims made within four years of, inter alia, the date an instrument was stamped by Revenue with effect from 31 October 2003. A valid claim is one where Revenue has been provided with all the information to enable them establish the extent of the overpayment. This measure was introduced with transitional arrangements.

(ii) Interest

Section 159B provides that with effect from 1 November 2003 interest on a repayment will only be paid where the repayment has not been made by Revenue within six months of receiving a valid claim for repayment. An exception to this general rule is that interest will be paid from the date of the event giving rise to the repayment, where Revenue has made an error in the operation of stamp duty. This section also provides that the new rate of interest on such repayments will be at the rate of 0.011% per day or part of a day (see Chart 12 for previous rates).

(iii) Assessments

Section 159C restricts the period with effect from 1 January 2005 within which Revenue may make enquiries or raise assessments in relation to under-payments of stamp duty to a period of four years from, inter alia, the date an instrument was stamped by Revenue. This restriction will not apply where the underpayment arises from fraud or neglect on the part of the taxpayer.

8.5.2 Surcharge

SDCA99 Pt2 The Finance Act 1991 introduced a surcharge as a penalty where the market value of the property has been understated by the accountable person.

With effect from 23 May 1994 the surcharge applies only when the submitted value is less than the ascertained value by more than 15% (previously 10%). The rates of surcharge (which apply to the total duty payable) are now as follows:

Amount of Understatement	*Surcharge %*
More than 15% but not more than 30%	25
More than 30% but not more than 50%	50
More than 50%	100

8.5.3 Appeals

SDCA99 Pt4 Up to the date of passing of the 1994 Finance Act any person aggrieved by a decision or determination of the Revenue Commissioners, had the right to appeal to the Appeal Commissioners, High Court or Property Arbitrators depending on the circumstances. As regards instruments executed after 23 May 1994 appeal provisions similar to those which apply for income tax apply for stamp duty purposes (See paragraph 1.1.12). In the case of appeals against the value of land, these are heard by the Land Values Reference Committee.

8.5.4 Payment of stamp duty on instruments

SDCA99 Pt2 This section enables the Revenue Commissioners to enter into agreements at their discretion for the payment of stamp duty under an agreement whereby, at regular intervals, stamp duty is paid in one sum equal to the total duty which would have been payable had each instrument been stamped individually. The 1994 Finance Act confirms that the duty is payable on the VAT exclusive consideration in the case of a conveyance, transfer or lease of property.

8.5.5 Anti-avoidance

SDCA99 Pt5 Ch2 (a) An anti-avoidance measure introduced by the Finance Act 1981 deems certain conveyances involving sub-purchasers to be voluntary dispositions inter vivos, thus rendering them liable to duty on the value of the property conveyed.

(b) Statutory Instrument No. 151 of 1985 which came into operation on 11 June 1985 contained anti-avoidance provisions in relation to the stamp duty chargeable on certain instruments. The instruments affected are as follows:

SCDA99 Pt5 Ch4 (i) A conveyance or transfer on sale where the vendor of property enters into an agreement for a long lease, or grants rights in relation to the property. In this case, any conveyance or transfer subject to the agreement, of the property by the vendor shall be charged to stamp duty as a conveyance or transfer on sale of the property for a consideration equal to the value of the property and the value shall be determined without regard to the agreement.

(ii) An instrument which evidences the surrender of a leasehold interest, or the merger of a leasehold interest in a superior interest. In this case, the instrument shall be charged to the same stamp duty as if it were a surrender of that leasehold interest.

SDCA99 Pt5 Ch2 (iii) A declaration by deed to the effect that a term in land is enlarged in a case where the term was created by an instrument executed within six years of the date of the execution of the deed. In this case, the instrument shall be charged to stamp duty as a conveyance or transfer on sale of that land for a consideration equal to the value of the land and that value shall be determined without regard to the term or any part thereof.

(c) Where an instrument effects a transfer of immovable property in the State in consideration for any other property (wherever situated and whether movable or immovable) duty will be payable on the value of the relevant immovable property situated in the State thereby conveyed or transferred.

SDCA99 Pt5 Ch8 (d) With effect from 27 March 1998 contracts for the sale of bearer shares are liable to stamp duty.

Chapter 9 Value-Added Tax

9.1 Value-Added Tax

9.1.1 Legislation

The principal pieces of Irish legislation governing the value-added tax system are as follows:

Value-Added Tax Act 1972 (Principal Act) – PA

Value-Added Tax (Amendment) Act 1978 – VAT (A)A

Value-Added Tax Regulations – R

While there is some Irish case law on VAT including decisions by the Appeal Commissioners, judgments from the European Court of Justice (ECJ) take precedence and are binding on all EU Member States.

9.1.2 European Union Directives

The EU Council issues VAT Directives to the Member States and the Member States must modify their VAT legislation accordingly. EU law takes precedence in the event of an inconsistency. The most important Directives are the Sixth, Seventh and Eight VAT Directives and the Second Simplification Directive.

Finance Act 2008 has updated the wording of the VAT Act to bring it in line with the recast of the EU Sixth Directive, i.e., EU Directive 2006/112/EC. The main focus in the 2008 Finance Act is the amendment of the definition of "taxable person" and the introduction of a new definition of an "accountable person".
A taxable person is now defined as "any person who independently carries out any business in the State" which now includes persons engaged in business activities irrespective of whether they are VATable or exempt business activities. Persons who are required to register and account for Irish VAT are now referred to as "accountable persons".

9.1.3 Charge

PA s2; VAT(A)A s3; PA s8; FA94 s94; FA95 s124; FA06 s94

Value-added tax is chargeable on the supply of goods and services within the State by a taxable person in the course or furtherance of any business carried on by him, and on goods imported into the State from outside the EU. VAT is also chargeable on the intra-Community acquisition of goods by VAT registered persons and on the intra-Community acquisition of new means of transport such as motor vehicles, boats, etc. by either a registered or unregistered person.

The amount on which VAT is chargeable is the total consideration which the person supplying goods or services becomes entitled to receive. In addition, in certain circumstances, a VAT charge may arise where no consideration is payable, such as the supply of canteen facilities free of charge.

Accountable persons account for VAT on their outputs and they are allowed credit against this liability for tax borne on business purchases and other inputs as evidenced by correctly prepared VAT invoices. Accountable persons must be registered with the Revenue Commissioners for VAT purposes. A detailed definition of "accountable person" is included in section 8 of the Value-Added Tax Act 1972 as amended.

9.1.4 Supply and self supply of goods

PA s3 The term "supply" includes:

VAT(A)A s4; FA89 s54 (a) The transfer of ownership of goods by agreement, including the transfer of ownership of goods to a business providing hire purchase services (effective from 1 May 2007), whether or not accompanied by a transfer of possession of the goods.

FA92 s167; FA95 s120; FA07 s76 (b) The handing over of possession of goods under a hire purchase contract. With effect from 1 May 2007 the sale of all repossessed goods is liable to VAT. Previously the sale was only liable to VAT if the customer was entitled to a VAT input credit.

FA96 s89 (c) The sale of movable goods pursuant to a contract under which commission is payable on purchase or sale by an agent or auctioneer who concludes agreements in his own name but for the account of another.

(d) Compulsory acquisition or statutory seizure.

(e) The application by an accountable person for the purpose of any business carried on by him of goods which he has acquired, except where a full input credit would be allowable to him in respect of the application of the goods.

(f) The appropriation by an accountable person of goods, on which an input credit was wholly or partly deductible, for a non business purpose, or the disposal of such goods free of charge.

(g) Intra-Community transfers (with certain exceptions).

(h) Where a liquidator, receiver or trustee in bankruptcy sells business assets in satisfaction of a debt of an accountable person or in the course of the winding up of a company, the sale is deemed to be a supply of goods by the accountable person in the course of business.

FA01 s182 The disposal of goods by an insurer in connection with an insurance claim is not a supply of goods where the insured was not entitled to deduct any part of the VAT incurred on the acquisition of the goods.

FA07 s76 Changes to the VAT treatment of businesses providing hire purchase services are effective from 1 May 2007. The provisions clarify that the transfer of ownership of goods, by a hire purchase provider pursuant to a hire purchase contract, is deemed not be a supply of goods.

9.1.5 Place where goods supplied

PA s3 The place where goods (other than goods sold by mail order or distance selling) are supplied is deemed to be:

(a) Where the supply requires their transportation, the place where the transportation begins.

(b) In the case of the supply and installation or assembly of goods where the goods are installed or assembled. Where a non-established trader sells goods by means of a supply-and-install contract in Ireland to either:

 (i) a VAT registered person;

 (ii) a Department of State, local authority or body established by Statute; or

 (iii) a person involved in a VAT exempt activity

 the customer rather than the supplier is required to self-account for VAT on a reverse charge basis.

(c) In any other case the place where the goods are located at the time of the supply.

(d) With effect from 1 January 1993 in the case of the intra-community acquisition of goods, where the dispatch or transportation ends. This is modified, however, so that where the person acquiring the goods quotes his VAT registered number the acquisition is deemed to be within the territory of the Member State which issued that number.

(e) The supply of gas and electricity to a taxable dealer, a person whose principal activity is the acquisition of natural gas and electricity for the purpose of resale, will be taxed where the taxable dealer has his business.

(f) The supply of gas and electricity to a person other than a taxable dealer will be the place where the recipient uses and consumes those goods.

Paragraph (e) and (f) will have effect from 1 January 2005 and these new provisions were introduced to incorporate the EU Council Directive 2003/92/EC into Irish VAT legislation.

Conversely, where a foreign taxable entity supplies gas and electricity to an Irish recipient which constitutes one of the following, i.e., an accountable person, a State Department or local authority, a body established by statute or an exempt entity, the Irish recipient shall be considered as an accountable person and shall be liable to account for Irish VAT on the reverse charge basis.

9.1.6 Supplies by VAT-registered traders in Ireland

Where an accountable person in the State supplies goods to a VAT-registered trader in another Member State, the supply is zero-rated in Ireland and is liable to VAT as an intra-Community acquisition in the other Member State. However, the Irish supplier must ensure the purchaser in the other Member State is registered for VAT before zero-rating the supply of goods.

9.1.7 Mail order and distance selling

Special rules apply regarding the place of supply in the case of mail order and distance selling (i.e., where the supplier arranges for the goods purchased to be transported to a private individual or to any other non-accountable person in another Member State). Where a mail order or any other type of distance selling business, located in another Member State, sells goods with a value in excess of €35,000 in Ireland in any one year, the goods are taxable in Ireland rather than in the Member State where the seller is located and the seller is obliged to register and to account for VAT in Ireland.

9.1.8 Private individuals

As regards goods purchased by individuals in other Member States (other than a new means of transport or purchasing goods by way of mail order or distance selling) VAT is payable in the Member State of purchase at the rate of VAT applicable there and no intra-Community acquisition arises. Private individuals are therefore free to purchase goods at VAT-inclusive prices in other Member States and are not liable to an additional Irish VAT charge provided the purchases are for personal and not business use.

9.1.9 Place where services supplied

PA s5;
FA95 s123;
FA97 s99
FA99 s121
FA05 s101

In general the place of supply of services is where the business of the establishment. Problems can arise, however, in the case of the supply of international services and the following are general guidelines in this regard.

(i) Immovable goods

The place where services connected with immovable property are supplied is the place where the property is situated.

(ii) Transport services

These are deemed to be supplied where the transport takes place. The 1992 Finance Act, however, amended the position relating to intra-Community goods transport services. The changes provided that, where a customer is registered for VAT, supplies of intra-Community goods transport and related ancillary and agency services are treated as being supplied in the Member State of issue of the customer's VAT number.

Where a customer is not registered for VAT, the place of supply is deemed to be the place of departure in the case of transport and transport agency services and the place where the services are physically performed as regards ancillary services and associated agency services.

(iii) Telecommunications services, radio or television broadcasting services

These are deemed to be supplied in the State in cases where they are supplied to private individuals in the State by non-EU suppliers

(iv) Means of transport

Where a means of transport, supplied by a lessor in Ireland is used outside the EU, the place of supply is deemed to be outside the EU.

VAT(A)A s27 ***(v) "Fourth Schedule" services***

These include advertising services, consultancy, legal and accounting services, data processing services, banking, financial and insurance services, the provision of staff, transfers and assignments of copyright patents, licences, trade marks and similar rights, hiring out of movable goods (other than means of transport), telecommunication services, radio and television broadcasting services, electronically supplied services and access to, and transport/transmission through gas and electricity systems and directly related services. There are complicated provisions determining the place of supply of these services and this will vary according to the place of residence or establishment of the customer and according as to whether or not the services are supplied for business purposes (See Chart 33). Generally, any person within the State acquiring a Fourth Schedule service for business purposes from a foreign supplier is chargeable to Irish VAT as if he had himself supplied the service. The Finance Act 2007 provides that, following a Ministerial Order (which had not issued at the time of writing) the legislation will not apply to a Department of State, local authority or a body established by statute. The amount on which the tax is payable is the consideration for the service supplied. Such tax is available for deduction, as a tax borne on inputs in the normal way. Although vehicle leasing is not a Fourth Schedule Service, an Irish trader leasing a vehicle from a foreign supplier will be chargeable to Irish VAT as if he himself had supplied the service to another person. These provisions will apply in situations where no VAT is effectively payable in the supplier's country.

PA 5A ***(vi) Electronically supplied services from outside the EU***

Finance Act 2003 introduced a new scheme for non EU businesses that supply electronic services to private consumers in the EU. Under this scheme the trader can opt to register for VAT in one EU Member State, make electronic supplies to private consumers in other Member States and remit the VAT due in each Member State to the

Member State in which he is VAT registered. That Member State will then remit the VAT due to the Member State of consumption.

The place of supply of electronically supplied services is the State, when these services are supplied to a private customer in the State by an accountable person from an establishment outside the EU, even if the person also has an establishment in the EU.

(vii) Money transfer services

The place of supply of intermediary services associated with money transfer services is the State, when these services are supplied to a non-EU principal and used and enjoyed in the State.

(viii) Intermediary Services

Effective from 1 January 2008 the place of supply of intermediary services where the person acts in the name of and for the account of another person (other than in relation to intra-Community transport of goods or ancillary activities) is the place where the underlying transaction of the principal is supplied for VAT purposes.

9.1.10 Sub-contractors services

FA08 s92(D) From 1 September 2008, the charge a sub-contractor makes to a principal contractor will not include VAT. Instead the principal contract calculates the VAT on the amount charged by the sub-contractor and pays the VAT directly to the Revenue Commissioners through his/her VAT return or where applicable he/she can self account for the VAT due under the reverse charge mechanism.

9.1.11 Telecommunications services

FA97 s99; FA00 s108 Significant changes were included in the 1997 Finance Act and these came into force on 1 July 1997. Their effects are as follows:

(a) A user, other than a private individual, purchasing telecommunications services from outside the EU, must self-account for and pay the VAT on those services.

(b) The same applies where a user, other than a private individual, purchases the services from another Member State.

(c) Where a non-EU service provider supplies services to private individuals in the State, the service provider must register for VAT here.

The definition of telecommunication services includes access to the internet.

9.1.12 Option not to register

VAT(A)A s6; F(No 2)A81 s11; FA07 s78 The following persons are not obliged to register for VAT unless they otherwise elect:

(a) A farmer (see definition below).

FA08 s92(e) (b) A person whose supplies of taxable goods or services consist exclusively of the following:

   (i) supplies to accountable persons of unprocessed fish caught by him in a sea fishing business, or

   (ii) supplies of the kind mentioned at (i) along with either or both of the following:

      (1) supplies of machinery, plant or equipment which have been used by him in the course of a sea fishing business, and

      (2) supplies of other goods and services the total consideration for which has not exceeded and is not likely to exceed €37,500 per annum.

(c) Persons whose receipts do not exceed €75,000 per annum, provided that 90% of their total receipts arises from the supply of taxable goods. This does not apply, however, in the case of persons supplying goods chargeable at the 21% rate where these goods were produced or manufactured by the accountable person wholly or mainly from materials chargeable at the zero rate.

(d) Persons whose receipts do not exceed €37,500 per annum and to whom (a), (b) or (c) do not apply. Where two or more persons, one of whom controls one or more of the others, supply goods or services of a similar nature, the total consideration for such supplies will be aggregated to determine if the €37,500 exemption limit is exceeded.

9.1.13 Farmers

VAT(A)A s6 A farmer is defined as a person who engages in at least one Annex A Activity and whose supplies of taxable goods and services in the course of business consist exclusively of:

(a) Supplies of agricultural produce (i.e., goods produced by the farmer in the course of an Annex A Activity).

(b) Supplies of agricultural services (i.e., any Annex B Service supplied by the farmer with his own or his employees' labour and using his farm machinery) excluding insemination services, stock minding and stock rearing, the total consideration for which has not exceeded and is not likely to exceed €37,500 per annum.

(c) Supplies of agricultural services (i.e., any Annex B service supplied by the farmer with his own or his employees' labour and using his farm machinery) excluding insemination services, stock minding and stock rearing which, in addition to supplies by retail of horticultural produce and supplies of bovine semen, the total consideration for which has not exceeded and is not likely to exceed €37,500 per annum.

(d) Supplies of race horse training services the consideration for which has not exceeded and is not likely to exceed €37,500 per annum.

(e) Supplies of other goods and services the consideration for which has not exceeded and is not likely to exceed €37,500 per annum.

(f) Supplies by retail of horticultural produce or supplies of bovine semen or a combination of both, the total consideration for which has not exceeded and is not likely to exceed €75,000 per annum.

Annex A Activities – These relate to agricultural production activities such as crop production, stock farming and cultivation, forestry and fisheries. (See 9.2 for further details).

Annex B Services – These relate to the supply of agricultural services which normally play a part in agricultural production. (See 9.3 for further details.)

As stated above farmers are not obliged to register for VAT purposes.

9.1.14 Flat-rate farmer

VAT(A)A s11

A flat rate farmer is a farmer who is not an accountable person. Where such a farmer supplies agricultural produce or agricultural services to an accountable person the accountable person is entitled to an input credit of 5.2% of the tax exclusive consideration for the supply. An invoice must be prepared by the accountable person showing the tax exclusive price and the VAT. The rate of 5.2% applies as and from 1 January 2007.

9.1.15 Farm buildings, etc.

PA s20

A flat-rate farmer who has borne tax on expenditure on the construction or improvement of farm buildings, farm structures, fencing, drainage and land reclamation may reclaim the tax. Repayment will be withheld if the farmer's tax affairs are not up to date.

9.1.16 Group registration

VAT(A)A s6; FA91 s79; FA06 s95 FA07 s79) FA08 s92(f)

Where the Revenue Commissioners are satisfied that it would be in the interests of efficient administration and that no loss of tax would be involved, they may treat a group of persons such as a number of interlinked companies, as a single accountable person. In these circumstances only one member of the group will submit VAT returns for the taxable period and such returns will cover the activities of all the members of the group. However, all parties to the group registration are jointly and severally liable for all the VAT obligations of the other group members. In addition the necessity of issuing tax invoices in respect of inter-group transactions is avoided.

To qualify for group registration the Revenue Commissioners must be satisfied that:

(i) the persons seeking the group registration are all established in the State and at least one of the group members is a taxable person.

(ii) they are closely bound by financial, economic and organisational links.

(iii) the granting of the VAT group registration seems necessary or appropriate to them for the purpose of efficient and effective administration, including collection, of VAT.

The granting of group registration is at the discretion of the Revenue Commissioners and there is no right of appeal. Legislation provides that Revenue may compulsorily group register connected businesses.

The Revenue Commissioners may defer payment of VAT where the business activities of one or more persons are so interlinked that group registration could be imposed and one or more of the persons has not made VAT returns or remitted VAT due.

9.1.17 Supplies to certain taxable persons – 13A holders

FA93 s90; FA95 s95

The 1993 Finance Act provided for the zero-rating of supplies to taxable persons whose output is mainly supplied to other EU states or exported out of the EU. A "qualifying person" is an accountable person whose turnover from supplies of goods (including certain contract work) either supplied outside the EU or dispatched or transported to a registered person in another EU state amounts to 75% of his total annual turnover from the supply of goods and services. The effect of this provision is that traders authorised for this purpose will no longer have to pay VAT to their suppliers and subsequently reclaim it from the Revenue Commissioners. Authorisation will be granted by the Revenue Commissioners on application by the appropriate persons and will be valid for a certain period only. An authorised person must notify the Revenue Commissioners if he is no longer a "qualifying person". The authorised person is obliged to provide a copy of the authorisation to all his suppliers in the State. This ensures that such suppliers will be aware of his authorised status. There is an obligation on the supplier in the State to quote the relevant authorisation number on the invoice on making a zero-rated supply.

9.1.18 Intra-community acquisitions – registered persons

FA95 s121; PA s3A; FA97 s97

Where a trader who is registered for VAT in Ireland makes an intra-community acquisition from a trader in another Member State, the VAT implications are as follows:

(i) the goods are liable in Ireland to tax on the intra-Community acquisition at the VAT rate applicable here;

(ii) the VAT payable is accounted for through the normal periodic VAT return, and

(iii) the tax payable is simultaneously deductible;

(iv) where goods have been subject to VAT under the margin scheme, the auction scheme or the special scheme for second-hand means of transport in another Member State, they are not treated as an intra-Community acquisition on arrival in the State and are not subject to Irish VAT, unless re-sold.

A number of transitional measures were included in the Finance Act 2004 to deal with goods in transit between Ireland and the accession countries.

9.1.19 Intra-Community acquisitions – unregistered persons

Traders who make an intra-Community acquisition but who are not registered for VAT in Ireland because their turnover is below the registration threshold are not taxable in the State if the annual value of their intra-Community acquisitions remains below €41,000. Instead, VAT is payable in the Member State of purchase (i.e., the country of origin) at the VAT rate applicable there. Where the threshold in respect of intra-Community acquisitions is exceeded, the trader must register for VAT in the State and will then be covered by the system already described in the preceding paragraph.

9.1.20 Non-taxable entities

In relation to non-taxable entities such as Government departments or exempt businesses such as insurance companies or banks that acquire goods in other Member States, an intra-Community acquisition arises. As in the case of small traders, such intra-Community acquisitions are not taxable in Ireland if the annual value of acquisitions remains below the €41,000 threshold already referred to above. VAT is instead payable in the Member State where the goods were purchased at the VAT rate applicable there. Where a non-taxable entity or exempt business exceeds the intra-Community acquisition threshold, it must register for VAT and is liable to tax in Ireland on its intra-Community acquisitions.

9.1.21 New means of transport

The intra-Community acquisition of new means of transport (including motor vehicles, boats and aircraft) is always taxable in the Member State of arrival. Special arrangements apply in respect of the payment of VAT on new means of transport acquired by private individuals or by traders not entitled to a deduction. A transfer by an entity in the State to the territory of another Member State is an intra-Community supply.

9.1.22 Cultural, artistic, entertainment and similar services

The Finance Act 2002 amended the VAT treatment of cultural, artistic, entertainment and similar services. Previously such services were deemed to be supplied where physically performed. Accordingly, foreign performers had to register for VAT when performing in Ireland. The amendments may be summarised as follows:

(i) Performer not established in the State

The new position as regards VAT treatment is as follows:

(a) Supplier of such services is not established in the State.

(b) Is no longer an accountable person.

(c) The acquirer of the services is now the accountable person (assuming the services are not acquired in a private capacity).

(d) Acquirer is liable to VAT as if they had supplied the service themselves.

(e) The reverse charge procedure applies.

In most cases a promoter, agent or similar person commissions the performer's service and that person is deemed to have received the service.

If the acquirer of the service from the foreign performer has been in receipt of Arts Council funding in last three years then:

(a) The acquirer may request a deferment of these provisions from Revenue.

(b) A deferment may be granted by Revenue to 1 March 2003.

(ii) Promoter not established in the State

If the promoter, agent or similar person, deemed to be the recipient of the service, is not established in the State, then the owner, occupier or controller of where the performance is to take place must provide certain specified information to Revenue in advance of the performance, as follows:

(a) Name and address of promoter.

(b) Details including dates, duration and venue.

(c) Other information as specified by regulations.

If the premises provider fails to provide this information, he/she may be held to be jointly and severally liable with the promoter for any VAT liability arising and must pay the VAT if not paid by the promoter.

9.1.23 Mobile traders

Where a person who owns, occupies or controls land (called the premises provider) allows a non-established person sell goods on the land (called the mobile trader) for a period of less than seven consecutive days, that person must supply certain information to Revenue in advance, as follows:

(a) Name and address of mobile trader.

(b) Dates of supplies.

(c) Address of lands.

(d) Other information as specified by regulations.

If the premises provider fails to do so, he/she may be held jointly and severally liable with the mobile trader for VAT liability and must pay the VAT if not paid by the mobile trader.

This provision is designed to place within the Irish VAT net casual foreign traders such as, weekend furniture dealers, vendors of clothing and merchandising outlets at concerts.

9.1.24 Rates

VAT(A)A s9; FA06 s97

Exempt -	Details are set out in the First Schedule to the Principal Act (See Chart 29). Those carrying on exempted activities cannot, with some minor exceptions, register for VAT.
Zero Rate -	Details of goods and services taxable at this rate are set out in the Second Schedule to the Principal Act (See Chart 30).
5.2% Rate -	This rate applies to livestock which includes live cattle, sheep, pigs, goats, deer, horses and greyhounds. (See Chart 47 for earlier rates)
10% Rate -	Details of goods and services taxable at this rate are set out in the Third Schedule to the Principal Act (See Chart 31).
13.5% Rate -	Details of goods and services taxable at this rate are set out in the Sixth and Eight Schedules to the Principal Act (See Chart 32).
21% Rate -	All goods and services which do not fall into the categories mentioned above are liable to VAT at this rate (see Chart 33).

9.1.25 Package rule

VAT(A)A s11

Finance Act 2006 sets out new rules for determining the rate of VAT applicable to the supply of a "package" comprising two or more elements which attract VAT at different rates. The new rules provide that, in the case of composite supply, i.e., where there is a principal element to which the other elements are ancillary, the VAT rate for the composite supply will be the VAT rate applying to the principal element. In the case of multiple supplies, i.e., where a number of individual supplies are made together for a single overall consideration, the consideration should be apportioned between the various supplies involved, and each supply will be taxed at the appropriate rate of VAT.

9.1.26 Amount on which tax is chargeable

PA s10; FA95 s125; FA97 s102; FA99 s124; FA05 s102; FA05 s106; FA05 s109; FA06 s97 FA07 s80 FA08 s102

Broadly speaking this is the total consideration which the person becomes entitled to receive in respect of a supply of goods or services, including all taxes, commissions, costs and charges whatsoever, but not including VAT chargeable in respect of the supply. The main exception to this relates to certain supplies of immovable goods. The 1995 Finance Act prohibits the deduction for the trade-in value of goods received in exchange which had applied heretofore. It also provides that the taxable amount of goods sold under a hire purchase agreement is the open market price of the goods or the total amount received by the person supplying the goods, whichever is the greater. The 1997 Finance Act provides that a person who gives a reduction or discount to a customer cannot adjust his VAT liability until a proper VAT credit note has been issued to the customer.

The 1999 Finance Act provides that, in accordance with the Sixth VAT Directive, tax should be based on cost price rather than open market price for certain transfers of goods to other Member States. It also provides that cost price should be used to establish the tax due in the case of certain intra-community acquisitions following transfers in other EU countries.

Finance Act 2005 provides a legislative basis for the Revenue Commissioners to obtain independent valuations of property for VAT purposes. It provides for the Revenue Commissioners to authorise persons to inspect properties and it requires occupiers to allow the right of entry to authorised persons at all reasonable times. It also provides for a penalty of €1,265 for obstructing a person authorised by Revenue to value a property or for failing to allow a valuation to take place.

Finance Act 2005 provides, in relation to the continuous supplies of utilities (i.e., gas, electricity and telecommunications) supplied to non-VAT registered persons that VAT is due at the time the supplier issues a statement of account, which should issue at least once every three months.

Finance Act 2006 provides that the taxable amount in respect of the supply of services consisting of the private use of business assets, and the supply of services free of charge by an accountable person for non-business purposes, is the cost to the accountable person of providing the service. It also provides that the taxable amount in respect of the supply of services diverted by a business to a non-deductible business use is the open market price of supplying the service.

Finance Act 2007 provides that Revenue may, in relation to transactions between connected parties, determine that VAT is chargeable based on the open market value of the transaction. The legislation is intended as an anti avoidance measure and is directed at transactions where the customer would not be entitled to fully recover the VAT charged or the supplier is engaged in activities that are not fully liable to VAT and a price below market value is charged for those goods or services

Finance Act 2008 provides that, with effect from 13 March 2008, where a customer pays a deposit but subsequently cancels the transaction and the supplier does not refund the deposit, the supplier may reduce his or her tax liability for the taxable period when the cancellation occurs by the amount already accounted for on the deposit.

9.1.27 Vouchers

The Finance Act 2002 provided for a change in the VAT treatment of the supply of vouchers in response to the tax planning opportunity that arose as a result of the decision of the European Court of Justice in the Argos case.

Prior to the changes made by Finance Act, 2002 where a right to receive goods and services, other than telecommunications services, for an amount stated on any token, stamp, coupon or voucher was granted for consideration, the consideration was disregarded for VAT purposes, except to the extent that the consideration exceeded the face value. The tax point arose at the time of redemption.

With effect from 25 March 2002, when a token, stamp, coupon or voucher is supplied for consideration to a person who acquires it in the course or furtherance of business, and that person on supplies them for consideration, both supplies and considerations are subject to VAT at 21%, and are no longer ignored. Now the redemption of such vouchers is ignored, and the face value disregarded as consideration in the hands of the person handing over goods or services on redemption of the voucher.

9.1.28 Cash basis

PA s14; FA92 s177; FA94 s97; FA95 s131 FA07 s87 FA08 s99

With effect from 1 July 1994 the following have the option to account for VAT on the basis of cash received in a taxable period rather than on the basis of sales.

(a) A person who satisfies the Revenue Commissioners that taking one period with another, not less than 90% of his turnover is derived from taxable sales to unregistered persons.

(b) A person who satisfies the Revenue Commissioners that the total consideration which he is entitled to receive in respect of his taxable supplies has not exceeded and is not likely to exceed

€1,000,000 in any continuous period of twelve months. (This limit was increased from €635,000 with effect from 1 March 2007.)

With effect from 13 March 2008, the cash received basis will no longer apply to transactions where a supplier on the cash receipts basis does not issue a credit note following the grant of a discount to its customer. In those circumstances, VAT should then be accounted for on the full invoiced amount and not on the amount received.

9.1.29 Invoice basis

PA s19
FA025 s106

Prior to 1 May 2002, the accountable persons who accounted for VAT on the invoice basis had a tax point where there was an advance payment. There was a deemed supply of part of the goods or service as was equal in value to the amount received. However, with effect from 1 May 2002, this provision no longer applies to an accountable person accounting for VAT on the invoice basis.

Accordingly it is the issue of the VAT invoice that is now the only tax point, when accounting on the invoice basis. There is no obligation to issue a VAT invoice under the Value-Added Tax Act, 1972 until the fifteenth day of the month following the month in which the supply of the goods or service was completed.

9.1.30 Tax deductible

PA s12;
FA94 s96;
FA95 s129;
FA98 s106;
FA99 s128;
FA00 s112;
FA06 s98

Provided that the goods and services to which such tax relates are used for the purpose of the taxable supply of goods and services, or for the purposes of qualifying activities abroad, VAT paid on the following inputs is deductible in computing liability.

(a) Tax charged to an accountable person by other accountable persons on supplies of goods and services to him.

(b) Tax paid or payable by the accountable person on goods imported by him.

(c) Tax payable on self supplies of goods or services.

(d) Tax payable on purchases from flat rate farmers.

(e) Tax on imported Fourth Schedule services.

(f) Residual VAT in relation to a supply of second-hand means of transport or agricultural machinery.

(g) Tax payable by a lessee in accordance with the provisions of section 93, Finance Act 1994.

(h) Tax payable on certain purchases of second hand goods as provided in Regulations.

(i) Tax payable on the intra-Community acquisition of goods.

(j) Where not previously allowed, any residual VAT contained in the value of goods transferred from a branch of a business within the State to a branch of the same business in another Member State.

(k) Post-letting expenses of a landlord who has made a long lease of commercial property.

(l) Tax in relation to the installation and assembly of goods where the Irish recipient is deemed to be the taxable person, subject to the recipient's normal entitlement to recover VAT.

(m) Tax in relation to the purchase of gas and electricity from abroad where the Irish recipient is deemed to be the accountable person and has to account for VAT on the reverse charge basis as included in the Finance Act 2004, subject to the recipient's normal entitlement to recover VAT.

(n) The issue of new shares or other securities for the purpose of raising capital for the person's VATable supplies.

Up to 23 March 2000 the allowable proportion of VAT on costs, which were incurred for both vatable and non-vatable purposes, could be reviewed annually by reference to turnover. Since then this no longer applies and apportionment can be made on any basis, provided the basis chosen correctly reflects the dual use.

9.1.31 Tax not deductible

VAT(A)A s10; FA87 s41; FA95 s129

No deduction is allowed in respect of tax paid on expenditure on the following:

(a) The provision of food, drink, accommodation or other personal services supplied to the accountable person, his agent, or his employees. Effective from 1 July 2007 a taxable person can, subject to stringent criteria, recover the VAT on accommodation costs of attending conferences for his employees or agent in the course of furtherance of the accountable person's business. Specific records have to be kept in relation to the conference and the conference must be for a minimum of 50 delegates.

(b) Entertainment expenses incurred by the accountable person, his agent or his employees.

(c) The acquisition, hiring or leasing of motor vehicles (as defined) other than as stock in trade or for the purposes of a business which consists in whole or part of the hiring of motor vehicles or for use in a driving school business for giving instruction. With effect from 1 May 2007 the exclusion applicable to motor vehicles shall not apply to purchases by hire purchase businesses of motor vehicles that will be the subject of hire purchase agreements.

(d) The purchase of petrol otherwise than as stock in trade.

(e) Expenditure incurred on food, drink, accommodation or other entertainment services as part of an advertising service is not deductible in the hands of the person providing that advertising service.

(f) Any VAT incurred by an accountable person in a transaction where the margin or auction schemes apply.

(g) A person from outside the EU who makes supplies in Ireland under the scheme for non-EU businesses that supply electronic services to private consumers in the EU is not entitled to deduct input VAT but is entitled to refunds under the 13th VAT Directive.

9.1.32 Bad debts

PA s10; FA94 s95

Sub-section 3(c) of section 10, PA provides for relief from VAT for bad debts incurred. An amendment contained in the 1994 Finance Act removes the relief where the bad debt occurs in the case of the long-term letting of immovable goods. This operates with effect from 23 May 1994.

9.1.33 Margin scheme

FA95 s126 FA99 s125 FA01 s185

The Seventh VAT Directive includes measures for the elimination of double taxation in relation to the sale of second-hand movable goods, works of art, collectors items and antiques. The margin scheme allows a dealer to account for VAT on resale of the goods, on his profit margin at the appropriate rate of VAT. This scheme is optional. Agricultural machinery which benefits from the new special scheme for agricultural machinery is excluded from the margin scheme. Certain goods acquired by an insurance company qualify as margin scheme goods.

9.1.34 Agricultural machinery

FA99 s131; FA00 s114 FA08 s96

A new scheme for agricultural machinery came into effect from 1 September 1999. It provides that where a dealer in agricultural machinery buys machinery from an unregistered farmer the dealer can claim back the residual VAT contained in the price. The Finance Act 2000 introduced further relief for repossessed machinery.

With effect from 1 July 2008, the definition of taxable persons has been extended to finance houses who are engaged in leasing agricultural machinery.

9.1.35 Auction scheme

FA95 s127 FA01 s185

A scheme similar to the margin scheme exists for auctioneers where the auctioneer's commission is the basis for calculating the profit margin. Specific sales of second hand goods by insurers are covered by the scheme.

9.1.36 Second-hand means of transport

FA95 s130
FA01 s190

A taxable dealer may claim a deduction for "residual VAT" where he purchases or acquires second-hand means of transport from certain categories of persons – broadly those not in a position to supply a VAT invoice. Included in the category of persons are insurance companies disposing of vehicles in connection with an insurance claim on which they are not liable to charge VAT.

9.1.37 Transfer of business

PA s3; FA91 s75; FA98 s105 FA01 s182 FA05 s99 FA01 s183 FA01 s191

The transfer of ownership of goods in connection with the transfer of a business or part of a business to another accountable person is not a supply of goods, and therefore, no VAT is payable on such a transfer. With effect from 25 March 2005, the transfer of business relief only applies where the transferred assets constitute an undertaking or part of an undertaking capable of being operated on an independent basis. If, however, the goods are diverted to non-business use, this is treated as a self-supply. A deduction is allowed in respect of VAT borne on services (e.g., auctioneer's fees) directly related to the transfer of a business from one accountable person to another.

The transfer of goodwill and other intangible assets in connection with the transfer of a business are not liable to VAT when transferred to another accountable person or flat rate farmer.

Where a property is transferred in connection with the transfer of a business to a person who is not entitled to full VAT recovery, that person will suffer a claw-back of VAT based on the remaining VAT life of the property.

9.1.38 VAT on property rules from 1 July 2008

Sale of property

FA08 s82-s91

With effect from 1 July 2008, there are new VAT rules that apply to the sale of property. In general, the sale of "new" buildings are automatically subject to VAT at 13.5% and "old" buildings are exempt from VAT but with an option to tax the sale at 13.5%. The sale of residential properties remains subject to VAT at 13.5%.

Special rules ("transitional rules") apply to properties that were acquired or developed before 1 July 2008 and are sold from 1 July 2008 onwards.

A "new" building is a building that has been developed in the previous five years or an existing building that has been redeveloped in the last five years where the redevelopment materially altered the use of the building and cost 25% or more of the VAT exclusive sales price of the building. Excluded from the definition of a "new" building is a building, newly developed or redeveloped, that was previously sold and occupied for an aggregate of at least two of the five years.

An "old" building is any building which does not come within, or is excluded from, the definition of a "new" building.

The sale of an exempt property will give rise to a claw back for the vendor of the VAT incurred on the acquisition/redevelopment costs of the property. To avoid this cost, the seller and the purchaser can opt to tax the sale, (see below), which would result in the vendor retaining the right to recover the VAT incurred on the costs of acquisition/development of the building.

For VAT purposes, the sale of a property includes an agreement that provides for a change in rights in respect of the property and the payment of 50% or more of the VAT exclusive sale price of the property before, or within, five years of the agreement. The concept of change of rights in property is quite broad and includes the creation, alteration or termination of rights but specifically excludes mortgages.

Sale of residential property

Residential properties sold by a developer (or by a person connected to the developer) where the developer was entitled to recover the VAT on the acquisition/development of the property are subject to VAT at the 13.5% rate. This treatment is generally applied regardless of whether the property is old or new.

Sale of undeveloped land

The sale of undeveloped land remains exempt from VAT. However, where a person supplies land and in connection with that supply there is an agreement to develop the land the sale is subject to VAT at the 13.5% rate.

Option to tax a VAT exempt sale of property

The vendor and a business purchaser can agree in writing to opt to tax the sale of an otherwise VAT exempt property. Revenue has stated that the option to tax will not apply to letting of residential property. Where they jointly opt to tax the sale VAT, is chargeable on the sale at the 13.5% rate and the purchaser should account for the VAT due on a reverse charge basis.

Properties owned before and held on 1 July 2008

Properties which had been acquired or developed prior to 1 July 2008 and have not been disposed of by that date will be subject to transitional rules, (referred to hereafter as "transitional properties").

Where a person has no entitlement to recover VAT on the acquisition/development of a transitional property, and that property has not been redeveloped since 1 July 2008, the sale of such a property is not subject to VAT. However, the seller and purchaser can still jointly opt in writing to charge VAT on the sale.

If the vendor of a property was entitled to recover VAT on the acquisition/development of a transitional property, the disposal of such a property is subject to the new rules, i.e., the sale is subject to VAT if it is a new building, it is exempt from VAT if it is an old building with the joint option to tax the sale.

Where a vendor has partial VAT recovery on the costs of acquisition/ development of a transitional property, the sale is chargeable to VAT and the vendor is entitled to an additional VAT credit which is based on an adjustment imported from the Capital Goods Scheme. (see below).

The assignment/surrender of a transitional property is chargeable to VAT where the person was entitled to recover at least part of the VAT incurred on acquisition/development of the property. Otherwise VAT is not chargeable.

The amount on which VAT is chargeable in respect of an assignment or surrender is based on the following formula;

$$T \times \frac{N}{Y}$$

T = *VAT on acquisition/development.*
N = *No. of full intervals plus one, that remain in the adjustment period.*
Y = *Total no. of intervals in the adjustment period.*

Lettings of Property

Commercial Lettings

With effect from 1 July 2008, there is, for VAT purposes, no distinction between leases of 10 years or longer and leases of less than 10 years. All leases are in principle exempt from VAT. Consequently, a landlord would have no entitlement to recover VAT on the acquisition/ development costs attributable to a property that it intends to let. To avoid this cost, the landlord could opt to charge VAT on the rent payable under the letting.

Option to tax lettings

In broad terms the "waiver of exemption", (see below), is replaced by a similar concept known as an "option to tax".

Generally speaking, to charge VAT on a letting acquired or developed after 1 July 2008 there must be either, a provision in the lease agreement that the landlord is opting to tax the lease or the landlord must notify the tenant in writing that VAT is chargeable. The option to tax is property specific. The option to tax is terminated if the above documentary conditions are not satisfied, the landlord and tenant agree to terminate the option or the property is used for residential purposes.

An option to tax a letting will not be available, or will be terminated, where landlord and tenant are connected persons and the tenant is not entitled to at least 90% VAT recovery or where the occupant of the property is "connected" to the landlord. The definition of a "connected" person is very broad so care in this area is required.

The termination of an option to tax will generally give rise to a VAT cost for the landlord under the Capital Goods Scheme (see below).

Waiver of exemption

Prior to 1 July 2008 a person could waive his exemption from VAT in respect of short-term commercial lettings and charge the tenant VAT on the rent. However, a waiver of exemption from VAT cannot be put in place after 30 June 2008.

If a waiver is in place on 30 June 2008 and carried forward into the new regime it will:

(i) apply to property held on 30 June 2008 and let after that date, but

(ii) not apply to property acquired, developed or let after 30 June 2008.

However, if a property is let after 30 June 2008 and it was being developed for or on behalf of the landlord on 18 February 2008 and the landlord had a waiver in place on that date, the waiver can extend to that letting.

There are also specific rules regarding the application of the waiver on or after 1 July 2008 where the tenant is "connected" to the landlord and is not entitled to recover at least 90% of the VAT that he incurs or the occupant, not being the tenant, is connected to the landlord. With effect from 1 July 2008, there is a minimum amount of VAT which must be payable in respect of such lettings on an annual basis. If this condition is not met, a waiver that is in place is automatically cancelled for that letting and a payment should be made to Revenue based on the difference between the VAT reclaimed on the acquisition/development of the property and the VAT accounted for on the rents to date. Where the waiver is cancelled, it will only be in respect of the individual letting between connected persons and the waiver will, subject to usual rules, continue to apply to other commercial lettings.

Residential Lettings

Lettings of residential properties on or after 1 July 2008 will be exempt from VAT. Unlike commercial lettings, an option to tax a residential letting is not available and a business will suffer restrictions in the recovery of VAT incurred on the acquisition/development of a residential property.

Capital Goods Scheme

The Capital Goods Scheme ("CGS") applies to the supply or development of property on which a business was charged VAT, or would have been charged VAT but for the transfer of business relief under section 3(5)(b)(iii) VAT Act 1972, or "exporters relief" under section 13A VAT Act 1972, on the acquisition or development of the property.

CGS is a mechanism whereby the initial VAT claimed is adjusted over a period of up to 20 years to reflect the taxable use of the property over that period. Therefore, if, subsequent to the initial deduction, the taxable use increases, a further amount of input VAT can be claimed and if the taxable use decreases, part of the input tax already claimed must be repaid to Revenue. CGS ensures that a person's VAT deductibility in relation to a property is proportionate to the person's taxable use of the property.

The adjustment period for properties is generally 20 "intervals" except in the case of refurbishment in which case it is 10 "intervals". The initial interval is the first 12 months, the second interval is from the first day after the end of the initial interval to the person's accounting year-end and subsequent intervals are based on accounting years. Consequently, other than the first two adjustment intervals subsequent adjustment intervals will be measured in accounting years.

The CGS rules can be complex and there are special rules that apply to the disposal of a property where VAT would have been charged but for the operation of section 3(5)(b)(iii) VAT Act 1972 (transfer of business relief). There are also special rules where the entitlement to VAT recovery relating to a property has changed by 50% or more.

9.1.39 VAT on Property Rules up to 30 June 2008

PA s4; VAT(A)A s8; FA95 s122

Certain activities involving immovable goods (land and buildings together with all fixtures attached thereto) are liable to VAT at 13.5%. This rate applies in cases where the value of any movable goods supplied as part of the contract does not exceed two-thirds of the full contract price.

VAT(A)A s10

The activities involved are as follows:

FA95 s122; FA97 s98

(a) The development of land including drainage and reclamation, the installation of fixtures in building and the repair and decoration of buildings in the course of business.

(b) The development of land or buildings and the disposal of a freehold interest in them.

(c) The granting of a lease of land or building for a period of at least 10 years or the disposal of a leasehold interest under a lease which, at the time it was created, was for a term of at least 10 years (or if less than 10 years contained an option to extend it to 10 years or more).

(d) The disposal of an undeveloped site in connection with which another accountable person enters into a contract with the purchaser to carry out development in relation to the site.

R19 It should be noted that the activities mentioned at (b) and (c) above
FA94 s93 do not attract liability to VAT unless all of the following conditions are satisfied:

(i) The property must have been developed wholly or partly after 31 October 1972.

(ii) The vendor must have disposed of a taxable interest in the course of business. Such an interest would be either the freehold or leasehold interest mentioned at (b) or (c) above.

(iii) The vendor must have been entitled to a tax credit in respect of any tax suffered on the development of the property or on the acquisition of his interest in the property.

Where the activity involves the granting of a lease of land or buildings for a period of at least 10 years VAT is payable on the capitalised value of the rent reserved. In making this calculation it is open to the tax payer to provide evidence by a competent valuer of what the value should be. In the absence of such evidence leases are valued at either of the amounts arrived at by the following formulae:

(i)

$$R \times \frac{3}{4} \times N$$

where:

R = The annual amount of the rent

N = The number of complete years for which the rent has been created

(ii)

$$R \times M$$

where:

R = The annual amount of the rent.

M = The "multiplier" which, at the time of writing (June 2007) is 21.27. The up to date multiplier can be obtained from Revenue. (See Chart 35 for earlier multipliers.)

Prior to 25 March 2002, where the lease included a rent review during the first five years of the lease it was not possible to use the above formulae to value the lease. In cases, however, where the formulae applied, the lower of the amounts arrived at by the formulae had to be used.

Where a person creates a lease of 10 to 20 years he is disposing of his interest for the period of the lease but retaining his right of reversion at the end of the period. This gives two elements to the transaction as follows:

(a) The creation of the lease, any VAT on which will be chargeable to the tenant.

(b) The retention of the reversion, any VAT on which is a self-supply to the landlord and is irrecoverable.

Section 93 Finance Act 1994 provides that, subject to approval by the Revenue Commissioners, where the lessee is entitled to a repayment of all the VAT charged it will not be necessary for the lessor to charge VAT on the capitalised value of the lease. Instead, the lessee will be liable to pay the tax as if he had supplied the goods in the course or furtherance of business and he will also be in a position to claim a simultaneous input credit, thus removing the need to finance the VAT charge. A joint application for this treatment, if required, must be supplied by the lessor and lessee along with such further information as may be required by the Commissioners. Where approval has been received from the Commissioners the invoice issued by the lessor must include an endorsement specifying the lessee's accountability for the VAT liability arising on the transaction. This provision has effect from 7 July 1995.

Finance Act 2003 provides that accountable persons involved in property transactions must retain records for the VAT life of the property plus six years.

1997 Finance Act Provisions

FA97 s96, s98, s102 Detailed amendments to the provisions on the taxation of leasehold interests are included in the 1997 Finance Act and came into effect on 26 March 1997. The main amendments are summarised as follows:

(a) The definition of the disposal of a leasehold interest is extended to include a surrender or assignment of a lease.

(b) The surrender or assignment of a lease will be valued in the same way as the creation of a lease, i.e., the capitalised value of the lease is added to any sum payable on the surrender or assignment of the lease.

(c) A surrendered or assigned lease is taxable in the hands of the new leaseholder ("reverse charge"). This applies where the new leaseholders are accountable persons, the State or local authorities and most exempt persons. It does not apply to private individuals nor to those involved in the medical, dental, educational and sporting fields. Accountable persons are entitled to an input credit for the tax paid.

(d) To avoid the possibility of lease values being reduced artificially it is specified that rental values for the purposes of calculating the capitalised value of a lease are to be based on the unencumbered open market rents.

VAT(A)A s24; FA97 s101 Rents receivable under leasehold interests which when created, are for a term of less than 10 years are not liable to VAT unless the recipient elects to be taxable - referred to as a "waiver of exemption". If he/she so elects, he/she becomes taxable on all rents which in the absence of such election would have been exempt. An exception to this treatment arises where under the 1997 Finance Act amendments a short term letting follows the taxable surrender of a leasehold interest. It is possible to waive the exemption in this situation without affecting the exempt status of other rents. A further amendment contained in the 1997 Finance Act provides that where a person cancels his election, there is a claw-back of input credits to the extent that the input credits exceed the VAT charged on the rents. Rents receivable from the following activities are always liable to VAT:

(a) Letting of machinery or business installations when let separately from any other immovable goods of which such machinery or installations form part.

(b) Letting in the course of carrying on a hotel business.

(c) Provision of parking accommodation for vehicles by the operators of car parks.

(d) Hire of safes.

Disposals of Sites and Buildings Separately

Under a technical interpretation of section 4 a property developer could dispose of a site separately from a building and not charge VAT on the value of the site. The Finance Act 2004 amended the relevant existing provisions with the effect that VAT is chargeable on the disposal of the site as well as on the building with effect from 4 December 2003.

Finance Act, 2002 – leases "Economic Value" test

PA s4 (3A) The Finance Act, 2002 introduced a new subsection into section 4 of the Value-Added Tax Act, 1972, as amended. The core of the new legislative changes is now contained in section 4(3A) of the Value-Added Tax Act, 1972. These changes are anti-avoidance in nature, and, like previous property VAT anti-avoidance provisions, affect all leases. The legislation is influenced by the European Court of Justice decision in the Dutch case Stichting '*Goed Wonen v Staatssechretaris van Financien*' (Case C-326/99). The term "economic value" was borrowed from that case.

Section 4(3A) can essentially be divided into two parts:

1. What must happen for the new legislation to apply and
2. What happens when the new legislation applies.

1. Application of new legislation

Three things must happen for the new legislation to apply, as follows:

(a) A person must have acquired and hold an interest in a property to which section 4 of the Value-Added Tax Act, 1972 applies and

(b) That person must surrender possession of that property in any of the following ways:

   (i) The creation of a long leasehold interest (i.e., one of ten years or more);

   (ii) The assignment of a long leasehold interest;

   (iii) The surrender of a long leasehold interest and

(c) The value of the lease, assignment or surrender for VAT purposes must be less than its "economic value". S.I. No. 219 of 2002 made changes to Regulation 19 with effect from 25 March 2002 to remove the condition regarding the five-year rent review and to allow in effect three methods of valuing a leasehold interest in immovable property.

The new legislation specifically excludes the disposal of a freehold interest from these provisions.

2. Effect of the application of new legislation

If the value of the creation, assignment or surrender of the leasehold interest for VAT purposes is less than the "economic value" of the lease, assignment or surrender then the creation, assignment or surrender of the leasehold interest is not treated as a supply of immovable goods/property for VAT purposes, but is treated as an exempt letting of that property, without a right of waiver, giving rise to a locked in VAT cost.

Economic value

The "economic value" of a lease, assignment or surrender is broadly defined as the sum of two elements as follows:

(a) the amount on which VAT was chargeable in relation to the acquisition of the property, plus

(b) the amount on which VAT was chargeable in relation to the development of the property.

Thus if a property was acquired, which was not subject to VAT, the economic value would be considerably less than if VAT applied to the acquisition cost.

Reduced economic value

In recognition of the real world of commercial transactions and economic value, the new legislation provides for, in certain circumstances, what has been termed "the economic value of a lesser interest". Where there has been no development of immovable goods since acquisition, and there is a disposal of a lesser interest (including a surrender or assignment) derived from the interest held, and the lesser interest is not greater than 35 years, the economic value of the lesser interest being disposed of is calculated by the formula:

$$E \times \frac{N1}{N2}$$

where:

E = Economic value of interest held

N1 = Length of lesser interest

N2 = Length of interest held (Note max for N2 is 35 years. N2 = 35 years in the case of a freehold interest.)

However, where the lesser interest being disposed of is by way of the creation of a lease, the reduced economic value as calculated above cannot be less than 75% of the economic value of the greater interest held.

With effect from 25 March 2002, all leases, assignments and surrenders must pass the so-called economic value test. If a lease, surrender or assignment fails this test, it is an exempt letting with no right of waiver. Obviously such a test failure may give rise to considerable irrecoverable VAT costs.

Waiver of Exemption

VATA s7 **(a) General**

Section 7(1A) VATA 1972 restricts the type of letting in respect of which a waiver will be permitted. Essentially a waiver is no longer permitted in respect of a letting of residential accommodation.

Accordingly a person who did not have a waiver in place at 2 April 2007, is prohibited from waiving with effect from that date in respect of residential accommodation.

A person who had a waiver in place at 2 April 2007 may continue that waiver but only in respect of lettings in place at that date i.e., he cannot extend the waiver to any residential buildings he acquires or develops after that date. There is some relief provided by s7(1A)(b) VATA 1972 which provides that the property will be regarded as having been acquired when the person enters a binding written contract for its acquisition or construction while it may be considered developed when an application for planning permission for its development as a house, apartment or similar establishment has been received by a planning authority. This measure helps accelerate the acquired/developed test so that the property may be regarded as acquired/developed prior to 2 April 2007 and therefore subject to the persons' waiver.

PA s8 (8) **(b) Short-term letting within a VAT group**

Prior to the 25 March 2002, a company in a VAT group could acquire property, recover VAT on acquisition costs, grant a short-term letting to another group member without a waiver of exemption being in place, and there was no exempt supply. Subsequently, when the lessor or lessee left the VAT group, there was no claw-back of the VAT credit obtained on the property.

Finance Act 2002 introduced changes with effect from 25 May 2002 where there is a short term letting (i.e., less than 10 years) of property within a VAT group, and the lessor was entitled to recover VAT on his acquisition and/or development of the property. As a result, the short-term letting is deemed to take place when either the lessor or the lessee leaves the VAT group, or when the VAT group breaks up. If the lessor does not have a waiver of exemption in place at the time he leaves the VAT group, or the lessee leaves the VAT group, or the VAT group breaks up, then the short term letting/surrender of possession is deemed to take place on the first exit of either party from the VAT group. Thus there is a self-supply of the property at this time with a VAT liability arising.

Change of use of property from VATable to exempt use

FA05 s100
FA05 s104

Prior to the Finance Act 2005 the diversion, by a landlord, of a property from a VATable use to a VAT exempt use gave rise to a self-supply of the property resulting in a claw-back of the VAT reclaimed on the purchase and development of the property and the subsequent supply of the property was VAT free. Finance Act 2005 provides that the amount of the VAT claw-back on a property that has been diverted from VATable to exempt use will be reduced according to the length of time that the property was used for VATable purposes before it was diverted to exempt use and is eliminated if the property is diverted to exempt use after 20 years. However, the subsequent sale of the property will be subject to VAT. In certain circumstances, the vendor will be entitled to an additional VAT input credit based on a proportion of the VAT incurred on the acquisition and development of the goods. The tax payable on the sale is reduced for any VAT clawed back as a result of the appropriation to exempt use.

9.1.40 Sale of a property with a sitting tenant

FA05 s100

The Finance Act 2005 provides that the disposal of a reversionary interest in a property with a sitting tenant who has developed the property is liable to VAT only if the property has been developed for and on behalf of or for the benefit of the landlord.

9.1.41 Holiday homes

FA00 s110
FA05 s113

Section 110 Finance Act 2000 was enacted to prevent people abusing the VAT election and cancellation rules in such a way as to obtain a holiday home almost VAT free.

With effect from 23 March 2000, the section provides for the payment of a cancellation fee to Revenue where the cancellation takes place within 10 years after the date of registration. There is no cancellation amount due to Revenue where the cancellation takes place after the end of this 10 year period. The cancellation fee during the 10 year period is based on a sliding scale under the following formula:

$$A \times \frac{10 - B}{10}$$

where:

A = The amount of the VAT deductible or the amount that would have been deductible if the transaction were not covered by the transfer of business rules; and

B = The number of full years for which the holiday home was used by the person. (A full year is any continuous period of 12 months).

Finance Act 2005 clarifies that, with effect from 1 July 2005, lettings in the short-term guest or holiday sector are taxable at 13.5%.

9.1.42 Repayments to foreign traders

PA s13; FA98 s113

There are provisions for the repayment to such traders of tax borne on services supplied to them within the State and on goods purchased within the State or imported for business purposes. These provisions apply broadly speaking to a person who satisfies the Revenue Commissioners that he carries on business outside the State and that he supplies no goods or services within the State.

9.1.43 Retail export scheme

PA s13; FA97 s106, s109, s111; FA99 s132

Detailed provisions are contained in the VAT (Export of Goods) Regulations 1992 as amended by the 1997 Finance Act to allow for the zero-rating of goods purchased by non-EU visitors.

9.1.44 Bankruptcy and winding up

FA76 s62

Unpaid VAT is a preferential debt in cases of bankruptcy or company winding up. The tax which ranks as a preferential debt is confined to that due for taxable periods ending not more than 12 months before commencement of bankruptcy or winding up proceedings.

9.1.45 Unjust enrichment

FA98 s114

Section 114 FA 1998 provides that an accountable person will be entitled to a refund of tax overpaid by him as a result of a mistaken assumption. This is subject to the person not being unjustly enriched by the refund. There are detailed provisions contained in the legislation concerning the question of what constitutes unjust enrichment. Finance Act 2003 extends the unjust enrichment provisions to interest on repayments.

9.1.46 Taxable periods

PA s1

Accountable persons must make returns and payment of VAT between the 10th and 19th days following the end of a taxable period. Each taxable period is a period of two months beginning on the 1st day of January, March, May, July, September or November. Failure to make the returns and payments can give rise to interest charges and/or penalties. If the aggregate of deductible inputs exceeds the VAT payable on outputs for a taxable period the Revenue Commissioners will make a repayment of the excess.

A person outside the EU who makes supplies in Ireland under the scheme for Non-EU businesses that supply electronic services to private consumers in the EU must submit special VAT returns and pay the VAT due in respect of supplies in all Member States each calendar quarter.

9.1.47 Paying by direct debit

PA s21
FA01 s195 Where a person pays their VAT by direct debit and where the balance at the end of the accounting period is more than 20% of the VAT liability for that period, Revenue will in certain circumstances charge interest.

PAs5 A person outside the EU who makes supplies in Ireland under the scheme for non-EU businesses that supply electronic services to private consumers in the EU must submit special VAT returns and pay the VAT due in respect of supplies in all member states each calendar quarter.

9.1.48 Annual accounting for VAT

PA s10;
FA89 s58;
FA95 s134 Section 58, Finance Act, 1989 enables the Collector General to authorise persons to make an annual VAT Return and pay their VAT on an annual basis. The features of this provision are as follows:

(a) The Collector General may determine that Returns be submitted for any number of taxable periods not exceeding six.

(b) The accountable person may continue to operate VAT on a two-monthly basis if he so wishes.

(c) The period covered by the authorisation is defined as the accounting period.

(d) VAT Returns and payment must be submitted between the 10th and 19th days of the month following the end of the accounting period.

(e) The Collector General must consider certain factors before issuing an authorisation, and the authorisation may be issued conditionally or unconditionally.

(f) The Collector General may terminate the authorisation, having taken account of certain factors.

(g) The accountable person has the option to align the date of his annual VAT Return with his commercial accounting period.

(h) There are provisions for a deemed termination of authorisation on cessation of trading, or liquidation, bankruptcy or death of the accountable person as appropriate.

(i) Where the deemed termination arises on the death of an accountable person, his personal representative is deemed to be the accountable person.

FA01 s194 (j) An accountable person who operates on an annual basis may be required to pay their VAT by monthly direct debit.

9.1.49 Appeals

PA s25; FA95 s137; FA97 s109

Any person aggrieved by a determination of the Revenue Commissioners in relation to VAT may lodge an appeal against such a determination. The same rights attach to such an appeal as attach to appeals against income tax assessments (see 1.1.11).

9.1.50 Time limits

FA98 s114; FA98 s115

The time limits for claiming refunds of VAT and for making an estimation or assessment by Revenue are reduced from six years to 4 years from 1 May 2003. If a claim relates to a taxable period before May 2003, the six-year limit for making a claim for a refund of tax will apply provided the claim is submitted by 31 December 2004.

9.1.51 Documentation

FA92 PtIII

Arising from the 1993 changes, certain VAT registered traders are required to complete the following returns and statements.

FA95 s132, s133

(i) Intrastat Return - to be completed monthly by any trader who imports more than €190,500 per annum from, or exports more than €635,000 per annum to, other EC Member States.

(ii) VIES – to be completed either quarterly or monthly by traders who export to a VAT registered trader in another EC Member State.

(iii) Upon request by an authorised officer an accountable person must give details to the Revenue Commissioners of any gifts or promotional items given in connection with taxable supplies and services.

9.1.52 Invoicing

FA01 s193

Prior authorisation from Revenue is not required when issuing or receiving electronic invoices as long as the systems are secure and both supplier and recipient comply with regulations.

The Finance Act 2003 provided for the outsourcing of invoicing operations to third parties, modified rules for self billing by the customer and introduced rules governing the storage of invoices when stored outside the State.

With effect from 1 January 2004 an Irish supplier of goods or services must issue an invoice not only to other accountable persons but also when making supplies to State Departments, local authorities, bodies established by statute or to exempt recipients.

In addition, the Finance Act 2004 introduced a new provision under which an Irish supplier is now also obligated to issue an invoice when supplying Fourth Schedule services to a person in another Member State.

New regulations were also issued in relation to the format of invoices in accordance with EC VAT legislation with effect from 1 January 2004. The main additions to the necessary information contained on invoices are the inclusion of sequential invoice numbers, the recipient's VAT registration number when receiving Fourth Schedule services and an indication that the reverse charge applies.

9.1.53 Expression of doubt

FA02 s107 The Finance Act, 2002 introduced new provisions which provide for an expression of doubt facility in VAT legislation as follows:

(a) Doubt about the application of VAT to a transaction

Where an accountable person is in doubt about the correct application of any enactment relating to VAT to a particular transaction he can lodge an expression of doubt.

This must be done at the same time as he furnishes his VAT return for the taxable period in which the transaction took place. The expression must be lodged with the Revenue office that deals with the examination of that taxable person's books and records. The expression of doubt can only be lodged if the VAT return is lodged on time.

(b) Doubt about whether a person is taxable or not

Where a non-registered person is in doubt as to whether they are accountable person relation to a transaction they can also utilise the expression of doubt facility.

The advantage of filing an expression of doubt is that interest will not apply to any additional liability, subject to certain conditions. Interest will apply where Revenue do not accept the expression of doubt as genuine. This will arise where Revenue:

(i) has issued general guidelines as regards the application of VAT law in similar circumstances,

(ii) is of the opinion the matter is sufficiently free of doubt as not to warrant an expression of doubt, or

(iii) is of the opinion the person is acting with a view to VAT evasion or avoidance.

The Letter of Expression of Doubt must:

(i) Set out full details of the transaction.

(ii) Identify the amount of tax in doubt.

(iii) Be accompanied by relevant supporting documentation.

(iv) Be clearly identified as an expression of doubt.

(v) Be acknowledged by Revenue as having been made.

There is a right of appeal if a person is aggrieved by a Revenue decision that an expression is not genuine.

9.1.54 Interest

The rate of interest on overdue tax is 1% per month or part of a month from 1 April 1998 to 31 August 2002 and 0.0322% per day or part of a day from 1 September 2002 onwards. In addition, with effect from 1 September 2002, interest at the rate of 0.0322% per day or part of a day will be charged where VAT deductibility is over claimed.

PA21A The Revenue Commissioners will be obliged to pay interest on VAT refunds in certain circumstances at a rate of 0.011% per day or part of a day with effect from 1 November 2003.

9.2 Annex A Activities

I. Crop production

1. General agriculture, including viticulture.
2. Growing of fruit (including olives) and of vegetables, flowers and ornamental plants both in the open and under glass.
3. Production of mushrooms, spices, seeds and propagating materials; nurseries.

II. Stock farming together with cultivation

1. General stock farming.
2. Poultry farming.
3. Rabbit farming.
4. Beekeeping.
5. Silkworm farming.
6. Snail farming.

III. Forestry

IV. Fisheries

1. Fresh water fishing.
2. Fish farming.
3. Breeding of mussels, oysters and other molluscs and crustaceans.
4. Frog farming.

V. Where a farmer processes using means normally employed in an agricultural, forestry or fisheries undertaking, products deriving essentially from his agricultural production, such processing shall be regarded as agricultural production.

9.3 Annex B Services

Supplies of agricultural services which normally play a part in agricultural production shall be considered the supply of agricultural services, and include the following in particular:

- field work, reaping and mowing, threshing, baling, collecting, harvesting, sowing and planting
- packing and preparation for market, for example drying, cleaning, grinding, disinfecting and ensilage of agricultural products
- storage of agricultural products
- stock minding, rearing and fattening
- hiring out, for agricultural purposes, of equipment normally used in agricultural, forestry or fisheries undertakings
- technical assistance
- destruction of weeds and pests, dusting and spraying of crops and land
- operation of irrigation drainage equipment
- lopping, tree felling and other forestry services.

CHAPTER 10 TAX AMNESTIES 1993

10.1 Tax Amnesties 1993

The Waiver of Certain Tax / Interest and Penalties Act 1993 provides for a main and a general amnesty.

10.1.1 Main amnesty

The main amnesty covers income tax, sur-tax, capital gains tax, income levy, health contribution and employment and training levy, for the period up to and including 5 April 1991 which has not been paid by individuals (companies are excluded from the main amnesty).

Excluded from the scope of the main amnesty are:

- Tax already at enforcement stage on 25 May 1993.
- Tax which had been under appeal at 25 May 1993.
- Tax on income and gains derived from illegal sources.
- Tax not paid by virtue of a tax avoidance scheme which would have been payable on or before 25 May 1993.
- Individuals under investigation in respect of tax liability up to and including 5 April 1991.

To qualify for the amnesty, the individual must, on or before 30 November 1993, give to a Chief Special Collector, a full declaration of the amounts coming within the terms of the amnesty and must then remit 15% of that amount to the Chief Special Collector by 14 January 1994. He must also declare that the amounts do not arise from any illegal source or activity.

The Chief Special Collector will issue a certificate of receipt.

The Revenue will be precluded from commencing an investigation into the tax liability of an individual for any period up to and including 5 April 1991 which is paid to the Chief Special Collector if the individual produces a certificate of receipt. An investigation may proceed if the declarations made to the Chief Special Collector are shown not to be full and true declarations.

The Special Collectors, who will administer the amnesty are precluded from disclosing any information obtained in the course of their duties.

10.1.2 General amnesty

The general amnesty applies to all taxpayers and provides for an amnesty from the payment of interest in respect of arrears of certain taxes up to and including 5 April 1991.

The taxes in question are the same as those covered by the main amnesty plus PAYE, corporation tax, corporation profits tax, VAT, capital acquisitions tax, stamp duty and residential property tax. In order to avail of this amnesty, the full amount of tax arrears must be paid by 14 January 1994. Where arrears of VAT are being paid by an individual, who is availing of the main amnesty, the VAT may be remitted to the Chief Special Collector.

The benefits of both amnesties will be withdrawn if:

- in the case of an individual, a correct return for 1992/93 is not submitted on time and for companies, a correct return for any accounting period ending in the year to 31 December 1993;
- a declaration given to the Chief Special Collector is found to be false;
- the amount remitted under the general amnesty was less than the full amount of arrears.

New penalties are provided for failure to comply with or abuse of the terms of the amnesty and for future non-compliance. An individual who abuses or ignores the amnesty by failure to make the appropriate declarations or by falsely making such declarations and who has failed to make returns or has submitted false returns for any years covered by the amnesty will be liable to specified penalties which will consist of financial penalties or terms of imprisonment or both.

The ability to mitigate certain fines and penalties is to be restricted. From now on, it will only be possible to remit penalties to the extent of 50%. In cases where the amnesty has been abused or ignored no mitigation will be allowed.

In certain circumstances, the Revenue Commissioners may obtain from financial institutions, details of the accounts and certain ancillary financial information of a taxpayer resident in the State. The circumstances are that:

- the taxpayer has filed a return and the Inspector feels that it is unsatisfactory;
- the Inspector has reasonable grounds to believe that the taxpayer has an undisclosed account or that the financial institution has information which would establish that the taxpayer's return is materially false;
- the Appeal Commissioners issue a determination that the Inspector is justified in seeking details of accounts held by the taxpayer with a financial institution.

Index

C